THE
OF THE
HIGHER POTENTIAL

MW01180819

by

Robert Collier

PUBLISHED BY

THE BOOK OF GOLD

72 ORCHARD STREET, TARRYTOWN, N. Y.

PRINTED AND BOUND IN THE U. S. A. BY
KINGSPORT PRESS, INC., KINGSPORT, TENN.

THE LAW OF THE HIGHER POTENTIAL

containing

THE GOD IN YOU

THE MAGIC WORD

THE SECRET OF POWER

THE LAW OF THE HIGHER POTENTIAL

"Would you know Life abundant,
Love doubled for all you give?-
There is a means no surer
Than helping someone to live."

(The above verse by Ellen H. Jones expresses so well the whole purpose of this book, that we gladly subscribe our name to it here.)

Robert Collier.

TABLE OF CONTENTS

v

THE SECRET OF POWER

THE LAW OF THE HIGHER POTENTIAL

PROLOGUE

WHY IS IT that most of the great men of the world, most of the unusually successful men, started life under a handicap?

Demosthenes, the greatest orator the ancient world produced, stuttered! The first time he tried to make a public speech, he was laughed off the rostrum. Julius Caesar was an epileptic. Napoleon was of humble parentage, and so poor that it was with the greatest difficulty that he got his appointment to the Military Academy. Far from being a born genius, he stood forty-sixth in his class at the Military Academy. And there were only sixty-five in the class. His shortness of stature and extreme poverty discouraged him to such an extent that in his early letters to friends, he frequently referred to thoughts of suicide.

Benjamin Franklin, Abraham Lincoln, Andrew Jackson and a number of our Presidents started life in the poorest and humblest of homes, with little education and no advantages. Stewart, who started what is now the John Wanamaker Store in New York, came to New York with $1.50 in his pocket, and no place where he could hope to get more until he himself earned it. Thomas Edison was a newsboy on trains. Andrew Carnegie started work at $4 a month. John D. Rockefeller at about $6 a week.

Reza Khan, who became Shah of Persia, started as an ordinary trooper in the Persian army. Mustapha Kemal, late Ruler of Turkey, was an unknown officer in the Turkish army. Ebert, first President of Germany after World

War I, was a saddle maker. A number of our own Presidents were born in log cabins, without money, without education.

Sandow, the strongest man of his time, started life as a weakling. Annette Kellerman was lame and sickly, yet she became diving champion and one of the world's most perfectly formed women. George Jowett was lame and a weakling until he was eleven years old. An older boy bullied him and beat him until he aroused such a feeling of resentment in young Jowett that he determined to work and exercise until he could pay back that bully in kind. In two years, he was able to beat the bully. In ten years, he was the world's strongest man!

Why is it that men with such handicaps can outstrip all of those naturally favored by Nature? Why is it that the well-educated, well-trained men, with wealthy and influential friends to help them, are so often pushed aside, to make way for some "nobody" whose family no one ever heard of, but whose sheer ability and force make him a power to be reckoned with?

Why? Because men with early advantages are taught *to look to material things for success* . . . to riches or friends or influence or their own training or abilities. And when these fail them, they are at a loss where to turn next.

But when a man has no special skill or ability or riches or influence, he has to look to something outside these for success, something beyond material means. So he turns to the God in him, to his cell of the God-Mind, and of that cell he demands that it bring him fame or fortune or power or position. What is more, if he continues to demand it with persistent faith, HE GETS IT!

You see, in every adversity there lies the seed of an equivalent advantage. In every defeat there is a lesson showing you how to win the victory next time. The turning point in the lives of most successful men has come at some moment of crisis, when everything looked dark. when there seemed no way out. That was when they turned to their inner selves, when they gave up hope in material means and looked to the God in them for help. That was when they were able to turn each stumbling block into a stepping-stone to success.

> "Isn't it strange that princes and kings,
>   And clowns that caper in sawdust rings,
>   And common folks like you and me,
>   Are builders for eternity?
>
> "Each is given a bag of tools,
>   A shapeless mass, a book of rules;
>   And each must make, ere life is flown,
>   A stumbling block or a stepping stone."

You are one with the great "I AM" of the universe. You are part of God. Until you realize that—and the power it gives you—you will never know God. "We are parts of one stupendous whole, whose body Nature is, and God the soul." God has incarnated Himself in man. He seeks expression. Give Him work to do through you, give Him a chance to express Himself in some useful way, and there is nothing beyond your powers to do or to attain.

It matters not what your age, what your present circumstances or position. If you will seek your help outside your merely physical self, if you will put the God in you into some worthwhile endeavor, and then BELIEVE in Him, you can overcome any poverty, any handicap, any untoward circumstance. Relying upon your personal abilities or riches or friends is being like the heathen of old, whom the Prophet of the Lord taunted. "You have a God whom you must carry," he derided them. "We have a God *who carries us!*"

The God of personal ability or material riches or friends is one that you must continually carry. Drop him,

and immediately you lose everything. But there is a God
in you who will carry you—and in the doing of it, provide
you with every good thing this world can supply. The
purpose of this book is to acquaint you with this God *in
you, The God That Only The Fortunate Few Know.*

As the poet so well expressed it—

> "In your own self lies Destiny. Let this
> Vast truth cast out all fear, and prejudice,
> All hesitation. Know that you are great,
> Great with Divinity. So dominate
> Environment and enter into bliss.
> Love largely and hate nothing. Hold no aim
> That does not chord with Universal Good.
> Hear what the voices of the Silence say—
> All joys are yours if you put forth your claim.
> Once let the spiritual laws be understood,
> Material things must answer and obey."

Some might think that merely a poet's dream, but along
comes Dr. J. B. Rhine of Duke University to prove it
scientific fact as well.

In his new book "The Reach of the Mind," Dr. Rhine
points out that in the past, Science seemed to feel that man
was entirely material. It had discovered how glands regu-
late personality through their chemical secretions; it had
shown that the child mind matures only as the brain de-
velops; that certain mental functions are linked with
specific areas of the brain, and that if one of these is
injured, the corresponding mental function is lost.

So Science believed that it had accounted for all the
processes of thought and action, that it could show a
material basis for each.

But now Dr. Rhine and other experimenters have proved that
knowledge can be acquired *without the use of the senses!*

Not only that, but they have also proved that the powers of the mind are not bound by space or limited by time! Perhaps their greatest discovery is that the mind can influence matter *without physical means.*

This has been done through prayer, of course, since time began, but such results have always been looked upon as supernatural. Dr. Rhine and other experimenters show that any normal person has the power to influence objects and events.

To quote "The Reach of the Mind"—"As a result of thousands of experimental trials, we found it to be a fact that the mind has a force that can act on matter. ... There must, therefore, be an energy convertible to physical action, *a mental energy."*

The one great essential to the successful use of this mental energy seems to be intense interest or desire. The more keyed up a person is, the more eager for results, the more he can influence those results.

Dr. Rhine showed through many experiments that when the subject's interest is distracted, when he lacks ability to concentrate his attention, his mental energy has little or no power over outside objects. It is only as he gives his entire attention to the object in mind, as he concentrates his every energy upon it, that he gets successful results.

Dr. Rhine's experiments prove scientifically what we have always believed—that there is a Power over and above the merely physical power of the mind or body, that through intense concentration or desire we can link up with that Power, and that once we do, nothing is impossible to us.

It means, in short, that man is not at the mercy of blind chance or Fate, that he can control his own destiny. Science is at last proving what Religion has taught from the beginning—that God gave man *dominion* and that he has only to understand and use this dominion to become the Master of his Fate, the Captain of his Soul.

> "Body and mind and Spirit, all combine
> To make the creature, human and Divine.
> Of this great Trinity, no part deny.
> Affirm, affirm, the great eternal I.
> Affirm the body, beautiful and whole,
> The earth-expression of immortal soul.
> Affirm the mind, the messenger of the hour,
> To speed between thee and the Source of Power.
> Affirm the Spirit, the eternal I—
> Of this great Trinity, no part deny."
>
> ELLA WHEELER WILCOX

CHAPTER ONE

THE GOD IN YOU

THE DECLARATION OF INDEPENDENCE starts with the preamble that all men are born free and equal.

But how many believe that? When one child is born in a Park Avenue home, with doctors and nurses and servants to attend to his slightest want, with tutors and colleges to educate him, with riches and influence to start him in his career, how can he be said to be born equal to the child of the Ghetto, who has difficulty getting enough air to breathe, to say nothing of food to eat, and whose waking hours are so taken up with the struggle for existence that he has no time to acquire much in the way of education!

> Yet in that which counts most, these two are born equal, for they have equal access to the God in themselves, equal chance to give Him means of expression. More than that, the God in one is just as powerful as the God in the other, for both are part of that all-powerful God of the Universe who rules the world.

In effect, we are each of us individual cells in the great Mind of the universe—the God Mind. We can draw upon the Mind of the Universe in exactly the same way that any cell in our own body draws upon our brain for whatever it needs outside its immediate surroundings.

All men are born free and equal, just as all the cells in your body are equal. Some of these cells may seem to

be more fortunately situated than others, being placed
in fatty portions of the body where they are so surrounded
with nourishment that they seem assured of everything
they can need for their natural lives.

Others may be in hard-worked parts where they are
continually having to draw upon the lymph around them,
and through it upon the blood stream and the heart, and
where it seems as though they cannot be sure of sustenance from one day to the next. Still others may be in
little-used and apparently forgotten parts where they
seem to have been left to dry up and starve, as in the
scalp of the head when the hair falls out and the fatty
tissue of the scalp dries, leaving the cells there to shrivel
and die.

Yet despite their apparent differences in surroundings
and opportunity, all these cells are equal, all can draw
upon every element in the body for sustenance at need.

To see how it is done, let us take a single nerve cell in
our own brain, and see how it works.

Look up the diagram of a typical nerve cell in any
medical work, and what do you find? From one side of
the cell, a long fibre extends which makes connection with
some part of the skin, or some group of cells such as a
muscle. This fibre is part of the nerve cell. It is the telephone line, carrying orders or stimuli from the cell to
the muscle it controls, or from the sensory nerve in the
skin to the cell in the brain. Thoughts, emotions, desires,
all send impulses to the nerves controlling the muscles
concerned, and provide the stimuli which set these muscles
in action, thus transforming nervous energy into muscular
energy.

So if you have a desire which requires the action of
only a single muscle, what happens? Your desire takes the
form of an impulse to the nerve cell controlling that
muscle, the order travels along the cell-fibre to the muscle,

which promptly acts in accord with the stimulus given it. And your desire is satisfied.

But suppose your desire requires the action of more than one muscle? Suppose it needs the united power of every muscle in the body? So far we have used only the long nerve fibre or telephone line connecting the nerve cell with the muscle it controls. But on the other side of each nerve cell are short fibres, apparently ending in space. And as long as the nerves are at rest, these fibres do lie in space.

But when you stir up the nerve cells, when you give them a job that is greater than the muscles at their command can manage, then these short fibres go into action. Then they bestir themselves to some purpose. They dig into the nerve cells near them. They wake these and stimulate them in turn to stir up those on the other sides of them until, if necessary, every cell in the brain is twitching, and every muscle in the body working to accomplish the job you demand.

That is what happens in *your* body if even a single cell in your brain desires something strongly enough, persistently enough, to hold to its purpose until it gets what it wants. And that is what happens in the God-body when you put the same persistence into your desires.

You see, you are a cell in the God-body of the Universe, just as every cell in you is a part of your body. When you work with your hands, your feet, your muscles, you are using only the muscles immediately connected with your brain cells. When you work with the money you have, the riches or friends or influence you control, you are using only the means immediately connected to your brain cell in the mind of God. And that is so infinitesimally small a part of the means and resources at the command of that Great God-mind.

It is just as though you tried to do all the work required of your body today by using only the tiniest muscle in your little finger, when by stirring up the surrounding nerve cells, you could just as well draw upon the power of the whole mind, or of the entire body if that were needed. It is as though one of your nerve cells undertook to do the work of the whole body, and tried, with the single muscle at its command, to do it!

You'd think that foolish, if one tiny nerve cell out of the billions in your brain, undertook any such gigantic job. You'd know it was hopeless . . . that no one cell, and no one muscle, could ever accomplish all that work. Yet you, as a single cell in the God-mind, have often attempted just as impossible jobs. When all you had to do to accomplish everything you desired was to stir into action the cells around you!

How can you do this? In the same way that any cell in your own brain does it. *Pray!* In other words, get an urgent, insistent desire. The first principle of success is DESIRE—knowing what you want. Desire is the planting of your seed. It needs cultivation, of course, but the first important step is the PLANTING. Desire stirs the nerve cells in your brain to use the muscles under their control to do the work required of them. Desire will set your nerve cell in the God-mind vibrating, using the muscle under its command and stirring into action all the nerve-cells around it until they, too, are working with you to bring about the thing you wish.

That is the reason it was said in the Vedas thousands of years ago that if any two people would unite their psychic forces, they could conquer the world! That is the reason Jesus told us—"If two of you shall agree as touching anything they shall ask, it shall be done unto them. For when two or three are gathered together in My name, there am I in the midst of them, and I shall grant their request."

When two or more nerve cells unite for a certain action, they get that action, even if to bring it about they have to draw upon every cell in the whole body for help!

This does not mean that anything is impossible to a single cell or a single person—merely that when two or more are united for a common purpose, the results are easier. But there is no good thing any man can ask, believing, that he cannot get.

In the first chapter of Genesis, it is written that God gave man dominion over the earth. And it is true. It is just as true as that any nerve cell in your whole body has dominion over your body. If you doubt it, let one nerve be sufficiently irritated, and see how quickly it puts every nerve in your body to work to remove that irritation.

One nerve cell in your body, with a strongly held purpose, can bring into action every cell in your body to accomplish that purpose. One nerve cell in the God-body (in other words, one man or woman) with a strongly held purpose, can bring into action every cell in the Universe, if these be necessary to the accomplishment of that purpose!

Does that mean anything to you? Does it mean anything to know that the words of prophets and seers are true, that the promises of the Scriptures can be depended upon, that there really is a Power in the Universe that responds to the urge of the lowliest man or woman just as readily as to the command of the highest?

The world is yours! It matters not whether you be prince or pauper, blue-blooded or red, white-skinned, black, yellow or brown. The God-body of the Universe makes no more distinction between cells than do you in responding to the impulses of the nerve-cells in your own body.

Rich or poor—it's all one to you. Highly placed or low —one can cause you as much trouble, or give you as great satisfaction, as another. And the same is true of the God-body of the Universe. All men are created free and equal. All remain free and equal nerve cells in the God-mind of the Universe.

The only difference lies in our understanding of the power that is ours. How much understanding have you? And what are you doing to increase it? "Seek first understanding, and all things else shall be added unto you." Easier to believe that now, isn't it? With the right understanding, you could run the world. Can you think of anything more important than acquiring understanding?

What turned the complaining, discouraged, poverty-stricken and quite ordinary young Bonaparte into the greatest military genius of his age, "Man of Destiny" and master of most of Europe?

The Talisman of Napoleon, the Talisman of every great and successful man, the only Talisman that will stir the whole body of the Universe into action, is the same Talisman as that needed to put the entire physical body at the service of any one nerve cell—*a purpose so strongly held that life or death or anything else seems of small consequence beside it!* A purpose—and the persistent determination to hold to it until it is accomplished.

Love sometimes makes such a Talisman—the love that goes out to dare all and do all for the loved one. Greed oftentimes brings it into being—hence many of the great fortunes of today. The lust for power is a potent Talisman, that has animated men since time began. Greater still is the zeal of one who would convert the world. That Talisman has carried men through fire and flood, into every danger and over every obstacle. Look how Mohammed, a lowly camel driver, became the ruler of and prophet to millions.

Faith in charms, belief in luck, utter confidence in another's leadership, all are Talismans of greater or lesser power.

But the greatest of all is belief in the God inside YOU! Belief in its power to draw to itself every element it needs for expression. Belief in a definite PURPOSE it came here to fulfill, and which can be fulfilled only through YOU!

Have you such a faith? If not, get it! For without such a faith, life is purposeless, meaningless. What is more, until you lay hold of that Talisman, life will never bring anything worth while to you!

What was it won for Grant over his more brilliant opponents? The grim, dogged, persistent purpose to fight it out along those lines if it took all summer! What is it that has made England victor in so many of her wars, in spite of inept leadership and costly blunders? That same bull-dog determination, which holds on in spite of all reverses and discouragements, until its fight is won. What was it that wore out the unjust judge, in the parable that Jesus told?

> "And he spake a parable unto them to this end, that man ought always to pray, and not to faint; saying, 'There was in a city a judge, which feared not God, neither regarded man;
>
> " 'And there was a widow in that city; and she came unto him, saying, "Avenge me on mine adversary."
>
> " 'And he would not for a while; but afterward he said within himself, "Though I fear not God, nor regard man; yet because this widow troubleth me, I will avenge her, lest by her continual coming she weary me." '
>
> "And the Lord said, 'Hear what the unjust judge saith. And shall not God avenge his own elect, which cry day and night unto him, though he bear long with them?' "

If the nerve in a tooth keeps crying out that a cavity in that tooth needs attention, won't you finally drop everything and seek out a dentist who can satisfy that nerve's needs? And if any other nerve prays continuously for attention, won't you do likewise with it?

Well, you are a nerve in the God-body. If you have an urgent need, and keep praying and insisting and demanding the remedy, don't you suppose you will get it just as surely?

A definite purpose, held to in the face of every discouragement and failure, in spite of all obstacles and opposition, will win no matter what the odds. It is the one nerve cell working against the indifference, the inertia or even the active opposition of the entire group. If the cell is easily discouraged, it will fail. If it is willing to wait indefinitely, it will have to wait. But if it keeps stirring up the cells next to it, and stimulating them to stir those beyond, eventually the entire nerve system will go into action and bring about the result that single cell desires—even if it be only to rid itself of the constant irritation.*

You have seen young fellows determined to go to college. You have thought them foolish, in the face of the obstacles facing them. Yet when they persisted, you know how often those obstacles have one by one magically disappeared, until presently they found themselves with the fruition of their desires. A strongly held purpose, persisted in, believed in, is as sure to win in the end as the morrow's sun is to rise. And earnest prayer is to the God-body what a throbbing nerve is to yours. Hold to it, insist upon it, and it is just as sure of a hearing. But remember:

"He that wavereth is like the wave of the sea, driven by the wind and tossed; let not that man think that he shall receive anything of the Lord."

All are born free and equal. All may not start with the same amount of wealth or opportunity immediately available to them, but all can go to the Source of these and get

* See parable of the importunate friend, page 154.

just as much of them as is necessary to satisfy their desires.

We are surrounded by riches. We have available unlimited wealth. But we have to learn how to draw it to us.

Years ago, at Kimberley in South Africa, a poor Boer farmer tried to glean a living out of the rocky soil. His boys oftentimes picked up pieces of dirty looking crystal and used them as pebbles to throw at some wandering sheep. After years of fruitless effort, the farmer abandoned his attempts to make a living out of this rocky soil, and moved to a more fertile spot. Today, the farm he tried so hard to cultivate is the site of the Kimberley Diamond Mines, one of the richest spots on the face of the globe. And the bits of dirty crystal that his boys threw at the sheep turned out to be diamonds in the rough!

Most of us are like that poor Boer farmer. We strive and struggle, and frequently give up, because of ignorance of our powers, ignorance of the good things around us. We remain in poverty until along comes someone and shows that we were standing on a diamond mine all the time.

Russell Conwell tells the story of a Pennsylvania farmer whose brother went to Canada and became an oil driller. Fired with the brother's tales of sudden wealth, the farmer sold his land and went to Canada to make his fortune. The new owner, in looking over the farm, found that where the cattle came to drink from a little creek, a board had been put across the water to hold back a heavy scum which was washed down by the rains from the ground above.

He examined this scum, and thought it smelled like oil. So he had some experts come out and look the ground over. It proved to be one of the richest oil fields in the state of Pennsylvania.

What riches are you overlooking? What opportunities? "Opportunity," says a famous writer, "is like oxy-gen. It is so plentiful that we fairly breathe it." All that is necessary is a receptive mind, a willingness to try, and the persistence to see things through.

There is some one thing that YOU can do better than anyone else. There is some line of work in which you can excel—if you will just find that one thing and spend all your time and effort in learning to do it supremely well.

Don't worry if it seems to be some humble thing that anyone ought to be able to do. In a magazine some time ago, there was the story of a Polish immigrant who could speak scarcely a word of English, who had no trade or training and had to take any sort of job that offered. He happened to get one in a nursery, digging up dirt for the flowers. He dug so well that soon he was attending to the planting of many of the commoner varieties of flowers.

Among these were the peonies. He loved those big peonies, gave them such careful attention that they thrived and grew more beautiful than ever. Soon his peonies began to attract attention, the demand for them grew, until he had to double and then quadruple the space devoted to them. Today he is half owner of that nursery.

Two artists opened an office together, doing any kind of work they could get. One noticed that wherever he happened to do cartoons for people, the results were so effective that they came back for more. So he made an especial study of cartoon drawing. Today his earnings are in the $25,000 class, while his fellow artist is still barely making ends meet as a jack of all trades.

A retail clerk found that she had a special gift for satisfying complaining customers. She liked to straighten out the snarls that others had caused, and she did it so well that she soon attracted the attention of her employ-ers. Today she is head of the complaint department.

There is the switchboard operator with the pleasing voice, the reception clerk with the cheery smile, the salesman with the convincing manner, the secretary with the knack of saving the boss' time, the drummer with the jolly manner. Every one of us has something. Find out what one thing you can do best, cultivate it and you can be the biggest man in that line in the world.

Success is where you are and within yourself. Don't try to imitate what someone else is doing. Develop what YOU have. There is something in you that will enable you to reach the top in some one line. Put the spot light on your own characteristics, your own abilities. Find what you can do best, what people like you best for. Then cultivate that.

When the great Comstock Lode was first discovered, a fortune was taken out of it. Then the ore petered out. The owners presently gave up and sold out to a new group. These men spent several hundred thousand dollars in a fruitless attempt to locate the rich lode, and they too were ready to give up. But someone thought to try a bore hole to the side of one of the entries, and struck an almost solid mass of ore so rich that nearly $300,000,000 was taken from it.

In the early days of the prairie farms, newcomers were frequently able to buy for a song the homesteads of the original settlers, because the latter had been able to find no water. They had dug wells, but had been unable to reach the streams beneath. Oftentimes, however, by digging only a few feet further, the newcomers found water in abundance. The first settlers had quit when success was almost within their grasp. The greatest success usually comes from one step beyond the point where defeat overtook you. "He who loses wealth, loses much," says an old proverb. "He who loses a friend, loses more. But he who loses his courage, loses everything."

Three things educators try to instil into children:

1st—Knowledge
2nd—Judgment
3rd—Persistence.

And the greatest of these is Persistence. Many a man has succeeded without education. Many even without good judgment. But none has ever got anywhere worth while without persistence. Without a strong desire, without that inner urge which pushes him on, over obstacles, through discouragements, to the goal of his heart's desire.

"Nothing in the world can take the place of persistence," said Calvin Coolidge. "Talent will not. Nothing is more common than unsuccessful men with talent. Genius will not; unrewarded genius is almost a proverb. Education will not; the world is full of educated derelicts. Persistence and determination alone are omnipotent. The slogan 'Press on' has solved and always will solve the problems of the human race."

Russell Conwell, the famous educator and lecturer who founded Temple University, gathered statistics some years ago on those who succeed, and his figures showed that of 4043 multimillionaires in this country at that time, only 69 had even a High School education. They lacked money, they lacked training, but they had the URGE to get somewhere, the *persistence* to keep trying . . . and they succeeded!

Compare that with the figures Conwell gathered on the sons of rich men. Only one in seventeen died wealthy! Lacking incentive, having no urge within them to get ahead, they not only failed to make their mark, but they lost what they had.

The first essential to success is a feeling of lack, a need, a *desire* for something you have not got. It is the powerlessness of the cripple or invalid that makes him long for strength, gives him the necessary persistence to work for it until he gets it. It is the poverty and misery of their existence that makes the children of the Ghetto long for wealth, and gives them the persistence and determination to work at anything until they get it.

You need that same urgent desire, that same determination and persistence if you are to get what you want from life. You need to realize that whatever it is you want of life, it is there for the taking. You need to know that you are a cell in the God-mind, and that through this God-mind you can put the whole Universe to work, if necessary, to bring about the accomplishment of your desire.

But don't waste that vast power on trifles. Don't be like the fable of the woodsman who, having worked long and hard for the wishing Fairy and accomplished the task she set him, was told that he might have in reward any three things he asked for. Being very hungry, he promptly asked for a good meal. That eaten, he noticed that the wind was blowing up cold, so he asked for a warm cloak. With his stomach full and a warm cloak about him, he felt sleepy, so he asked for a comfortable bed to lie upon.

And so, with every good thing of the world his for the asking, the next day found him with only a warm cloak to show for his labors. Most of us are like that. We put the mountain in labor, just to bring forth a mouse. We strive and strain, and draw upon all the powers that have been given us, to accomplish some trifling thing that leaves us just where we were before.

Demand much! Set a worth-while goal. Remember the old poem by Jessie B. Rittenhouse from "The Door of Dreams" published by Houghton Mifflin Co., Boston.

"I bargained with Life for a penny
And Life would pay no more,
However I begged at evening
When I counted my scanty store.

"For Life is a just employer;
He gives you what you ask,
But once you have set the wages,
Why, you must bear the task.

"I worked for a menial's hire,
Only to learn, dismayed,
That any wage I had asked of Life,
Life would have paid."

Don't you be foolish like that. Don't bargain with Life for a penny. Ask for something worth putting the Universe to work for. Ask for it, demand it—then stick to that demand with persistence and determination until the whole God-mind HAS to bestir itself to give you what you want.

The purpose of Life from the very beginning has been dominion—dominion over every adverse circumstance. And through his part of dominion, his nerve-cell in the Mind of God and his ability through it to get whatever action he may persistently demand—man HAS dominion over everything.

There is a Spark of Divinity in YOU. What are you doing to fan it into flame? Are you giving it a chance to grow, to express itself, to become an all-consuming fire? Are you giving it work to do? Are you making it seek out ever greater worlds to conquer? Or are you letting it slumber neglected, or perhaps even smothering it with doubt and fear?

"And God said, Let us make man in our image, after our likeness; and let him have DOMINION over the fish of the sea, and over the fowl of the air, and over the cattle, and over all the earth, and over every creeping thing that creepeth upon the earth."

Do you know what is the Unpardonable Sin in all of Nature? Read the following chapters, and you will see!

Affirmation:

"And every morning I will say, There's something happy on the way. And God sends love to me. God is the light of my life, the Source of my knowledge and inspiration. God in the midst of me knows. He provides me with food for my thoughts, ideas for excellent service, clear perception, Divine intelligence."

CHAPTER TWO

THE GOAL OF LIFE

LIFE IS LOGICAL. The Power that rules the Universe does not deal in miracles, but in logical developments. The happenings which seem like miracles are merely those of whose logical sequence we are still in ignorance.

To understand this, you have only to follow life from the beginning and watch its logical growth and development. Nothing was accidental. Nothing hit or miss. It followed logical lines, trying first one experiment, then another, abandoning those which proved impractical, perfecting those which showed promise, working always toward the goal of *self sufficiency*—toward a creature which should not be dependent upon circumstances or surroundings, but should have dominion over these within itself.

AND NOW LIFE HAS ATTAINED THAT GOAL, THOUGH FEW AMONG MANKIND REALIZE IT OR KNOW HOW TO TAKE ADVANTAGE OF IT.

To grasp this vital fact, it is necessary to learn WHY all of life worked from the beginning of time towards this one end. To do this, let us go back to the start of life here upon earth—to the one-celled water-plants or Thallophytes which first peopled the warm waters of the ocean. Let us show how life started with them, and groped ever upward until it evolved the mind of man.

22

In the Atlantic Monthly some time ago, there was an article by C. D. Stewart which gives the germ of the idea:

"First in the order of creation," he tells us, "are the one-celled water plants floating and moving about. They have no evident organs but the single cells; and they take their food, as cells have always done, by absorbing it from the liquid in which they are immersed.

"Moss consists of such cells, but banded together. At first it was but a thin sheath of cells lying flat on the mud; then it became several cells thick, the moisture being passed from the cells below to those above by absorption.

"Finally *the great idea came to pass* in the form of the fern. Here was a vegetable mechanism with true, running roots, which the moss has not; and it possessed a woody stem provided with tubes for conducting water. With the invention of the fern, piping the water upward, while the roots struck down to bring it from below, nothing more was necessary to the making of a tree. It only remained for a company of cells to go ahead and, in modern parlance, construct a 'Bigger and better' plant.

"Imagine some primeval promoter addressing a company of those water-inhabiting cells and proposing the whole idea . . . 'Come now; our idea is to take a lot of you cells and build a tall plant living on land. Some of you are to be hung high up in the glare of the sun; you will stay aloft and absorb the hot energy of summer while you make food for cells that are differently engaged. You must become specialists; and you are to give up this one-cell, jack-of-all-trades idea. We are going to build a tree.'

"A shiver of fear and consternation would certainly seize upon any water-living cells that had the power to think. 'Impossible!' they would exclaim. 'We should all die. Water is our food and life. We must be immersed in the water. A thing like that would never do.'

"But that is just what came to pass. And every cell in

the top of a tree continues to be immersed in the life-giving water. Between a cell in the sea and one in the topmost twig there is no essential difference of situation."

And so at last a Mind was born. Each of those original one-celled plants had possessed a degree of intelligence, enough to enable it to take from the water around it the elements essential to its well being. But each was entirely absorbed in itself.

Now a Mind was born which had to consider the good of a group rather than of any one cell, which had to assign to various members of that group different tasks, each task essential to the life of the group . . . *and then to see that the tasks were done.*

A whole aeon was spanned in that one accomplishment. The pattern for all later life was formed then and there. In that moment, Utopia, the Millennium, Heaven itself was made possible, for in that moment, the whole idea of Government was born. Individualism was discarded in favor of general welfare. From that time on, the individual has been of secondary importance, except as he could impose his importance or his will upon the group.

In taking that first group of single-celled plants and putting it into a community undertaking, so to speak, Nature had started a new phase of life—a principle upon which all life has since been based. She had found the principle that she has since used in growing every form of vegetation. And it did not take her long to adapt that principle to animal life.

Starting with the lowly Amoeba, or single-celled water creature, she presently formed jelly-fish, corresponding roughly with the moss of plant life, and from them worked up into other of the soft, "squushy" forms of sea life. But here she began to meet with obstacles. Ferns and plants and trees she had rooted in the ground, and shown them how to burrow into the soil with their roots to reach the moisture and other elements they needed. But the animals were footloose and could be wafted here and there by tide or current. Some of them were bruised against rocky shores, some were left high and dry by the tide, some were devoured by bigger creatures of their own kind. They must have protection, means of living on shore or in water, ability to propel themselves away from danger.

Thus was born the crustacean. First its shell was no more than a thicker, tougher outer skin, like the callus on your hand. Then, as the need grew greater, more and more layers were added to that skin, greater toughness and hardness given to it, until it was capable of withstanding contact with the rocky shore, until its armor was impervious to attack from other creatures.

And as more and more of its time was spent out of water, it developed lungs to supplement its gills, legs to take the place of fins. That was how the first land creature came into being—a fish left high and dry by the tide half its time, which had to develop means of breathing and moving about on land—or perish. And nothing perishes from the earth which has the intelligence to know what it needs for survival, the persistence to keep demanding it until it gets it.

As the earth cooled and the waters receded, these half-land-half-sea creatures became necessarily wholly creatures of the land. And their new mode of life brought new needs, new methods of satisfying those needs.

Those creatures that were stolid and easily satisfied, contented themselves with the herbs and grasses which grew in abundance, and asked only that they be let alone. To these were given shells or tough hides for protection against the fiercer animals. The timid ones developed speed or learned to dig holes secure from their enemies.

Some grew wings that they might fly away from them, and build their nests far beyond their reach. Others—the fiercer ones—developed strength and great teeth and claws for attack.

In each type, *Nature sought to develop to the uttermost the quality which might give it self-sufficiency.* Stealth, speed, wariness, fierceness, strength, bulk, armor —all these and a hundred other qualities Nature tried. But all failed. No armor was so thick that something might not penetrate it. No defense so perfect that some form of offense might not overcome it. No flight so high, no speed so fast, no size so big, no strength so great, but something else was stronger.

Whether it was the fierce Tyrannosaurus, the enormous Gigantosaurus, the saber-tooth Tiger, the fleet deer, the soaring eagle, the wily fox, the venomous snake, or the lowly ant—each had its enemy which could bring all its strength or frightfulness or stealth to naught.

THE GOAL OF LIFE'S DEVELOPMENT—*SELF-SUFFICIENCY, DOMINION OVER CONDITIONS*— WAS TO BE FOUND IN NONE OF THESE.

And so, after trying every material means of reaching its goal, and failing utterly, Nature began to seek its end in the realm of the mind.

Looking back over the progress of life, we see that it is only as the mind in each creature sought greater expression that this creature developed above its fellows. Lloyd Douglas explains the idea graphically in "The Green Light." *

"Let us begin with the hypothesis," he says, "that from the very dawn of animate life there was a potential man in the making, related to present-day man much as an

* Published by Houghton Mifflin Co., Boston, Mass.

acorn is related to the oak it is to be. At one phase of this creature's upward progress, he closely resembled what we know as the harbor seal. Dissatisfied with his ocean, because he was possessed of an instinctive urge *to escape his limitations*, he climbed up on a rock and at the cost of who knows how much agony—endured by generations of his kind, he achieved a capacity for recovering oxygen from the air instead of the water. It is quite conceivable that of all these creatures who made the experiment, only a comparatively few had the fortitude to see it through.

"The next phase in the evolution of the most audacious was to crawl and flop along the ground, inland, Nature gradually helping them and their posterity to more suitable means of locomotion than flippers.

"The sub-plot concerns the creatures who were left behind. Some of them hadn't the courage to climb up on the rock, at all. Some climbed up and stayed a little while, but were glad enough to slip back into their sea. Some went through all the suffering necessary to achieve lungs to replace the old gills, but hadn't the valor to travel inland. They remained sprawling on the rocks, when they were not swimming about with all manner of things more or less like them.

"The most venturesome moved upon the land, leaving the harbor seals behind them. And the foolhardy ex-seal climbed a tree and developed legs. And when, after a few hundred thousand years, he decided to climb down and fight it out with the tigers, he left up there in the tree-tops a large number of creatures who, like himself, had been brave enough to go through all the pain of escaping from the sea, but weren't up to the job of forsaking the shelter of the forest. They chattered shrilly as they watched this little handful of daring daredevils build a hut, shape a stone axe, and hollow a log into a boat for more ambitious fishing.

"Then came the day when a smaller selected group decided on a long trek into the distant mountains, the large majority voting to stay where they were and take no further risks. Those who went forth encountered fresh hardships which taught them things they had never known in the jungle and bound them together socially for mutual defense.

"Our chief trouble in thinking about evolution is that we fail to understand that *it is going on today*. This creature with the irresistible desire to rise is still evolving. His physical readjustments to meet the imperative demands of new climates, new soils, and radically altered modes of existence seem to have been completed. But that does not mean that his evolution is finished. Any more than it means a baby's development is finished when the teeth he has cut at the cost of much pain have freed him from milk to meat. Man's evolution has been operating for some time in the field of his mental progress. He is now about to make long strides morally.

"The harbor seal who, at a frightful price, learned to breathe, but who at the one critical hour of deciding whether to justify this suffering by going on, inland, to possess the earth, is now sadly imitated by the people who have endured the pain and grief and anxiety of their existence but lack the courage to proceed toward the achievement of that peace and personal power which is their rightful wage. *Many who have fully paid for it* have no awareness of their own personal adequacy."

Later in the book, in speaking of the Dean of the Cathedral, who had come through great suffering to self-sufficiency and peace, Douglas puts these words into the Dean's mouth:

"Whatever I have been able to achieve, in personal poise, stability, adequacy, has come to me by way of the obstacles I have met. This has always been true of men, since the dawn. Emergencies have always been necessary to man's evolution. It was the darkness that produced the lamp. It was the fog that produced the compass. It was winter that clothed us, hunger that drove us to exploration. The aviator can taxi all day on the ground with the wind behind his back, but if he hopes to rise, he must drive into the face of it.

"In spite of all the painful circumstances I have met, my course is upward. I know that the Universe is on my side. It will not let me down. I have been detained at times, but eventually I go on through.

"I go on through. I have suffered, but I know that I am destiny's darling. You have suffered, but you, too, can carry on through. Take it from me. I know. In spite of all the little detainments, disappointments, I get the lucky breaks. I get the signal to go forward. I have been delayed, long, long, but at length I get the Green Light."

"The Green Light"—the signal to go ahead, to move onward toward our goal.

Just as no athlete ever developed muscles without exercise, just as no musician ever developed skill without practice, so no creature ever developed new faculties without encountering and overcoming obstacles and difficulties. It is only as you have urgent NEED for new faculties that you are able to call upon the elements necessary to produce them. It is only as you struggle with obstacles that you are able to climb upon them and make them stepping-stones to something better.

In every man there is a Seed of Life, with infinite power to draw to itself whatever it conceives to be necessary to its expression. It doesn't matter who you are, what your environment or education or advantages, the Seed of Life in you has the same power for good.

What is it makes a poor immigrant boy like Edward Bok, overcome every handicap of language and educa-

tion, to become one of the greatest editors the country
has known?

What is it accounts for the fact that, as before-men-
tioned, of 4043 multimillionaires in this country a few
years before the first World War, all but 69 started so
poor that they had not even a high school education?

Isn't it that the more circumstances conspire to repress
it, the stronger becomes the urge of the Life in you for
expression? The more it lacks channels through which to
expand, the more inclined it is to burst its shell and flow
forth in all directions?

It is the old case of the river that is dammed, generating the most power. Most of us are so placed that some
opportunity for expression is made easy for us. And that
little opportunity serves like a safety valve to a boiler—
it leaves us steam enough to do something worth while,
yet keeps us from getting up enough power to burst the
shell about us, and sweep away every barrier that holds
us down.

Yet it is only such an irresistible head of steam as that
which makes great successes. That is why the blow which
knocks all the props from under us is often the turning
point in our whole career. Take the case of a man I know
who, five years after losing his job, reached his goal as
head of a rival company and the greatest authority on his
product in the country. Do you suppose he would ever
have won these rewards had he continued as salesman
for his original company?

No, indeed! He was getting along too well. He had a
comfortable home, a fine family, a good income and con-
genial working conditions. Why should he disturb them?
The old fable of the dog with the bone looking at his reflection in the water, keeps many a man from taking a
chance at a better opportunity when he has a reasonably

good one within his grasp. He's afraid he may be giving up the real for the chimera.

Yet playing safe is probably the most unsafe thing in the world. You cannot stand still. You must go forward— or see the world slide past you. This was well illustrated by figures worked out by one of the big Economic Services. Of all those who have money at 35, 87% lose it by the time they are 60.

Why?—Because the fortunes they have take away the need for initiative on their part. Their money gives to them easy means of expressing the urge in them, without effort on their part. It gives them dozens of safety valves, through which their steam continually escapes.

The result is that they not only accomplish nothing worth while, but they soon dissipate the fortunes that were left them. They are like kettles, the urge of life keeping the water at boiling point, but the open spout of ease letting the steam escape as fast as it forms, until presently there is not even any water left.

Why do the sons of rich men so seldom accomplish anything worth while? Because they don't have to. Every opportunity is given them to express the urge in them through pleasant channels, and they dissipate through these the energies that might carry them to any height. The result? They never have a strong enough "head of steam" left to carry through any real job.

With us ordinary mortals, however, sooner or later comes a crisis in our affairs, and how we meet it determines our future happiness and success. Since the beginning of time, every form of life has been called upon to meet such crises. So the goal of life has always been DOMINION—a means of overcoming all obstacles, of winning dominion over circumstances.

In "Weekly Unity" Magazine, some years ago, there was the story of a couple who wanted to dispose of their house and move to another town. But the so-called "Depression" was on at that time, and houses were a drug on the market. Real Estate Agents held out no hope, so "Why not try prayer?"—a friend asked. "What can we lose?" they asked each other. So they sat down together and tried to realize—

1. That there is only one Mind, that they were parts of that Mind, and that those to whom they must sell were also parts of it.
2. That this God-Mind is working for the good of all—for their good and for that of those who were seeking just such a home as theirs.
3. That this God-Mind was glad to help them, glad to help those seeking such a home, so all they had to do was to put their home in His hands, and leave the working out of the problem confidently and serenely to Him.

Within a short time, they sold the house for a good price for CASH. In another issue, "Unity" told about a dealer who had bought a number of pianos on credit, and borrowed some of the money from the bank to pay for them. The pinch came, and the bank notified him that his note must be paid by a certain date. He went home worried and miserable. With the help of his wife, however, he was able to throw off the worry and put it up to the God Inside Him to find the necessary funds.

That afternoon, one of the clerks came to him and said there was a man cursing and swearing about something he had bought from him the day before. He went over to the man and found him ranting and raging about an inexpensive article he had purchased for his son, on which some of the strings had broken. The shopkeeper promptly gave him a better article to replace it. That took all the wind out of the complaining customer's sails, and he became so apologetic that he felt he had to buy something else to make up for his boorish behavior. It developed that he was planning to get a fine piano for his daughter's birthday, and the money he promptly paid for this proved to be more than enough to take care of the dealer's note at the bank.

The goal of life since the beginning of time has been DOMINION over just such circumstances as these, and only through the God in you can you win it. "My soul, wait thou only upon God," bade the prophet of old, "for my expectation is from Him."

But don't limit the channels through which His help can come to you. Don't insist that it should be through a legacy from some rich uncle, or a raise in your pay or the winning of some prize or order. Develop any channel that looks promising, but leave ALL the channels open. And then act as though *you already possessed the thing you want.*

Don't say—"When this bill is paid—or this crisis past —I shall feel so relieved." Instead, say—"I AM relieved, I feel so content and peaceful now that this load is off my shoulders."

How will you act when you get the thing you want? Well, act that way now, think that way—and before you know it, you will BE that way. Remember the lines by Ella Wheeler Wilcox—

> "Thought is a magnet; and the longed-for pleasure
>   Or boon or aim or object is the steel;
>   And its attainment hangs but on the measure
>   Of what thy soul can feel."

How would you conduct yourself if you fully realized your one-ness with God, if you could truly believe that He is constantly offering you life, love and every good thing your heart can desire? Well, that is exactly what He is doing!

So act as if you already had the thing you want. Visualize it as yours. See the picture clearly in every detail in your mind's eye. Then LET GOD make it manifest. Do what you can, of course, with what you have, where you are, but put your dependence upon God, and LET His good gifts come to you.

Look at the first chapter of the Scriptures. When God wanted light, did He strive and struggle, trying to make light? No, He said—"*Let* there be light."

When you want something very much, instead of trying to MAKE it come your way, suppose you try asking for it and then LETTING it come. Suppose you just relax, and *let* God work through you instead of trying to *make* Him do something for you. Suppose you say to yourself —"I will do whatever is given me to do. I will follow every lead to the best of my ability, but for the rest, it is all up to the God in me. God in me knows what my right work is, where it is, and just what I should do to get it. I put myself and my affairs lovingly in His hands, secure that whatever is for my highest good, He will bring to me."

Emerson used to say that when we discern Truth, we do nothing of ourselves but allow a passage for its beams. They express the same thought in electricity through the equation—$C = E \div R$: The current delivered at any given point is equal to the voltage divided by the resistance. With too much resistance, no current is delivered, no matter how much may be available.

When we worry and are tense and fearful, we set up so great resistance that God finds it difficult to get through to us. We have to LET GO before we can become good conductors. Like John Burroughs, we must be able to say—"Serene I fold my hands and wait, nor care for wind or tide or sea. No more I strive against time or fate, for lo! Mine own shall come to me."

Unity has a favorite Prayer of Faith, written by Hannah More Kohaus, which all of us might well use when we are worried or sick or in need. If you will relax and repeat it slowly aloud, it is calculated to help you in any crisis:

"God IS MY help in every need;
God does my every hunger feed;
God walks beside me, guides my way
Through every moment of the day.

"I now am wise, I now am true,
Patient, kind, and loving, too.
All things I am, can do, and be,
Through Christ the Truth that is in me.

"God is my health, I can't be sick;
God is my strength, unfailing, quick;
God is my all; I know no fear,
Since God and love and Truth are here."

CHAPTER THREE

YOUR MENTAL BROWNIES

You have read of the fall of man. You have been told how Adam and Eve ate of the fruit of the Tree of Knowledge of Good and Evil, and thereafter felt naked and ashamed. And you have probably regarded the Scriptural story as a parable or legend which you have interpreted in your own way.

But do you know that back of this story is a groundwork of basic truth?

For what are the facts of the Scriptural narrative? Man lived in a Garden of Eden, where "he toiled not, neither did he spin." The fruits of the trees were his for the taking. He went about naked and unashamed. That might easily be the tale of any primitive people, might it not, especially if they happened to live in a tropical clime? It is true until comparatively recent years of the natives of some of the South Sea Islands.

You see, primitive man possessed only simple consciousness—the same consciousness as the higher animals such as the dog, the horse and the elephant. He was conscious of himself, of what he saw and felt, but he did not know he was conscious of them. He could look out upon the objects around him, he knew which gave him pleasure and which pain, but he could not reason out the whys and the wherefores, he could not look at himself from the outside and reason or plan ahead. As Schopenhauer put it—"He perceived *things* in the world, but not the world;

36

his own actions and passions, but not *himself*." His was a world of sensations.

He could feel and enjoy, but he was incapable of sin, because he knew no such thing as sin or shame. He did what he liked and took what he wanted. He did little work, because everything was free. There was no labor but the effort of gathering food.

That was primitive man in the childhood of the race. He could not sin because he was not conscious of himself as a separate entity. He could not know toil or worry, because he never planned ahead far enough for that.

But he ate of the Tree of Knowledge of Good and Evil—in other words, he became *self* conscious. For the first time, he became aware of himself as a separate entity. For the first time, he began to analyze his desires, his needs, his passions. He found that others sometimes desired the same things as he. Thence came strife. He learned that his needs could best be met by planning and working for them. Thence came labor and worry. He became conscious that his emotions were evident to others. Thence came shame and secret sin.

That was the fall of man. It was less a fall than a rise to a higher plane of consciousness, but because it is the "in-between" plane, between the Eden of mere animal sensations and the heaven of the higher consciousness, because it means a purgatory of toil and sweat and suffering, mankind has been prone to look back with longing upon the peace and content of his early days, and to wish himself back in that bucolic state where he knew no sorrow or labor or shame. And upon occasion, he betakes himself there by putting his higher faculties to sleep with drink or drugs.

But there is no turning back. His only hope lies in the forward road—the road to the heaven of a higher consciousness where he can win to *dominion* over all conditions.

Since first he was driven from Eden, man's lot has been made more bearable by the promise that some time, some day, there would come a Messiah who should lead him into this Promised Land.

That Messiah has come—and gone—but few were they who understood His message. "Go forth unto all the world," He bade His disciples, "and preach, saying—The Kingdom of Heaven is at hand."

But mankind was too ignorant, too far down in the scale of self-consciousness to be ready for that message. The Kingdom of Heaven had to be postponed a couple of thousand years. Only today are our eyes being opened to it. Only today are men in any large number reaching out for that higher consciousness which is the "Heaven in us" to which Jesus so often referred.

Mankind, like Ancient Gaul, can be divided into three parts.

1st—Those who are still in a state of simple consciousness, living, acting and thinking as the animals do. Men and women in this class can be said to exist—nothing more.

2nd—Those in a state of self-consciousness. This comprises the great bulk of the higher races of mankind. They reason, they study, they work, they sorrow and enjoy. But they are forced to depend for all good things upon their own efforts and they are subject to all manner of circumstances and conditions beyond their control. Theirs is a state of struggle.

3rd—Those entering into or who have reached the intuitional or higher consciousness, that state which Jesus termed the Kingdom of Heaven within us.

Just as, in the childhood of the race, there was brought forth an Adam and Eve with such advanced receptual in-

tellects that they presently developed conceptual ideas
(i.e. named impressions and the ability to classify them,
compare them and draw conclusions from them), so today are to be found here and there the advance guard of
the Mental Age—men and women as far ahead of the
ordinary conceptual intellect of their fellows as this is in
advance of the simple consciousness of the animal.

You see, the animal recognizes only images. Each
house is to him a new house, with its own associations of
food or famine, of kindness or blows. He never general-
izes, or draws conclusions by comparing one house with
another. His is the simple or receptual consciousness.

Man, on the other hand, takes his recept or image of a
house and tabs it. He names it a house and then classifies
it according to its kind. In that way, he turns it from a
mere image into an idea or concept. It is as though he
were traveling on a railroad train and keeping a tally of
every house he passed. To the animal, it would mean filling his mind with the pictures of a hundred or more
houses. To a man, it would be merely a matter of jotting
down in the tablets of his memory—"100 houses, 25 of
the Colonial type, 15 Tudor style, etc."

If his mind were too full of images, there would be no
room in it to work out conclusions from those images, so
man classifies those images into concepts or ideas, and
thus increases his mental capacity a millionfold.

But now the time has come in his mental development
when his mind is so full of concepts that a new short cut
must be found. Here and there a few have already found
this short cut and penetrated to the highest plane of consciousness—the intuitional or "Heaven" consciousness.

What is this higher consciousness? Bucke calls it the
Cosmic Consciousness, and defines it as a consciousness of
the world about us, a consciousness that does not have to
stop and add concept to concept like a column of figures,

but which can work out the answer immediately, intuitively, as a "lightning calculator" can work out a problem in mathematics, apparently without going through any of the intermediate stages of addition and subtraction, of labored reasoning from premise to conclusion.

You see, the conscious you is merely that aggregation of images and sensations and concepts known as the brain. But beyond and above this reasoning mind is your intuitive mind—the Soul of you—which is one cell in the great Oversoul of the Universe, God. It is the connecting link between God and you. It is part of Him. It shares in all His attributes, all His power and wisdom and riches. And at need it can draw upon the whole of these. How? In the same way that any cell of your body can draw upon the vitality of the whole body—by creating the need, *by using what it has.*

There is nothing mysterious about the way life works. It is all a logical growth. In the intellect, the young child first registers impressions, then it recognizes and tabs them, finally classifying them and using them as the basis for reasoning out ideas. By the use of impressions and images, the child can know the world it sees and feels. By concepts, it can construct in imagination the world it has not seen. Is this all? Is it the end?

"No!" answers Bucke in "Cosmic Consciousness." "As life arose in a world without life; as simple consciousness came into existence where before was mere vitality without perception; as self-consciousness soared forth over land and sea; so shall the race of man which has been thus established make other steps and attain to a yet higher life than any heretofore experienced or even conceived.

"And let it be clearly understood that the new step is not merely an expansion of self-consciousness, but as distinct from it as that is from simple consciousness, or as is this last from mere vitality without any consciousness at all."

But how shall we know this new sense? How recognize its coming? The signs are evident in every man and woman of high mentality. You have seen accountants who could write down a column of figures and give you the total without consciously adding one to another. You can recall instances when you have anticipated word for word what someone was about to say to you, when you have answered the telephone and known before he spoke who was at the other end of the wire, when you have met a stranger and formed a "snap judgment" of him which afterwards turned out to be marvelously correct. We call this intuition. It is the first stage of the Cosmic Consciousness. It is a perfectly logical step in the growth of the intellect.

In the jump from Simple Consciousness to Self-Consciousness, man combined groups of recepts or images into one concept or idea, just as we combine the three Roman numerals III into the one symbol 3. No longer did he have to hold in his mind each individual tree in a forest. He grouped them all together under one heading of trees, and called the group a forest.

Now he is advancing a step farther. Instead of having to first study each tree individually to learn the properties of that forest, he is getting that knowledge from the soul within him, which is part of the great Oversoul of the forest and of the Universe, and therefore knows all things. In other words, he is getting it intuitively.

That is the first step in reaching the Heaven consciousness—to cultivate your intuitions, to encourage them in every possible way. Your soul is a cell in the great God-body just as every cell in your body is part of you. And as part of the Oversoul of the Universe, it has access to all the knowledge of the Universe. But it needs exercise, it requires development.

When you want to develop any cell or set of cells in your body, what do you do? You exercise them, do you not? You use them to the limit of their abilities. Then what happens? They feel weak, exhausted. They become thin and emaciated. Why? Because you have broken up those cells, used the energy in them, and they have not yet had time to draw upon the blood stream for more. For the first few days or weeks that you continue that hard usage, they remain weak and nerveless. Again why? Because the amount of energy your "governor" is accustomed to apportioning those cells is not sufficient for such heavy work. But keep persevering, and what happens? Those cells not only harden until they are equal to any call you can make upon them, but they grow in size and power. They have put in a permanent order upon the "governor" for more life-giving energy, and as long as they can find use for it, that energy will keep coming to them.

That is the first thing you must do to grow in intuitive consciousness—cultivate what you have, use it on every possible occasion even though you seem to strain it beyond its powers at first. Listen for that still, small voice. And listen *to* it. "And thine ears shall hear a word behind thee," promised the Prophet of old, "saying—This is the way, walk ye in it, when ye turn to the right hand, and when ye turn to the left."

What is the vision of the artist, the inspiration of the writer, the discovery of the chemist or inventor, but his intuitive consciousness at work? Ask almost any great author, and he will tell you that he does not work out his plots. They "come to him"—that's all. "The key to successful methods," says Thomas A. Edison, "comes right out of the air. A real new thing like a general idea, a beautiful melody, is pulled out of space—a fact which is inexplicable."

Inexplicable—yes, from the viewpoint of the conceptual intellect—but quite understandable from the intuitive point of view.

So much for the first step. It is one possible to any man or woman of high intellect. When it involves a problem or a work of art or a story or a new discovery, it requires only filling the mind with all available concepts related to the desired result, then putting it up to the God in you to work out the answer.

The second step is the earnest desire for a higher consciousness. That sounds simple enough. Everybody would like to be able to learn without going through all the labor of adding percept to recept, making concepts of these and then figuring out the answers. So if the earnest desire is all that is needed, it ought to be easy.

Yet it is not. It is the hardest step of all. Why? Because the desire must be your *dominant* desire. It must not be merely a means to the end of obtaining riches or winning to high position.

All agree on this: This Heaven consciousness comes only as the result of a tremendous desire for spiritual truth, and a hunger and thirst after things of the spirit.

Perhaps that can be better understood when you remember how many ordinary people have had partial glimpses of it when almost at the point of death, or when coming out from under the influence of anaesthetics.

What, then, are the necessary conditions?

First, an understanding of the power latent in you, an understanding that, regardless of how much or how little education you have received, there is in you a power (call it the subconscious, or your soul, or your good genii or what you will) capable of contacting the Intelligence which directs and animates all of the universe.

Second, the earnest desire for spiritual growth. To possess this, a man need not be an ascetic, or give up his family or his business. In fact, he should be the better husband and father and business man for it. For the man of business today is no longer engaged in cheating his neighbor before the neighbor can cheat him. He is trying to *serve,* and to the extent that he succeeds in giving more and better service than others, he succeeds. Can you conceive of any finer preparation for the Heaven consciousness?

Third, the ability to thoroughly relax. As Boehme put it—"To cease from all thinking and willing and imaging. Your own 'self-conscious' hearing and willing and seeing hinder you from seeing and hearing God."

"When a new faculty appears in a race," says Bucke, "it will be found in the very beginning in one individual of that race; later it will be found in a few individuals; after a further time, in a larger percentage of the members of the race; still later, in half the members; and so on until, after thousands of generations, an individual who misses having the faculty is regarded as a monstrosity."

The Heaven consciousness, or Cosmic Consciousness as Bucke calls it, has reached the point of being found in many individuals. When a faculty reaches that point, it is susceptible of being acquired by all of the higher type of members of that race *who have reached full maturity.*

And it is never too late to develop this Intuitive Consciousness, for your mind never grows old. In his book, "The Age of Mental Virility," Dr. Dorland points out that more than half of mankind's greatest achievements were accomplished by men over 50 years old, and that more of these were done by men over 70 than by those under 30.

In tests made by Dr. Irving Lorge of Teachers College, Columbia University, it was found that while SPEED of learning might decline with years, the mental

powers do not decline. When the speed penalty was elimi-
nated, people of 50 and 60 made higher scores than those
around 25. Dr. Lorge sums up his tests in these words:

"As far as mental ability is concerned, there need be no
'retiring age.' The probabilities are that the older a person becomes, the more valuable he becomes. He possesses
the same mental power he had in his young manhood,
plus his wealth of experience and knowledge of his particular job. These are things that no youngster, however
brilliant, can pick up."

You have an Intuitive Consciousness, which has evidenced itself many a time in "Hunches," and the like. Remains, then, only to develop it. Robert Louis Stevenson
pointed the way when he told how he worked out the plot
for Dr. Jekyll and Mr. Hyde.

"My Brownies! God bless them!" said Stevenson,
"Who do one-half of my work for me when I am fast
asleep, and in all human likelihood do the rest for me as
well when I am wide awake and foolishly suppose that I
do it myself. I had long been wanting to write a book on
man's double being. For two days I went about racking
my brains for a plot of any sort, and on the second night
I dreamt the scene in Dr. Jekyll and Mr. Hyde at the
window; and a scene, afterward split in two, in which
Hyde, pursued, took the powder and underwent the
change in the presence of his pursuer."

You have had similar experiences. You know how,
after you have studied a problem from all angles, it sometimes seems worse jumbled than when you started on it.
Leave it then for a while—forget it—and when you go
back to it, you find your thoughts clarified, the line of reasoning worked out, your problem solved for you. It is
your little "Mental Brownies" who have done the work
for you!

The flash of genius does not originate in your own

brain. Through intense concentration you have established a circuit through your subconscious mind with the Universal, and it is from IT that the inspiration comes. All genius, all progress, is from the same source. It lies with you merely to learn how to establish this circuit at will so that you can call upon IT at need. It can be done.

"There are many ways of setting the Brownies to work," says Dumont in "The Master Mind." "Nearly everyone has had some experience, more or less, in the matter, although often it is produced almost unconsciously, and without purpose and intent. Perhaps the best way for the average person—or rather the majority of persons—to get the desired results is for one to get as clear an idea of what one really wants to know—as clear an idea or mental image of the question you wish answered. Then after rolling it around in your mind—mentally chewing it, as it were—giving it a high degree of voluntary attention, you can pass it on to your Subconscious Mentality with the mental command: *'Attend to this for me—work out the answer!'* or some similar order. This command may be given silently, or else spoken aloud—either will do. Speak to the Subconscious Mentality—or its little workers—just as you would speak to persons in your employ, kindly but firmly. Talk to the little workers, and firmly command them to do your work. And then forget all about the matter—throw it off your conscious mind, and attend to your other tasks. Then in due time will come your answer—flashed into your consciousness—perhaps not until the very minute that you must decide upon the matter, or need the information. You may give your Brownies orders to report at such and such a time—just as you do when you tell them to awaken you at a certain time in the morning so as to catch the early train, or just as they remind you of the hour of your appointment, if you have them all well trained."

Have you ever read the story by Richard Harding Davis of "The Man Who Could Not Lose?" In it the hero is intensely interested in racing. He has studied records and "dope" sheets until he knows the history of every horse backward and forward.

The day before the big race he is reclining in an easy chair, thinking of the morrow's race, and he drops off to sleep with that thought on his mind. Naturally, his subconscious mind takes it up, with the result that he dreams the exact outcome of the race.

That was mere fiction, of course, but if races were run solely on the speed and stamina of the horses, it would be entirely possible to work out the results in just that way. Unfortunately, other factors frequently enter into every betting game.

But the idea behind Davis' story is entirely right. The way to contact your subconscious mind, the way to get the help of the "Man Inside You" in working out any problem is:

First, fill your mind with every bit of information regarding that problem that you can lay your hands on.

Second, pick out a chair or lounge or bed where you can recline in perfect comfort, where you can forget your body entirely.

Third, let your mind dwell upon the problem for a moment, not worrying, not fretting, but placidly, and then turn it over to the "Man Inside You." Say to him—"This is your problem. You Can do anything. You know the answer to everything. Work this out for me!" And utterly relax. Drop off to sleep, if you can. At least, drop into one of those half-sleepy, half-wakeful reveries that keep other thoughts from obtruding upon your consciousness. Do as Aladdin did—summon your Genie, give him your orders, then forget the matter, secure in the knowledge that he will attend to it for you. When you waken, *you will have the answer!*

"The smartest man in the world is the Man Inside," said Dr. Frank Crane. "By the Man Inside I mean that Other Man within each one of us that does most of the things we give ourselves credit for doing.

"I say he is the smartest man in the world. I know he is infinitely more clever and resourceful than I am or than any other man is that I ever heard of. When I cut my finger it is he that calls up the little phagocytes to come and kill the septic germs that might get into the wound and cause blood poisoning. It is he that coagulates the blood, stops the gash, and weaves the new skin.

"I could not do that. I do not even know how he does it. He even does it for babies that know nothing at all; in fact, does it better for them than for me.

"When I practice on the piano I am simply getting the business of piano playing over from my conscious mind to my subconscious mind: in other words, I am handing the business over to the Man Inside.

"Most of our happiness, as well as our struggles and misery, comes from this Man Inside. If we train him in ways of contentment, adjustment and decision, he will go ahead of us like a well-trained servant and do for us easily most of the difficult tasks we have to perform."

Read that last paragraph again. "Most of our happiness, *as well as our struggles and misery,* comes from this Man Inside."

How, then, can we use him to bring us only the good things of life?

By BLESSING instead of ranting and cursing, by TRUSTING instead of fearing. Every man is what he is because of the dominating thoughts that he permits to occupy his mind and thus suggests to the Man Inside. Those thoughts that are mixed with some feeling of emotion, such as anger or fear or worry or love, magnetize that Man Inside and tend to drive him to such action as will attract to you similar or related thoughts and their logical reactions. All impulses of thought have a tendency to bring about their physical equivalent, simply because they set the Man Inside You to work trying to bring about the physical manifestations of your thought images. Jesus understood this when He said—"By their fruits shall ye know them."

What, then is the answer?

1. Realize that your thoughts are the molds in which the Man Inside You forms your circumstances, that "As a man thinketh, so is he."

2. Remember that there is nothing in all of God's Universe which you need to fear. For God is Love, and you are one with God. So make friends with your problems. Don't try to run away from them. Walk up to them, bring them into the open, and you will find that they are not obstacles, but stepping-stones to something better.

3. If you are worrying or fearful, stop it. Put your affairs into the hands of the God in You—and forget them! Remember that all things are possible with God, and all things are possible with you when you realize that you are one with Him. So look to God instead of to your difficulties. Look to the things you WANT—not to those you fear.

4. Forget the past. Remember—"Now is the accepted time. Now is the day of salvation." Look ahead to the great things that are before you—not backward at the regrets of the past. Look to what you want to see manifested. Think of each day as in itself a life, and say each morning—"I wake to do the work of a man."

5. Bless all things, for under even the most unprepossessing exterior lies a kernel of good. Remember that "When Fortune means to man most good, she looks upon him with a threatening eye."

In "Unity Weekly," the story is told of a farmer who,

when he plows a field, blesses every seed he puts into it, and visualizes the abundant harvest it will bring. His neighbors marvel at the size of his crops.

In another issue, they tell of a guest in a western hotel who was impressed by the atmosphere of joy and peace in the room she occupied. Living in it seemed to be an inspiration. She was so filled with the presence of good in it that she asked the maid who had occupied it before, to give it such a restful atmosphere. The maid told her it was not the occupant, but herself; that whenever she worked in a room she blessed it, and as she left it, she stood in the door for a moment affirming peace and restfulness for it and blessing for the one who would occupy it.

Arthur Guiterman has written a blessing for every home that each of us might well use:

> "Bless the four corners of this house,
> And be the Lintel blest;
> And bless the hearth, and bless the board,
> And bless each place of rest;
> And bless the door that opens wide
> To stranger, as to kin;
> And bless each crystal windowpane
> That lets the starlight in;
> And bless the rooftree overhead,
> And every sturdy wall;
> The peace of God, the peace of man,
> The peace of love, on all."

CHAPTER FOUR

THE SEED OF LIFE

How DID THE ELEPHANT get its trunk, the camel its hump, the lobster its shell, the birds their wings? How has every creature's need been met since time began?

By impressing its need so strongly and so urgently upon the Life Force inside that it said in effect—*"Save me or I perish!"*

The elephant was a great, lumbering creature. It could not bend down to get the succulent grasses it must have to sustain its vast bulk. It would have worn itself out with bending. So it sent out its distress signal—*"Give me a means of picking up food or I perish!"*

The camel was a wanderer in the waste places. It must be able to exist for days at a time without food or water. So it required a place to store these—a reserve supply it could draw upon in between oases. Result? Its hump of fat for energy, its four stomachs to hold a reserve water supply.

The Fundamental Law of the Universe is that every form of life holds *within itself* vitality enough to draw to it every element it needs for growth and fruition. But it is only as it casts off all outside support, and puts its dependence solely upon the life force that created it and left its spark within it, that it is able to draw to itself the elements it needs for complete growth and fruition.

If the elephant had been able to go to the local inventor and get him to rig up a patent reaping and feeding machine, do you suppose he would ever have grown a trunk? If the camel had been able to buy a special pack-saddle which would carry reserve supplies of grain and water, would he ever have grown his hump? If you are able to go to some rich relative, or to the government, whenever you lack for the necessities of life, are you ever going to develop dominion over circumstances?

"It is only as a man puts off all foreign support and stands alone that I see him firm and to prevail," wrote Emerson. "He is weaker by every recruit to his banner." In other words, it is only as a man puts his dependence solely upon the God *inside HIM* that he becomes master of his own fate, that he is able to draw to himself whatever he needs for support.

Take the giant redwoods of California. By no law known to man can they draw water to their foliage hundreds of feet in the air! Yet they do draw it—hundreds of gallons every day.

It is not done through pressure from below—from the roots. It is done by pull from above! In other words, the need is first established, then the need itself provides the means or the "pull" to draw to it the elements it must have for expression!

All through Nature, you will find that same law. First the need, then the means. Use what you have to provide the vacuum, then draw upon the necessary elements to fill it. Reach up with your stalk, spread out your branches, provide the "pull" and you can leave to your roots the search for the necessary nourishment. If you have reached high enough, if you have made your magnet strong enough, you can draw to yourself whatever elements you need, no matter if they be at the ends of the earth!

God formed a Seed of Himself in you. He gave it power to attract to itself everything it needs for its growth, just as He did with the seed of the tree. He gave it power to draw to itself everything it needs for fruition, just as He did with the tree. But He did even more for you. He gave your Seed of Life power to attract to itself everything it needs for its *infinite expression!*

You see, Life is intelligent. Life is all-powerful. And Life is always and everywhere seeking expression. What is more, it is never satisfied. It is constantly seeking greater and fuller expression. The moment a tree stops growing, that moment the life in it starts seeking elsewhere for means to better express itself. The moment you stop expressing more and more of Life, that moment Life starts looking around for other and better outlets.

The only thing that can restrict Life is the channel through which it works. The only limitation upon it is the limitation you put upon it.

The secret of success lies in this: There is inside you a Seed of God capable of drawing to you any element you need, to bring to fruition whatever of good you desire. But like all other seeds, its shell must be broken before the kernel inside can use its attractive power. And that shell is thicker, harder, than the shell of any seed on earth. Only one thing will break it—*heat from within*—a desire so strong, a determination so intense, that you cheerfully throw everything you have into the scale to win what you want. Not merely your work and your money and your thought but the willingness to stand or fall by the result—to do or to die. Like the Master when He cursed the fig tree for its barrenness, you are willing to demand of the Seed of Life in you that it *bear fruit or perish.*

That is the secret of every great success. That is the means by which all of life, from the beginning of time, has won what it needed.

What was it gave to certain animals protective shells, to others great speed, to still others a sting, to those who needed them claws or horns? What gave to the bold and strong the means to destroy, to the weak and cowardly facilities for hiding or escape? What but the Seed of Life in each, giving to every form of life the means that form craved to preserve its skin.

Go back through the ages and you will find that as conditions change, the forms of life change with them. When the whole earth was covered with water, the only forms of animal life were in the sea, so they breathed through gills. Then parts of the land began to emerge and the changing tides left certain forms of sea-life high and dry half the time. Did they perish? No, indeed! They grew lungs to use in the air to supplement the gills they needed in the water. The Glacial periods came and a large part of the earth was covered with ice. Did the animal life freeze? Again, no. Those forms that were subject to cold grew fur, those in warm climes hair, while the birds which alternated between heat and cold grew feathers.

Always the seed in each form of life responded to the call of that life—*"Give me so-and-so or I perish."*

Since the very creation of the earth, Life has been threatened by every kind of danger. Had it not been stronger than any other power in the Universe—were it not indeed a part of God Himself—it would have perished ages ago. But God who gave it to us endowed it with unlimited resource, unlimited energy. No other force can defeat it. No obstacle can hold it back.

What is it that saves men in dire extremity, who have exhausted every human resource and finally turned to God in their need? What but the unquenchable flame of God in them—the Seed of Life He has given to each of us— with power to draw to us whatever element we feel that we need to save us from extinction.

The story is told of a little girl four years old, who had been taught to believe in a protecting Deity. She got lost one day, and was gone for hours. Her mother was on the verge of desperation when at last she saw her child coming home. She was all alone, yet seemed to be holding somebody's hand and her lips were moving as if she were carrying on a sprightly conversation. Her mother opened the front door just in time to see her drop the invisible hand and to hear her say:

"You may go now, God. This is where I live. And thank you very much!"

It was all quite simple as she explained it to her mother. She had wandered about until she got tired and hungry. Then she realized that she didn't know the way home.

"I knew I was losted, Mother," she said, "so I asked God to take me home. I knew that He knew the way. Then I started for home and God showed me where to go. And here I am."

"Why, then," some will ask, "does not the God in you exert itself to bring you food when you are hungry, drink when you are thirsty, clothing when you are cold, money when you are in debt?" Why? Because you don't put your dependence upon it for these. You look for these things to your hands or your friends or some means within the power of those around you. It is only when you despair of all ordinary means, it is only *when you convince it* that it must help you or you perish, that the Seed of Life in you bestirs itself to provide a new resource.

That is why psychological or metaphysical means so seldom cure a patient who continues to put some of his dependence upon drugs or treatments. It is not that the spirit in you is a "jealous God." It is that it takes a real need to stir Him into action. As long as you show that you feel there is a chance of your being saved through some other means, the Seed of Life in you is not going to bestir itself to help you. And as long as it sees that you are depending upon your friends or the stock market or some other method to supply your urgent need of money, it is not going to worry itself about it.

"Unity Weekly" tells of a woman alone in a big city, jobless, anxious and discouraged, and worried about her husband who was seeking work in another town.

Because there was no one else to whom she could look for help, she prayed until she was able to put utter faith in God, to believe that He would look after her and to put all her dependence upon Him. Then she was able to go out into the street with springy step, with a heart full of confidence and a face that radiated belief in herself and in her ability to do things. She threw away her sheet of Want Ads, and on impulse, turned into a cheerful looking building and found a desirable job! Within a day or two after, an unexpected check came to her in the mail, and a letter of good news from her husband.

Another case was that of a subnormal boy, about to be rejected by a school. His mother had taught him to believe in God, so he kept repeating to himself—"God will tell me what to do." God did—to such good purpose that a few years later he graduated at the head of his class!

Then there was a woman who was expected to die from a seemingly incurable and painful disease. She asked that her bed be moved to a window, and as she looked out at the starry spaces in the long hours of the night, she thought of God—of His power, of His goodness, of His love for every creature, of Jesus saying that not even a sparrow fell without His marking it. And as she pondered all this, belief in His ability and His willingness to cure her came to her, until presently there began to flow into her consciousness the belief that she WAS cured, and she amazed her attendants by sitting up and asking for something to eat. Today she is alive and well.

How can YOU stir the boundless force of the God in

you into action? How can YOU draw upon its infinite resource for your urgent needs?

How did the early forms of life wake it from its lethargy? By putting it squarely up to the Seed to *save them or perish with them,* did they not? Those early forms of life had no means of reasoning out their troubles. They only knew that conditions were too much for them, so they went straight to the power that animated them and cried—*"Save us or we perish."*

Utter faith, utter dependence—that is the only answer. No half-way measures will do. If you want help and have exhausted all the methods that physicians and surgeons and practitioners can offer you, and want now to go direct to the Source for new Life, new health and strength, you cannot keep on dabbling with drugs and treatments and hope to stir the Seed of Life in you into action. You must drop everything else. You must put your whole dependence upon the infinite power of that Seed of God in you. You must get the attitude of our revolutionary patriots— "Sink or swim, live or die, survive or perish, I give my hand and my heart to this cause. Either I live by it or I die with it!"

Get that attitude of mind, and the stirring of your Seed of Life into action is simple.

Say to yourself—"I am one with the Life Force that runs the Universe, the great I AM of which Jesus said— 'Before Abraham, was I AM.' I AM energy. I AM power. I AM filled with omnipotent life. The vitality of God permeates every fiber of my being. I AM well and whole in every part of my body. I AM made up of billions of cells of Intelligent Life, and that Intelligence is guiding me to Health and Happiness and Prosperity."

E. Stanley-Jones, author of CHRIST OF THE INDIAN ROAD, tells how he broke down completely with nervous exhaustion and brain fatigue at the end of eight

years of missionary work in India, just when he had
learned the ways of the people, and conditions seemed
ripe for him to do the most good.

He was terribly depressed and disappointed, until one
night in the midst of his prayers, he seemed to hear a
voice saying—"Are you yourself ready for this work to
which I have called you?" "No, Lord," he answered, "I
am done for. I have reached the end of my resources."
"If you will turn that over to me," the voice told him,
"and not worry about it, I will take care of it." "Lord,"
he responded gladly, "I close the bargain right here!"

That was many years ago. The Doctors had just told
him he would have to leave India and go back home for a
couple of years to rest. Instead, he threw himself with
renewed energy into his work, and he never before knew
such health as he has had since. He seems to have tapped
a new source of life for body, mind and spirit. *Yet all he
had to do was to take it!*

Does this mean that you are to make no effort to help
yourself? By no means! This was never meant for a lazy
man's world. The whole purpose of existence is growth,
and all of nature is continually growing. Whenever anything stops growing, it starts to die.

We were given hands to work with, brains to think
with. We were expected to use these.

For while it is not the roots that send the moisture to
the tops of the tall trees, it is the roots that dig down to
the moisture and nutriment to start it flowing. It requires
an urgent need to draw to you resources beyond the power
of your hands, just as it requires the evaporation of the
moisture in the leaves to pull the water to the tops of the
tallest trees, but unless the hands or the roots do their
part first, that need will never be satisfied. The trouble
with most people is that they go as far as their hands or
their immediate abilities will take them, and stop there.

It is as though a tree sent up its stem only as high as the root pressure carried the water from the earth. That would give us a forest of stunted trees, just as dependence upon their hands gives us the masses who live in poverty and misery.

It is only when you multiply your hands by thousands, it is only when you conceive and start great projects impossible of attainment by you alone, that you call forth the power of the Seed of Life in you, to draw to you every element you need for complete growth and fruition.

When George Mueller of England started his first orphanage, he had no money, no backers, no material resources to depend upon. He saw the need, that is all, so he went as far as he could in supplying that need. And each time, when he had reached the end of his resources, yet kept confidently trying, the need was met! In fifteen years, he built five orphanages and spent more than $5,000,000—all without a single visible means of support!

When St. Theresa proposed to build an orphanage, she was asked how much she had on which to start. When it developed that her total wealth was only three ducats, her superiors laughed at the idea. "It is true," she answered them, "that with only three ducats I can do nothing, but with God and three ducats I can do anything!" And she proceeded to prove it by building the orphanage whose good work made her famous.

In the fields of philanthropy and religion, you can find hundreds of similar stories. And in the fields of business, you find many thousands more. How many times have you read of some great institution that was founded on nothing but hard work and the faith of its founder. Henry Ford began on little else. Stewart started what is now the John Wanamaker store with a total cash capital of $1.50.

Sometimes, in fact, it seems to be an advantage not to have enough money when you start a new project.

Then you don't put your faith in the money—you put it in IDEAS. In other words, you look to MIND to supply the means.

Someone expressed it well when he said we must work as if everything depended upon us, and at the same time, pray as if everything depended upon God.

What does an oculist do when you go to him for glasses? Fit your eyes with glasses that take away ALL the strain and enable you to see perfectly? No, indeed! The best oculists give you glasses a little short of the strength necessary to take all the strain off your eyes. They relieve you of the heavy burden, but they leave your sight just enough short of perfection to keep your eyes working towards that end.

The result? When you go back six months or a year later, your eyes are stronger—you can take glasses which do less of your work—until in time you do without them altogether.

What do business leaders advise young people today? Live within your income? No, indeed! *Go into debt!* Reach out! Spread yourself! Then dig the harder to catch up!

You are entitled to just as much of the good things of life as Ford or Rockefeller or Morgan, or any of the rich men around you. But it is not THEY who owe it to you. And it is not the world that owes you a living. The world and they owe you nothing but honest pay for the exact service you render them.

The one who owes you everything of good—riches and honor and happiness—is the God inside you. Go to him! Stir him up! Don't rail against the world. You get from it what you put into it—nothing more. Wake up the God inside you! Demand of him that he bring you the elements you need for riches or success. Demand— and make your need seem as urgent as must have been the need of the crustacean to develop a shell, of the bird to grow wings, of the bear to get fur.

Demand—and KNOW THAT YOU RECEIVE! The God in you is just as strong as ever He was in those primitive animals in pre-historic days. If He could draw from the elements whatever was necessary to give the elephant its trunk, the camel its hump, the bird its wings, and to each creature the means it required to enable it to survive, don't you suppose He can do the same today to provide YOU with the factors you consider essential to your well-being?

The answer is that you have already brought into being your "hump" or your "trunk" or whatever it was that you felt you must have. You are, in short, what your thoughts and fears and beliefs have made you. *Your present condition reflects the successful result of your past thought!*

Astonishing as it may sound to many people, you are now living in a world of your own making. But you don't have to keep on living there if you don't like it. You can build a new world in exactly the same way you built that one—only it would be well to build it on a different model.

It is the Einstein doctrine of the extended line, which must return to its source. An evil thought or act goes out upon its course, but the Eternal Lawmaker has decreed that it must return to its creator. A good act or thought is governed in the same way. "By their fruits, ye shall know them."

So don't complain of your lot. Don't rail at the difficulties and obstacles that confront you. Smile on them! Treat them as friends. *Bless them*—for they can be made to bless you!

You see, they have not been sent from Heaven to punish you. You asked for them yourself. They are of your own making, and they are your friends, because they call forcibly to your attention some wrong method you have been using. All you have to do is to change your methods, and the results will automatically change with them. It is just as though you were doing some problem in multiplication, and you kept saying—"One times one is two." That would throw your whole result out of balance, and it would stay out until you learned your mistake and made one times one equal one.

> "You are not higher than your lowest thought,
> Or lower than the peak of your desire.
> And all existence has no wonder wrought
> To which ambition may not yet aspire.
> O Man! There is no planet, sun or star
> Could hold you, if you but knew what you are."

What, then, is the method to be used to get what you want from life?

1st—DESIRE. Decide what it is you want. Make it something so worthwhile that all other things will seem small and unimportant beside it, something so urgent that you can say to the God Inside You—*"Give me this or I perish!"*

2nd—*See yourself having it.* Visualize the thing you want. See yourself with it. Try to get the FEEL of having it, the joy and thankfulness you would get out of it. In Burton Rascoe's Memoirs, he tells how he worked out his life on a predetermined schedule, in which everything came true because he thought it, he desired it and he BELIEVED it. Here are a few typical lines from it:

"When I was fifteen years old, I wanted to live in Chicago some time and I *knew* I would; the university I wished to go to was the University of Chicago and I *knew* I would; there was only one newspaper in the world I ardently wished to work on—the Chicago Tribune—and I *knew* five years in advance that I would some day work there; when I was a reporter I *knew* I would be some day literary editor.

"When I was literary editor of the Chicago Tribune I *knew* I would some day live in New York and be literary editor of the New York Tribune.

"In 1927 I wanted $50,000 and *knew* I would get it; within less than a year I had over $100,000, almost without any effort on my part."

3rd—*Be thankful for having received it.* Remember the admonition of the Master—"Whatsoever things ye ask for when ye pray, believe that ye RECEIVE them, and ye shall have them." You cannot believe that you actually receive the things you ask for without being thankful for them. So give thanks, sincere thanks, for having received the things you prayed for, and try to FEEL grateful. Remember to SMILE! Repeat aloud daily Adelaide Proctor's poem—

"My God, I thank Thee, who has made the earth so bright;
So full of splendor and of joy, beauty and light;
So many glorious things are here, noble and right.

"I thank Thee too that Thou hast made joy to abound;
So many gentle thoughts and deeds circling us round,
That in the darkest spot of earth Thy love is found."

4th—*Act as though you HAD already received* the thing you asked for. Faith without works is dead. Do some physical thing each day such as you would do if you had the object you prayed for. If you are asking for money, for instance, GIVE a little, even though it be only a dime, just to show the freedom from money worry that is now yours. If you are asking for love, say a kindly word to each of those with whom you come in contact. If you are asking for health, dance about your room, sing, laugh, do some of those things you will do when you have fully manifested the good health you crave.

5th—*Show your affection* for the thing you asked for. Give your love to it, pour it out just as you would if you had the object in your hands. Only by making it REAL to you in your thoughts can you materialize it in your life.

We go, you know, in the direction of our thoughts. What we long for—*and expect*—that we are headed towards. So look for the kind of things you want to see. Look for them in your own life—and in the lives of those around you. Look for them—AND BEGIN DOING THEM! Remember those lines of Goethe's:

> "Are you in earnest? Seize this very minute;
> What you can do, or dream you can, begin it;
> Boldness has genius, power, and magic in it.
> Only engage, and then the mind grows heated;
> *Begin, and then the work will be completed.*"

CHAPTER FIVE

AFTER ITS KIND

Do YOU KNOW what is the most important lesson in the whole Bible? Do you know what principle was considered so vital that God is said to have used it on three of the six days of creation, and it is repeated no less than six times in the first chapter of Genesis alone? Just this:

"Everything Reproduces After Its Kind!"

Go back over the miracles of increase in the Bible. What do you find? When the widow of Zarephath gave Elijah her oil and meal, what did she get? MORE OIL AND MEAL, did she not? Not gold, or riches, but IN-CREASE AFTER ITS KIND.

When another widow begged Elisha to save her sons from bondage, he asked—"What hast thou in the house?" And when told—"Naught save a pot of oil," it was the *oil* he increased, was it not?

When the multitude lacked for bread and the Apostles asked Jesus what they should do, He did not turn the stones into bread, or bring forth gold with which to buy. No, He asked—"How many loaves have you?" And when told five, and two fishes, He based His increase upon *them*.

You see, it all comes back to terms of electrical energy, for what is energy but power, and what are personality, skill, ability, riches, but different forms of power? If you want to increase your stock of these, what must you do? Put them to work, must you not? Put them out at interest, as in the parable of the talents. No energy ever expanded until it was released. No seed ever multiplied until it was sown. No talent ever increased until it was used.

You want more power, more riches, greater ability, a wider field of usefulness. How are you going to get them? *Only by putting out at interest that which you have!*

And the way to do this lies—NOT in working for riches as such—BUT FOR INCREASE IN THE FORM OF ENERGY YOU HAVE!

Now, what have YOU in the house? What seed can you plant, what service can you give?

In Weekly Unity some years ago, there was the story of a mother who had been well-to-do, but had lost everything and was now hard put to it to provide food and clothing for her small boys. It was near Christmas, and she was bewailing to a friend the fact that she could buy no gifts for her children, much less remember old friends and relatives.

The friend smiled. "Money is not what you need," she told her. "Can money buy the gifts that live in your heart? If I were in your place, I should stop repining and, instead, seek the guidance of your Inner Self."

The mother took the advice, and one night, as she dropped off to sleep after having prayed for guidance, she saw a beautiful tree, lighted with tapers, and beneath each light hung a small envelope. As she looked more closely, she saw that the names written on the envelopes were those of friends and relatives to whom she longed to give.

Opening one of the envelopes, she found a piece of blank paper and she seemed to hear a voice saying: "Write, and let that which you write bear witness of Me. As you write, give from your heart the treasures that are stored there in My name. I will fulfill every blessing according to your word."

The mother woke, and going immediately to her desk, began to write her blessings. She wrote words of life and wholeness for an aunt who had been bound with rheumatism for months; words of courage for an uncle who was having a difficult time with his farm; words of guidance for a young cousin who had seemed to lose her way a bit. Inspired by that Inner Self, she wrote ten blessings that night.

She had never thought that she could write, but her own heart thrilled at the beauty of the words that came to her, and she was lifted up by their power and simplicity. "Don't ever again say you have nothing to give," one of her friends told her later. "I never received so richly in all my life." And throughout the years, the blessings that this mother gave out have continued to bear fruit.

"Give me gold," prayed Levesco, "that I may be helpful, not helpless. Give me gold that I may taste the pure joy of making others happy. Give me gold that I may see the beauties of this world in moments of leisure. Give me gold that I and mine may be secure in our declining years."

A worthy prayer, indeed. But prayer alone is not enough. You must plant the seed before you can hope to reap the harvest. You must give before you can get.

"DO THE THING," said Emerson, "and you shall have the power. But they who do not the thing, have not the power. Everything has its price, and if the price is not paid—not that thing but something else is obtained. And it is impossible to get anything without its price.

"For any benefit received a tax is levied. In nature nothing can be given—all things are sold.

"Power to him who power exerts."

Russell Conwell, the famous lecturer, who built the Baptist Temple in Philadelphia and founded Temple University, was in the beginning merely the pastor of a very poor flock. His congregation consisted of working people, and many of them were in need. So he was continually offering prayers for money.

One Sunday, it occurred to him that the old Jewish custom had been to make a gift or offering first, and then pray for what you wanted. So he announced that the following Sunday, he would reverse his usual method of procedure. Instead of offering his prayer first, he would first take up the collection, and he wanted all who had special favors to ask of God to give freely as an "Offering." We quote the result from "Effective Prayer":

"The question was asked afterward if anyone who made a special offering on that particular day had not been answered, and there was no exception in the mass of testimony to the efficiency of each prayer that day. The recitals of the marvels which followed that prayerful offering were too startling for general belief. The people had complied with the conditions, and God had answered clearly according to His promise. They had brought the tithes into the storehouse, and the Lord had poured out the blessings as an infallible result.

"Cases of sudden and instantaneous recovery of the sick were related by hundreds. One poor man whose child was insane prayed for her recovery. That afternoon when he went to the sanitarium, she met him in her right mind.

"A lady sold her jewelry and brought the proceeds as an offering as she prayed for healing from sciatic rheumatism. She fell going from the Church, and arose to find the rheumatism gone.

"One old gentleman involved in a ruinous lawsuit brought all the profits of the previous week and deposited them as he prayed for a just outcome. Within the week, the suit was withdrawn.

"A woman with an overdue mortgage on her home determined to risk all on one prayer, and gave all she had as she prayed. When plumbers came to repair a leak the following week, they discovered a loose board in the floor under which her father had hidden all his money. The sum was more than enough to pay off the mortgage in its entirety.

"There were probably fifty such cases."

You have to sow before you can reap. You have to give before you can get. And when you sow, when you give, you must give freely, with no strings to it. As Jesus put it—"Except a kernel of wheat fall into the ground and die, it abideth alone. But if it die, it beareth much fruit."

You remember the old-fashioned hand-pumps that are still to be found on many farms. To start them, you had to pour in a bucket of water, in order to create a vacuum and thus be able to draw water from the well. The same principle applies in using a siphon. You pour in water to drive out the air and create a vacuum. Once the vacuum is formed, your water flows, and you can get unlimited quantities of it without having to give more. But you get none from pump or siphon until you first give some.

You must give to get. You must sow the seed you have before you can reap the harvest. You cannot merely lend it. You must GIVE it, freely and fully. "Except a kernel of wheat fall into the ground and DIE," said the Master. Except your seed of riches be given freely and fully, you get nothing from it. "But if it die, it beareth much fruit." If it be dead to you—if it is gone beyond hope of return, then you can look for a harvest.

"He that findeth his life shall lose it," said the Master on another occasion, "but he that loseth his life for My sake shall find it." He that gives all he has in the service of his fellows shall find that in so doing, he has planted seeds which will bring him a harvest of happiness and plenty.

You have probably read the story of Charles Page, as given in the American Magazine a few years ago. Page was then a millionaire oil operator in Oklahoma, but a few years before he had little or nothing, and his wife was so sick he feared he was going to lose her as well. The surgeons at the hospital had given up hope for her, so as all other avenues seemed closed, Page turned to God.

"Oh, Lord," he prayed, "don't take her away from me. I just couldn't bear it."

The words rang in his ears—and they had an empty ring. As a prayer, it seemed to fall flat. Why should the Lord interfere for him, if the only reason he could offer was that he couldn't bear it? Plenty of husbands just as devoted as he had lost their wives. Why should the Lord specially favor him?

The thought came home to him with the power of a blow. What had he ever done that the Lord should go out of His way to help him? What reason had he to look for special consideration from above? None! He'd been a decent enough citizen, but no more so than the average, and kneeling there he couldn't recall a single thing he had done which would entitle him to ask favors from the Lord.

The thought appalled him. What chance had he? Must he then lose the one dearest to him in all the world, just because he had never done enough to be worthy of keeping her? No! No! That was unthinkable. It wasn't too late. He would start that very minute. What was it the Master had said? "Whatsoever ye do unto the least of these My brethren, ye do it unto Me."

The next morning a poor widow was in transports of

joy to find under her doorsill money enough to carry her safely through the winter.

But that evening inquiry at the hospital elicited the information that Page's wife was no better. For a little his faith faltered. Then, as he thought back over the reason for his act, it flamed up anew. Why had he helped the widow? Not because he was interested in her welfare, not even because it was the right thing to do, but because he was trying to buy off the Lord. Thinking of it in that light, it sounded ridiculous. He got down on his knees again.

"I ain't makin' a bargain with You, God," he promised. "I'm doin' this because it's the *right thing* for me to do."

This time it seemed to him his message carried. He felt strangely cheered and relieved. His prayer had gone through.

Now comes the remarkable part of this incident. His wife, much to the astonishment of the surgeons, took a turn for the better, and within a comparatively short time was well!

From that day to this, Charles Page has never failed in his Covenant with God. Times there were when everything looked black. Times when it meant a real struggle to find the Lord's share. But his faith never faltered. He knew if he did his part, he could depend upon God for His.

For a long time, he gave a tenth of all his earnings. Then he increased it to a fourth. Later to a half, and finally to all except what he needed for personal and family expenses. He has given away literally millions.

"But don't get the idea," he warns, "that I'm telling you how to get rich. It's the *giving*, not the *getting*, that is important. Personally, I believe that it's only playing fair to tithe, or give a part of your income to God. But it must be a gift, not an investment. Do you get the difference? If you tithe in the right spirit, you will get your reward just as sure as a gun's iron; but the reward may not come in the form of money. Often it's something far better than money . . ."

"What you keep to yourself you lose," wrote Munthe. "What you give away, you keep forever." And Irene Stanley expressed much the same thought in her little poem—

> "You have to let go of the rung below
> When you reach for the round above.
> There is no other way to climb, you know,
> You *have* to let go of the rung below.
> Each upward step brings more of the glow
> And warmth of the Sun of Love,
> You have to let go of the rung below,
> When you reach for the round above."

You see, God incarnates Himself through you. But He cannot be shut up. He must be given out, expressed. You put Him into everything you do, whether towards failure or success. You are inseparable from the creative force. You are part of the fountain head of supply.

What then must you do to win riches and success? GIVE ! Give freely of what you have.

> "Give, and it shall be given unto you; good measure, pressed down, and shaken together, and running over, shall men give unto your bosom. For with the same measure that ye mete withal it shall be measured to you again."—Luke 6:38.

Does that require too great faith? You do not marvel at the farmer who freely throws all his seed into the ground, knowing he will never see it again, but must depend upon its fruit for his increase. He shows perfect faith. Should you show less?

Remember the first Law of Life, the law that was considered so important that it was repeated six times in the first Chapter of Genesis:

"Everything increases after its kind."

Do you expect that law to be changed for you? Do you expect to reap without sowing? "There is that scattereth and increaseth yet more," said that wisest of ancient sages, King Solomon. "And there is that withholdeth more than is meet, *but it tendeth to poverty.*

"The liberal soul shall be made fat, and he that watereth, shall be watered himself."

You see, Life is logical. Life follows definite, fundamental laws. One of these laws is that you reap as you sow, that "He that hath a bountiful eye shall be blessed."

For all motion is cyclic. It circulates to the limit of its possibilities and then returns to its starting point. Thus any unselfish expenditure of energy returns to you laden with gifts. Any unselfish act done for another's benefit is giving part of yourself. It is an outward flow of power that completes its cycle and returns laden with energy.

Everything we get, we pay for—good or bad. Personal gain comes through impersonal service. Personal loss comes through selfishness.

As Emerson puts it—"A perfect equity adjusts its balance in all parts of life. *Every act rewards itself.*"

Any act of ours that injures another, separates us from God. Any act of ours that helps others, brings us closer to God and Good. One may think that his cheating of another is a secret between them, but by his cheating, he has shaken the trust of another in human brotherhood and damaged his idealism. Isn't that a definite affront that is going to stand between him and God when the one who cheated tries to enlist God's help in enlarging the activities of his own life?

Wouldn't it have been better to say to himself: "God gives me all my money. Surely He has given me enough for all the needs of my business, or if He hasn't already given it, it is on the way. If I need more, He will give me more. So I am not even going to think about trying to make 'easy money' by taking advantage of others. God provides me with plenty, and I am going to run this business as if He were always here beside me."

One on God's side is a majority. You are always together with God. So make Him an active partner in your business. Look to Him for its needs, give the same loving service you feel that He would give. Then cast off all worries, all fears, and *put your business lovingly in His hands.* When the future looks dark, when problems confront you, just say to yourself:

> "God lights the way; no more I grope,
> Nor stumble on in troubled hope.
> I sow no seeds of care and strife;
> But those of love, and joy, and life.
> No more I strive to plan my lot;
> The Father fills my cup unsought."

What is the Unpardonable Sin? What but damming the sources of God's supply. What but trying to shut up the God in you, trying to keep Him from expressing Himself.

When the giant monsters of antiquity ceased developing, and depended upon their size and strength and fierceness, they perished. When the vast Empires of China and Greece and Persia and Rome stopped reaching out and tried merely to hold what they had, they died. When the rich man or big business of today stops giving service and merely hangs on to his fortune, he loses it.

You cannot stand still. You must go forward—or die. There is a God in you seeking expression. You cannot keep Him shut up. You must give Him channels through which to express Himself, or He will rend you and come out of you.

What would you think of a man who spent years in developing great muscles, then tried to keep them great by not using them, by not wearing them out? You'd call him a fool, wouldn't you, because everyone knows that the only way to develop muscles is to use them, the only way to keep them strong is to continually exercise them.

What everyone does not seem to know is that all of life works in the same way. You cannot hold on to anything good. You must be continually giving—and getting. You cannot hold on to your seed. You must sow it—and reap anew. You cannot hold on to riches. You must use them and get other riches in return.

The Unpardonable Sin is to stand in the way of progress, try to stop the cycle of life.

You must give to get. You must sow to reap. The unprofitable servant in Jesus' parable was not the first or the only one to be cast into outer darkness where is weeping and gnashing of teeth, from burying his talent. The ones who became rulers over many things were those who freely used what they had—who started riches *flowing!*

So when a "talent" is given you, don't try to hide it away or bury it. Don't dam up the channels of supply with the few dollars you have, and thus prevent the unlimited riches of God from flowing to you.

Set up your generator, which is the service you have to offer your fellowman. Turn on the steam by giving to it all the power, all the skill, all the intelligence you have. Then start the flow of riches with your faith by cheerfully pouring into the channel of service all that you have. That means buy the things that are necessary to your development and that of your family. Pay your just debts, though it leaves you without a cent in your purse. Put your dependence—NOT on the few dollars you have in hand, but on the great ocean of supply above and about you. Use the few dollars you have to create the vacuum which shall poke a hole in the bottom of that ocean, and start the unending flow of riches pouring into you.

You remember that Jesus once likened the power of God to the leaven in bread. You put a tiny yeast cake into a great pan of dough and it affects the whole mixture. It makes it GROW. Apparently it INCREASES the quantity of flour, milk, eggs and other ingredients—certainly it makes them bulk to several times their original size.

That yeast is the "God in you" that you put into your circumstances, your affairs. Put it into fears and worries, and it will increase them until they can hardly be borne. Put it into your expenses, and it will make them ever greater. Put it into love and life and good work, and it will bring these back to you increased a hundredfold.

"Let's have a league of optimists,"
  writes Elizabeth Swaller in LET'S HAVE IT,
"To boost the world along.
  We are so weary of the thought
  That everything is wrong!

"We're surfeited with talk of lack,
  Depression, gloom and fear.
  If we but think of brighter things,
  Good times will soon be here.

" 'Tis time to turn and face about
  And court conditions fine.
  By boosting, I shall prosper yours,
  And you will prosper mine."

Put your yeast into optimistic thoughts, into kindly words, into loving acts of service. Remember, the hardest part of anything is the start. If you want something, pray for it—*then START* doing, being, giving—whatever is needful to set the yeast acting. *You* don't have to make the dough expand when you put the yeast into it. The yeast attends to that. All you have to do is to give the yeast a chance to get in its work!

So if you want to receive something of good, show your faith by GIVING of what you have. Put a little yeast into your affairs. It doesn't matter how poor you are, how much in debt, how weak or sickly. You can always give something. But remember that everything increases after its kind, so give of what you want to receive. Sow the seeds of the harvest you want to reap, whether it be love, energy, service or money.

And PRAY! Nearly 2,000 years before Christ, it was said in the Vedas that if two people would unite their psychic forces, they could conquer the world. Then came Jesus, to put it even more definitely: "Again I say unto you, that if two of you shall agree on earth as touching anything that they shall ask, it shall be done for them of my Father which is in Heaven. For when two or three are gathered together in my name, there am I in the midst of them."

In one of his books, Russell Conwell tells of a little group in his church who were in such straitened circumstances that they decided to get together and see if, by uniting their prayers, they could not improve their finances.

So they met at the house of one of their number who happened to be a bookbinder by trade, and decided that each week the whole group would unite their prayers to solve the difficulties of some one member.

The bookbinder was the first one chosen. He owed a

great deal of money, and had no means of paying his debts. So that evening, the group prayed that he might receive help in meeting his obligations. It was then agreed that at noontime every day until the next meeting, each member would stop whatever he was doing, and spend a minute or two in silent prayer that the bookbinder's needs might be met.

The meeting was on Tuesday evening. The next day after lunch, as was his custom, the bookbinder dropped into a publishing house nearby for a chat with some friends. He met there a man from Washington who told him that "for the first time in his life, he had forgotten his train," and must now get back home on some urgent business, without placing a contract which he had intended to give to a New York bookbinder.

The bookbinder suggested that he also was in that business, and possibly could help him, but the other objected that the particular class of work he wanted could be done only in New York. Upon the binder persisting, however, he explained his needs, and being convinced that they could be filled right there in as satisfactory a way and on more reasonable terms than in New York, he not only gave the binder the contract, *but advanced enough money to more than take care of his difficulties!*

The binder hurried to the other members of his group and told them of his good fortune. His problem was so completely solved that he felt they ought to start work at once for some other member, because all were so badly in need. All felt so elated over their success in helping the binder solve his problem, that they chose the most difficult case of all as the next.

This was a jeweler who had grown so old and forgetful that his business was in a deplorable condition. Bankruptcy seemed so sure that his son had moved out of town to avoid sharing the disgrace.

Two or three days after the group started working on the jeweler's problem, the son came to town for a day to attend a funeral. On the return trip from the cemetery, he fell into conversation with one of the other mourners, in the course of which the latter mentioned that he was looking for an expert in clockmaking to superintend a new factory he was erecting in another city.

The son told him his father was a master of that art, but no good at managing finances. The upshot of it was that the jeweler applied for the position, at the same time explaining his present financial difficulties. The manufacturer liked his letter, went over the whole situation with him, and ended by taking over the store as a retail outlet, paying off the old debts, and forming a business connection with the jeweler which prospered both amazingly.

An old lady who owned a small notion store was next. Soon after the group united in prayer for her, a fire destroyed the store next door to her. The owner decided to build bigger than before, and offered her not only an attractive price for her store, but an interest in his business, which paid her enough to live in comfort the rest of her days.

Every Member of that Group Became Prosperous!

Do you, too, want something very much? Then give— *and pray!* Get yourself a small toy bank—a paper one will do. Each day put something into it, even though it be only a penny. Give that money to God. Give it to Him at the time you put it into the bank, but leave it there until it amounts to a dollar or more. Then use it for any good charitable purpose that presents itself.

Don't give it to some panhandler. Try to use it where it will do the recipient some good. Use it to help him to help himself, as in buying some book for him that will show him the way out of his difficulties.

And as you give, *pray!* Pray not only for yourself, but for others.

Every morning at seven, we shall pray for protection for our own family, and for all students of this Course who will join with us in "uniting their psychic forces" by "agreeing as to the thing they should ask." For this prayer, you cannot do better than repeat the Ninety-first Psalm.

Every day at noon, we shall pray for abundant supply for all of those among our readers who will join with us in praying for the whole group. For this prayer, hold in your hand any money you intend to give that day for any good purpose, and any checks or money you intend to use to pay bills, and say with us:

"I bless you . . . and be thou a blessing. May you enrich all who touch you. I thank God for you, but even more I thank Him that there are billions like you where you came from. I bless that Infinite Supply. I thank God for it and I expand my consciousness to take it in. (Here try to see in your mind's eye a Niagara of money flowing to you and to all who are praying with you. See yourself and all of us bringing in a great net full of money like the nets the Apostles pulled in bursting with fish.) I release that Infinite Supply through all my channels and the channels of all the students of this Course just as I freely release the money I hold in my hand, giving it where it will do the most good. The Spirit that multiplied the loaves and fishes for Jesus enters into this money, making it grow and increase and bring forth fruit an hundredfold. All of God's channels are now open and flowing for us. The best in ourselves for the world—the best in the world for us."

Then PREPARE for prosperity. When the Israelites of old were suffering from drought, and begged the Prophet Elisha to help them, what was the first thing he told them to do? Fill the valley with ditches—prepare to RECEIVE the water that they asked for!

You see, prayers and affirmations are not for the purpose of influencing God. He has already done His part. All of good is always available to each of us. Our prayers and affirmations are for the purpose of bringing our own minds to the point where we can ACCEPT God's gifts! We don't need to work on conditions—we need only to work on ourselves. The only place we can cure our lacks and our troubles *is in our own minds!* When we have done it there, we shall find that they are cured everywhere.

"Whatsoever things ye ask for when ye pray," the Master assured us, "believe that ye HAVE RECEIVED them, and ye shall HAVE them."

> That is the basis of all successful prayer, whether for the healing of our bodies, or for material benefits. Once you convince your Higher Self, which is the God in you, that you HAVE the thing you want, *it will proceed immediately to bring it into being!*

But how, you may ask, can I convince my Higher Self that I have riches or any other good thing, when my common sense tells me that I am in debt up to my ears and creditors are hounding me day and night?

You can't—if you keep thinking and acting DEBTS. But here is a psychological fact: The Higher Self accepts as fact anything that is repeated to it in convincing tones often enough. And once it has accepted any statement as fact, it proceeds to do everything possible to MAKE IT TRUE!

That is the whole purpose of affirmations—to bring the God in You to accept as true the conditions that you desire, to the end that He will then proceed to bring them into being. It is a sort of auto-suggestion. You keep saying to yourself that you ARE rich, that you HAVE the things you desire, until the constant repetition is accepted by the Higher Self and translated into its physical equivalent.

Debts? Don't worry about them. Remember that the shadow of growing grain kills the weeds. Keep your mind on the good you want and it will kill off the evil you fear, just as the turning on of light dispels darkness. A farmer does not have to hoe the weeds out of growing wheat, any more than you have to sweep the darkness out of a room. Neither do you have to worry about debts or lack. Put all your thoughts and all your faith in the riches you are praying for, and let them dispel the debts.

But don't worry if you can't summon such faith right out of the blue. Most of us have to lead up to it gradually. Start with Coue's well-known affirmation—"Every day in every way we are getting richer and richer." Use that to prepare your Higher Self for the stronger affirmations. Then, when your faith has grown stronger, *claim the thing you want!* Affirm that you HAVE it— and insofar as possible, ACT AS THOUGH YOU HAD IT!

Write it in your heart that each day is the best day of the year, that NOW is the accepted time, NOW is the day of salvation. Then thank God for the good you have been praying for, believe that you HAVE received and give thanks.

Remember this: God's will always works when you offer no resistance to it. So pray—and then LET His good come to you. Don't fight the conditions about you. Don't try to overcome the obstacles in your path. BLESS them—know that God is in them—that if you will LET them, they will work WITH you for good. Have faith not only in God, but in people and things. Don't look for a miracle to happen. Don't expect an angel from Heaven to come and open the way. Know that God works through ordinary people and things, and it is through them that your good will come.

So bless THEM. Serve them as you would the Lord, doing each thing that is given you to do as though you were the greatest genius. And all day long, as the thought occurs to you, keep repeating to yourself—"Every day in every way I am getting richer and richer," or whatever it is that you desire.

A prayer for health and happiness, to be used at ten in the evening, will be given in the next Lesson.

There is something about praying for *others* that oftentimes does one more good than praying for oneself. You see, you cannot give anything to others without first possessing it yourself. When you wish another evil, you draw that evil to yourself first and you usually get a part of it. When you bring good to another, you bring it through yourself, and you share in it.

Remember the experience of Job in the olden days. Despite his lamentations and prayers, he lost all his riches, and his afflictions remained with him. But then misfortune fell upon his friends as well, and in his sympathy for them, Job forgot his own ailments and prayed for his friends. And it is written that—"The Lord turned the captivity of Job, *when he prayed for his friends*. And the Lord gave him twice as much as he had before."

> "For who upon the hearth can start a fire,
> And never warm the stone?
> Or who can cheer another's heart,
> And not his own?
> I stilled a hungry infant's cry,
> With kindness filled a stranger's cup,
> And lifting others,
> Found that I was lifted up!"

CHAPTER SIX

THE SPIRIT OF LIFE

THE LAW OF LIFE is the law of division and growth. Our life cells divide, grow and divide again. That is the principle of all cell life. Use them—break them up—and the more you release, the more the Life in you will expand and draw new life to you.

The Law of Life is no different from the Law of Supply. You must give to get.

In the material sense our bodies are nothing but plants, and to thrive must have the same four elements that plants require—food, water, sunshine, air. Why? Because the essence of growth lies in breaking each minute cell in two, and then drawing to each part the elements necessary to rebuild it to the size of the original cell. As stated before, the Law of Life is the law of division and growth.

Air, sunlight and exercise heat the cells, causing them to expand and break up. Food and water provide the elements necessary to their growth.

Experiments have shown that the inmates of insane asylums are more easily managed when kept in the sun; that the intelligence of school children is increased nearly 100% by keeping them exposed to solar radiations. Why? Because stupidity and insanity are frequently due to inactivity of the thyroid gland, whose secretions are necessary to the activity of the brain cells. And sunlight tends to increase that activity.

The only material curative agents known to man are

these four—food, water, air, sunshine. They can be imitated to a degree. They can be counterfeited by drugs and appliances and treatments. But the best doctors will tell you that no drug ever discovered, no process ever invented, compares with these four methods of Nature.

Drugs will break up your cells, alcohol will stimulate them, but the stimulus of both is unnatural, therefore it tends to react in the opposite direction, and the reaction often leaves you worse off than before.

The principle of all healing lies in a change of "potential." You have an accident, let us say. You have a bad cut here, an ugly bruise there, a broken bone somewhere else. What happens?

1st, the blood coagulates (condenses) in the open wound to keep you from losing too much liquid.

2nd, the edges of the wound heat (go into a higher potential) in order that they may fuse together again.

3rd, the ends of the broken bone, when brought together, do the same.

4th, the bruised part represents broken cells. These also heat, and throw off those parts which are damaged beyond repair, drawing frantically upon the blood stream for new parts, new elements for rebuilding.

5th, all three places are sore and tender to the touch. Why? Because they are heated to a higher potential while the fusing process goes on. The cells are expanded. More blood is drawn upon. Damaged and worn-out cells accumulate.

What can drugs do to speed up these processes? Certain drugs, like Iodine, Dakin's Solution and Penicillin, can cleanse. But other than this, there is little good that drugs can do. The way the process of healing can best be expedited is from within—through the mind which controls those blood streams, which directs the building and rebuilding.

At the 156th Annual Meeting of the Massachusetts Medical Society, Dr. Richard C. Cabot, Professor-Emeritus of Medicine at Harvard University, said in part:

"When you sprain your wrist, it stiffens, swells and pains. That is the body's way of forming a splint. When the doctor places a splint on the wrist, it is only to imitate and aid the body forces.

"I remember an autopsy on a man who had been killed by an automobile. He was 65, had never been sick a day in his life and always felt in perfect health. We found his body harboring four usually fatal diseases; but his system had set up defenses which rendered all of them perfectly harmless.

"The body simply has a superwisdom which is biased in favor of life rather than death. It doesn't win every time, and often needs our help—but it is ten times as powerful as medicine's imitation. And it is a force that doesn't make as many wrong diagnoses as I did when I was in practice."

And Dr. O. H. Robertson, Professor of Medicine at the University of Chicago, reports that in pneumonia, the disease which causes most deaths in the winter months, the lungs of those who get well really furnish their own cure. They manufacture a large "police" cell which travels through the lungs engulfing and killing the germs of pneumonia!

What can you do to help that cure along? 1st, relax— let go of your fear of the disease. 2nd, have faith in the power and the willingness of the God Inside You to cure you.

The creative order, you know, is from states to conditions—from states of mind to conditions of the body. Stir up the life in any organ that is manifesting a diseased condition, believe that you HAVE the perfect organ made in God's image, and it necessarily follows that the

God Inside You will remold it in the form of that perfect organ.

This is all that medical men try to do with their drugs —stir up the life that has settled into the wrong molds, and hope for the best that it will settle next time in the right ones. They don't expect their drugs to heal anything. They are like a small boy with one of these toys where you try to put several balls into their right compartments—they keep shaking them out of the wrong holes, knowing that if their patience lasts and the toy holds together, the balls will eventually drop into the right compartments.

The God in us tries hard to show us how to heal, but we think we know more than He and persist in working against Him. What is fever but the God Inside Us raising the body to a higher potential in its efforts to get rid of the impurities in the system? What is a swelling but a localized fever to accomplish the same purpose? What is pain but a signal that it is time to re-condense that life-energy into a lower potential? Pain causes one to writhe, to strain, to harden—therefore to condense.

The body does not need drugs. What toxics it needs, it manufactures for itself. As Dr. Bertram Ball put it— "Narcotics are not necessary in the treatment of disease. The human body manufactures its own toxics, and an individual's chemistry can be attuned without the aid of narcotics so as to expel internal poisons."

What the body does need in time of sickness is to stir up the life latent within it. Stir it up to such a potential that it will draw to itself whatever elements it needs for its growth and perfect fruition. Alcohol will do this to a slight extent and for a limited time. So will drugs. But the poisons they leave in the system frequently do it more harm that the temporary exhilaration they produce can do good.

The only stirring of the life forces in you that will ever do you any real and permanent good is a mental stirring, a stirring of the God Inside You. That stirring-up comes best from yourself.

Whether you work alone or with another, remember this: *No seed ever germinated without first heating within.* The seed of life in you is no different. There are two prerequisites to every healing: 1st, Faith in the ability of someone or something to heal you. 2nd, Emotion, the *feeling* that you HAVE been cured. Faith puts the God Inside You to work, emotion bursts the shell in which your life is now confined and enables the God in You to pour it into the perfect image He holds of you.

So, when sickness or accident assails you, don't worry about the particular part affected, but bless the God in You and stir Him into action.

Then *let go!* Don't try to heal yourself. You don't know the first principle of it. But the Spirit of Life in you knows all about it. So let Him do the work. All you have to do is to relax *and let Him work.* Remember that one on God's side is a majority. You and God together can overcome anything.

A writer in one of the metaphysical magazines tells of a time when she was sick and discouraged and burdened with responsibilities. An understanding friend kept reminding her—"God is with you. Keep your mind fixed on that, for it is true. Tell yourself and KNOW—'I am together with God.'" Her friend's faith quickened her own, lifted her for a moment into a different world, brought her a sense of peace and protection that enabled her to relax, to let go of her troubles and let the God in her solve them.

The Easterners, you know, have a theory that water is the most irresistible element, because it is the most non-resistant. Put an obstacle in its way, and it will flow around it. Dam it, and it will either seep through, or else wait until enough of it accumulates to flow over the top.

Most of our ills and difficulties come from resistance. You have seen how electric heaters work. The current flows through the wires to the central coil, with no resistance upon the part of the wires, therefore no heating, no wear and tear. But the coil is made of special alloys that *resist* electricity. Result? Those alloys HEAT, and continue to heat whenever the electricity tries to flow through them, until they finally wear out and become fused and useless from the force of their resistance.

"Resist not evil," St. Paul bade us, "but overcome evil with good."

Suppose you or someone you dearly love has a serious accident or illness, that seems likely to put an end to your well-being and usefulness for the rest of your days. The prospect appalls you, naturally. You resent it and fight against it with every atom of your being, and every drug and appliance at the command of your physician.

Result? CONFLICT! You have dubbed your problem "Evil," you have fought it and tried to disown and get rid of it. Naturally it fights back. Naturally it does you all the harm possible.

Yet if, instead of fighting against it, you will recognize it as "Good" in disguise, it can be the greatest friend you have ever known! Remember—"When Fortune means to man most good, she looks upon him with a threatening eye." That is true of every phase of life.

Time was when maggots in a wound were looked upon as a sure sign of corruption and death, yet in the Chaco war in South America, surgeons found maggots to be one of their greatest allies in healing dangerously infected wounds. Fever has always been looked upon with dread, and every means used to allay it, yet today malaria fever has been found to be one of the surest means of ridding the patient of the plague of syphilis, and doctors are inducing artificial fevers to cure a number of ailments. Germs have long been looked upon as enemies of mankind, but recent experiments with animals have shown that those with the normal quota of germs are far healthier than those raised under ideal germ-proof conditions.

In other words, all of life is working with us for good —*provided we will LET it* and not continually fight against it. God is in everything, and God's will always works for our good—*if we offer no resistance to it.* Try to know of everything that happens to you that it is of God, and God is good. Then *LET IT COME!*

Let it come, and BLESS IT! Say aloud to yourself, whenever you think of it—"All things are working together for my good, and I am working with them in the wisdom and power of the Spirit. I put myself and all of my affairs lovingly in the hands of the Father, in the childlike trust that whatever is for my highest good will come to me."

Bless the germs, bless the accident, bless the loss, bless any seeming misfortune that comes to you—NOT in a spirit of pious resignation—but with the active faith that it is working WITH you for your greatest good. Feel the perfect trust betokened in Lenor Anthony's little poem—

> "Secure that like the trees my days are planned,
> That my whole patterned life is in Thy hand."

Brown Landone told an interesting personal experience along these lines in an article in Nautilus Magazine.

"I am King of some 4,000 kingdoms and five hundred billion subjects," he said.

"I have twelve empires of brain and nerve cells, and these alone consist of some 80,000,000,000 living individuals! Of course, you may have called them mere 'cells' but each cell is a living individual and performs its functions more intelligently than most human beings.

"We now know more about a cell than we dreamed of knowing ten years ago. We now know of its body, its brain, and its nervous system. We even know the responses of its emotions and feelings.

"Have you ever tried to manage even forty house servants, or forty office workers? If so, then think of the gigantic work my spirit and your spirit must do, to keep our hundreds of billions of subjects working together in harmony.

"What *method* shall we use?

"In the past, I have tried to secure perfect harmony among my subjects by *decree*. But as I tried to control my more than 400,000,000,000 subjects by will power, I caused resentment and racial strikes among them, and these strikes caused me aches and pains and disease.

"So of late years, I have become a little wiser. Human life and cell life want love and understanding, and each wants to feel that he is willingly working in harmony with others, with one unified desire.

"Now let me tell you of my heart.

"Up to five years ago, I had been working my heart cells under command, constantly demanding—without even thinking about it—that they do their work and keep going as many hours per day as 'I' wished to work. Oh, I was very autocratic and very unjust to them.

"As a result, five years ago, there was complete heart exhaustion, *even a wearing out of the structure of the heart*. The best specialists, examining it by every means known to science, concluded that I would be very lucky if I could live ten days, possibly not more than 10 hours.

"Now what did I do? Instead of blaming the cells of my old heart for my condition, instead of thinking that they were failing me, I began blessing them for all they *had* done. I apologized to them for the way in which I had used them. I began giving them a little more rest, and loved them every day, every minute.

"I do not expect this heart to live a thousand years, but I do know that it actually rebuilt itself. Other parts of my body are being reconstructed, too."

The methods used by Brown Landone are sound psychology. If you go back to the first forms of life on earth, you remember that they were individual cells, each with an intelligence of its own. When groups of cells united to form multi-cellular animals, they did not give up their individual intelligences. They merely subordinated these to the group intelligence, just as good soldiers subordinate themselves to their commanding officer. But each cell works intelligently for the body's good. And each is not only a faithful servant, but a friend and partner.

Scientists tell us that the cells of our body plan their work and build their body structures just as intelligently as ever an architect or builder put up a skyscraper.

Having individual intelligence, then, is it not natural that every cell in our body should partake of our moods, should feel downcast when we are discouraged, should be peppy and active when we are joyful, should be lazy or slothful or energetic and determined, according to the way we think?

Why is it that martial music can stir you to such an emotional pitch? Why is it that revivalists, faith healers and all who want immediate group action always start with the community singing of some familiar old hymns? Why is it that mob psychology can so quickly turn an ordinary human being into a blood-thirsty lyncher or an arrant coward, even as it can turn a coward into a brave man?

Why? Because the emotionalism engendered arouses

the billions of individual minds in the cells that make up the body, and unites them all on a common thought. It is the reason that a person under hypnotic spell can do things impossible to his conscious self. And it is the reason that *you can be healed instantaneously of any ill* of body or mind or affairs.

Go back through the Old Testament, and see how many times you are adjured to *be thankful, be joyful,* to sing the praises of God, as a necessary corollary to health and prosperity. "Let them shout for joy and be glad . . . Yea, let them say continually, Jehovah be magnified, Who hath pleasure in the prosperity of His servant." "Blessed be the Lord, who daily loadeth us with benefits, even the God of our salvation." "Let the people praise Thee, O God; let all the people praise Thee. Then shall the earth yield her increase, and God, even our God, shall bless us."

Praise, give thanks, be joyful—how otherwise can you convince those billions of tiny intelligences that you HAVE the thing you pray for, how else can you stir them into action to bring it into being?

We quote below part of a prayer written by Walter DeVoe of the Eloist Ministry, because it so well expresses that idea of praise and joy:

"I praise Thy healing life and intelligence in every organ, in every nerve, in every atom of my flesh. I praise Thy glorious wisdom which is illuminating my soul and purifying my mind of every limiting thought. I praise Thy tender, healing love which invigorates and upholds me and dissolves away all fear. O Living Father, this is Thy holy temple. Thou art making it a perfect dwelling place from which shall radiate Thy healing love and wisdom to all Thy children. Father, Thou art glorifying me with Thy healing power, that I also may glorify Thee."

What do you tell YOUR army of intelligent worker-cells each day? Do you assure them that Divine Love goes before them and prepares the way? Do you tell them that Infinite Wisdom guides them and shows them what to do? Do you set them an example of energy and courage, do you face every difficulty with serenity and confidence, do you act as a real leader should?

What would you think of a commanding general who went into battle downcast and discouraged, who let every soldier know that he was beaten before he started? What would you do to a factory superintendent who came to work each morning looking as though he had no interest in what was going on, ready to drop into the nearest chair and let the world go by?

Yet that is exactly the way that many men handle the army of workers that make up their bodies. They fill them with fear, worry, anxiety, dread. They make them doubt themselves and all their fellow-workers. They tell them they cannot be depended upon to do their work properly, so outside help in the form of drugs and medicaments must be called upon.

And when the little cell-workers accept these suggestions of incompetency and helplessness, they make them even more hopeless by telling them they are sick, that they are ageing, that soon they must die. What else can the poor things do but carry out the suggestions given them? What recourse have they but to bow to the greater intelligence above them?

"Are you suffering with the conviction that you have kidney disease?" writes a famous psychologist. "If so, do you know what you are doing while you are holding this conviction? The kidneys are as sensitive to our thoughts as the stomach or any other organ, and you are sending a lot of anxiety and fear into their cells. Instead of encouraging them when they need your encouragement, instead of giving them stimulus and uplift, you are sending to them despair and despondency.

"What is the result? Chemical poisoning, of course. You are putting extra burdens on these little cell minds which are trying to throw off any abnormal conditions of the kidneys. Instead of helping, you are hindering them, you are depressing and disheartening them. This seriously interferes with their normal functioning, and materially aids the development of any possible disease tendency that may be lurking there. You should give the little cell minds of your kidneys, as you should all the cell minds of the other organs of your body, the benefit of your encouragement, your uplifting thought, so that they will function normally.

"The stomach likewise is sensitive to our thought. When we receive a telegram containing bad news of those dear to us, of their dangerous illness or death, of some accident or other unfortunate thing that has befallen them, we know how quickly the follicles of the stomach become fevered, parched, and refuse to secrete the gastric juices. Digestion cannot go on until the gastric follicles are normal again, and this cannot be while the unfortunate news remains in the mind and is dwelt upon, because the stomach cells are in sympathy with the brain cells and all the other cells of the body.

"Knowing that the cells thus respond to the thought we give them, if we expect them to be friends to us, to work for us instead of against us, and to function normally, we must be friends to them.

"There are tremendous possibilities in this idea of sending into the cell life of various organs of the body indications of what we want of them and encouraging them to respond, just as we would children, who would never amount to anything if we were always discouraging, scolding, blaming and condemning them. We can send messages of despair or hope, joy or sorrow, the expectancy of good things to come or the reverse, to the cell intelligence of every organ and thus build into our life joy, health, hope, success, or despair, disease, pessimism. In other words, we must hold thoughts, the convictions which we wish to come true.

"If you persistently maintain a hopeful, healthful, joyous mental attitude you will soon get encouraging results on the physical plane. Your habitual thought, your fixed belief, is the strongest force in your life, and your life processes will follow your beliefs. Train your subconscious mind to expect health, to expect the normal functioning of all your organs. *By an inexorable law, what we expect tends to come to us.*"

You have seen men, under hypnotic suggestions, perform prodigies of strength. You have seen them stretched between two chairs, their head on one, their feet on another, supporting the weight of several people, when they could not ordinarily hold up the weight of their own bodies in that position. If the cells of the body can do that, under outside suggestion, what can they not do under proper suggestions from their own rightful master?

As a man thinketh in his heart, so is he. Easier to believe that now, isn't it? Easier to believe that the thoughts you hold in your mind become imaged in your body, acting as the blue-print from which all your little cell-workers build.

The ancient Greeks understood this, and surrounded themselves with beautiful statuary and lovely pieces of art. The fable of Pygmalion and Galatea was but their way of saying that each man is his own sculptor, his own creator, and the image of his body that he holds in mind is the one which shall presently breathe the breath of life.

So give those willing fellow-workers of yours a worth-while model to build from. Give them thoughts of youth and beauty and life. Don't discourage them with thoughts of age or decay. Age is in no wise necessary. Biologically speaking, there is no reason why your body should not live forever, and remain as youthful and virile as in its prime. Dr. Alexis Carrel has proven this by taking the heart of an embryo chick and keeping it alive and growing indefinitely.

There is only one reason for age. There is only one reason for decay. That is the "letting down" of your cell-workers—the clogging of your pores, the failure to throw off all the wastes and poisons of the body. Keep your cell-workers on the job, and this will never happen to you. Keep them encouraged, uplifted, working on a pattern of youth and virility, and they will build you a body you can be eternally proud of.

If you want help in this, if you believe—as we do—that you get best results by uniting your prayers with those of others, and helping them even as you want them to help you, then every night at ten pause for a few minutes to join with us and other students in the following, which is adapted partly from a prayer given in Unity Weekly:

"I am of God, and God is all good. I am energy, I am strength, I am power, I am filled with omnipotent life. And as I am, so are all those others who are praying now with me to demonstrate life. The vitality of God permeates every fibre of our beings. Grace and poise are ours. We radiate life and love and riches and understanding, and as we give out these, we attract more and more of good to each other and to ourselves. The Spirit of God, which is active in us, flows through our bodies in a purifying, cleansing, healing stream that removes all obstructions and brings peace, health and harmony to our bodies. We are well, strong and vital. We are eternally youthful. We are happy, buoyant, free. We shall arise in the morning filled with energy, radiance, and the power to accomplish whatever we find to do."

> "Love that keeps thee all the day
> Care for thee tonight;
> Love that drives all care away
> Give thee peace and light.
> When the darkness seems to hide,
> When the shadows fall,
> Fear thou not; thou shalt abide
> Where His love is all!"
>
> —ETHEL B. CHENEY

CHAPTER SEVEN

THE GOD UNBORN

YOU REMEMBER THE STORY of the wise king who, fearing
that his son would be spoiled by the adulation of courtiers
and servants, put him in charge of a peasant couple, to be
brought up as their own son.

The child knew nothing of his royal birth, of his riches
or power. He worked and studied and played like any
other peasant child. It was not until he had grown into a
strong, self-reliant young fellow that the king sent for
him and revealed his true position.

Most of us are like that child. Brought up in ignorance
of our Divine Sonship, we think we are poor and powerless. Emerson says that Christ alone, of all those who
have lived upon this earth, correctly estimated the greatness and the unlimited possibilities of man. "I came that
ye might have LIFE," He said, "and have it more abundantly." And again and again He reminded us that we
are all of us Sons of God.

There is no such thing as a human nobody. Every one
of us has a God in him. Every one can put that God to
work for him, and become as great as the greatest.

> "Within me is the sum of all things past;
> Within me are the years that yet remain;
> And heaven has not a space too high or vast
> That I may not within myself contain;
> Nor is there an accomplishment divine
> That is not slumbering in this soul of mine."

99

The trouble is that most of us put the God in us to work—NOT for success—BUT FOR FAILURE! Have you read Dorothea Brande's "Wake Up and Live!"? In it she shows that if we would only use to good purpose the time and energy we spend in making failures of ourselves, we could be certain successes. It takes energy to fail, she points out. We fill life so full of energy-consuming, *but secondary* activities that we have no time for success. We give to our vast army of intelligent cell-workers a pattern of failure on which to build. Can you wonder that the finished result is FAILURE?

We must act, says Dorothea Brande, as though it were impossible to fail. Most of us have had the experience of finding ourselves in great danger, or being up against some impossible situation, and in desperation doing the one right thing to get us out which we should at ordinary times have regarded as impossible.

How do we do it? "Because," according to WAKE UP AND LIVE, "we dare not fail. Every alternative to success has been wiped out. So by ceasing to let fear hold its frustrating sway, we come into the use of already existing aptitudes which we formerly had no energy to explore."

In the Arabian Nights Tales, there is the story of a fisherman who found in his net a tightly sealed vase. On opening it, a great Genie came forth, who first threatened to kill the fisherman, but who, when the fisherman learned to control him, brought him riches and power beyond his wildest dreams.

There is in every one of us a God unborn. We can keep Him locked up all our lives, or we can bring Him forth and let Him be the motive power of everything we do.

Most of us let this God slumber all our lives, or if we bring Him forth, we put Him into labors of failure rather than of success.

We start Him off each morning with thoughts of failure, or give Him work in no way related to what we have to accomplish. Take your average day, as an instance; you get up in the morning morosely, regretfully, wishing you had gone to bed earlier the night before, or that you had not eaten or drunk this or that. You start telling all the billions of cells in your body that they have not been doing much of a job, but that not much can be expected of them, because the foods you gave them were not right for them, and the things you did would naturally fatigue them, and at your age they should be beginning to dry up and decay anyway.

That accomplished, you pick up the morning paper and read all the murders, scandals, robberies and failures, telling your God He can't expect to do much in a world like this, where anything evil may happen and where there is no telling from one day to the next when you may be the victim.

Your God-mind well impregnated with this idea, you go on to work, crowding and being crowded so that when you arrive at the office or shop, you feel ready to drop down and rest. Once securely seated, you find a score of minor, unimportant things to occupy your time, and give you excuse for not trying to do any difficult, creative work. You open the mail, you look up minor facts, you examine the previous day's figures . . . in short, you occupy yourself with all the trifling details that any clerk could handle as well as you, just so you will not have to TRY to succeed.

You put your God to work bringing you failure, when you might be using His infinite energies in making you the greatest success in your life!

Remember that this God can incarnate Himself only through you. He is an inseparable part of Creative Force, for good or ill. He goes in the direction of *your* thoughts.

He brings to you the things you visualize, whether they be the ills you fear or the success and happiness you desire. Whatever you give Him to do, with serene and confident assurance, that He does.

If He sees that you do not believe in success, that all your time is put in on unimportant work that leads only to failure, naturally He will work with you for failure, since He assumes that failure is what you want. If He sees that you expect sickness, He will do his best to bring sickness to you. If he gets the idea from your reading and conversation and habits of thought that you are looking for trouble and misery, be sure He will bring you as much of these as you can stand.

If He is led to believe that you have no hope of ever becoming rich or successful, and are content to merely scrape along as best you can, He will be just as content to loaf on the job and let you scrape along. He is the perfect servant, doing exactly what you expect of Him, no more, no less.

But if you expect good from Him, and let Him know that you are putting all your dependence upon Him to get that good, He will be just as faithful in bringing it to you.

Emerson said, you remember, that man is weak to the extent that he looks outside himself for help. It is only as he throws himself unhesitatingly upon the God within himself that he learns his own power and works miracles. It is only when he throws overboard all other props, and leans solely upon the God in him that he uncovers his real powers and finds the springs of success.

The chief characteristic of the religion of the future, said Dr. Eliot, will be man's inseparableness from the great Creative Force of God, which finds its outlet through the God within himself.

We are part of the Fountain Head of all supply. We are in touch with Omnipotence. Yet most of us have been entirely impotent, at the mercy of every wind of circumstance. Why? Because we put our God into images of impotence. We are dwarfs of what we might be, because we do not believe in our own power. We have unlimited capabilities, yet we do the work of pigmies. We go through life without even scratching the surface of our potentialities.

And all because *we are afraid!* We fear to trust the God in us. We fear to let go ourselves, and leave the work to Him. Like a man learning to swim, we are afraid to trust to the water to keep us afloat—we must struggle until we wear ourselves out, when if we would just relax and trust in it, the water would bear us up without effort on our part.

What is it that YOU fear? When you are reluctant to tackle a job, when you hesitate to call on someone, when you dawdle over little things rather than get at the real work that awaits you, nine times out of ten it is because you are afraid of something.

DO THE THING—and you will overcome your fear. You may not rid yourself of the hesitation the first time, or even the tenth, but keep doing the thing, and you will overcome all fear of it.

You remember when the children of Israel were wandering in the desert, they brought upon themselves a plague of serpents, which bit them and caused them great distress. Moses devised a cure for the wounds which has been a model for the cure of all fears since. He fastened a serpent of brass upon a pole and bade all the people gaze upon it. And all who had been bitten were cured by gazing upon that serpent of brass.

Bring your fear out into the open. Bring it out where you can look upon it. When you see it clearly, you will laugh at your fears. When you face it boldly, you will find it to be only a shadow of your own imagining.

"The whole course of things," said Emerson, "goes to teach us faith. We need only obey. There is guidance for each of us, and by lowly listening, we shall hear the right word."

But before we can hear it, we must listen. And to listen, we must TRUST.

Have you ever noticed that when you take medicine regularly to help the functioning of any organ, that organ soon stops functioning of itself, and waits for you to do all its work? The bowels, for instance. Get the habit of taking cathartics, and soon the bowels will not act without a cathartic.

The same is true of the God inside you. As long as you feel that the entire direction of your affairs is up to you, as long as you put your dependence upon your own abilities or your income or other material things, you will get no action except from these material means. To set the God in you to work, you must put your dependence upon Him. You must throw overboard all other dependences. You must put everything into His hands, and say to Him —"Help me or I perish!"

If you are in need, and your only hope of succor seems to lie in a rich aunt, *forget her!* Forget every material means. Throw them overboard, figuratively speaking. Remember that Life tried every material means of winning dominion and failed. If IT could not succeed that way, you cannot. So forget the material means, forget friends and rich relatives and speculation and the like.

Mentally put everything you have into the hands of the God in you, give Him the job of finding the way out of your difficulties, and then leave it to Him. "My God shall supply all my needs, according to His promise." *Let Him!*

Throw the burden entirely upon His shoulders, and don't interfere. Say to yourself, when thoughts of fear and worry intrude upon you—"I don't give a darn. I have given the job to the God in me. It is His worry now. If He cannot work it out, we'll go down together. But, sink or swim, it is up to Him."

God incarnates Himself through you. But only YOU can put life into the seed He gives you. You have heard how the female shad seeks the warmer waters of the rivers in the Springtime and lays its eggs in their shallows. Those eggs lie dormant until they die, unless the male shad comes along and releases the sperm which fertilizes them and quickens them into life and growth.

God has put a seed of Himself into you, but it remains dormant until YOU furnish the spark which quickens it into life. And that spark lies in giving the God in you work to do, then putting your dependence solely upon Him to accomplish it.

What was it made Napoleon? Simply his colossal belief in his destiny—in the God in him. He gave it a big job to do, and it did it—just as long as Napoleon put his faith in it. With ragged, ill-trained levies, he crossed the Alps into Italy and defeated well-equipped armies twice his size. He brought France out of chaos and made it the greatest power on earth.

Then his success went to his head. He thought it was HIS brain, HIS abilities, that had done all this. He put his faith in HIS strategy, HIS well-trained armies—and what happened? His Star, neglected, went into eclipse, and Napoleon himself quickly followed.

God incarnates Himself through you, but it rests with *you* to give life and expression to the God in YOU. You must give Him channels through which to express Himself. You must do your part, but look to Him for results.

What is the Unpardonable Sin? It is quenching the divine spark in yourself. It is smothering it with fear or worry, refusing it the chance of expression.

What was it brought the great empires of antiquity to ruin? When Athens was still a village, Rome not yet dreamed of, Europe a savage playground, China had become a civilized country where people rode in carriages, lived in fine houses, dressed in silks, ate from dishes and tables, even carried umbrellas. Today China is the football of the powers. Why? Because she built a wall around herself and stood still for 2,000 years. She stopped giving out, stopped progressing—and perished.

What puts an end to great fortunes, so that "Three generations from shirtsleeves to shirtsleeves" has become a byword? They stop making them, try to merely hold on to what they have. Result? They perish. You cannot stand still. The God-life in you is dynamic—not static. It must be finding new channels of expression or it goes out of you.

Give it a chance. Stop trying to hold on to what you have and, instead, sow it like seeds. Each night throw everything you have and are back into the lap of God, and put it up to the God in you to mold it anew, nearer to the Heart's Desire.

To do that, you need to be able to let go mentally of everything—of all your possessions, your abilities, your honors, everything. Throw everything back into the lap of God. You can't hold out on Him. You can't say—You take care of this and I'll look after that. Everything must go. It must be a complete new deal.

You remember the old Egyptian conception of God as the central sun, with rays shooting out in all directions, and at the end of each ray a hand, symbolizing a man. Some of the hands were open, and through them God's good gifts were poured out on the world. Some were

clenched tight, trying to keep for themselves all of God's
good. That is the Unpardonable Sin, trying to hold all
the good for ourselves, and thus shutting off a channel
of expression for God.

"He who would be great amongst you must be the servant of all." He who would win fortune, must make himself a channel for good to all about him.

"Charity begins at home, it is true," says a well known
writer. "But it does not stop there. To have only a beginning, without a continuing or an ending, is to be a
futile thing. Charity is not static; once started, it keeps on
going until it arrives."

Every good thing must be shared with others, before
you can get the full benefit of it. A new invention brings
the inventor nothing until he gives others the benefit of
it. A new idea, a new discovery, a new truth brings you
little joy until you share it.

What is the Fundamental Law of the Universe? It is
the law of the "Open Hand." It is the law that he who
would reap, must first sow. It is the law that before you
can get, you must give. It is the Law of the Higher Potential, that power must always flow from a higher to a
lower potential, that water must run down hill, that you
must get above your troubles before you can overcome
them.

And the only way you can get above your difficulties
is to put yourself on a higher plane mentally than they,
on a plane from which you can look down upon them and
laugh at them.

Our deepest griefs come not from the loss of those who
have ministered freely to our comfort and contentment,
but when we lose someone to whom we have given the
best of our time, our thought and our energy. And the
reason? Because we have lost a part of ourselves that we
had given to the object of our love.

Obviously, the best way to heal that wound is to give again, to find someone in urgent need of just such care and affection as we have been lavishing upon the lost one, and to give freely to him.

The watchword of the higher plane is—"Give!" Just as with Job, when he forgot his own sorrows and cares and losses in giving help to his stricken friends, he regained all and more than ever he had had before. "And the Lord turned the affliction of Job, when he prayed for his friends."

How, then, shall we order our lives?

1st. Find some worthy channel through which the God in you can express Himself. It does not matter how small or unimportant that channel may be in the beginning. Remember that the Master said that he who gave even a cup of water in His name should have his reward. Do the thing that is given you to do. Take advantage of the opportunities for expressing God that are near at hand. When you have done these, have no fear but that other opportunities will be given you.

2nd. Put your faith—NOT in your friends or your abilities or your resources—but in the God in you. Remember that He is a God who will carry you—not One that you have to carry. So go at every job cheerfully, attack every difficulty confidently, knowing that if you will do your utmost and still keep trying, the God in you will take up the task from there on and carry it to a successful conclusion.

3rd. Get above your troubles. Remember that power flows only from a higher to a lower potential, so get on a higher plane than any difficulty that assails you. Say to yourself, when you meet something beyond your powers to overcome, "I don't give a darn. The God in me can do anything. I should worry if my human powers have failed. The God in me cannot fail, for all of Life and all of Intelligence are working with Him for good. I have no fear, for the God in me is carrying on from where I left off, and nothing can stop him."

4th. Each morning when you awake, and each night when you go to bed, imagine yourself the commander of a great army of intelligent soldiers, or the sales manager of a vast group of salesmen. Then make the sort of speech to them that you would if you were such a commander or sales manager. Give them confidence in themselves and in you. Put pep and enthusiasm into them. Show them that, working together for any common aim, they are invincible. Then tell them their goal, and start them towards it.

5th. Work for your health in the same way. Dr. Charles Northen has shown that healthy plants, grown in soil containing all the mineral elements in proper balance, will resist most insect pests—without spraying, without outside help.

He took an orange grove infested with scale, and by restoring the mineral balance to the soil around certain trees, rid them completely of scale, though all the trees around them were still infested with it. By the same method, he grew healthy rose-bushes between rows that were riddled with insects, and the insects would not touch the bushes grown in soil with proper mineral balance. He even intertwined healthy cucumber and tomato plants with diseased plants. The bugs ate the diseased plants, *and refused to touch the healthy ones!*

It has been similarly proven that a healthy body can resist the attacks of any disease. As one nutrition authority recently put it—"One sure way to end the American people's susceptibility to infection is to supply through food a balanced ration of iron, copper and other metals. An organism supplied with a diet adequate to, or preferably in excess of, all mineral requirements, may so utilize these elements to produce immunity from infection quite beyond anything we are at present able to produce artificially."

From the material point of view, that is the ideal way to keep the body healthy. From the mental, there is an even more effective way—by appealing to the intelligence of the billions of cells that make up your body.

In his book—"Man, the Unknown"—Dr. Alexis Carrel brought out the fact that, at need, the body manufactures its own chemicals. It shows a knowledge of its own needs, and a resourcefulness in taking care of them, such as no human intelligence could muster.

Why then feed drugs and the like to an organization capable of manufacturing any chemical it may require? Why call in physicians to diagnose a trouble which the Intelligence within us understands a million times better than any doctor? Why not appeal to that Intelligence first?

"My old disorder returned as violently as ever," wrote John Wesley in his Journal. "The thought came to my mind, why do I not apply to God at the beginning rather than at the end of my illness? I did so, and found immediate relief so that I needed no further medicine."

So when next some ailment troubles you, instead of running to the medicine chest or the family doctor, just call together that army of cells of yours and remind them that they know more about this body of yours than all the scientists and physicians in the world, that they have a chemical laboratory which can turn out more effective drugs and serums than any made by man, and that their combined intelligence is such that they can use these chemicals to immediately cure any ailment that can attack you.

Remind them of all this, and ask them why, with all these resources at their command, you should call upon outside help. There can be but one answer—you shouldn't. Furthermore, you WILL NOT. It is their job, and you are going to put your dependence entirely upon them. If they choose to lie down on the job, it is just too bad, but —sink or swim—it is up to them.

6th. Take the same attitude towards riches and success. Success in life is a matter of the use of your intelligence. Well, here are a hundred billion cells, each with intelligence. Give them a common aim, and they can do anything. Set them seeking riches or any other good thing for you, and riches you will have.

"My God shall supply all my needs, according to His promise." Remember that. Your God can supply all your needs. He is a God Who can and will carry you—not One you must carry. But you must hold Him to the job. You must give Him definite work to do, and let Him know that you are putting your sole dependence upon Him to do it.

Give Him a goal. Set Him a mark to shoot at. Then DEMAND of Him that He win it, and BELIEVE in Him!

Suppose you were commander of an army. What would you expect if you got out and begged them to fight for you?—if you whined and pleaded? Well, you ARE the commander of an army—an intelligent army that does what is really expected of it.

Give them a goal—then cheer them to it! Put all your life, all your faith and enthusiasm into your efforts to win that goal, into your belief you will do it. Tell them they've got to win or perish—to keep attacking until they get there or die in the attempt, but that you know they CAN do it—ARE DOING IT! Then thank God for them. Be proud of them. Rejoice that they ARE successful.

That's the sort of talk that makes an army victorious. That's the sort of feeling that will make the God in you win. Can you give it to Him? Have you the courage to put your fate to the toss, to win or lose it all? Are you the Master of your fate? Are you the Captain of your soul? Then PROVE it!

Lastly, learn to forgive. Remember that after "Give us this day our daily bread," comes the line—"And forgive us our debts, as we forgive our debtors."

No matter how anyone may have wronged you, give him your blessing. Say to yourself, whenever resentful thoughts occur to you—"God is the only presence and power, therefore everything that happens to me is for good. I do not resist, antagonize or condemn anyone and my mind is filled with peace."

Charles Kingsley used to say, you remember, that we know our relations to God only through our relations to each other. And Carlyle defined wealth as the number of things we love and bless, which we are loved and blessed by.

You have seen these electric cranes that are used to pick up scrap metal and the like. A great disc hangs at the end of the rope, with wires connected to it. When it is desired to pick up anything, the electric current is turned on, the disc magnetized and it will then lift huge masses of scrap. To let go, all that is necessary is to turn off the current, and down drops the load.

We are all like that. Magnetize us with love, and we can do or attract any good thing. Fill us with fear or hate, and our attractive power is gone. So let's LOVE our jobs, our business associates, our neighbors. Let us do everything as to the Lord, thanking Him and rejoicing for work and pay. God always helps—if we will but let Him.

And let's rid ourselves of those twin devils of fear and hate. Let's start by forgiving all who have wronged us. Here is a little poem by Bonnie Day, clipped from Unity, which expresses the idea better far than we could:

"I NOW forgive. If any have offended
  Through ignorance or malice, be it known
  The debt is canceled and the matter ended,
  There's nothing to atone.

"I NOW forgive, my thought goes out in blessing,
  And love erases every trace of wrong—
  Father, what lifts the weight that has been pressing
  So sorely, and so long?

"CHILD, 'twas the weight of your own condemnation,
  The self-inflicted load that burdened you,
  By your own act of reconciliation,
  You are forgiven, too.

"FOR while you held your brother as a debtor,
  Your bitter thinking shackled your own soul,
  The self-same act that broke for him the fetter
  Has made you free and whole."

THE MAGIC WORD

CHAPTER EIGHT

THE LAW OF INCREASE

"I am Success, though hungry, cold, ill-clad,
I wander for a while, I smile and say,
'It is but for a time, I shall be glad
Tomorrow, for good fortune comes my way.
God is my Father, He has wealth untold,
His wealth is mine—health, happiness and gold.'"
—ELLA WHEELER WILCOX

IN A PAMPHLET written by Don Blanding, he tells of a time during the trying years of the Great Depression, when he found himself financially, mentally and physically "broke." He was suffering from insomnia and from a physical lethargy amounting almost to paralysis. Worst of all, he had a bad case of "self-pity," and he felt that the self-pity was fully justified.

He was staying at a small Art Colony (on credit), trying to rebuild his wrecked life and wretched body. Among those at the Colony was Mike, an Hawaiian boy. Mike seemed to be always cheerful. Mike seemed to be always prosperous. And, naturally, Blanding wondered why. For Mike, when he had known him before, had been blessed with few of this world's goods.

So one day he asked Mike what good fairy had waved her wand over him and turned all that he touched into gold.

For answer, Mike pointed to a string of letters he had pasted over his bed—"L-I-D-G-T-T-F-T-A-T-I-M."

Blanding read them, but could make no sense out of

them. "What are they, the 'Open, Sesame' to the Treasure Cave?"

"They have been the 'Open, Sesame' for me," Mike told him, and went on to explain how they had helped him. It seems that Mike, too, had experienced his ups and downs, but in the course of one of his "downs," he had happened upon a teacher who showed him the power of PRAISE and THANKFULNESS.

"There is an inherent law of mind," says Charles Fillmore, "that we INCREASE whatever we PRAISE. The whole of creation responds to praise, and is glad. Animal trainers pet and reward their charges with delicacies for acts of obedience; children glow with joy and gladness when they are praised. Even vegetation grows better for those who love it. We can praise our own ability, and the very brain cells will expand and increase in capacity and intelligence, when we speak words of encouragement and appreciation to them."

God gave you dominion over the earth. Everything is your servant, but remember it is said in the Scriptures that God brought every beast and fowl to Adam, *to see what he would call them*. You are like Adam in this, that you can give to everything and everybody with whom you come in contact the name you like. You can call them good or bad. And whatever you call them, that is what they will be—good servants or evil. You can praise or curse them, and as you do, so will they be to you.

There is one unfailing Law of Increase—"*Whatever is praised and blessed, MULTIPLIES!*" Count your blessings and they increase. If you are in need of supply, start in now to praise every small piece of money that comes to you, blessing it as a symbol of God's abundance and love. Salute the Divinity represented by it. Bless Him and name Him Infinite and Abundant Supply. You will be surprised how soon that small piece of money will increase to many pieces. Take God into your business. Bless your store, bless every one that works for you, each customer that comes in. Know that they represent the Divinity called Abundance, so bless them as such.

If you are working for someone else and want a better job or more pay, start by BLESSING and being THANKFUL *for what you have.* Bless the work you are doing, be thankful for every opportunity it gives you to acquire greater skill or ability or to serve others. Bless the money you earn, no matter how little it may be. Be so thankful to God for it that you can give a small "Thank Offering" from it to someone in greater need than yourself.

Suppose the Boss does seem unappreciative and hard. Bless him just the same. Be thankful for the opportunity to SERVE faithfully, no matter how small the immediate reward may seem to be. Give your best, give it cheerfully, gladly, thankfully, and you will be amazed how quickly the INCREASE will come to you—not necessarily from your immediate boss, but from the Big Boss over all.

I remember reading a letter from a woman in the drought belt in which she said that they, unlike most of their neighbors, had an abundant supply of water, and excellent crops. "When my husband plows a field," she writes, "I ask God to bless each furrow. Each seed that goes into the seeder is blessed, and the realization held that it will produce abundantly according to His righteous law. Our neighbors marveled at the abundance of hay that we cut this year. The hay was sold before the third cutting was put up.

"Each day, in the silence, I put the ranch 'Lovingly in the hands of the Father.' I ask God to bless everybody that comes in contact with the ranch."

Few realize the power of praise and blessing. Praise

may be called the great liberator. You remember the
story of Paul and Silas. They lay in jail bound with
chains, but they did not despair. They rejoiced and sang
hymns of praise, and lo, the very walls were shaken down
and they were set free.

Praise always magnifies. When we praise God and then
look about us and praise His invisible presence in all that
we see, we find that the good is so magnified that much
becomes evident that we ordinarily fail to see. Running
through all of Jesus Christ's acts as well as His teachings
we find the glowing element of praise. When He looked
at five loaves and two small fishes and realized that He
had a multitude to feed, His first thought was a thought
of praise. "And looking up to heaven, he blessed."

Go back over the Old Testament and see how often you
are adjured to "Praise the Lord and be thankful, that
THEN shall the earth yield her increase." Probably no
life chronicled in the Scriptures was more beset with
trials and dangers than that of King David. And what
was his remedy? What brought him through all tribulations to power and riches? Just read the Psalms of David
and you will see.

> "Jehovah reigneth; let the earth rejoice;
> Let the multitude of isles be glad.
> Bless Jehovah, O my soul;
> And all that is within me, *bless* his holy name ...
> Who forgiveth all thine iniquities;
> Who healeth all thy diseases."

"If anyone could tell you the shortest, surest way to
all happiness and all perfection," wrote William Law,
"he must tell you to make it a rule to yourself to thank
and praise God for everything that happens to you. For
it is certain that whatever seeming calamity happens to
you, if you thank and praise God for it, you turn it into

a blessing. Could you therefore work miracles, you could not do more for yourself than by this thankful spirit; for it turns all that it touches into happiness."

How then can YOU increase your supply? How can you get more of riches and happiness and every good thing of life? In the same way as the Wise Men and the Prophets of old. In the same way that Jesus twice fed the multitudes. In the same way that He filled the disciples' nets to overflowing with fish, after they had labored all night and caught nothing.

By EXPANDING what you have! And the way to expand is through love, through praise and thanksgiving —through saluting the Divinity in it, and naming it Infinite and Abundant Supply.

Throughout the Bible we are told—"In everything by prayer and supplication WITH THANKSGIVING let your requests be made unto God." Again and again the root of inspiration and attainment is stressed. *Rejoice, be glad, praise, give thanks!*

And that was what our Hawaiian boy had done. That was the secret of his prosperity and success. The Talisman he had pasted over his bed meant—"Lord, I do give Thee thanks for the abundance that is mine." Every time he looked upon it, he repeated those words of thankfulness. The happy ending lies in the fact that these words of praise and thanksgiving proved to be as potent a talisman for Don Blanding as they had for Mike, the Hawaiian.

"Whoso offereth praise, glorifieth Me," sang the Psalmist of old. And it is as true today as it was thousands of years ago. Praise, thankfulness, understanding—these three supply the golden key to anything of good you may desire of life.

In "Think What You Want" magazine, some time ago, H. W. Alexander told how praise helps. "Sincere praise is money in your pocket," he said. "It is a spiritual and moral uplift. It is a tonic to the giver and the receiver. It rebounds to both a thousand times. I know a company whose sales during the depression went from $2,600,000 a year to $8,000,000. Praise was the inspiration.

"In a divorce court not so long ago was recorded the story of a man who from a laborer's job climbed to the Presidency of his business. A friend asked him why he quit his almost lifetime companion, though she was well provided for. Said he, 'Well, my wife of today appreciates my ability, tells me right along, whereas my childhood sweetheart knows my weaknesses and tells me about them. I like appreciation.' His income tax is on a $100,000 salary.

"Little things count. Your secretary has a new dress, a new hat, a fashionably fluffy ruffle—tell her so. The file clerk finds your letters quickly—tell her so. The cop on the beat is sure to see the school boys are safely over with a wave of his hand. Tell him he is tops.

"One of the finest persons who worked for me was an elderly servant woman. She had a tough time in life, poorly educated, used split infinitives, came early in the morning to clean the house. She often said to me as I left in the morning, 'Sure, you look good today. You've got a big job, you work hard, you'll win.' She *thought* I was good, and when I went out I *was* good. Top executives who read this know very well the truth of what the chauffeur, maid, gardener—who gives them a cheery word of praise, means to them at market time, conference time, or directors' time—it rings in their mind—oh, yes, they remember. You can't fly too high.

"And the mother who *thinks* her boy or girl is about right, aids them on as no one else can.

"I have this belief—that big or little, praise does win friends, wins respect for yourself, wins you a monetary return, and it helps a Pullman porter, a housewife, an industrialist, to bigger, better things. It costs you nothing but a smile—but do be sincere.

"To the wives who may read this: You know your man. He can't fool you. But be just as honest as you can, praise him, send him out to his private automobile, his street car, his bicycle, his train, or his walk, with a smile, with praise, and you'll wear sables—try it."

Like attracts like. Praise and appreciation bring back greater praise and appreciation to you. If you want health, happiness, in your life, if you are seeking riches and success, attune your thoughts to these. BLESS the circumstances that surround you. Bless and praise those who come in contact with you. Bless even the difficulties you meet, for by blessing them, you can change them from discordant conditions to favorable ones, you can speed up their rate of activity to where they will bring you good, instead of evil. It is only lack of RESPONSIVE-NESS to good that produces the lacks in your life. Good works on the plane of EXPANSION. Good revolves at a high rate of activity. You can key your activity to that same rate by an expectant, confident state of mind. You can bring all your surroundings and circumstances up to that same level by BLESSING them, PRAISING the good in them, saluting the DIVINITY in them.

In the pages that follow, we shall show you how the practice of blessing and praising all things has brought good to all who have tried it, how you can use these same methods to attract every good thing *you* may desire.

"Into whatsoever house ye enter, first say—'Peace be to this house!'"

CHAPTER NINE

IN THE BEGINNING

"For life is the mirror of king and slave,
'Tis just what we are and do;
Then give to the world the best you have,
And the best will come back to you."

WE OFTEN SPEAK of psychology and metaphysics as new sciences, and think that the study of these began within the last half-century. Yet if you refer to the very first book of the Bible, you find more profound examples of applied psychology than in any textbook of today.

Take the story of Jacob as an instance. You remember how Jacob agreed to serve Laban seven years for the hand of Rachel in marriage. And how, through the guile of his father-in-law, Jacob had to serve a second seven years. Even then, when he would have gone back to his own country, Laban begged him to tarry yet a while longer, and agreed to pay Jacob as wages "all the speckled and spotted cattle, and all the brown cattle among the sheep, and the speckled and spotted among the goats."

Since Laban first removed from the herds all cattle of this kind, the chances of Jacob's getting rich on the speckled offspring of solid-colored cattle seemed poor indeed.

But Jacob evidently knew his Scriptures, and the idea we think so new, that first comes the "word" (or mental image), then the physical manifestation, was in his mind even when he made the bargain.

For what did he do?

"And Jacob took him rods of green poplar, and of the hazel and chestnut tree; and pilled white strakes in them, and made the white appear which was in the rods.

"And he set the rods which he had pilled before the flocks in the gutters in the watering troughs when the flocks came to drink, that they should conceive when they came to drink.

"And the flocks conceived before the rods, and brought forth cattle ringstraked, speckled, and spotted.

"And Jacob did separate the lambs, and set the faces of the flocks toward the ringstraked, and all the brown in the flock of Laban; and he put his own flocks by themselves, and put them unto Laban's cattle.

"And it came to pass, whensoever the stronger cattle did conceive, that Jacob laid the rods before the eyes of the cattle in the gutters that they might conceive among the rods.

"But when the cattle were feeble, he put them not in; so the feebler were Laban's, and the stronger Jacob's.

"And the man increased exceedingly, and had much cattle, and maidservants, and menservants, and camels, and asses."

You have heard of the English cuckoo. Too lazy to rear and care for its own young, it goes to the nests of other birds when they are off seeking food, notes the markings on their eggs, then comes back later *and lays in their nest eggs of those same exact markings!*

Various saints of the middle ages are said to have had markings on their hands, feet and sides similar to those on the crucified Saviour, acquired from constant contemplation of His image. And only recently I read of an adopted child, which was reported to have developed markings similar in all respects to those of the real son of its foster-parents, although the son had died some months before the adopted child was born. The parents were satisfied it was a case of reincarnation, but it seemed to me merely a materialization in the foster-child of the images in the mother's mind. She had grieved inexpressibly over her loss. She had adopted the waif to try to fill the void left by her own little boy. And striving to see in his every action some reminder of her lost one, those images so strongly held in her mind actually expressed themselves in the body of her foster-child.

It all comes back to that first line of the first chapter of the Gospel of St. John—"In the beginning was the Word." For what is a "Word"? A mental image, is it not? Before an architect can build a house, he must have a mental image of what he is to build. Before you can accomplish anything, you must have a clear mental image of what it is you want to do.

Turn to the Scriptural account of the creation of the world. What is the outstanding fact you find there?

IN EVERY THING GOD CREATED, THE "WORD" CAME FIRST—THEN THE MATERIAL FORM!

Just listen: "And God said, Let there be light . . . And God said, Let there be a firmament . . . And God said, Let us make man . . ."

First the "word," then the material form. Scientists tell us that words denote ideas, mental concepts—that you can always judge how far a race has advanced in the mental scale by the number of words it uses. Its vocabulary is the measure of its ideas. Few words—few ideas, few mental images.

Therefore, when God said—"Let the earth bring forth grass," He had in mind a clear mental image of what grass was like. In other words, He had already formed the mold. As the Scriptures put it—"The Lord God made the earth and the heavens, and every plant of the field *before it was in the earth,* and every herb of the field *before it* grew." He made the mental image, the mold. It needed then only to draw upon the energy about Him to fill that mold and give it material form.

And that is all you, too, need to do to give your word of power material form—first make the mental image, the mold, then pour into it the elements necessary to make that image manifest for all to see.

What do you want first? — Health — Happiness? Riches?

For perfect health, begin by taking the life out of every distorted image of sickness or imperfection. Charge those nerve centers of yours to withdraw their supporting hands, and let your image of disease collapse like the pricked bubble it is.

THEN IMAGE THE PERFECT MOLD OF WHATEVER ORGAN HAS BEEN DISEASED. Image the perfect mold of it so vividly that you can clearly see it in your mind's eye, then charge The God in You to reach out with its millions of hands for all the elements it needs to make that perfect image manifest.

First the word (the mental image), then the creation. But the creation will never become manifest without faith. So when you have made your image, when you have set The God in You to work pouring into it the elements it needs for life, *"believe that you receive!"* See with the eyes of your mind that perfect organ functioning as it was meant to, *and thank God for it!*

For riches, the same principle holds true. Take your life out of every image of debt, of lack, of unfulfilled obligation. The God in you is a God of plenty. He cannot owe money. He cannot be limited. There are no circumstances powerful enough to force Him to live in poverty or want.

Yet He, remember, is devoted entirely to your advancement. So how can you be tied down by debt or limitation of any kind?

How? Because YOU have insisted upon it. Instead of a God of plenty, you have worshipped one of want. Instead of reaching out for what you needed, you have tied the hands of The God in You and tried to do their work with the paltry powers of your material hands.

Unloose The God in You! Give Him a job and set Him to work. Make your mental image of the great business or other service you long for, then set The God in You to work bringing to you every element you need to make that image real. And don't wait until you receive the whole of it, but as fast as any element becomes manifest, USE it!

If you have only 10¢, USE it to start your great idea. If you have only the idea, START it, even though you can take only the first step. First the word, remember, then the creation. And there can be no creation without faith.

Show your faith by using each element as fast as it makes itself manifest, even though there be no sign that any other element is following, and before you know it, your whole structure will be complete.

Have you ever read Genevieve Behrend's account of how she got $20,000, when, from all material points of view, her chances of ever seeing that amount of money were just about nil?

"Every night before going to sleep," she writes, in YOUR INVISIBLE POWER, "I made a mental picture of the desired $20,000 which seemed necessary to go and study with Troward. Twenty imaginary $1,000 bills were counted over each night in my bedroom, and then, with the idea of more emphatically impressing my mind with the fact that this twenty thousand dollars was for the purpose of going to England, and studying with Troward,

I wrote out my picture, saw myself buying my steamer ticket, walking up and down the ship's deck from New York to London, and finally saw myself accepted as Troward's pupil. This process was repeated every morning and every evening, always impressing more and more fully upon my mind Troward's memorized statement: 'My mind is a center of Divine operations.' I endeavored to keep this statement in the back part of my consciousness all the time, with no thought in mind of how the money might be obtained. Probably the reason why there was no thought of the avenues through which the money might reach me was because I could not possibly imagine where the $20,000 would come from. So I simply held my thought steady and let the power of attraction find its own way and means.

"One day while walking on the street, taking deep breathing exercises, the thought came: 'My mind is surely a center of Divine operation. If God fills all space, then God must be in my mind also; if I want this money to study with Troward that I may know the truth of Life, then both the money and the truth must be mine, though I am unable to feel or see the physical manifestations of either. Still,' I declared, 'it must be mine.'

"While these reflections were going on in my mind, there seemed to come up from within me the thought: 'I AM all the substance there is.' Then, from another channel in my brain the answer seemed to come, 'Of course, that's it; everything must have its beginning in mind. The Idea must contain within itself the only one and primary substance there is, and this means money as well as everything else.' My mind accepted this idea, and immediately all the tension of mind and body was relaxed. There was a feeling of absolute certainty of being in touch with all the power Life has to give. All thought of money, teacher, or even my own personality, vanished in the great wave of joy which swept over my entire being. I walked on and on, with this feeling of joy steadily increasing and expanding until everything about me seemed aglow with resplendent light. Every person I passed appeared illuminated as I was. All consciousness of personality had disappeared, and in its place there came that great and almost overwhelming sense of joy and contentment.

"That night when I made my picture of the twenty thousand dollars it was with an entirely changed aspect. On previous occasions, when making my mental picture, I had felt that I was waking up something within myself. This time there was no sensation of effort. I simply counted over the twenty thousand dollars. Then, in a most unexpected manner, from a source of which I had no consciousness at the time, there seemed to open a possible avenue through which the money might reach me.

"Just as soon as there appeared a circumstance which indicated the direction through which the twenty thousand dollars might come, I not only made a supreme effort to regard the indicated direction calmly as the first sprout of the seed I had sown in the absolute, but left no stone unturned to follow up that direction, thereby fulfilling my part. By so doing, one circumstance seemed naturally to lead to another, until, step by step, my desired twenty thousand dollars was secured."

For happiness, the method is no different. Your God is a God of love, and real love can know no unhappiness, for love gets its happiness from giving.

There are laws to interfere with almost every other activity of humanity, but none to keep you from giving as much as you like. An unselfish giving results in getting, just as surely as planting results in harvesting. Give with no thought of reward but the good of the one you are helping, and good is bound to flow back to you.

Love begets love, you know, so take your life out of every thought of enmity, of repining, of unhappiness. In place of these, see yourself in your mind's eye giving every manner of happiness to all whom you would have love you. Image that in your mind's eye, then set The God in You to work bringing you opportunities to make all these loved ones happier. And as fast as each opportunity presents itself, USE it! No matter how tiny an opportunity it may be, *use it!* No matter if it be merely the chance to say a pleasant word, to give a kindly smile, to bring a happy thought, *use it!*

And in the using, you will find that doubly great happiness has come to you.

Each of us is a miniature sun, his circumstances and surroundings his solar system. If debts and disease and troubles form part of your system, what is the remedy? *Let go of them, of course!* If you want new planets of riches and youth and happiness, how can you get them? In the same way the sun does, and only in that way—by throwing off from yourself.

Remember this: Nothing can come into your solar system except from you or through you. If it comes from outside, it is not yours and has no power over you until you take hold of it mentally and accept it as yours. If you don't want it, you can refuse to accept it, refuse to take hold of it, refuse to believe in its reality—then put in the place it seems to occupy, the perfect condition of your own imaging.

If there is something lacking in your solar system, you have only to "speak the word"—create the mental image, then hold to that image in serene faith until The God in You has filled it with those elements that make it visible to all.

It is your own fault when you allow yourself to become the victim of personal impotence or of undesirable external situations. As Emerson put it—"Nothing external to you has any power over you." You fear these negative seemings simply because you BELIEVE in them, when all the time it is only that BELIEF that gives them power and authority.

Remember, YOU are the central sun of your own solar system. YOU have dominion over everything within that system. YOU can say what shall enter, what shall stay there. And you have infinite attractive power to draw to you anything of good you may desire. Nothing stands between you and your fondest desires but lack of understanding of or faith in this power of attraction.

But once you send out the desire, you must have perfect faith in the result. You cannot accomplish anything by expressing a desire and then spending your time fearing and worrying lest you will not find the work you seek, or not have the money in time to pay your bills, or that some other evil thing will happen to prevent good from coming to you. The law of attraction cannot bring both good and evil at the same time. It must be one or the other. And it is up to YOU to decide which it shall be.

"After any object or purpose is clearly held in thought," says Lilian Whiting, "its precipitation in tangible and visible form is merely a question of time. Columbus saw in vision a path through trackless waters around the world. The vision always precedes and itself determines the realization."

Dare you to say—"Every day in every way I am getting richer and richer"? If you dare—and will follow up the word with the mental image of yourself HAVING all the riches you desire—Spirit substance will make your word manifest and show you the way to riches.

You were designed by the Father to be master of your

fate and captain of your soul. If you are not exercising that mastery, it is because you are lying down on the job. Instead of mastering your thoughts and mental images, you are letting them bow down before mere things.

No thing can make you unhappy if you will exercise your divine power of love and blessings towards it. Everything is good in its essence, and that good essence will respond to your call of blessing, and its good will come forth to meet you.

"The world stands out on either side
No wider than the heart is wide;
Above the world is stretched the sky—
No higher than the soul is high;
The heart can push the sea and land
Farther away on either hand;
The soul can split the sky in two,
And let the Face of God shine through."

CHAPTER TEN

TREASURE MAPPING FOR SUPPLY

So MANY PEOPLE have won to success and happiness by making "Treasure Maps" to more easily visualize the things they wanted, that Nautilus Magazine recently ran a prize competition for the best article showing how a "Treasure Map" had helped to bring about one's heart's desire. Caroline J. Drake won the contest.

"I had been bookkeeper," she wrote, "in a large department store for seven years when the manager's niece, whose husband had just died, was put in my place.

"I felt stunned. My husband had died ten years previously, leaving a little home and some insurance. But sickness and hospital bills had long since taken both home and money. I had supported the family for eight years and kept the three children in school, but had not been able to save any money. The eldest child, a boy, had just finished high school but as yet had found nothing to do to help along.

"Day after day I looked for work of any kind to do which might pay rent and give us a living. I was thirty-five years old, strong, capable and willing; but there was absolutely no place for me. For the first time in my life I was afraid of the future. The thought that we might have to go on relief appalled me.

"Thus three months passed. I was behind two months with the rent when the landlord told me I would have to move. I asked him to give me a few days longer in which to try and find work. This he agreed to do.

"The next morning I started out again on my rounds. In passing a magazine stand I stopped and glanced over the papers and magazines. It must have been the answer to my many prayers that led me to pick up the copy of a magazine which stared me in the face. Idly I opened it and glanced at the table of contents. My mind was in such a turmoil that I was barely conscious of the words which my eyes saw.

"Suddenly my eye was caught by a title about 'treasure-mapping' for success and supply. Something impelled me to buy a copy of the magazine which proved to be the turning point in our lives.

"Instead of looking for work, I went home. Still under the influence of that 'Something' (which I did not then understand) I began to read the magazine. Strange and unreal as it then seemed, still I did not doubt. I read each article eagerly and in its order. When I came to the article about treasure-mapping to bring success and supply, something about the idea seemed to hold me in its grip. As a child I had always loved games, and this idea of making a treasure-map reawakened that old desire.

"I read the article several times. Then, with a bunch of papers which I hunted up, I set to work to make my treasure-map of success and supply. So many things came into my mind to put on that treasure-map! First, there was the little cottage at the edge of town. Then there was a little dress and millinery shop which I had always longed for. Then, of course, a car. And in that cottage would be a piano for the girls; a yard in the back where we could work among the flowers of an evening or a morning. My enthusiasm grew by leaps and bounds. From magazines and papers I cut pictures and words and sentences—all connected with the idea of success and abundance.

How I Made the "Treasure-Map"

"Next I found a large sheet of heavy white paper and began building that map. In the center I pasted a picture of a lovely little cottage with wide porches and trees and shrubbery around it. In one corner of the map I put a picture of a little storeroom and underneath I pasted the words, 'Betty's Style Shop.' Close to this I pasted pictures of a few very stylish dresses and hats.

"At different places on the map I placed sentiments and mottoes—all carrying out the idea of success, abundance, happiness and harmony.

"I do not know how long I worked on that treasure-map which was to be the means of attracting into our lives the things which we had need of and desired. I could already feel myself living in that cottage and working in the little dress shop. Never had I felt so completely fascinated and thrilled with an idea as with that treasure-map and what I was sure it would bring us. I tacked the map on the wall of my bedroom, right in front of my bed, so that the first thing I saw in the morning and the last thing at night would be that treasure-map of my desires.

"Every night and morning I would go over every detail of that map until it fairly seemed to become a part of my very being. It became so clear that I could call it instantly to mind at any moment in the day. Then in my Silence period I would see myself and the children going through the rooms of the cottage, laughing and talking, arranging the furniture and curtains. I would picture my daughters at the piano singing and playing; I would see my son sitting in the library with books and papers all around him. Then I would picture myself walking about my shop, proud and happy; people coming in and going out. I would see them buying the lovely hats and dresses, paying me for them and going out smiling.

"During all this time, I was learning more and more of the power of the mind to draw to us the things and conditions like unto our thoughts. I understood that this treasure-map was but the means of impressing upon my subconscious mind the pattern from which to build the conditions of success and harmony into our lives. Always, after each of my Silence periods, I would lovingly thank God that the abundance and harmony and love were already ours. I believed that I *had* received; for mentally living in the cottage and working in the shop was to me the certain fact that I would take possession of them in the material world just as in the mental.

"When the children found out what I was doing, they entered heartily into the spirit of the game and each of them soon had a treasure-map of his own.

"It was not many weeks before things began to happen. One day I met an old friend of my husband's and he told me that he and his wife were going west for several months and asked if we would come out and take care of their house for the rent. A week later we were settled in that cottage, which was almost the very picture of the one I had on my treasure-map. A little later my son was offered work evenings and Saturdays in an engineering office, which proved the means of his entering college that fall.

"We had been in the cottage nearly two months when I saw an advertisement in the local paper for a woman to take charge of a lady's dress shop. I answered the ad and found that the owner was having to give up the shop for several months, perhaps permanently, on account of her health. Arrangements were quickly made so that I was to run the business and share half the expenses and the profits.

"Within six months after we started treasure-mapping for supply, we had accomplished practically everything that map called for. When the owner of the cottage came back several months later, he made it possible for us to buy the place and we are still here.

"The business, too, is mine now. The lady decided not to come back, so I bought the business, paying her so much a month. It is a much larger and more thriving business now—thanks to the understanding of the power of thought which I gained through my study and practice."

In another article in Nautilus, Helen M. Kitchel told how she used a "Treasure Map" to sell her property. She pasted an attractive picture of her house on a large sheet of paper, put a description of it underneath and then surrounded picture and description with such mottoes as—"Love, the Divine Magnet, attracts all that is good" —and others of a similar nature. She hung her map where she could see and study it several times a day, and repeated some of the affirmations or mottoes whenever the thought of making a sale occurred to her.

She also started a little private letter box which she called "God's Box" and in it, whenever the thought occurred to her, she placed a letter written to God telling of her needs and desires. Then each month she went over the letters, taking out and giving thanks for those that had been answered.

Within a year her house was sold, on the very plan she herself had outlined in one of her "Letters to God," on the exact basis and for the exact price she had asked in that letter.

Another method is to "Talk with God." Go somewhere where you can be alone and undisturbed for a little while, and talk aloud to God exactly as you would to a loving and understanding Father. Tell Him your needs. Tell Him your ambitions and desires. Describe in detail just what you want. Then thank Him just as you would an earthly father with whom you had had a similar talk and who had promised you the things you asked for. You will be amazed at the result of such sincere talks.

"My word shall not come back to me void, but shall accomplish that whereunto it was sent." Whatever you can visualize—and BELIEVE in—you can accomplish. Whatever you can see as yours in your mind's eye, you can get. "In the beginning was the Word." In the beginning is the mental image.

Corinne Updegraff Wells had an article in her little magazine "Through Rose Colored Glasses" that illustrates the power of visualizing your ambitions and desires. "Many years ago," she says, "a young girl who lived in a New York tenement was employed by a fashionable Fifth Avenue modiste to run errands, match samples and pull basting threads.

"Annie loved her job. From an environment of poverty she had become suddenly and miraculously an inhabitant of an amazing new world of beauty, wealth and fashion. It was thrilling to see lovely ladies arrive in fine carriages, to watch the social elite preen before Madam's big gold framed mirrors.

"The little errand girl, in her starched gingham, soon became filled with desire and fired with ambition. She began imagining herself as head of the establishment instead of its most lowly employee. Whenever she passed before mirrors she smiled at a secret reflection she saw of herself, older and more beautiful, a person of charm and importance.

"Of course, nobody even suspected the secret existence of this make-believe person. Hugging her precious secret, Annie smiled confidently at that dazzling reflection in the mirror and began playing an exciting game. 'I'll pretend I'm already Madam. I'll be polite and look my best and have grand manners and learn something new each day. I'll work as hard and take as much interest as though the shop were really and truly mine.'

"Soon fashionable ladies began whispering to Madam: 'Annie's the smartest girl you've ever had!' Madam herself began to smile and say: 'Annie, you may fold Mrs. Vandergilt's gown if you'll be very careful,' or 'I'm going to let you deliver this wedding dress,' or, 'My dear, you're developing a real gift for color and line,' and, finally, 'I'm promoting you to the work-room.'

"The years passed quickly. Each day Annie came more and more to resemble the image she alone had seen of herself. Gradually, the little errand girl became Annette, an individual; then Annette, stylist; and finally, Madam Annette, renowned costume designer for a rich and famous clientele.

"The images we hold steadfastly in our minds over the years are not illusions; they are the patterns by which we are able to mould our own destinies."

"You never can tell when you do an act
Just what the result will be,
But with every deed you are sowing a seed,
Though the harvest you may not see.
Each kindly act is an acorn dropped
In God's productive soil;
You may not know, but the tree shall grow
With shelter for those who toil.

"You never can tell what your thought will do
In bringing you hate or love,
For thoughts are things and their airy wings
Are swifter than carrier doves.
They follow the law of the universe—
Each thing must create its kind,
And they speed o'er the track to bring you back
Whatever went out from your mind."
                              —ELLA WHEELER WILCOX

CHAPTER ELEVEN

"WANTED: RAIN!"

"From one to two inches, and free from hail if possible. Is badly needed to save remaining crops and fill the reservoirs. Must be delivered soon to do any good. Will pay highest market price.

"Can be delivered any place; prefer general rain. Showers gratefully accepted, but prefer real, honest-to-goodness downpour.

"This offer made by the following firms for the general good of the community, and in the general belief that anything worth having, is worth asking for."

BELLE FOURCHE, South Dakota needed one thing—RAIN—to save remaining crops and fill the reservoirs. Why not advertise for it, thought L. A. Gleyre, publisher of THE NORTHWEST POST. A novel idea—advertising to the Lord—never been tried in just that way before, but at least there was no harm in trying. The prayerful advertisement reprinted above was the result.

"We proposed to each merchant in town," says Mr. Gleyre, "that he pay $2.50 for his name at the bottom of the page ad, with the provision that if no material rain fell between the date of the advertisement and the following Tuesday midnight, the ad was entirely at our expense.

"The idea took immediately . . . we could probably have filled a double truck. While the week was rolling by, our people had a new one to think about—their minds were actually taken off the scarcity of rain and made to function along the line of whether THE NORTHWEST POST was going to make good with their ad. The majority of our merchants were pleased with the idea. Some actually believed we had some inside information from the weather bureau which prompted our offer. A few, including one or two preachers, while not saying so to us, took occasion to say it was sacrilegious, etc.

"During the specified week, light rains fell in some parts of our territory. Belle Fourche had three very light sprinkles—not enough to count, for we agreed that the rain should be a downpour. Toward the end of the week excitement ran rife and interest continued to grow. Some of our warm friends made bets we would win. Others openly hoped we would, while everyone agreed that it would be tremendously helpful if we did win.

"*We won*—but lost. Just six hours after midnight, Wednesday morning, it rained pitch-forks-and-saw-logs-for-handles. It was exactly what we advertised for—a swash-buckling, rip-snortin' downpour of rain. It measured from one-half to two inches, and one remote point reported seven inches of rainfall!

"But we didn't charge any merchant a cent. We lost by six hours.

"I think it attracted more attention than anything we have done in years. To this day we are asked to advertise for something needed."

Where did that rain come from? Did the advertisement bring it? Does the Rain Dance of the Hopi Indians bring it? Did the prayer of Elijah bring it, as told in the Bible?

Yes! At least, so we believe, and we think we can show you good reason for that belief. Not only that, but we believe that back of these answers to prayer is the fundamental law of life and supply!

For of all the promises of Jesus, there is but one that

promises us WHATEVER WE ASK shall be done for us! That one positive assurance is *based on this condition*—"If two of you agree on earth as touching anything they shall ask, it shall be done for them of my Father which is in Heaven."

And again He said—"Where two or three are gathered together in My name, there am I in the midst of them." Why is this? Why the necessity for several to unite in asking for a thing in order to be sure of getting it?

A good many years ago, Professor Henry of Princeton made an experiment with a charged magnet. First he took an ordinary magnet of large size, suspended it from a rafter and with it lifted a few pounds of iron.

Then he wrapped the magnet with wire and charged it with the current from a small battery. Instead of only a few pounds, the now highly charged magnet lifted 3,000 pounds!

That is what happens when one person prays, believing, and another adds his prayers and his faith. In effect, the second person is charging the magnet of the first one with his current, MULTIPLYING the power of the other's prayer a dozen times over.

In Nautilus Magazine some months ago, Elizabeth Gregg told how five people prayed—agreeing—and the most pressing personal problem of each was soon solved. It seems that the husband of a Mrs. A. had been sick with ulcerated stomach for months. She had prayed repeatedly, without result, so one day she picked four of her friends whom she knew to be badly in need of help in different ways, and got them to agree to meet together on a certain day each week and see if, by uniting their prayers in perfect agreement, they might not improve their condition.

At the first meeting, it was decided to pray for the recovery of Mrs. A.'s husband, so these five women, sitting in silence, mentally pictured the husband strong and well, going about his work in a happy way. Then they gave thanks that their prayer had been answered.

"It was agreed," the article goes on to say, "that promptly at twelve o'clock noon each day until the next meeting, each of the five women would stop whatever she was doing and spend five minutes in silent prayer, agreeing with each other, that the husband be freed from sickness.

"Three days after that first meeting, the husband was entirely free from pain. By the end of the week, he was on his way to complete recovery.

"Next came the problem of Mrs. B., a widow whose home was to be sold in six weeks for failure to meet her payments. With earnestness and faith the women concentrated at the stated time each day upon the desire that the way would open for her supply. And true to the law, the way did open. Just a day before the week was up a well-to-do lady in the town called and asked Mrs. B. if she would take care of her children, eight and ten, for a few weeks while she, the mother, was away. The sum she offered would take care of the back payments on the home and provide living expenses. Shortly after the lady returned she made arrangements for Mrs. B. to take care of an invalid aunt, which gave the widow a steady and lucrative income.

"Next was the problem of Mrs. C., whose husband had been out of work for several months. A few days after the week of agreement was up the husband received a letter from a cousin living at a short distance offering him work in his lumber mill. So, again the law was fulfilled.

"Then the case of little Miss D., who for years had been estranged from her family, came under the law for solution. But in this case it was several weeks before any outward sign of fulfillment appeared. However, love had entered the heart of Miss D. during this time and for the first time since the estrangement she gave way to her new feeling and wrote to each of the family asking forgiveness for what she now acknowledged had been intolerance on her part. By return mail came letters from her family, letters also filled with the spirit of love. Thus, for the fourth time in the work of these women did the law work unfailingly.

"The last problem was that of Mrs. E., who owned a little dress shop but whose business had been almost ruined since the larger and newer shop just across the street had opened. Envy and hate had filled the heart of Mrs. E. so that she resisted all overtures at friendship which the owner of the new shop had made. Then, from her study of Truth she learned that no one need compete with anyone; that there is full abundance for all when we learn how to claim it. So, instead of envying, she now joined with the others in sending out love and good will to her competitor, as she had called her.

"A few weeks later the owner of the new store called and asked if Mrs. E. would take over the management of her store for six months while she was in the East on business. She explained that when she returned it might be advantageous to both of them to form a partnership. This was later done and today Mrs. E. is half owner of a thriving dress and millinery shop and there is perfect harmony between her and the woman she once hated."

Russell Conwell, author of "Acres of Diamonds," tells of dozens of such cases. He tells of a kidnapped child returned unharmed through the power of united prayer; of a lost child found in the same way; of men and women cured of apparently incurable diseases; of businesses saved, of positions won, of love renewed and families reunited. There is no good thing you can ask, believing, that shall not be given you.

"What will you have?" quoth God. "Pay for it and take it." And the paying consists of complying with the law of agreement, by praying—if you pray alone—that the good you are asking for yourself shall be given to all others as well, by "agreeing as to what ye shall ask" if you are praying in a group.

Did you ever read the diary of George Mueller covering the early days of his great work? George Mueller, you know, was the man who started an orphanage with no money in hand, no rich patrons, no prospects—just absolute trust in God. Read the following extracts from his diary and see how that trust was justified:

"Nov. 18, 1830. Our money was reduced to about eight shillings. When I was praying with my wife in the morning, the Lord brought to my mind the state of our purse, and I was led to ask Him for some money. About four hours after, a sister said to me, 'Do you want any money?' 'I told the brethren,' said I, 'dear sister, when I gave up my salary, that I would for the future tell the Lord only about my wants.' She replied, 'But He has told me to give you some money.' My heart rejoiced, seeing the Lord's faithfulness, but I thought it better not to tell her about our circumstances, lest she should be influenced to give accordingly; and I also was assured that, if it were of the Lord, she could not but give, I therefore turned the conversation to other subjects, but when I left she gave me two guineas.

"On March 7. I was again tempted to disbelieve the faithfulness of the Lord, and though I was not miserable, still, I was not so fully resting upon the Lord that I could triumph with joy. It was but one hour after, when the Lord gave me another proof of His faithful love. A Christian lady brought five sovereigns for us.

"April 16. This morning I found that our money was reduced to three shillings; and I said to myself, I must now go and ask the Lord earnestly for fresh supplies. But before I had prayed, there was sent from Exeter two pounds, as a proof that the Lord hears before we call.

"October 2. Tuesday evening. The Lord's holy name be praised! He hath dealt most bountifully with us during the last three days! The day before yesterday five pounds came in for the orphans. O how kind is the Lord! Always before there has been actual want he has sent help. Yesterday came in one pound ten shillings more. Thus the expenses of yesterday for housekeeping were defrayed. The Lord helped me also to pay yesterday the nineteen pounds ten shillings for the rent.

"I saw more clearly than ever that the first great and primary business to which I ought to attend every day was to have my soul happy in the Lord. The first thing to be concerned about was not how much I might serve the Lord, how I might glorify the Lord; but how I might get my soul into a happy state, and how my inner man might be nourished.

"Review of the Year 1838

"As to my temporal supplies. The Lord has been pleased to give me during the past year 350 pounds, 4 shillings, 8 pence. During no period of my life has the Lord so richly supplied me. Truly, it must be manifest that, even for this life, it is by far the best thing to seek to act according to the mind of the Lord as to temporal things. We have to make known our need to God in prayer, ask His help, and then we have to believe He will give us what we need. Prayer alone is not enough. We may pray never so much, yet, if we do not *believe* that God will give us what we need, we have no reason to expect that we shall receive what we have asked for."

"In the heart of man a cry, in the heart of God supply."
But as Mueller said, prayer alone is not enough. If we
do not BELIEVE that God will give us what we ask for,
we have no reason to expect that we shall receive it.

How can we cultivate such belief? Jesus gave us the
cue. "Unless ye be converted (turned about) and become
as a little child, ye shall in no wise enter the Kingdom of
Heaven." And again—"Unless a man be born again, he
shall not enter the Kingdom."

How can we become as a little child? How can we be
born again? The first essential would seem to be to determine what there is about a child that we must imitate.
What one thing is universal with all little children? DE-
PENDENCE, is it not? Utter dependence upon those
around them, utter faith in them to provide their needs.
And the greater the dependence, the better those needs
seem to be supplied.

Take the embryonic child in its mother's womb, for
instance. At inception, it measures only .004 centimeters.
In nine months, it multiplies in size a billion times. That
is what happens to it during its state of most utter dependence. In the next eighteen to twenty-one years, when
it comes to depend more and more upon itself, it increases
only sixteen times.

Does that mean we should make no effort ourselves?
By no means! The admonition given us was—"Work
and pray!" And the "work" is emphasized first. But it
does mean that when we have done all that is in our
power, we can confidently and serenely leave to the Lord
whatever else is necessary to the accomplishment of our
desire.

Three thousand years ago, there was a poor woman
whose husband had just died and left her with two small
sons and a heavy burden of debt.

The amount was not much, as debts go today, but when

you have not a cent, even a small debt looks big as a mountain. And the widow had nothing at all.

So in the fashion of those days, her creditor purposed to sell her sons into bondage. For even in those semi-barbaric times, property was more valuable than life. The right of human beings to life, liberty and the pursuit of happiness had never even been heard of—in fact, any man would have been considered a Bolshevik and a menace to the community who suggested so heretical a doctrine.

In our enlightened times, of course, they would do the things differently. The widow would only have to move to the slums, take her boys out of school and set them to selling papers, while she took in washing or some similar uplifting and exhilarating work.

But in those bad old days, there were no tabloids for them to sell, so they just made slaves of them. This widow's creditor was about to sell her boys into slavery. So she, having nowhere else to turn, went to the Prophet Elisha, and begged him to help her in her need.

And what do you suppose Elisha did? Took up a collection? Or appealed to the fund for widows and orphans? Not he! "What have you in the house?" he asked.

Just that. "What have you in the house?" He did not suggest that she go to the Chamber of Commerce or some philanthropical society, or stage a demonstration at the White House, or ask Congress to adopt the "dole." Not he! He believed in using the means at hand, believing that God always provides unlimited supply if we but have the courage and faith to use what we have.

So he merely asked what the widow had to start with, and when told—"Naught save a pot of oil," he bade her borrow vessels from the neighbors *and pour out into them the oil that she had.* In other words, she was to *start the flow.* And it is written that so long as she had vessels to receive it, *the oil kept flowing.*

When the vessels were all filled, Elisha bade her sell the oil and pay her debt, and then start afresh with her sons beside her.

What have YOU *in the house?* When troubles assail you, do you sit back and bemoan your fate, waiting for some friend to help, or do you take stock of what you have, and set to work using it?

You remember the story of the man who came from the hospital after an accident, completely paralyzed. Of all his body, he could move only one finger. In those circumstances, wouldn't you have given up? But he didn't. "If I can move but one finger," he decided, "I'll use it to do more than one finger ever accomplished before!" He did—and lo and behold! In a little while, the fingers next that one began to show life, too. Before many months had passed, he was using every muscle in his body.

I know of a man who lost everything he had in the clothing business. From an expensive apartment, he had to move his family into the poorest rooms in town, where they and their neighbors did not know from one day to another, where the next meal was coming from. They were downcast—yes. But discouraged? No!

He went around to some of his old creditors—got them to trust him for a few knit neckties that they could not sell anywhere else—found a printer who would give him credit for a few hundred envelopes, letterheads and postage—and sent those ties to lists of men culled from the occupational directory of the telephone book. As fast as the money for them came back, he bought more ties and mailed them out, he and his family doing the work of enclosing, addressing and stamping in their cramped little apartment. Before that type of selling became passé, *he had made two hundred thousand dollars out of it.* Yet most men in the same circumstances give up and quit. Life's biggest mistake, according to Harrington Emerson, is to under-estimate your power to develop and to accomplish. Ella Wheeler Wilcox says:

"Ships sail east, and ships sail west,
    By the very same breezes that blow;
    It's the set of the sails, and not the gales,
    That determine where they go."

Success is not a thing—not a guerdon that awaits you at some far-off shrine. Success lies in doing well whatever thing you are doing *now*. It is more a matter of mental attitude than of mental or physical capacity. You have all the fundamentals of it right now. But it is only the USE of them that can make you successful.

"All very well," perhaps you say, "but look at the handicaps I am under. There is Jim Jones, whose father left him a million—and all mine left was some debts to add to my own."

Have you ever read Emerson's comparison of Alaska and Switzerland? Alaska, according to him, is in six respects much better off than Switzerland. It has tremendous resources of virgin forests; Switzerland has practically none. It has great stores of gold and silver and copper and lead and tin and coal; Switzerland has practically none. It has fisheries—the greatest in the world; Switzerland has none.

It has in proportion to its area, greater agricultural possibilities than Switzerland—over a hundred thousand square miles suitable for agriculture. It has a tremendous seacoast; Switzerland none. And yet if Alaska were supporting the same number of people to the square mile as Switzerland, it would have 120,000,000 inhabitants.

Now the Swiss have marketed what? Natural resources? No! The Swiss are a people who take a block of wood that was worth ten cents and convert it into a carving worth a hundred dollars.

They will take a ton of metal, steel, brass, and so on, and put it together in such form as to make it worth several million dollars.

They take cotton thread that they buy from this country at twenty cents a pound, and they convert it into lace worth a couple of thousand dollars a pound.

And because as a nation they have learned the art of utilizing their latent capacities, they have prospered abundantly.

What is the moral? Simply this: It is not money that counts. It it not natural resources. It is the way *you use what you have!* You can succeed with what you have at this moment, if only you learn to use it rightly.

"Ask not for some power that has been denied you. Ask what ability you have which can be made to develop into something worth while. *What is in your hand?*"

"We are too apt to think," says Bruce Barton, "that if we had some other man's equipment or opportunity, we could do great things. Most successful men have not achieved their distinction by having some new talent or opportunity presented to them. They have developed the opportunity that was at hand."

Great successes are simply a group of little successes built one upon another, in much the same way that John MacDonald's first great subway was merely a long line of little cellars—*strung together!* As Professor James put it—

"As we become permanent drunkards by so many separate drinks, so we become saints in the moral, and authorities and experts in the practical and scientific spheres, by so many separate acts and hours of working. Let no one have any anxiety about the upshot of his work or education, whatever the line of it may be. If he keeps faithfully busy each hour of the working day, he may safely leave the final result to itself. He can with perfect certainty count on waking some fine morning, to find himself one of the competent ones of his generation, in whatever pursuit he may have singled out."

What makes a great musician? Practice—keeping everlastingly at it until playing becomes second nature. What makes a great artist, a great lawyer, a great engineer, a great mechanic or carpenter? Persevering study and practice. You may have a natural liking for a subject, so the study of it is easier to you than to others, but the big successes in life have seldom been the brilliant men, the natural wonders, the "born orators" or the talented artists. The great successes have been the "grinds."

"A few years ago," said Dr. John M. Thomas, President of Rutgers University, "Rutgers had a student called a 'greasy grind' by some of his classmates. This was S. Parker Gilbert, Agent-General for Reparations under the Dawes plan. He may have been a 'greasy grind,' but at thirty-two he was earning $45,000 a year. And, according to Owen D. Young, Chairman of the Board of Directors of the General Electric Company, Gilbert held for several years the most important political position in the world."

A good many men in and out of college have an idea that to study is foolish. "No one ever gets anywhere from studying," they say. S. Parker Gilbert is only one of thousands of cases that prove to the contrary.

The most important job in the world for you is the one above yours. And the way to get it is to study—to "grind"—until you can put more of knowledge, more of skill, more of initiative into it than any man around you. Only thus can you win success.

Why do so many fail? Because they do not try hard enough, work persistently enough. The doors of opportunity are always closed. They have been since the world began. History tells us of no time when you could walk down a street and find any doors of opportunity standing open and inviting you to come in. Doors that are worth entering are usually closed, but the resolute and courageous knock at those doors, and keep knocking persistently until they are opened.

You remember the parable of the importunate friend:

"And He said unto them, Which of you shall have a friend, and shall go unto him at midnight and say unto him, Friend, lend me three loaves; for a friend of mine in his journey is come to me, and I have nothing to set before him?

"And he from within shall answer and say, Trouble me not; the door is now shut, and my children are with me in bed; I cannot rise and give thee.

"I say unto you, though he will not rise and give him because he is his friend, yet because of his importunity he will rise and give him as many as he needeth. And I say unto you, Ask, and it shall be given you; seek, and ye shall find; knock and it shall be opened to you."

Why do so many fail to receive that for which they ask? Because they are not importunate enough. They do not convince the God in them that their prayer is something they MUST have. They ask and knock once or twice, and because the door is not immediately opened, they give up in despair. Remember—"He that wavereth is like a wave of the sea, driven with the wind and tossed. Let not that man think that he shall receive anything of the Lord."

> "If you have faith in God or man or self,
> Say so; if not, push back upon the shelf
> Of silence all your thoughts till faith shall come.
> No one will grieve because your lips are dumb."
> —ELLA WHEELER WILCOX

CHAPTER TWELVE

CATALYSTS OF POWER

"Doubt not, fear not, work on, and wait;
As sure as dawn shall conquer dark,
So love will triumph over hate,
And Spring will bring again the lark."

—Douglas Malloch

NEARLY TWO THOUSAND YEARS before Christ, it was said in the Vedas (the sacred writings of the Hindoos) that if any two people would unite their psychic forces, they could conquer the world, even though singly they could do nothing.

Then came Jesus to tell us even more positively that if two of us agree as touching anything we may ask, it shall be done for us.

Jesus never made any such positive promise of certain results when we pray alone. Why should it be necessary for two to unite their desires or prayers in order to be sure of results? If you add 2 to 2, you get only 4. If you add your muscular power to mine, you can lift only twice as much as either of us could lift alone. Yet if you add your prayers to mine, you get—not merely twice the power, but a hundred or a thousand times as much.

Why should this be? We have the word of many great psychologists that it is so. Judge Troward of England, who was to the British Empire what Professor Wm. James was to America, is authority for the statement, as is Brown Landone and a score of psychologists of lesser note. What is the reason?

Perhaps the answer lies in what chemists call CATA-LYSTS. In chemistry there are certain substances which, when added to others, release many thousands of times as much power as they themselves contain. These catalysts, without losing any of their own energy, multiply the energy in other substances by thousands and sometimes even by millions! Perhaps that is what happens when two or more unite as touching the thing they shall pray for. Perhaps one is a CATALYST, multiplying the power of the other by thousands upon thousands of times. Certain it is that even Jesus, when those about Him were not in sympathy with Him and did not believe in Him, as on the occasion of His visit to Nazareth, worked no mighty works. Perhaps that is why, when He sent out His disciples to heal the sick, He sent them out "two by two."

Be that as it may, one thing is sure: If two or more of you will get together for a minute or two each day, and really agree as touching the thing you shall ask and the way you shall ask for it, you will get amazing results. Mind you, it is not enough to merely pray together for the same thing. You must unite your thought. You may ask me to pray with you that you may be healed of an ulcerated stomach, and when we pray, you may be picturing those sores and thinking of the pain and trouble they have been causing, while I am picturing the perfect organ that God gave you. That is not uniting our forces. That is setting them in opposition. We must both think health. We must both see in our mind's eye the thing we WANT—not the one we fear or wish to be rid of.

The same is true of debts. You may be thinking of all the money you owe, of the mortgage that is falling due, of the cut in pay you had to take, while I am trying to help you by thinking of the Infinite Supply that God is sending you. We'll never accomplish much that way. We've BOTH got to think of and visualize RICHES— not debts or lack. We've got to remember that the debts or other wrong conditions are merely the LACK of riches or health or other good thing, and that when we provide the good, the evil disappears as naturally as darkness disappears when you turn on the light. So what we must think of and see in our mind's eye is the light—i.e. the riches or the perfect health or the love or other good thing we desire.

If two can unite in doing that, there is no good thing they can ask, believing, that they cannot get. In the preceding chapter, we quoted the article by Elizabeth Gregg in Nautilus, telling how five women prayed together, and every prayer was answered. And in Chapter Five, we told of a similar group in Russell Conwell's church who accomplished even more marvelous results through united prayer.

You have problems too great to be solved by you alone. And you have friends with problems that they are unable to handle. Why not get together and unite your forces? Why not meet for fifteen minutes once a week, talk over your difficulties, decide upon the case that seems most pressing, and then at a certain time each day, all of you drop whatever you are doing and give a minute or two to uniting your thought and your prayers? You CAN do it, and you will be amazed at the power of your united prayers. There is nothing of good you can ask, believing, that cannot and will not be done for you.

"No star is ever lost we once have seen.
We always may be what we might have been."

CHAPTER THIRTEEN

THE FIRST COMMANDMENT

"If with pleasure you are viewing
  Anything a man is doing,
If you prize him, if you love him,
  Tell him now.
Don't withhold your approbation
  Until the Parson makes oration
And he lies with many lilies on his brow.

"For no matter how you shout it
  He won't really know about it,
He won't count the many teardrops
  That you shed.
If you think some praise is due him,
  Now's the time to pass it to him.
For he cannot read his tombstone when he's dead."

"WHAT SHALL I DO to be saved?" asked the rich young man of Jesus 1900 years ago. And today most of us are asking essentially the same question—"What shall I do to be saved from poverty and sickness and unhappiness, here and now as well as in the hereafter?"

"Keep the commandments!" was the Master's answer to the rich man. And later, when asked—"What is the greatest commandment," He told His hearers: "Thou shalt love the Lord thy God with all thy heart, and with all they soul, and with all thy mind: *This is the first and great commandment.* And the second is like unto it.

158

Thou shalt love thy neighbor as thyself. On these two commandments hang all the Law and the Prophets."

Sounds simple enough, but just what is "loving God"? Is it going to Church and being a professed Christian? Or is it simply BEING THANKFUL AND HAPPY!

Going to Church and being an example to your neighbors is excellent, but is there any way in which you can show your love for God better than by being happy? Happiness implies praise, satisfaction with what God has done, thankfulness for His good gifts. Happiness means that you are enjoying life, appreciating it to the full, radiating joy to all about.

And loving your neighbor is just making him happy, too—praising him and blessing him and doing what you can to help him.

Can you think of any commandment, any law, that would do as much towards universal peace, towards settling the strife between labor and capital, towards bringing the millenium, as these two?

1. Be thankful and happy yourself.
2. Try to make your neighbor happy.

"On these two commandments hang all the Law and the Prophets."

Someone has wisely said that the first step towards universal peace is to have peace in our own hearts—to wish our neighbors well, to bless and praise even those who have used us despitefully. Evelyn Gage Browne expressed the thought when she wrote—

> "This old world needs the tender touch,
> The kindly word, the lifting hand,
> The love that blesses us so much,
> And friendly hearts that understand."

It is said that a woman once went to Krishna and asked him how to find the love of God. "Who do you love most?" he inquired. "My brother's child," she answered. "Go back and love him more," advised Krishna. She did so, and lo! Behind the boy, she saw the form of the Christ child.

The same thought is expressed in the old legend of the group that went out to find the Christ child. There were knights and great ladies and monks and clergymen and all manner of people, and among the latter was a kindly old shoemaker. Everyone laughed at the idea of his going out when so many of the great ones of the earth were ahead of him. But after they had all come back disappointed, the bent little shoemaker walked joyfully in, accompanied by the Christ child himself.

"Where did you find Him?" they asked. And the Christ Child answered for him—"I hid myself in common things. You failed to find me because you did not look with the eyes of love."

Millions of books have been written about love, but most of them know not even the meaning of the word. To them, love is passion, self-gratification. Real love is not that. Real love is GIVING. It seeks only the good of the loved one. Yet in giving love freely, you get it, for it is like energy in that it expands only as it is released. It is like a seed in that it multiplies only when you sow it. As Ella Wheeler Wilcox put it—

> "Give love, a:.d love to your heart will flow,
> A strength in your utmost need;
> Have faith and a score of hearts will show
> Their faith in your word and deed."

Carlyle defined wealth as the number of things a man loves and blesses, *which he is loved and blessed by.*

Who are the unhappiest creatures on earth? Not the

poor or the sick—but those who keep all their love for themselves. They may be worth millions, they may have dozens of servants to attend to their every want, but they are bored to extinction. They are miserable. Why? Because they have stopped giving, and as the words of a beautiful hymn expresses it—

"For we must share, if we would keep
That blessing from above.
Ceasing to give, we cease to have—
Such is the Law of Love."

Life is expansion, mentally and physically. When you stop growing, you die. That is literally true in the case of your body cells, and figuratively true mentally, for when you cease to progress mentally, you are as good as dead. The undertaker may not call for a year or two, but so far as useful purposes are concerned, you might as well be buried.

And just as life is action, so is happiness service. For in helping and praising others and making them happy, you win happiness for yourself. Charles Kingsley once said that we know our relations to God only through our relations with each other. No man can love God while he hates his neighbor. No man can love God while he is himself unhappy or deliberately makes another unhappy.

To be unhappy implies a criticism of God. An unhappy man cannot be grateful, he cannot be trustful, he cannot be at peace—and without these, how can he love God?

Yet if he lives only for himself, he is bound to be unhappy. "For whosoever shall save his life shall lose it," said the Master. "But whosoever shall lose his life for My sake, the same shall save it." He who loses himself in the service of others shall find therein life and love and happiness.

Longfellow tells of sending first an arrow into the air,

and then a song, and seeming to lose them. But presently he found the arrow in an oak tree, and the song, from beginning to end, he found in the heart of a friend.

"He prayeth well," wrote Coleridge, "who
   loveth well both man and bird and beast.
He prayeth best, who loveth best
All things both great and small;
For the dear God who loveth us,
He made and loveth all."

When Jane Addams graduated from college, the doctors told her she had only six months to live. If a doctor told you that, what would you do? Most of us would simply sit down and die, and feel very sorry for ourselves in the doing of it.

Not so Jane Addams. "If I have only six months to live," she said, "I'll use those six months to do just as much as I can of the things I want most to do for humanity."

And she so lost herself in the work that she forgot to die. Eight years after the time predicted for her demise, she started Hull House, the Chicago settlement that is known the world over. Not only that, but her health was as good or better than that of the doctors who had prophesied her end.

Everyone has heard of Luther Burbank and of the marvelous success he had in growing things. He could take even a prickly cactus plant and from its shoots grow a plant without thorns or prickers, from which cattle could get sustenance on even the dryest soil.

How did he work such wonders with all manner of growing things? Through the magic of love! He blessed each little plant, he praised and nursed and loved it. And the life in it responded by giving him such results as no man before him had ever dreamed of. Here is the message that Luther Burbank sent to his friends on his last birthday:

"As you hold loving thoughts toward every person and animal and even toward plants, stars, oceans, rivers and hills, and as you are helpful and of service to the world, so you will find yourself growing more happy each day, and with the happiness comes health and everything you want."

"Love and you shall be loved," said Emerson. "All love is mathematically just, as much as the two sides of an algebraic equation." The old philosopher who said— "Take out of life anything you want, *and pay for it,*" stated an eternal truth. You get as you give. It is well to remind one's self of this frequently by repeating now and then, when inclined to be disturbed by seeming difficulties—"I so love that I see all good and give all good, *and all good comes back to me.*"

The most universal desire in all the world is man's natural desire for happiness. It is the purpose of existence. It is God's plan—to make man WIN happiness through struggle and service, through adding to the happiness of others.

Why is it that a moving-picture actor makes a thousand times as much as a teacher, or as an average business man or even a clergyman? Because he makes many thousand times as many people happy. He enables them to forget their troubles, to live their ideals, their dreams, through his picturing of them. When the rest of us find some way to make as many people happy, we shall share in like rewards.

A long time ago, Emerson wrote—"He who addresses himself to modes and wants that can be dispensed with, builds his house off the road. But he who addresses himself to problems every man must come to solve, builds his house on the road, and every man must come to it."

Just ask yourself—What have I to GIVE that will add to the happiness of those around me? You will be surprised how many simple little ways of brightening the lives of others will present themselves, and how great the reward these ways can bring, when multiplied by hundreds or thousands.

A man down in Washington was too poor to buy his child toys, yet he wanted above everything to make that child happy. So with his pocket-knife, he carved out of discarded pieces of lumber a rough sort of Kiddie-car. It made such a hit, not only with his own youngster but with every child around, that he took it to a manufacturer and made a fortune out of it.

Years ago, a young veterinary over in England had a mother who was confined to a wheel chair. To soften the jolts for her, he fastened a strip of rubber around the iron tires. Those strips of rubber, through constant improvement, developed into the famous Dunlop tire, which have sold by the million.

There are similar stories to be found by the hundred. The only limit to your opportunities is the limit of human happiness. And that has not yet been reached.

"My husband died a short time ago," writes a poor, harassed widow, "leaving his estate so involved that it looks as though we shall lose everything. What can I do? I have two young children to clothe and feed and educate, and I've never made a penny in my life. Tell me, is it wrong to pray for death, for I don't know what else we can do?"

Is it wrong to pray for death? What do *you* think? Is praying for death showing love for God, confidence in Him? What did the Prophet of old, in similar case? "My husband is dead," wailed the widow to Elisha, "and the creditor is come to take unto him my two sons to be bondmen." Did Elisha demand that God rain down gold upon her? On the contrary—he asked what she had in the house, and with it he helped her to win her own salvation.

Read the story of Mary Elizabeth, and you will find an almost exact parallel. A widow with three children, no money, and the creditor "Poverty" demanding those children for bondservants. But the oldest of them asked herself—"What have we in the house?"—and found an ability to make others happy through delicious candy. Today the whole family is independently wealthy.

> "You have no talent? Say not so.
> A weaker brother you can lift
> And by your strength help him to go
> Renewed and blessed—this is your gift.
>
> "No talent? Some one needs a word
> Of courage, kindness, love, and cheer—
> Which only you can speak—to gird
> His spirit against grief and fear.
>
> "Yours is a special gift that none
> But you can use. Oh, lift your heart!
> So much of good will be undone
> Unless you do your own great part.
>
> "You are God's helper day by day;
> He comforts, guides, and speaks through you;
> He needs just you in this blest way.
> No talent? Oh, that is not true!"
> —EVELYN GAGE BROWNE

The ancient Greeks had a legend that all things were created by love. Everyone was happy, because love was everywhere, and each vied with the other to make those around him happy.

Then one night while love slept, fear crept in, and

with it came disease and lack and all unhappiness. For where love attracts, fear repels. Where love gives freely, fear is afraid there will not be enough for all, so holds on to everything it has.

What was the knowledge of good and evil against which God warned Adam in the Garden? Wasn't it a knowledge of things to *fear?*

In the second chapter of Genesis, we are told that Adam and Eve were naked and were not ashamed. Why? Because they knew no evil—therefore they feared no evil.

But they ate of the Tree of Knowledge of good and evil. They learned about evil. They hid themselves in the Garden in fear of evil. And immediately evil things began to happen to them, and have continued happening to their descendants ever since.

In the Garden of Eden, everything was abundance. The earth gave of its fruit bountifully. Then man learned fear. And having been given dominion over the earth, his fear reacted upon it. He feared it would hold back its fruits. He feared there would not be enough for all. He feared the snake and the wild animal, which before had been docile to his love.

What was the result? Instead of giving of its abundance gladly, he had to wrest its fruits from the earth. Instead of the luscious fruits and herbs of the Garden, the earth gave him the product of his fears—thorns and thistles. Instead of friendship between him and the beasts of the forest, there was the natural fruit of fear—suspicion and enmity.

From the time he ate of the Tree of Knowledge of Good and Evil, man has reaped the fruits of fear. And as long as his belief in evil holds, he will continue to reap the fruits of fear.

God is love. And what is the first characteristic of love?

To give. God is constantly giving to us *all that we will accept.*

But that is, alas, woefully little. For the first characteristic of fear is to shut up every opening, whether of income or outgo. Fear repels. Fear holds on to what it has, lest it should be unable to get more. Fear takes only what it can grab. It will not open its doors and let good come in. It is too much afraid of evil.

The result is that good comes to us through fear only after great struggle and suffering, even though the good be all the time trying to manifest itself. It is like a fortress built upon the highest peak of a great mountain. It is so fearful of evil coming to it that it has put itself as far as possible away from good as well.

Love opens the petals of the flowers and the leaves of all growing things to the sun, giving freely of its fragrance, and thereby draws to itself every element it needs for growth and fruition.

Love asks—What have we in the house that will make others happy?—and thereby attracts to itself everything necessary for its own happiness.

What is the first and greatest commandment? To give out love, to make the world a happier place than you found it. Do that, and you cannot keep happiness from coming to you, too.

"I often wonder," says Andrew Chapman, "why people do not make more of the marvelous power there is in Kindness. It is the greatest lever to move the hearts of men that the world has ever known—greater by far than anything that mere ingenuity can devise, or subtlety suggest. Kindness is the kingpin of Success in life; it is the prime factor in overcoming friction and making the human machinery run smoothly. If a man is your enemy, you can not disarm him in any other way so surely as by doing him a kind act."

The Lady or the Tiger

In ancient times, it is said that there lived a king whose methods of administering justice were original in the extreme.

He built a huge arena to seat himself and all his people. Under it, he put two doors. When a culprit was brought before him, accused of any crime, the king gave him his choice of which door he would open. If the accused man chose the right door, there came forth from it a beautiful lady, who was forthwith wed to him. But if he chose the wrong door, there came out of it a fierce and hungry tiger, which immediately tore him to pieces.

The king had a beautiful daughter, and upon a time it came to pass that a handsome young courtier fell in love with her and she with him. That was a grievous crime, for it did not at all suit the king's plans that his daughter should marry a commoner, no matter how well favored he might be. So the poor suitor was promptly clapped into a cell, and informed that on the morrow he must stand trial in the arena like any common culprit.

The princess was heartbroken. She tried prayers, she tried tears, but her father was adamant. Any common man who dared lift his eyes to her deserved death, and death he should have—death, or marriage to someone in his own station.

Failing to move her father, the princess tried the guards. But no amount of gold would persuade them to free her lover. This much she did accomplish, though—she learned from which door the tiger would come, from which the lady. More, she learned who the lady was, and horror of horrors, it was one she had seen more than once casting amorous glances at her lover!

The morning found her torn between love and jealousy. She could not see her lover killed before her eyes—and yet, would it not be better to suffer that moment of agony, and be able to remember him as loving only her, than to see him day after day in the arms of another, see the triumph in that other's eyes, see his own eyes turn away from her to the beauty in his arms?

As in a dream, she took her place on the dais at her father's right hand. As in a dream, she saw her lover step forth, saw him look to her for a sign, saw herself signal to him to choose the right hand door—then hid her face that she might see no more.

Which had she chosen—the Lady or the Tiger? Which would you choose in like circumstances? Judging from the newspapers of the day, all too many, even in our so-called civilization, would choose the tiger. Why? Because they would rather see their lover dead than in the arms of another. Their idea of love is passion, self-gratification, and if they can't have their loved one for themselves, they don't want anyone else to have him, regardless of how he or the other may suffer.

At some time and in one modified form or another, that choice of the Lady or the Tiger comes to most people, and your answer depends solely upon what kind of love yours is. If it is real love, you will not hesitate for a moment, for real love is selfless and free from all fear. (And that is all jealousy is—*fear!*) Real love gets its happiness from giving. It lavishes itself upon the object of its affections without thought of return. And by its very prodigality, it brings back real love to itself.

For love is a magnet. Like the magnet of iron which gives off electricity, by its very giving it draws to itself its own. And again like the iron magnet, when its strength is done, when all power has gone out of it, it has only to rub against a stronger magnet to be renewed!

What is it that makes men and women fall in love? Not beauty; that attracts attention. But love requires

more than beauty. Love requires personality, *charm,*
MAGNETISM!

And what is magnetism? What but the power you
GIVE OUT! It is vitality, it is abounding interest in
people and things, it is LOVE!

You cannot be self-centered and still give out magnetism. You cannot think only of the gratification of your
own desires and still expect to win or hold another's love.

Love gives out a current of love, and all who come
within its aura are attracted to it. Selfishness, jealousy,
hate, are like layers of insulation around a magnet. They
not only shut off all love from going out, but they keep
any from getting in. A selfish man, a jealous man, an
angry man, has no magnetism. He repels everyone he
comes in contact with. He has shut off his own current,
and insulated himself against any from the outside.

I remember reading a story of a man who had become
involved in a serious law-suit. He was bitter and resentful, for he felt that his opponents had been most unfair
and unjust. But the suit was apparently going against
him.

He went to a teacher of the mental sciences and laid
his case before him. The teacher told him he would never
get anywhere with his case until he rid himself of his
resentment and hatred. "Bless your opponents," he advised. "Know that in some way not yet apparent they are
doing you a favor. Say to yourself, whenever thoughts of
resentment creep in—'I live by the law of love.' And then
try to do just that."

The man tried it, and found that he could not keep
saying and using this affirmation without its affecting
everything he did. There came a most unexpected opportunity to do a great favor for his opponents. Re-
luctantly he did it, and lo and behold, it opened the way
to a fair settlement of the whole case—a settlement that

proved eventually far more profitable to him than winning the case would have done.

"Doubt not, fear not, work on and wait; as sure as dawn shall conquer dark, so love will triumph over hate." So writes Douglas Malloch, and in a recent issue of Nautilus Magazine, Sonia Shand tells of a "Love Game" which bears out the same idea.

It is based, she says, on Shakespeare's "Taming of the Shrew." You remember, in the play, no matter what Katharine said or did, Petruchio acted as though she were falling in with his wishes, and the more contrary she became, the more he would praise her for her sweet submission to his every wish. Well, this game is as simple as that. No matter what happens during the time you are playing your game of Love, you smile and say it is good and wonderful.

Whether a feared bill collector comes blustering to your door, or the neighbors' children pull up your favorite flowers, or any one of the hundred annoying things that are part of your daily existence happen, just smile and give thanks for them as though they were great blessings instead of annoying trials.

Release the feeling of love toward each and every annoying thing as though it were the best that ever happened to you. You will be amazed at the results that come from this little game, because in love, no matter how tiny the grain of it, there is unlimited power for good, and it is never wasted.

You have heard the old adage that a soft answer turneth away wrath. This game has the same principle incorporated in it, with a lot more added to it. Non-resistance is one thing, but by itself it is negative. Add your praise and blessings to it, and you turn it into a positive force for good.

To love all things is our natural heritage. It was what

made Adam and Eve so happy in the Garden of Eden. The snake of Fear crept into their hearts and turned them out of Eden, but we can each of us get back in if we will use the game of Love.

Try it. And while you are playing it, be sure to glorify *yourself*. See yourself as the perfect individual you always had hoped some day to become. Be the charming, gracious, noble self, who is raised by the powers of Love to a level above all sordid, petty, annoying and ugly things of life. Be that for one hour each day, and you will be amazed how quickly you will be that all the day.

You can use this Love Game in the home, in business, in whatever you are doing and wherever you are working.

If you are a business man, perhaps worried by a heavy load of debts and obligations, bless your creditors with the thought of abundance as you begin to accumulate the wherewithal to pay off your obligations. Keep the faith they had in you by including them in your prayer for increase. Begin to free yourself at once by doing all that is possible with the means you have, and as you proceed in this spirit the way will open for you to do more. For through the avenues of Spirit, more means will come to you and every obligation will be met.

If you are a creditor, be careful of the kind of thoughts you hold over your debtor. Avoid the thought that he is unwilling to pay you or that he is unable to pay you. One thought holds him to be dishonest and the other holds him to be subject to lack, and either of them tends to close the door to the possibility of his paying you soon.

Declare abundant supply for both creditors and debtors, and thus help them to prosper. Pray and work for their good as well as for your own, for yours is inseparable from theirs. You owe your debtor quite as much as he owes you and yours is a debt of love. Pay your debt to him and he will pay his to you.

Take anything in your life that seems not to be going well, and give a few minutes each day to "treating" it. Remind yourself first that harmony and true success are the Divine purpose of your life, that there are no exceptions to this law, therefore this particular difficulty must come under it. That being so, this thing that troubles you cannot be inharmonious or negative, once you know the truth about it. Know, therefore, the truth must be that in some way this difficulty is working out for your good, that beneath its hard and ugly outer shell, there is a kernel of perfect good for you. So bless the good within.

How does the kernel of the black walnut break its tough shell and send up a green shoot that presently grows into a great tree? By heating within! And that is the way you have to break the shell of every difficulty and trial that confronts you—by BLESSING the kernel of good you know to be within it, by praising and loving it until it expands and bursts its shell and springs forth as the fragrant plant of good for you.

Praise, blessing, thanksgiving, LOVE—these will solve any difficulty, tame any shrew of sickness or trouble. Start each day by saying—"This is the day which Jehovah hath made; I will rejoice and be glad in it. I thank God for abundant life, I thank God for enduring love. I thank God for joy, I thank God for glorious health, I thank God for infinite supply. I have awakened to a new day. I join the birds and all created things in glorious praise and thanksgiving. Lord, I do give Thee thanks for the abundance that is mine."

> "If I have faltered more or less
> In my great task of happiness;
> If I have moved among my race
> And shown no glorious morning face;
> If beams from happy human eyes
> Have moved me not; if morning skies,

Books and my food, and summer rain
Knocked on my sullen heart in vain;
Lord, Thy most pointed pleasure take
And stab my spirit broad awake."
—ROBERT LOUIS STEVENSON

Exercise for Chapter Thirteen

Remember, in "Vanity Fair," the owner of a fine estate who always carried acorns in his pocket, and when strolling about his grounds, if he came to a vacant spot, he would dig a little hole with his foot and drop an acorn into it. "An acorn costs nothing," he was fond of saying, "but it may spread into a prodigious bit of timber."

The same is true of words of praise, of blessing. They cost nothing, but when planted in the waste places of human consciousness, they become tremendously productive of happiness. As Willa Hoey expressed it—

"It's the little things we do and say
That mean so much as we go our way.
A kindly deed can lift a load
From weary shoulders on the road,
Or a gentle word, like summer rain,
May soothe some heart and banish pain.
What joy or sadness often springs
From just the simple, little things!"

Write it on your heart that each day is the best day of the year. There is no tomorrow, you know; there is no yesterday. There is only the eternal NOW. So make the most of your happiness *now*, while you can.

You create your own environment, so only YOU are to blame if some existing situation seems unhappy. That being so, only YOU can rectify it. You must cure it in your own thought before it can be remedied anywhere else. "Nothing is evil, but thinking makes it so."

Instead of thinking unhappy thoughts, sickly thoughts, thoughts of poverty and lack, talk to the God in You about the good things you want. Start with what you have, and suggest to him each day that you are getting stronger, healthier, richer, happier. Talk to Him as to a rich and loving Father, describing the improvements you see in your affairs, the finer body you have in your mind's eye, the more important work you should be doing, the lovelier home, the richer rewards. Talk them over for ten minutes each day when you are alone with Him. You will be amazed at how readily He will help you to carry out your suggestions.

Don't worry about how He is to bring about the conditions you desire. Just talk to Him confidently, serenely, happily—and then leave the rest to Him. And for your prayers, here is an affirmation used by Unity which has been found unusually effective:

"My Father-God, I place all my dependence in Thee, Thou giver of every good and perfect gift. Thou who art the source of my being art also the source of my supply. All that I shall ever need is in Thy mind for me, prepared for me from the beginning. Omnipresent substance, the garment with which Thou clothest Thy universe, with which Thou nourishest all Thy creation, is also mine to have and to use for my every desire and for the blessing of others of Thy children. I open myself fully through my faith in Thee, through my vision of Thy abundance, through my expectancy of its manifestation for me. I open my hands, my pocketbook, my wardrobe, my business, my bank account, and from Thy rich storehouse Thou dost fill every vessel that I hold out to Thee full to overflowing with Thine own omnipresent good and in Thine own good measure, pressed down, shaken together, running over. I thank Thee, my Father-God, that through the Christ in me I can touch Thine omnipresent substance and all my world be clothed with Thy opulence. I praise and give thanks that now and throughout eternity I am one with Thee and that in this union all Thine is mine and mine is Thine forever and ever."

Throughout this book, we shall give you numbers of affirmations to use for different conditions. Don't try to use them all at once. Use one until it becomes so familiar that you find yourself repeating it too parrotlike. Then change to another. All are helpful. The mere statement —"I am good," "I am strong," "I am capable," is an upbuilding affirmation that tends to start your subconscious trying to bring about that condition in you, just as negative statements such as "I am poor or sick" tend to make those conditions true. So try to remember always to PRAISE God in every thing and every condition that confronts you. Praise Him and look for the Divinity in each.

"Praise God that Good is everywhere;
Praise to the Love we all may share—
The Life that thrills in you and me;
Praise to the Truth that sets us free."

CHAPTER FOURTEEN

THE THREE LAWS OF LIFE

IT HAS BEEN CONSERVATIVELY estimated that 60% of the causes that make for success or failure in business lie outside a man's own control, entirely apart from his particular ability or methods.

They are the fundamental trends, the seasonal ebb and flow of the tides of business which cast so many upon the rocks. To the extent that men swim with the tide of fundamental forces, they make success easy. To the extent they fight against it, they make things more difficult for themselves.

Three Laws of Life govern man—and two of them at least govern you whether you wish it or not. You can disregard them if you like. You can remain ignorant of them. And you can continue to be the sport of circumstance.

Or you can learn these laws, understand how they operate, and work *with* them to get any good thing of life.

The first of these laws is to many the most hopeless of all of Nature's laws. It seems inexorable as the Car of Juggernaut. It has caused more sorrow, more poverty and misery than all other laws together. It is—

The Law of Averages!

Under it, man has come to accept evil as a necessity, feeling that he must take the bad with the good. Under it, he has become accustomed to seeing corrupt politicians, bootleggers and evil-doers of the worst type prosper, while the decent elements in the community pay. Under it, he expects to fail more often than to succeed.

Why? Because that is the Law—the Law which brings forth enough fish to choke the sea, then lets the many die that the few may live; the Law which puts enough riches in the earth to make us all millionaires, then lets the many serve that the few may enjoy.

That is the Law of Averages. That is the law which makes it hard for people to believe in a just God. That is the law which rules in the Country of the Blind, where more than two billions live. That is the law which has been governing *you!*

But that is the law which need govern you no longer, for there is a law that overrides the Law of Averages. It is called "The Law of Capillary Attraction."

For thousands of years, philosophers have wrangled over the problem of why men without scruple or conscience should so often succeed, while good men of equal ability fail. Some tell us it is because the wicked have their innings in this world and will suffer for it through eternity, while we shall have our turn at happiness and plenty then. That is a bit unsatisfying, especially when those near and dear to us are suffering for lack of things we should be able to give them. But for many, it has to suffice.

But not for all! A few have learned that there are definite laws governing success—just as definite and just as certain of results as the laws of Physics.

These basic laws govern everything you do. They rule all of mankind, whether mankind likes it or not. They are unlike man-made laws in that they govern high and low alike. They defer neither to rich nor to poor, to weak nor to powerful—only to those with an understanding heart. It was with them in mind that the wisest of ancient kings bade us seek first understanding, and all things else would be added to us. Summed up, those laws are:

1. *The Law of Averages,* under which man in the mass is no better off than the animals, his chances of happiness and success in life but little better than one in a hundred.
2. *The Law of Tendency,* which is towards Life-GIVING. To the extent that a man allies himself with this great fundamental force of nature, to that extent he improves his chances for success.
3. *The Law of Capillary Attraction,* which gives to every nucleus the power to draw to itself those things necessary for its growth and fulfillment. It is through this third law that man is able to rise above the Law of Averages. It is by using it with the Law of Tendency that he is able to reach any height, attain any goal.

Under the Law of Averages, man in the mass is subject to alternate feast or famine, happiness or misery—just as the animals are. Nature seems carelessly profligate. She brings forth enough fish to choke the sea—then lets the many die that the few may live. She gives life with a prodigal hand—then seems entirely careless of it, letting the mass suffer or perish so long as the few survive.

To man she has given inexhaustible riches—but the few have most of it while the many toil to serve them.

That is Nature's Law of Averages in the animal kingdom. That is Nature's Law of Averages for man in the mass. But for man the individual she reserves a different fate.

As long as he chooses to be governed by the Law of Averages, man must be content with his one chance in a hundred of prosperity and happiness. But let him separate himself from the mass, and he can choose his own fate.

And the way to separate himself from the mass is—
not to journey to some desert or forgotten isle, not to
mew himself up in a solitary cell—but to hitch his wagon
to the star of some strong purpose, and thereby pull
himself out of the mass of self-centered, self-seeking,
merely animal humanity, and ally himself with the great
fundamental Law of the Universe which carries all mankind upon its crest.

The word "Man," you know, means steward or dis-
tributor. The purpose of man here on earth is to utilize
and distribute God's good gifts. To the extent that he
cooperates in this purpose, he is allying himself with the
forces behind all of nature. To the extent that he looks
out only for his own selfish ends, he is opposing it. "I
came," said Jesus, "that they might have life, and have
it more abundantly." And He demonstrated His mission
by giving more of life to all who sought it.

And what is "Life"? Life is energy. Life is power. Life
is supply. Life is the creative force out of which the world
and everything in it was made in the beginning, and is
made now.

As I see Him, God is the Life-Principle which permeates and directs the universe. His "sons" are the individual subconscious minds or Spiritual Selves back of
each of us, pouring Life into us, guiding and governing
(to the extent we permit them) all the complicated functions of our bodies, all our outward circumstances and
conditions.

These "sons" are like vast Genii, possessing all riches,
all happiness, all wisdom on their own plane, but forced
to reflect those God-like gifts upon the material plane
only as we (their mirrors) can understand and express
them.

They pour their Life-energy through us in a continuous
stream, like the strips of steel that are fed into stamping

machines in a steel mill. Going in, it is potential life, potential power, potential riches. But like the strips of steel, coming out it is only what we have expressed through it—what our stamping machine (our innermost beliefs) has impressed upon it.

Whatever we truly believe, whatever we love and bless and hold constantly in thought as our own, it brings into being in our lives, in our bodies, in our circumstances. Like light shining through a prism, it is broken up into its component colors in passing through our conscious minds. But like the prism, our minds can be darkened by fear and worry to shut off all the happier colors. It is a perfect stream of Life-Energy that starts through us, but just as a poorly made die in a stamping machine can cut crude and ugly patterns on the best of steel, just as a faulty prism can turn beams of sunshine into shadows, so can your beliefs turn perfect Life-Energy into manifestations of sickness and poverty and misery. God does not inflict them upon you—you do.

The first essential, then, is to change the pattern—to watch your beliefs as the Director of the U. S. Mint watches the molds which cast the golden eagles he turns out. Instead of picturing the things you FEAR, and thus stamping their mold upon the Life-Energy passing through you, picture the conditions you WANT. "What things soever ye ask for when ye pray," said Jesus, "believe that ye RECEIVE them, and ye shall HAVE them!"

What do YOU want? Know that your spiritual self HAS it. Like the perfect flower in the tiny unopened bud, it is all there, needing only the sunshine of your faith to bring it forth.

You have seen trees in the winter, all the twigs bare, with no sign of the brilliant foliage soon to spring from them. Yet the leaves are already there, perfectly formed, waiting only for the warm sunshine to bring them out. In the same way, the things YOU want are already around you, no matter how bare everything may look. They need only the sunshine of your faith to bring them forth.

That is the first step, *to have faith!* That is the pattern which molds all your circumstances—*your beliefs.* Get that pattern right. It is there that unscrupulous men get ahead of their less understanding brethren. Knowingly or unknowingly, they have hit upon the fact that the first essential of material success is to believe in themselves, believe that the world belongs to them, believe that it *owes* them a living. They may not knowingly BLESS the things they want, but they LOVE them, long for them, put them above everything else in life, and since God is love, it sometimes seems that we have only to love a thing greatly to get it.

To that extent, they are right. Their trouble is that they do not bother to look around for right sources from which to draw their supply. They take whatever is not nailed down, and sooner or later they run afoul of the Law of Tendency and end in ruin.

This Law of Tendency is our next step, for it *requires co-operation* with the Life-Giving forces of the universe— *swimming with the tide.*

The Law of Tendency is based upon the fact that the whole purpose of Life is growth. The forces of nature are Life-GIVING forces. Its fundamental trends are towards the advancement of life, the good of the world. Those businesses and those individuals whose work is in line with that tendency are swept forward by the great tide of good. Those whose work tends to hinder the forward movement of life are sooner or later brushed aside and cast upon the rocks.

Ella Wheeler Wilcox expressed the thought beautifully when she wrote—

"The world has a thousand creeds, and never a one have I,
  Nor church of my own, though a million spires are pointing
    the way on high.
  But I float on the bosom of faith, that bears me along like a
    river:
  And the lamp of my soul is alight with love, for life, and the
    world and the Giver."

"But," I can hear you say, "I know many worthy men whose efforts were always for good, yet who are hopeless failures." True—but so do I know many swimmers who cannot keep afloat a hundred yards, even with the strongest tide behind them. The tide is the second step. The first step is to get your pattern right—in other words, learn how to swim. And having the tide with you makes that first step none the less necessary.

Believe in yourself. Look upon yourself as one of the Lords of the Universe. Know that it belongs to you. BELIEVE THAT YOU *HAVE* the things you want. Love them. Bless them. Thank God for them, even before they seem manifest. "Lord, I do give Thee thanks for the abundance that is mine."

That is the first essential. The second is to USE your powers for good—*get on the side of the Life*-GIVING *forces.*

"Sounds well," perhaps you will say, "but I'd like you to tell me how I am going to use riches for good, when my principal reason for taking this course is to learn how to GET riches to keep the wolf from my own door!"

The first essential in the creation of anything—be it a house or an automobile or a fortune—is the mental picture or image. Before God made man, He "imaged" him —He formed a mental picture of him. Then He poured His Life-Energy into that image, and it became man. Before an architect builds a house, he draws a mental picture of it, he "images" it upon paper. Then he pours materials and energy into that image and it becomes a house. Before you can build a fortune, you must form it in your mind's eye. You must "image" it on the mental plane, and in that mental image you must think of it as already yours. In other words, "believe that you HAVE it!" An easy way to do this is the "Treasure Mapping" outlined in Chapter X.

One of the startling facts of modern science is that this universe is not a finished product. Creation is going on all around us—new worlds being formed, cosmic energy taking shape in a million different molds.

> But a far more startling fact to most of us is that WE ARE CREATORS, and that we can form today the world we personally shall be living in tomorrow.

People blame their environment, their education, their opportunities, their luck, for their condition. They are wrong. There is one person to blame—and only one— THEMSELVES. They are today the result of their thoughts of yesterday and the many yesterdays that preceded it. They are forming today the mold for what they will be in the years to come.

For there is no such thing as failure. Whether you are poor and sickly, or rich and strong, you have succeeded in one thing. You have compressed the cosmic energy about you into the mold that you held before the mind's eye of your inner self. You have named the forces that worked with you "good" or "bad," and as you named them, so have they been to you as servants—Good, or Evil.

But there is a happy ending. You don't need to leave things as they are. If you don't like the present results you can rename those servants. You can bless and praise the good, no matter how tiny it may seem, and by your praise and blessing, you can expand it a thousand-fold.

Which brings us to the third step—"The Law of Capillary Attraction."

Scientists tell us, you know, that everything in this world starts with a nucleus—a whirling bit of energy microscopically small, but with the power of attracting to itself everything of a like nature which it needs for its growth. Plants, animals, man himself, are started by just such a nucleus. And so-called inanimate matter is formed in the same way.

Plant a seed of corn in the ground, and it will attract to itself from the earth and the water and the air everything it needs for its growth. Plant the seed of a desire in your mind and it forms a nucleus with power to attract to itself everything needed for its fulfillment. But just as the seed of corn needs sunshine and air and water from which to draw the energies necessary to bring forth the perfect ear, so does your seed of desire need the sunshine of a perfect faith, the fruitful soil of a will-power held steadfast to the one purpose.

This is the Alpha and Omega of all accomplishment— that every seed has in it the perfect plant, that every right desire has in it the perfect fulfillment, for Desire is God's opportunity knocking at your door. The seed must be planted, it must have nourishment and sunshine. The desire must be definitely planted by the work of starting the initial step in its accomplishment, it must be nourished by a will-power which holds it to its purpose, and it must have the warm sunshine of perfect faith. Given these, it will attract to itself whatever else is necessary to its fulfillment.

You see, the Law of Capillary Attraction is based upon the principle of growth from the vitality inherent in the seed or idea itself. It is like a snowball which starts with only a handful of snow, yet by gathering to itself all it comes in contact with, ends as an avalanche!

First the seed, the desire. Next, the planting—the initial step necessary to start its accomplishment. Third, the cultivation—the continual working towards the one end. You can't just WILL a thing into existence, you know. But you can use the will as the machinist uses a vise—to hold the tool of your purpose until it accomplishes its end. Fourth, the sunshine—FAITH—without which all the others are as nothing. Without sunshine, the seed will rot in the ground, the plant will wither on the stalk. Without faith, your desire will die still-born. Believe that you RECEIVE. See the perfect plant in the seed. See the perfect accomplishment in the desire.

Prof. Wm. James of Harvard, the greatest psychologist this country has known, wrote—"If you only care enough for a result, you will almost certainly attain it. If you wish to be rich, you will be rich; if you wish to be learned, you will be learned; if you wish to be good, you will be good. Only you must, then, really wish these things, and wish them exclusively, and not wish at the same time a hundred other incompatible things just as strongly."

But be careful that your desire tends towards Life-GIVING, towards the furtherance of Good. You can't make much of a snowball pushing up hill. If you do, it will presently grow bigger than you, get beyond your control, and engulf you in the resultant catastrophe. The fruit you bring forth is going to partake of the same nature as the seed you plant. If there is no kindliness in the seed, no love of your fellow-man, nothing but self-gratification, the fruit of your tree will be the same kind. It will be bitter to others—it will turn bitter in your own mouth.

Now how does this apply to you? There are certain things you want from life—Success, Riches, Fame, Honor, Love, Happiness, Health, Strength. All of these are worthy desires. All of them are entirely possible of fulfillment for you. How are you to go about getting them?

Your job here on earth is to distribute certain God-given gifts—certain goods, certain services, certain abilities—to the end that the world may be more livable for your having been in it.

In ancient Egypt, it was believed that each person was given at birth a "Ka" or "Double", which was his REAL SELF. It had infinite power for good. The body was merely its reflection, seen through the glass of the conscious mind.

So it is with you. Your REAL Self is God's image of you—the God in You. He gave it dominion over all the earth. Can you imagine it, then, as powerless under any circumstances, as poverty-stricken, as in doubt where its supply is coming from?

If you believe in God at all, you must believe in His intelligence. And if He is intelligent, He made nothing without a purpose. Everything fits into His plan. YOU, for instance—He created you for the purpose of performing certain work. That being so, it would seem pretty certain that He gave you every ability, every means necessary for the perfect performance of that work, would it not?

But how are you to know what that work is? Easily enough, if you stop to analyze your ambitions and desires. They are your subconscious promptings. Not, of course, the merely selfish desires for the gratification of some personal vanity or passion. But the big, deep down ambitions that come to you in exalted moments. They are the promptings of The God in You, urging you to EXPRESS on the material plane the work he is already doing in the mental realm.

You have an idea, let us say, which will short-cut the work of the world, make life easier and happier for any number of its inhabitants. You take whatever steps seem good to you to accomplish that idea. But you presently reach a point where lack of money or lack of knowledge or other circumstances leave you high and dry—seemingly at your rope's end. What are you to do then?

PRAY! And how are you to pray? Jesus gave us the formula—"Whatsoever things ye ask for when ye pray, believe that ye RECEIVE them, and ye shall HAVE them."

But how can you believe that you HAVE when you are at the end of your resources and there is no possible way out in sight? How? By knowing that The God in You, your REAL SELF, already HAS the answer in the realm of the REAL. By seeing the finished result there, imaging it in your mind's eye, and then putting it up to that God in You to show you the next step necessary to reflect that result on the material plane, in the serene confidence that, since he has worked out the answer, the EXPRESSION of it step by step through you is simple.

Tell yourself—and KNOW—you ARE rich, you ARE successful, you ARE well and happy and possessed of every good thing you desire. Use your "Treasure Map" to picture these things—then believe that you HAVE them.

No matter how limited your education, no matter how straitened your circumstances, the God in You HAS the knowledge and the means and the power to accomplish any right thing you may desire. Give him a job—and it is DONE! You HAVE it! And you have only to see that finished result in your mind's eye—"BELIEVE THAT YOU RECEIVE"—in order to begin to reflect it on the material plane.

Therein lies the nucleus of every success—the nucleus which has such life that it draws to itself everything it needs for its full expression—*the belief that you HAVE.*

It is the secret of power, the Talisman of Napoleon. To acquire it takes just three things.

1. Know that this is a world of Intelligence. Nothing merely happens. You were put here for a purpose, and you were given every qualification and every means necessary to the accomplishment of that purpose. So you need never fear whether you are big enough, or smart enough, or rich enough to do the things required of you. "The Father knoweth that ye have need of these things," so do the things that are given you to do in the serene knowledge that your needs will be met.
2. Know that The God in You which is your REAL Self is already DOING this work you were given to do, so all that is required of you is to SEE that accomplished result, and REFLECT it step by step on the material plane, as the way is opened to you. "And thine ears shall hear a word behind thee, saying—This is the way. Walk ye in it."
3. Have serene faith in your God's ability to express the finished results through you. When you can SEE that result in your mind's eye as already accomplished, you will realize that you don't need to fear or worry or rush in and do things foolishly. You can go serenely ahead and do the things that are indicated for you to do. When you seem to reach a cul-de-sac, you can wait patiently, leaving the problem to The God in You in the confident knowledge that at the right time and in the right way he will give you a "lead" showing what you are to do.

The fundamental Law of the Universe, you remember, is the Law of Attraction. You attract to you whatever you truly love and bless and believe is YOURS.

Knowing that The God in You HAS the fruition of your desire—knowing that the perfect leaf is in the bare twig of your present circumstances—it is easy to pour such life, love and blessings into that leaf that it bursts its bonds and blossoms forth for all to see.

So, like the Egyptians of old, let us commune with The

God in Us night and morn, much as our reflection in the mirror might commune with us:

> Reality of me, I greet you and salute you the perfect "me" God created. You have a perfect body, made in the image and likeness of God. Make that perfect body manifest in me. You have infinite riches—dominion over all things. Use that dominion, I pray you, to uncover and bring out in my life, my work and my surroundings the perfect reflection of (whatever your particular desire may be).

Then SEE, in your mind's eye, The God in You doing those things you wish to do, emphasizing the traits you wish to cultivate, displaying the riches or possessions you want. Know that he HAS these. And that as soon as you can SEE them through the prism of your conscious mind, as fast as you can *realize* their possession, *you, too, will reflect them for all the world to see!*

OUR PRAYERS ARE ANSWERED
By Bonnie Day

"Our prayers are answered: each unspoken thought
And each desire implanted in the mind
Bears its own harvest, after its own kind;
Who dreams of beauty has already caught
The flash of angel wings. Who seeks to find
True wisdom shall assuredly be taught.
But thorns of fate have thorny thoughts behind;
For out of our own hearts our lives are wrought.

"Be on thy guard, my soul, lest wind-blown seed
Into the fertile soil of thought should fall
And lodging place within the garden wall
Be given to bitter rue or noxious weed.
Unspoken prayers bear fruitage. Love thoughts call
Forth into being every loving deed.
Idle or earnest, still our prayers are all
Answered according to our inward creed."

CHAPTER FIFTEEN

A PRAYER FOR WORK

"Lord give me work. All work is Thine.
Help me to make Thy business mine.
Give me my part, and let me share
Thy joy in making life more fair;
My part, and with the part the will
To make my life Thy plan fulfill.
Thus every day, Lord, help me see
My simplest task as done for Thee."
—ESTHER ANN CLARK

ALL DAY LONG and every day, the God in You keeps repeating—"I AM." But He lets YOU end the sentence. You can add "poor" or "rich", "sad" or "happy", "sick" or "well," as YOU choose. God can do for you only what you ALLOW Him to do THROUGH you. You praise and bless Him, only when you see the good and true and beautiful. You dishonor Him when you call yourself weak or sick or poor.

So claim the good! Praise God for it, thank Him and bless Him for all His good gifts.

If you are out of work at the moment, know that the Spirit of the Lord is upon you, directing you to your right work. The Spirit of God goes before you to make plain your way. It works through you to make you efficient, successful, prosperous and of real worth to your employer and associates.

Know this—and then open your channels! Give of what

you have of service to others. Start where you are. Distant fields always look greener, but opportunity lies right where you are. Take advantage of every opportunity of service, even if it be only to wash dishes or do chores around your own home. Show God that you are a channel for good NOW. The more you can prove that, the greater will be your opportunities, and soon those opportunities will take the form of just the right job for you.

Each night and morning, and whenever the need for a job occurs to you, repeat this affirmation:

> "God in me knows what my right work is, where it is and what I ought to do to be actually engaged in it. Let this knowledge be quickened in me as a revelation to my conscious mind so I shall know what is my right work, where it is and what there is for me to do to be established in it."

Remember it is from within, and not from without, that you get in touch with all of Good. Every ill, every lack, every discordant condition, must be cured in your own thought first. It is like a radio. The programs of all the world are in the air about you, but you have to tune in on the one you want. When you turn on the radio, the program that comes to you may be some sordid tale of crime or unhappiness, or it may be merely static noises. If so, that is all you will get—until you turn the dial. But you CAN get the program you want, if you keep turning away from the others and persistently try until you find the one you want.

But you must both affirm and ACT the part. To affirm prosperity and then act like a pauper with what substance you have is to show that you do not believe your own affirmation and do not expect anything from it. It doesn't matter if you have to force yourself to take some appropriate action. Take it—and thereby increase your faith.

Every affirmation should be matched by some action

expressing the faith that you HAVE received or ARE receiving, action of the sort you would engage in if the affirmed good were visibly and tangibly present.

That doesn't mean you must spend a lot of money recklessly, buy a lot of things such as you will when you have the riches you crave. It does mean you must take the mental attitude of BEING rich, HAVING the right sort of job, sprucing up, being confident and serene and unworried.

You can help others get the sort of place they want in the same way you can yourself. Here is an affirmation to use for others:

"Infinite Spirit, open the way for So-and-so's right position (or home or abundance or what-not), the position he is best fitted to fill, the position that needs him and which no one else can fill so well as he. Let him be led to the right people, the right place where he can give good service for good pay. Lead him to make the right contacts. I leave it with you, and I know all is well."

In a recent issue of Nautilus Magazine, Dortch Campbell tells how he prayed for a home—and found the one he had always dreamed of.

"The whole secret," he says, "lies in that beautiful thing called love. I prayed for a home. Every element in the answer that came was in accord with justice. The quality of love was not strained.

"A house that you can call your own home is not so easy to obtain these days. For me it was most difficult. Conditions have been serious in the Mississippi Valley for nearly a decade; the cotton problem has become acute. But the house where I had lived for a long time was taken away from me. I was homeless; there was no other available, for people have not been building houses in my country.

"I had to build my own home to find a roof for myself

and my loved ones. But there was no mortal way to build that home. I had not sufficient money to buy even a lot. Yet the home of my own became a reality in answer to my prayers as simply and as unostentatiously as a rose unfolds.

"I felt that we are far too selfish in our prayers, so I prayed for others when I prayed for myself. I asked that the contractor who should build my home should be blessed through me. I prayed for the owner of the land. I prayed for an harmonious association with the contractor. I asked that there be love and friendship between us and between all who might be associated in the undertaking. I prayed that he might find a way to finance my home and that I in turn should help him to succeed. I prayed for others as earnestly as I prayed for myself. I prayed for the landowners that they, through me, might sell other lots.

"I prayed in this fashion, loving them that they in turn might love me. Deep within me, I desired that all of us might equally profit in the building of my home. This was all. There was no domination on my part, no attempt to influence or control them, no direct thought to them.

"Step by step, that home came about. I obtained the lot for a very small outlay—a lot worth three times what I paid. The contractor himself actually gave me the money I required. The home became mine in such a gentle fashion that I, accustomed to prayer, stand amazed. Things—for example—like a driveway, were contributed free.

"But it was not only I who was helped, and this to me is the most beautiful part of the answer to that prayer. It has been my privilege since the house was constructed to help those who helped me in getting my home. More lots have been sold, more will be sold. The contractor has closed several contracts as a result of building my home.

"What we need is to be not only hearers but DO-ERS

of the Word. We find Truth by trying to live it. Since God is love, it may be that we have only to love a thing greatly to get it. Can it be that the long-lost key to attainment through prayer is in feeling the loving power of God within to give us that which the heart desires?"

"If I can do some good today,
 If I can serve along life's way,
 If I can something helpful say,
 　Lord, show me how.

"If I can right a human wrong,
 If I can help to make one strong,
 If I can cheer with smile or song,
 　Lord, show me how.

"If I can make a burden less,
 If I can aid one in distress,
 If I can spread more happiness,
 　Lord, show me how.

"If I can do a kindly deed,
 If I can sow a fruitful seed,
 If I can help someone in need,
 　Lord, show me how.

"If I can feed a hungry heart,
 If I can give a better start,
 If I can fill a nobler part,
 　Lord, show me how."
 　　　　—GRENVILLE KLEISER

CHAPTER SIXTEEN

FIRST CAUSES

"How CAN I TELL if I am working a-right?"—many students ask us.

And "How can I be sure I am following correct lines?" —is the question in the mind of many a man and woman when confronted by some unusual problem.

In his Edinburgh Lectures, Judge Troward gave so clear an answer to this question that I quote it here:

> "If we regard the fulfillment of our purpose as contingent upon any *circumstances,* past, present, or future, we are not making use of First Cause. We have descended to the level of *Secondary Causation,* which is the region of doubts, fears and limitations."

What is First Cause? Judge Troward defined it, too.

"If a lighted candle is brought into a room, the room becomes illuminated; if the candle is taken away, it becomes dark again. Now the illumination and the darkness are both conditions, the one positive resulting from the presence of the light, the other negative resulting from its absence. From this simple example we therefore see that every positive condition has an exactly opposite negative condition corresponding to it, and that this correspondence results from their being related to the same cause, the one positively and the other negatively; and hence we may lay down the rule that all positive conditions result from the active presence of a certain cause, and all negative conditions from the absence of such a cause. *A condition, whether positive or negative, is never primary cause, and* the primary cause of any series can never be negative, for negation is the condition which arises from the absence of active causation."

How can you be sure that you are working a-right? By asking yourself one question: "On what am I putting my dependence for the riches, or the health, or the success I am seeking?" If the answer is—"Upon my ability, or my doctor, or his drugs, or the help of my friends," then you can rate your chances of success as not more than one in ten, for you are working with secondary causes, and secondary causes are always undependable.

But if your answer is—"I am throwing everything I have into my work, but I am putting my dependence for success—NOT on these *means*—but on the unquenchable, irresistible power of the Seed of Life working through me," why then you can count your chances of success as nine out of ten.

You see, it all comes back to the Fundamental Law of the Universe—that each nucleus, each seed, contains within itself vitality enough to draw to it every element it needs for its complete growth and fruition.

But the seed must germinate, the nucleus must start whirling, before either has the slightest attractive power. Until they do that, they are so much congealed life, with no more "pull" to them than any other bit of inanimate matter around them.

Suppose you want something badly—more than anything else life can offer you at the moment. The desire for that something forms a nucleus, a seed, and like every other seed, it has latent in it the power to draw to itself the elements necessary for its complete growth and fruition. But until you *do* something about it, it is an inanimate nucleus, a seed that has not been planted, a nucleus with no power of attraction because no one has taken the trouble to start it whirling.

How can you put it to work? By PLANTING your seed—in other words, by making your start. What is the first thing you would do if you KNEW you would get your desire? What is the first step you would take in its accomplishment? TAKE IT! Do something to start, no matter on how small a scale. To begin, you know, is to be half done. Make the accomplishment of that desire the *sine qua non* of your existence, give to it all the thought and energy and riches you have to bring it into being, leave all other considerations in second place until you have won what you want.

That is the way great fortunes are made. That is the way miracles are performed. That is the only way you can put life into the nucleus of your desires and start them whirling and drawing to you whatever things you need for their manifestation.

Conditions, obstacles—they don't matter. Disclaim them, disregard them, and lay claim to the thing you want regardless of conditions. Like the seed in rocky soil, they may force your nucleus to work harder, to whirl faster, but give it vitality enough, and it will draw what it needs from the ends of the earth!

So don't work on poverty. Don't work on debts. That will merely bring more of these undesirables to you. Work on your idea, work on your nucleus—*believe that you receive*—and you will speedily draw to you all the riches you need to fill out the vacuums now caused by poverty and debts.

You have seen shoots of trees spring up on rocky ledges where there was scarcely enough nourishment to keep a bit of moss alive. And you have known such shoots to grow into mighty trees. How do they do it?

The seed of a tree is a nucleus. Plant it, and the first

thing it does after it heats and germinates is to burst its shell and send forth a shoot—*upward*—using for that purpose the energy latent in the seed itself. In other words, it reaches out first to express life. It uses all the power it has to bring forth fruit. When it finds it has not enough energy in itself to accomplish this, it puts forth roots to draw the necessary elements from the soil about.

But if it happens to have fallen on a rocky ledge, it soon finds there is not enough soil to give it moisture or nourishment. Does it then despair? Not a bit of it! It sends its roots into every tiny crevice until they reach moisture and nourishment. It actually splits giant rocks asunder in its search for nutriment. It burrows through or around any obstacle until it exhausts the last flicker of life in itself or gets what it wants. Wherever they are, whatsoever may stand between, the shoot of the tree sends its roots seeking every element it needs for its growth and fruition.

First the stalk—then the roots. First the need—then the means to satisfy that need. First the nucleus—then the elements needed for its growth. The seed is a primary cause. The need, the nucleus, both are primary causes. Conditions—they are secondary. Given enough life in the nucleus, it will draw to itself the necessary means for growth regardless of conditions. The life in the seed is what counts—not the place where it falls.

All through Nature, you will find that same law. First the need, then the means. Use what you have to provide the vacuum, then draw upon the necessary elements to fill it. Reach up with your stalk, spread out your branches, provide the "pull" and you can leave to your roots the search for the necessary nourishment. If you have reached high enough, if you have made your magnet strong enough, you can draw to yourself whatever elements you need, no matter if they be at the ends of the earth!

God formed a Seed of Life which is you. He gave it power to attract to itself everything it needs for its growth, just as He did with the seed of the tree. He gave it power to draw to itself everything it needs for the fruition of its DESIRES, just as He did with the tree. But He did even more for you. He gave your Seed of Life power to attract to itself everything it needs for its *infinite expression!* He asks of you only that you make your desires strong enough, your faith in their drawing power great enough, to attract to you anything necessary to their fruition.

You see, Life is intelligent. Life is all-powerful. And Life is always and everywhere seeking expression. What is more, it is never satisfied. It is constantly seeking greater and fuller expression. The moment a tree stops growing, that moment the life in it starts seeking elsewhere for means to better express itself. The moment you stop expressing more and more of Life, that moment Life starts looking around for other and better outlets.

The only thing that can restrict Life is the channel through which it works. The only limitation upon it is the limitation you put upon it.

Over in Japan, they have taken the shoots of oak trees, and by binding a wire tightly around the main root at the point where the trunk begins, they have stunted the growth to such an extent that instead of great oaks eighty or a hundred feet high, these shoots reproduce all their qualities in dwarfed trees twelve or fourteen inches in height! These stunted trees live as long as regular trees, but they express only the millionth part of the life an oak should manifest.

We look upon that as abnormal, and so it is, yet it is being done all around us every day. Men bind their subconscious minds with wires of fear and worry. They put clamps of limitation upon their channels of supply. Then they wonder why they don't express more life in their bodies, why more of happiness and comfort is not evidenced in their surroundings.

God put a seed of Himself into you. That seed He called DESIRE. He gave it infinite power to draw to itself whatever it needs for expression. But He gave you free will—in other words, He left it with you to direct that expression—to draw upon it to the full or to put clamps upon it, as you like.

There lies in you the aegis of a Napoleon, a Lincoln, an Edison—anything you wish. All that is necessary is to stir up the Seed of God in you, and give it channels for expression. You can be what you want to be, if you want it strongly enough, if you believe in it firmly enough to make it your dominant desire.

How did Annette Kellerman, from a hopelessly crippled child, become one of the world's most perfectly formed women? By stirring up the Seed of Life in her limbs, through her earnest DESIRE for strength and beauty, by giving them work to do, ways in which to express life! How did George Jowett, from a cripple at eleven, become the world's strong man at twenty-one? By stirring up the Seed of Life in him through his overmastering DESIRE to be strong—by giving his muscles first a little, then more and more of work to do.

How did Reza Khan, from an ordinary trooper in the Persian army, rise to the rulership of Persia? How did Stalin, from a poor student, become Dictator of Russia? How did a water boy win to the throne of Afghanistan?

One and all, they stirred up the Seed of Life in them through DESIRE and Faith. One and all, they reached up and out, using freely all the power they had in the serene confidence that there was plenty more behind. Obstacles? They knew that obstacles were merely negative conditions that would disappear as darkness disappears when you turn on the light. It was the *prize* they kept their eyes upon. And it was the *prize* that they reached out for and plucked!

A few years ago, if anyone had told the neighbors of these men that today they would be rulers, he would have been laughed at as crazy. "Why, just look at their position," he would have been told. "Look at their circumstances, their surroundings. Look at the condition of the country. Consider their lack of training, of experience."

Conditions—all of them. Secondary causes. And these men had the vision to see beyond them—to go back to the *primary cause*—the Seed of God in themselves. They opened new channels for it to express itself. They reached up their stalks and spread out their branches and the Seed of Life in them drew to itself every element needed to bring forth their fruit.

At the heart of you is a seed—the Seed of God, the Seed of Life. In it is a perfect body, just as in every acorn there is a perfect oak. Not only that, but there is the power in it to draw to you every element you need to manifest a perfect body.

What do you care if circumstances have conspired to make you sick, or crippled or weak or infirm or ugly or old? If you are, it is because you or those around you have put the clamps of your fears or wrong beliefs upon the Seed of Life in you, and certain of your organs are stunted or dying.

The remedy? It is simple. Remove the clamps! Disregard your infirmity? It is only a condition—a LACK of Life. Then stir up the Seed of Life in you. Stir it up and charge it to draw to itself every element necessary to fill out the perfect image of your body that is in the seed.

Impossible? Have you ever heard of anything that is impossible to God? It is a Seed of God that is in you, and there is NOTHING of good it cannot draw to you!

The Law is—Use what you have, and more will be given you.

"Let me not ask how difficult may be
The work assigned to me.
This only do I ask:
Is this my task?

"Let me not ask if I be strong enough,
Or if the road be rough.
I only ask today,
Is this the way?"
—CLAUDE WEIMER

"Every good tree bringeth forth good fruit," said Jesus. "But a corrupt tree bringeth forth evil fruit. Every tree that bringeth not forth good fruit is hewn down and cast into the fire. Wherefore by their fruits ye shall know them."

What did Jesus mean by "Bearing fruit"? Didn't He have in mind methods of expressing the Seed of Life in you, making opportunities for it to expand and reach out to all those you come in contact with, doing something that makes this world a better place to live in?

And how does a tree go about the bearing of fruit? It brings forth a fragrant blossom first, does it not? When the blossom goes, it leaves the pistil, which gradually ripens into the luscious fruit.

The blossom is any idea of service, any means for making life more comfortable or enjoyable for those you live or deal with. The pistil is the action of turning that blossom into the beginning of the fruit by taking the first step to start the service, no matter how small that step may be. The luscious fruit is the finished service.

"That's fine!" I can hear many say, "I have the blossom—oh, a most fragrant blossom—but no means for turning it into the pistil or the fruit."

What does the branch have with which to start fruit?
Enough nourishment for a start, but nothing over. Do you
see the branch worrying on that account? Not a bit of it!
It uses cheerfully everything it has, serene in the knowledge that providing more is the vine's problem. The
branch has only to supply the *need*. The more it finds use
for, the more it gets. Another branch may be just as big,
but if the first one bears twice as much fruit, it will get
twice as much nourishment, for the vine apportions its
life-giving forces—not by size, but by needs. Wasn't it
Jesus who said—"I am the vine, ye are the branches."
Can you draw on Him for more than He can provide?

"Straight from a mighty bow this truth is driven: They
fail, and they alone, who have not striven." They have
a proverb in the East that a road of a thousand miles
begins with a single step. Goethe expressed the thought
when he wrote—

> "Are you in earnest? Seize this very minute;
> What you can do, or dream you can, BEGIN it!
> Boldness has genius, power and magic in it.
> Only engage, and then the mind grows heated;
> BEGIN, *and then the work will be completed.*"

"If ye abide in me," promised the Master, "and my
words abide in you, ye shall *ask what ye will,* and it shall
be done unto you. For herein is my Father glorified, that
ye bear much fruit."

If you stir up the Seed of Life in you by strong DE-
SIRES, if you provide it channels through which to
express itself by taking the first step towards the accomplishment of those desires, you can ask for any element you need, and it will be given you.

But if you lose this day loitering, it will be the same
story tomorrow and the day after. That which you are

today is the fulfillment of yesterday's aspirations; that which you are tomorrow will be the achievement of to-day's vision. You can't stand still. You must go forward—or backward. Eternal progress is the Law of Being. If you meet its call, you will never fail to go on and on to greater and greater heights. As Florence Taylor so aptly put it—

> "Success is the sum of small efforts,
> Repeated day in and day out,
> With never a thought of frustration,
> With never a moment of doubt.
> Whatever your cherished ambition,
> Begin now to make it come true,
> Through efforts, repeated, untiring,
> Plus faith in the thing that you do."

Health, riches, love—they are all *means* to an end, they are all conditions. The Seed of Life in you is the only thing that counts—that, and the channels you give it for expression. There is your PRIMARY CAUSE—all else is secondary. So disregard all else, and keep going back to it.

Do you want love? The mere desire is a proof of the availability of the love you want, for someone has rightly defined desire as God tapping at your door with His in-finite supply. So plant the seeds of love by giving it to all you come in contact with. Plant the seeds freely, serenely, believingly, and the harvest is as sure as when you plant seeds of wheat in fertile ground.

Make it a practice to appreciate things and people. Use it all through the day whenever anything occurs that pleases you. Say silently, if you cannot do so audibly, "I appreciate you." And never miss an opportunity to say a kindly word of praise or thanks to those around you. As Amy Bower puts it—

"We never know
How far kind words may go.
There is no way to measure
Friendly smiles. They carry treasures
Of courage, faith and love of man.
And we may watch them grow
Until their warmth
Infolds a multitude; returns to bless
The giver too with bread of happiness."

A good affirmation to use is—"I so love that I see all good and give all good, and all good comes back to me."

Do you want riches? Then plant the seeds you *have* by releasing them to START the work you want to do. You remember the story of the two darkies, lounging on a river bank dreaming away a sunny afternoon. "What you thinking about?" asked one. "I was just wishing I had a million dollars." "If you had a million dollars," said the first one dreamily, "would you lend me ten?" "No, I wouldn't!" "What, if you had a million dollars, you wouldn't lend me ten?" "No, I wouldn't. If you ain't got gumption enough, niggah, to wish yourself what you want, I wouldn't lend you a cent!"

And that, in effect, is what is wrong with most people. They have enough gumption to WISH for what they want, but they have not a great enough DESIRE for it to DO the things they must to bring that wish to pass. They have not the faith to plant their seed. They have not the magnetism to draw to them what they need.

The great essential is to provide a need—to supply the "pull." An ordinary beech tree draws some sixty gallons of water from the earth every day. How does it do it? Through evaporation! It spreads out its leaves, the light and heat of the sun absorb their moisture, and they in turn draw it from the earth. The same tree, its branches and leaves dead, draws not even a pint of water. Why? Because there is no longer the need, the "pull."

And the way to supply the need, to provide the "pull", is to START DOING the thing you want. However hopeless and impossible its accomplishment may seem, start doing it to the degree that you are able to at present.

Most of us feel that we must get somewhere else, or accumulate certain things, before we can make our start. And we wonder and wonder how we can get to that place or get hold of the things we regard as so essential, instead of realizing that all there is to a start is to START!

> "Just where thou art, shine forth and glow;
> Just where thou art, 'tis better so;
> Serve thou the Lord with perfect heart,
> Not somewhere else, but where thou art."

Emerson had a saying that you could travel the world over in search of beauty, but unless you had it within yourself, you would never find it, and the same is true of every good thing of life. The first step to success lies right where you are and in what you are doing. Until you have learned the lesson your present work holds for you, until you have learned to do it joyfully, lovingly, as to the Lord, you have not taken that first step towards the goal of your ambitions. You have not really begun.

Supply is an active force. It goes only to those who are alive, who are providing so many and such powerful magnets for it that they can "pull" it to themselves regardless of what obstacles may come between.

But suppose it is health you want? Suppose you are crippled or blind or bed-ridden. What then?

Why, then your remedy lies in breaking up the congealed life in your afflicted organ, and pouring it anew into the perfect mold.

And the way to break it up is by giving all you have of

life to that one desire, by working up so intense a FEEL-
ING that it shall presently burst its shell and draw to it
every element it needs for its perfect expression.

You can't do that by dabbling in mental work, the while
you are depending partly upon drugs, partly upon other
means. You must FEEL so strongly that your salvation
lies in the Seed of God within you, you must BELIEVE
so utterly in its power, that you are willing to sink or
swim by it alone. Like Grant, you must have the grim
determination to "fight it out along those lines, if it takes
all summer!"

But it will not take "all summer." Once you get the
spirit of it, you will find it by far the speediest and surest
method there is. Often your relief will be immediate.

A writer in Unity tells of a friend who was suffering
from a physical inharmony that threatened to become
malignant, when all at once the thought came to her—"If
God can't heal me, what can *this* do?" "This" referred
to the drugs she was taking. Immediately she applied a
cleansing substance to the troublous part, threw away the
drugs and from that day had no further trouble.

In THE FORUM, recently, Winifred Rhoades told of
an amusing happening in India. It seems that a pack
animal slipped at a ferry in India some years ago, and a
case of medicines was spilled. The colored pills were
picked up and returned to their appropriate bottles, but
with the white pills it was impossible to tell one kind from
another. However, a young native gathered them up, and
in spite of the missionary doctor's warning of the danger
of using them ignorantly, he promptly made them the
foundation of a widespread reputation.

When the missionary next appeared in that region, the
young native greeted him with joy. "I owe all my prosperity to you!" he exclaimed. It seems that the bottle
containing the assorted white pills he had picked up was

the favorite in his shop. Patients came from far and near
to get them. And in answer to the horrified doctor's question as to how he could administer them if he didn't know
what they were meant for, he announced that he gave
them to patients only when he didn't know what was the
matter with them.

Dr. Richard C. Cabot of Harvard told a gathering of
his fellow-medicos—"The body has a super wisdom and
force which are biased in favor of life rather than death.
What is this force? It is God, the healing power which
supplies 90 percent of recovery." And on another occasion, he said—"If nature, assisted by the proper mental
and emotional moods, is capable of curing an ulcer in three
or four weeks, why isn't it possible for the same force to
heal the same ulcer in three or four minutes, when the
curative processes have been speeded up abnormally by
the subject's passing through an intense religious (emotional) experience?" In "Man, the Unknown", Dr. Alexis
Carrel told of having actually seen a cancerous growth on
a man's hand cured in a few minutes.

You see, underneath all its seeming hardness, life is
really a kindly force. Life is love. It is supply. It is health.
It has in it every element we need to satisfy any right
desire. So there is no need to look to this man, or that
drug, or some outside agency, for the things you need. Go
to the Primary Cause. Go to Life. Go to God!

"There is a time in every man's education," said Emerson, "when he arrives at the conviction that he must take
himself for better or for worse *as his portion;* that though
the wide universe is full of good, no kernel of nourishing
corn can come to him but through his toil on that plot of
ground given to him to till.

"The power which resides in him is new in nature, and
none but he knows what he can do. *Nor does he know
until he has tried."*

" 'You are sick,' they said, 'But that isn't the truth'—
And the woman shook her head.
'The Bible declares, he that dwelleth in God
Shall not say, I am sick,' she said.
And she held to the truth through a starless night,
Till morning proved that her words were right.

" 'You are tired,' they said. But she smiled at that.
'How can I be tired,' said she,
'When the only work is work for God,
And He is my life, you see?'
And she quietly went her busy way,
With a happy song in her heart all day.

" 'You are poor,' they said. But she only thought,
'How little they know! God speed
The day when the world awakes to find
That love is its only need.'
And she still maintained, as her fortune grew,
Not money but love—if they only knew!

"For the world knows not of the peace that comes
To a soul at one with God.
It is only those who are toiling on
In the path the Master trod
Who can feel, through the dark, that loving hand,
And holding it fast, can understand."

What was it that made Napoleon Master of most of
Europe? Not native genius. Not brilliant intellect. In his
class at the Military Academy, he stood forty-sixth—and
there were only sixty-five in the class!

The genius that made Napoleon was first his intense
DESIRE for power, and then *his colossal belief in his
own destiny!* He had no fear in battle, because he believed
the bullet was not made that could kill him. He had no
hesitation in attempting the seemingly impossible, because

he believed the very stars in their courses would stoop to sweep the obstacles from his path.

You see, the secret of success lies in this: There is inside you a Seed of Life capable of drawing to you any element you need, to bring to fruition whatever of good you desire. But like all other seeds, its shell must be broken before the kernel inside can use its attractive power. And that shell is thicker, harder, than the shell of any seed on earth. Only one thing will break it—heat from WITHIN—a *desire* so strong, a determination so intense, that you cheerfully throw everything you have into the scale to win what you want. Not merely your work and your money and your thought, but the willingness to stand or fall by the result—to do or to die. Like the Master when He cursed the fig tree for its barrenness, you are willing to demand of the Seed of Life in you that it *bear fruit or perish.*

That is the secret of every great success. That is the means by which all of life, from the beginning of time, has won what it needed.

What was it gave to certain animals protective shells, to others speed, to still others a sting, to those who needed them claws or horns? What gave to the bold and strong the means to destroy, to the weak and cowardly facilities for hiding or escape? What but the Seed of Life in each, giving to every form of life the means that form craved to preserve its skin.

Always the seed in each form of life responded to the call of that life—*"Give me so-and-so or I perish."*

Since the very creation of the earth, Life has been threatened by every kind of danger. Had it not been stronger than any other power in the Universe—were it not indeed a part of God Himself—it would have perished ages ago. But God who gave it to us endowed it with unlimited resource, unlimited energy. No other force can defeat it. No obstacle can hold it back.

What is it that saves men in dire extremity, who have exhausted every human resource and finally turned to God in their need? What but the unquenchable flame of God in them—the Seed of Life He has given to each of us—with power to draw to us whatever element we feel that we need to save us from extinction.

What do business leaders advise young people today? Live within your income? No, indeed! *Go into debt!* Reach out! Spread yourself! Then dig the harder to catch up!

You are entitled to just as much of the good things of life as Ford or Rockefeller or Morgan, or any of the rich men around you. But it is not THEY who owe it to you. And it is not the world that owes you a living. The world and they owe you nothing but honest pay for the exact service you render them.

The one who owes you everything of good—riches and honor and happiness—is the Seed of Life inside you. Go to it! Stir it up! Don't rail against the world. You get from it what you put into it—nothing more. Wake up the Seed of God inside you! Demand of it that it bring you the elements you need for riches or success. Demand— and make your need seem as urgent as must have been the need of the crustacean to develop a shell, of the bird to grow wings, of the bear to give it fur.

Demand—and KNOW THAT YOU RECEIVE! The Seed of Life in you is just as strong as ever it was in those primitive animals of pre-historic days. If it could draw from the elements whatever means it required to enable them to survive, don't you suppose it can do the same today to provide you with the factors you consider essential to your well-being?

True, these factors are different from those called for

in primitive times, but do you suppose that matters to the Seed of Life? Everything in this world is made up of energy. Don't you suppose it is as easy to pour that energy into one mold as into another?

Many seem to think that riches and success are a matter of luck. They are not luck. They are a matter of DEMANDING MUCH from the Seed of God inside you, and then insisting upon those demands being met.

The trouble with most people is that they are looking to some force outside themselves to bring them riches or happiness. The superstitious carry a rabbit's foot or an amulet, believing it will bring them luck. The religious carry medals or images or the relic of some Saint. It never occurs to them that they have the means of going direct to God. God seems too impalpable, too shadowy and far away. His apparent isolation, His seeming detachment from their work-a-day world, makes Him appear too unsubstantial to depend upon in real need. They want something they can see and feel and talk to. Something with a substance like their own. Hence the demand for statues and pictures and shrines and relics. Hence, too, the need for Saints and Priests—intercessors, nearer to the Great One than ordinary mortals can hope to reach.

But direct contact is always better than even the most potent intermediary. And you HAVE the direct contact, any time you want to use it.

You are a Tree of Life. The seed of you is a Seed of God—part of Him as much as the acorn is part of the oak. And that Seed has all the properties of God, just as the acorn has all the potential properties of the oak. It can draw to you every element you need to make yours the most perfect tree in the garden, the most fruitful.

So, instead of depending upon the stars, or a rabbit's foot, or an amulet, or even the Saints, put your faith in the Seed of God, which is the animating part of you. No matter what your circumstances may be, no matter what obstacles may conspire to hold you down, look—NOT merely to the means at hand, NOT to circumstances or conditions—but to that never-failing power of the Seed inside you to draw to you any element you believe you MUST have to survive.

That is the way to make your "Star", your "Destiny", work for you. Only the "Star", the "Destiny", is right inside YOU. It is the Seed of God, the Seed of Life in YOU which your desire, your faith, and your need have started into action. It is stronger than any circumstances. It can overcome any condition. So bless it and baptize it, *and stir it up!*

Bless it morning and evening, but when the urgent need arises—DEMAND! Demand that it bestir itself. Demand that it draw to you whatever elements you need. Demand—and *give all* as you demand all—make it a matter of life or death, survive or perish.

There is a point in the tree, you know, below which the "pull" of the leaves has little power. That is the point to which the roots must deliver the water, or the tree will never flower or bear fruit.

There is a point in your circumstances or your business at which the pull of your Seed of Life does not make itself felt. That is the point to which your efforts must deliver the fruit of your work, or your desire will die still-born.

So when you demand, first GIVE—throw every bit of effort you have into reaching the point at which the Seed of Life will take over the work. Give all that you can to the work in hand, and don't forget to give to the Lord as well.

It is this which makes so successful the prayers of those who, demanding riches, throw all their scanty store into the plate, and depend solely upon that Seed of God in them to supply their needs. When you can do this, believing, the world is yours.

> "When things go wrong, as they sometimes will,
> When the road you're trudging seems all up hill,
> When the funds are low and the debts are high,
> And you want to smile, but you have to sigh,
> When care is pressing you down a bit,
> REST—if you must—but don't you quit.

> "Success is failure turned inside out—
> The silver tint of the cloud of doubt,
> And you never can tell how close you are,
> It may be near when it seems afar.
> So stick to the fight when you're hardest hit—
> It's when things seem worse that you musn't quit."

Exercise for Chapter Sixteen

"All things therefore whatsoever ye would that men should do unto you, even so do ye also unto them; for this is the law and the prophets."

Someone in Omaha studied that Golden Rule, and out of it found the solution to much of Nebraska's jobless problem in the last big depression. He brought together a number of jobless men and women, and started them doing things to help others!

Forgetting their own troubles, they looked about them for ways to help others more unhappy and unfortunate than themselves and organized the All Omaha Self Help Society. They do farming, craft work and canning. They build houses, repair them, tend yards, do housework, care for children, and perform any service that offers which is of value to the community. Where money is available, they accept pay for their services and turn it into wheat and flour and fuel and shelter. They have improved their condition and that of all around them, without waiting for business to pick up or for some government agency to give them a lift. And in scores of parts of the country, similar groups have done the same.

In times of quandary, when you seem at the end of your rope, if you will only stop and think awhile, you will nearly always find that you have the BEGINNINGS of the solution of your problem in your mind, or somewhere ready to your hand. Use that beginning to start—no matter on how small a scale.

Alice Foote MacDougall built a business that, before the depression of the '30's, was worth $5,000,000. Yet she started with a little booth in Grand Central Station where she sold coffee. One blustery winter's day, everyone that came in seemed so cold and hungry that she sent home for her waffle iron and the necessary ingredients, and served waffles free to all who came for coffee. Those free waffles made her famous. They were the start that built for her a string of restaurants and a good-sized fortune.

The stories of that kind we might tell are legion. There was the poor farmer's wife who gave some of the strawberry preserves she was making to a youngster from High School who had stopped by for a drink. He thought them so good that he asked if he couldn't sell some of them to neighbors. From that start she built a profitable business.

The famous Jones Farm Sausage got its start from the talk of neighbors and friends who had tasted this delicious sausage at the Jones' table. And many another successful business has started on as small a scale.

The great thing is the start—to see an opportunity for service, and to start doing it, even though in the beginning you serve but a single customer—and him for nothing.

> "In life's small things be resolute and great
> To keep thy muscles trained.
> Knowst thou when Fate thy measure takes?
> Or when she'll say to thee
> 'I find thee worthy, do this thing for me!' "

CHAPTER SEVENTEEN

OLD MAN GRAVITY

OUT IN CALIFORNIA, when you meet a man who feels "down in the mouth" and ask how it is with him, he doesn't tell you that his digestion is bad or his liver off color, but, more likely, he will say—*"Old Man Gravity's got me."*

Sinbad the Sailor had the same idea away back in the times when the Arabian Nights were new. He called it The Old Man of the Sea, but it rode his shoulders just like "Old Man Gravity" does today. What is this Old Man?

When you lack ambition, when you feel discouraged and the world seems all awry, it isn't the fault of your liver. It's "Old Man Gravity."

When your feet weigh a ton, when there doesn't seem to be an ounce of energy left in your system, it isn't a pill that you need. It's some way of knocking "Old Man Gravity" off your shoulders.

Who is he? His full name is *"Gravitation."* He is our same friend whom we have met in so many guises before. Properly cultivated, he can be made a power to attract to you all of good. But when ignored or wrongly used, he is just "Old Man Gravity", weighing you down.

The Law of Gravity, you know, is the pull of the mass. It is the tendency of solid objects to draw to them every loose particle within their range of attraction. It is the constant struggle of inertia against ertia.

What has this to do with discouragement, lassitude and the like? Just this:

Your body is made up of solids and liquids. The solids are the mass of condensed energy. The liquids are the particles of "free" energy. The force of gravity in your body and in the earth is all towards attracting those free particles to the solid mass, and condensing them into a part of it.

But when those loose particles become congealed into one solid mass, *you're dead!* So the life-giving forces within you are all for freedom. They are "ertia", and from birth to death, they wage a constant fight against the forces of "inertia."

How are you to keep "Old Man Gravity's" hands off you? How are you to release his hold when he gets his clutches upon you?

How do you release his hold on water? By turning it into steam, do you not? How do you release his hold upon coal or oil? By vaporizing it, by turning it into gas!

You can't turn your body into steam or gas, but you can use the same idea. You know how martial music will put new life into soldiers who seem ready to drop. Why? Because stirring music wakes up the particles of "free" life in you and sets them whirling at a faster rate.

You know how a fragrant perfume will revive you when you are tired. Why? Because it, too, has the faculty of stirring up the life in you, whereas an obnoxious smell has just the opposite effect.

You know how a bright, sunshiny morning fills you with pep, whereas a gray, cloudy day gives you the blues. Why? Because sunshine wakens the life in you, and makes it expand.

Love, laughter, happiness, praise, all stimulate the "free" life in you—all make you feel better, regardless of what condition you may have been in before. Sorrow,

hate, fear, worry, depress the life in you, and make it easy
for "Old Man Gravity" to get in his work.

Why is it that sudden good news has often raised sufferers from their sick beds, sometimes after they had been
given up as lost? Because joy frees the life-energy in your
body. It breaks up the condensed particles and sends them
merrily about their appointed work.

Why is it that worry and fear bring so great a harvest
of sickness and old age and death? Because worry and
fear mean strain. And strain hardens—*congeàls*—the life-
energy in you. You hear of people being "scared stiff,"
and the expression is literally true. You read of "the lame
man leaping as an hart" for joy, and again it is literally
true.

Of course, sudden fright will sometimes loosen every
particle of free energy, and enable a paralytic or cripple
to perform prodigies of strength. Some years ago, for
instance, I received a clipping from a Los Angeles paper,
telling how "Frances Avita, frail and weighing only 100
pounds, lifted a heavy automobile off the head of her
brother and saved his life after an auto accident. Sum-
moning superhuman strength, the girl was able to lift over
900 pounds, a weight which no ordinary man could move."
And you have doubtless read of similar cases.

It is this sudden freeing of the life energy in him which
makes a badly scared man the most dangerous man on
earth. It is like the sudden freeing of energy that takes
place when you ignite any explosive. He has for the moment the strength of ten men, and he will use it in any way
to escape the danger he fears. But continued fear, like any
other continued nervous strain, dissipates that energy and
makes one powerless as the rabbit "charmed" by its an-
cestral enemy, the snake.

This is true not only of your body, but of your business, your home, your circumstances and surroundings.

Belief in yourself and your power over things, faith in the destiny that carries you on, will mold all the free life about you into factors favorable to your well-being and success. Pessimism, worry, fear, will congeal that life into a bleak and dreary waste.

Dr. Draper of the College of Physicians and Surgeons of Columbia University, is on record as stating that man's most destructive forces are within his own soul.

As though to confirm this, the Reader's Digest had an article saying that "Personal worry is one of the principal causes of physical ailments which send people to hospitals. The chances are better than even that if you are ill, worry is causing the symptoms."

In the Springfield Weekly Republican some time ago there appeared an article stating—"New proofs that worry can wear holes in people's stomachs are reported by Dr. Daniel Davies and Dr. A. T. Macbeth Wilson, both of London, in the form of records of 58 instances of severe stomach bleeding among 50 different patients. In 47 out of the 58 attacks, Doctor Davies and Doctor Wilson found that the bleeding was preceded by some kind of worry or emotional stress. One ship's captain was upset by a breakdown of his ship's engines, which he feared that an incompetent engineering staff would not fix in time to keep the ship from being lost.

"A businessman had unexpected trouble with his bankers and had to raise $75,000 within a few days. At the other end of the social scale, the proprietor of a one-man coffee stand had just failed and lost his business. An already worried nurse found herself suddenly responsible for the whole hospital, through illness of the sister in charge. An accountant bled from his stomach following an unexpected demand by his partner for dissolution of the business. A father had two attacks of bleeding, each following the birth of an addition to the family."

Dr. Loring Swaim, who is the Director of a famous clinic in Massachusetts, had under observation 270 cases of arthritis which were cured when they became free from fear, worry and resentment.

Dr. W. S. Inman of the British Medical Association says that *"Thinking* about babies often makes women get styes on their eyelids." And under the heading of "Anxiety and Illness" the Reader's Digest told of a man who was bothered by a troublesome skin disease. "Almost every Monday I have a breaking out like this," he said. Asked by the physician what he did on Sundays, it developed that he usually visited a young lady to whom he had been engaged for years, but who had repeatedly postponed the wedding day. Each Sunday he pressed for a decision. Each Monday was the day after frustration. And almost every Monday, his skin protested his anxious state by breaking into eczema.

"There is increasing evidence," said the article, "that pent-up, repressed anxiety which cannot be relieved in action is discharged in the form of disease. In many cases of high blood pressure, no organic cause can be traced. Dr. Erwin Moos reports the case of a man with a systolic blood pressure of 280, who was afflicted with a lung disorder, and whose urine showed traces of albumin. Rest and drugs brought no beneficial effect, but one day the patient remarked that he had done great wrong to his estranged wife. The doctor immediately arranged a meeting, and after a friendly discussion between the two, the man's blood pressure fell to 150, his lung symptoms abated, and the albumin disappeared. Several years later the patient was in good health, with a blood pressure of only 130.

"Fully fifty percent of the problems of the acute stages of an illness, and seventy-five percent of the difficulties of convalescence, have their primary origin—NOT in the body, but in the MIND of the patient," says Dr. Edward A. Strecker.

Perhaps the whole matter is best summed up in the words of John Wesley, written in his "Journal" under date of May 12th, 1759:

"Reflecting today on the case of a poor woman, who had continual pain in her body, I could not but remark on the inexcusable negligence of most physicians in cases of this nature. They prescribe drug upon drug, without knowing a jot of the matter concerning the root of the disorder. And without knowing this, they cannot cure, though they may murder the patient. Whence came this woman's pain (which she would never have told had she not been questioned about it)?

"From fretting for the death of her son. And what availed medicine whilst the fretting continued? Why then do not all physicians consider how far bodily disorders are caused, or influenced, by the mind?"

That this is often true even of the diseases of young children is indicated by an experience of Zola Somerville, as given in Unity Weekly:

Her little daughter had been on a coasting party one evening, somewhat against the mother's wishes, and late that night Mrs. Somerville became aware of a nagging, irritating cough from her daughter's room across the hall.

After thinking over a number of simple remedies she had in the house, and rejecting each, she began to ask herself—"What is a cough anyhow? What causes it?" The answer came clearly—"irritation. Yes, undoubtedly a cough is irritation." In fact, this particular one sounded very irritating to me. That answered the first question, but where it had come from or what caused it was not so easily answered.

Well, then, who was irritated, my daughter or I? Something deep down inside me seemed to say—"Aren't you irritated right now thinking that she shouldn't have gone out into the snow? Also because you are being kept awake when you think you want to sleep?" Admitting that, what was I to do about it? What is irritation? It seems real but does God make it? No, I felt sure He had not.

All right then, if God had not made irritation, what had He made? What is the opposite of irritation? Quick as a flash came back the answer—PEACE! Then I recalled that before Jesus left His disciples He said: "Peace I leave with you; My peace I give unto you." And there came to my mind the incident when the disciples were in the ship with Jesus and a great storm arose. "Peace, be still," He said to the sea, and there was a great calm.

Evidently there was great power in that word peace when it was uttered by one who knew the power of the spoken word and spoke it with authority. For a long time I was entirely unaware of anything about me except the consciousness of this wonderful gift of peace. How grateful I felt for such a rare gift.

When I thought of my daughter again, I realized how very quiet the house was. I listened for some minutes, but only the sound of quiet, regular breathing came from the room across the hall—no irritating cough to keep me awake. Another miracle had taken place, yet it was all divinely natural. My thoughts of worry and irritation had simply given place to the consciousness of the real kingdom of peace on earth.

The next morning, my daughter's cold had entirely disappeared—in fact, she showed no more signs of cold during the remainder of the winter.

Peace, relaxation—few things are more important to good health. At the Bailey Educational Service in New York, cranky children are taught to play a game of "shut-eyes." First the teacher, then the child, closes his eyes and keeps them closed for half a minute or so. Gradually this is extended to relaxing the arms, the hands, the legs and feet. "Relaxation," it is explained, "does not work miracles, nor are the benefits noticed at once. But gradually the child learns to do it himself. He rests himself, recharges his nervous system. Temper, tantrums and crankiness disappear."

To be able to teach your own child, you must first learn how to relax yourself. "The first thing to do," explains the school, "is to sit in a comfortable chair or couch. Fold the hands easily in the lap, or let them rest on the sides of the chair, completely limp. The eyes should be closed, the lips permitted to part, the head to fall to one side, where it is supported by the shoulder. The feet should be crossed at the ankles, the soles outward. Every muscle should slacken."

Such relaxation, if only for a half a minute, provides remarkable rest. "It is impossible for a thoroughly relaxed person to become angry," declares the head of the school. "Anger is a matter of the nerves, and is due to too much tension."

This statement is borne out by Dr. Howard W. Haggard of Yale University in his book "Devils, Drugs and Doctors."

"Paralysis of a limb may be a sign of serious disease," he says, "but a man may be paralyzed with fear, and he may be struck dumb or blind with terror. Diarrhea also is a symptom of disease, but it is likewise often a complication of emotion. King James I of England was prone to diarrhea from the emotion aroused by distressing matters of state. The excessive secretion of saliva, called salivation, may occur in disease, while in fever the mouth may dry out and become parched. The saliva is also secreted excessively when a savory food is merely thought of, and the mouth dries out with fear.

"This last is shown by the glass of water put before the public speaker; he drinks before he speaks because he is frightened and afterward because he has dried his mouth by talking.

"The dry mouth of fear was one of the early legal tests, a form of ordeal. The mouth of the defendant was filled with flour; if he was innocent and felt no fear, his saliva flowed and he was able to swallow the flour; if he was guilty, his fear kept his mouth dry and he choked.

"Vomiting may come from illness, and it may also come from fear or the smell of some disgusting substance. The pressure of the blood in the artery rises slowly as the kidneys harden with age, but it also rises even from the emotion caused by having a physician apply the apparatus to determine its height.

"The blood of a man with diabetes contains an abnormal amount of sugar and some of it finds its way into his urine; strong emotions suffered in restraint may temporarily cause both of these symptoms, as in the football substitute sitting on the side lines, or the student faced with a difficult examination.

"Most of the symptoms of disease can be counterfeited by the influence of the nervous system upon bodily functions. Mental irritation or depression can produce dyspepsia, jaundice, or a general decline. Fright may produce palpitation of the heart, and heart failure has resulted from business reverses. After cities are destroyed by earthquakes, men and women are found dead who show no signs of injury. The modern surgeon is worried by the patient who faces an operation with the conviction that he will die.

"There are on record a number of cases of persons mentally depressed, but not otherwise unwell, who have accurately predicted the time of their death. Thus Dr. John Billings mentions the case of an officer who had sustained a slight flesh wound at the battle of Gettysburg. The man, although unusually robust, became depressed mentally, and declared at the start that he would die, which he did on the fourth day. A postmortem examination showed that every organ was healthy and the wound was too trivial to cause death.

"Pain, which is the supreme subjective phenomenon of disease, is almost wholly mental. A man during rage feels no pain from injury until after his anger has cooled; the same man waiting in the anteroom of the dentist may suffer agony in anticipation.

"The gravest disturbances of the body are seen in a disease of the imagination called hysteria. Hysterical persons involuntarily counterfeit the symptoms of disease; the limb may be drawn up in a deforming contracture, or palsied. Persons with hysteria may become mute or blind, their sensations may be perverted, they may vomit obstinately or lose their appetite and waste away."

Dr. Haggard goes on to point out that such conditions may continue for years, yet be suddenly and completely relieved by some highly emotional experience, such as a fire or an earthquake, or just the exaltation of a fervent belief in some relic or "healer."

If conditions of such long standing can be instantly and completely cured—and every physician will agree that such cures have been made—then, in our opinion, ANY *condition can be just as quickly and completely cured!*

For everyone knows that if you keep a bone or muscle in one position for months and years, it will grow that way. It matters not why you assumed the position at the beginning, whether from hysteria or accident or disease. "As the twig is bent, the tree is inclined."

I remember reading the case of a healthy young farmer who went to Chicago to find work. Unable to get a job, he presently drifted around to one of the many "flop houses" for the night. There an acquaintance "put him onto the racket" of posing as a cripple and begging alms at some street corner. He tried it; it proved profitable beyond anything he could earn by honest work; so he became a professional cripple and mendicant.

For ten years he sat on street corners twelve and fourteen hours a day, his limbs pitifully hunched up, the while he begged coins from gullible passers-by. At the end of those ten years, do you suppose he could use his limbs? No more than if they had been crippled by accident or disease! It took him years to regain their power.

So when faith or emotion or understanding instantly cures a condition of long standing, what does it matter how that condition occurred? It has been allowed to GROW that way, and the growth is just as stubborn, just as "set" if caused by hysteria, as though it had been started by serious accident or disease.

Therefore, when doctors admit that one kind of palsied or deformed limb can be cured (as they do) by faith and emotion, they are by that very admission giving evidence that ANY kind may be cured!

Brown Landone showed how you can help others to be healed in one of his articles in Nautilus Magazine: "A patient had a very lame leg. Its muscles were so sore that it was almost impossible for her to take a step on her left foot.

"By the old method," Landone explained, "the practitioner would have refused to recognize the reality of the lameness and pain, and then idealized the Divine idea of a perfect human limb. By the new method, the practitioner did this, and then something *more*. She told the patient to go home and to imagine that she was again a little girl, running and skipping at play in a field of flowers, to *feel* that she was a child again, skipping rope and playing tag and having a glorious time.

"Then when the patient was gone, the practitioner herself identified herself with the joyous vital activity of a child. In other words, the practitioner *lived* in spirit the very activities she had asked her patient to imagine and feel. And the healing took place within an hour.

"Here is another case. About four weeks ago an elderly gentleman came to me, exhausted. Although he had been using mentalized Truth for many years, he felt he had come to an age when there was little strength left in him and that he could not go on actively as he had previously done. I talked with him of the energy he would have, and the good times we could have together, if he would only *feel* as young as I do.

" 'Well,' he said, 'I know there is no time or age in spirit and I have affirmed youthfulness for years, and yet I haven't the energy and pep now which I used to have.'

" '*Affirming* youthfulness is not enough,' I replied. 'Affirmations are thoughts *about* youthfulness. What you need is to *feel* youthful, to awaken powers deep down underneath thought.'

" 'Anyway,' he said, 'I haven't the energy to act like a kid!'

" 'Well,' I said, 'I'm older than you are and I am going to give you a treatment by taking two hours off this afternoon to have a glorious time!'

"I went to the beach with five young men and all the time I was enjoying myself and acting like a kid—whether bathing, rowing, or skipping up and down the beach. I identified myself with the vitality and strength of youth, and also with the *love* of youthfulness and the love of that 'old' man!

"That night when I returned to the city, I had a telephone call from him. He said, 'About *three o'clock* this afternoon, I began to feel a return of energy such as I have not had for twenty years. It is astounding.' (And it was twenty minutes to three when the young men and myself left our auto and took our first skip down the beach.)

"That was four weeks ago, and the man is gaining in strength and vitality every day."

> If thou wouldst right the world,
>   And banish all its evils and its woes,
> Make its wild places bloom,
>   And its drear deserts blossom as the rose—
> *Then right thyself!*
>
> If thou wouldst turn the world
>   From its long, lone captivity in sin,
> Restore all broken hearts,
>   Slay grief, and let sweet consolation in—
> *Turn thou thyself!*
>
> If thou wouldst cure the world
>   Of its long sickness, of its grief and pain,
> Bring in all-healing Joy,
>   And give to the afflicted health again—
> *Then cure thyself!*
>
> If thou wouldst wake the world
>   Out of its dream of death and dark'ning strife,
> Bring it to Love and Peace,
>   And Light and Brightness of Immortal Life—
> *Wake thou thyself!*
>   —JAMES ALLEN *in Epoch*

Exercise for Chapter Seventeen

At the Bethlehem Steel Mills men were loading cars with pig iron, each man carrying twelve and one-half tons a day. Frederick W. Taylor, efficiency expert, advanced the unbelievable theory that, according to foot pounds and calories, the men should carry three times that amount. He put it to the test merely by making the men sit down and rest every few minutes—*before they tired* instead of after. If you sit down before you tire, the body repairs itself, or rests, much more quickly; you require less time for resting in the long run and almost never slow up your work because of fatigue.

Well, this simple rule enabled the men to carry forty-seven and a half tons of pig iron the very first day and to continue at that rate—three times as much as formerly. That tells the story. It is almost never your work that tires you, but *how you work.* You should rest before you tire, or the moment you begin to tire, instead of postponing rest until the next hour or day or week.

In the days of ancient Greece, there was probably no exercise or work that took as great a toll of heart and nerve as long-distance running. Yet many of these runners lived to be old men and were almost as speedy and enduring at fifty as when young.

How did they manage? The moment they finished a run, they relaxed utterly. And the way they relaxed was to lie on their backs, with their legs up against a tree or other support, their feet as high as they would go!

The reason? To send the blood to the head and the back of the neck, where many of the glands are located that have so much to do with injecting new energy into the heart and nervous system.

What is it that makes the stomach sag, the cheeks become jowls, the whole figure flop? What but the pull of GRAVITY. Keep a rabbit in an upright position for two hours and it will die. Why? Because its vital organs have been pulled out of place.

Yet man stays in an upright position most of his time. Perhaps that is one of the reasons man lives only two to three times maturity, on the average, while the animals live five to seven times theirs. His vital organs bog down from the continual pull of gravity. Even his brain, some believe, sags like an egg with an air bubble at the top, bringing on senility.

The Success School of New York utilizes this idea. They have found that the one way to reduce without leaving the jowls flapping over the neck like a turkey gobbler's, and without making the skin of the cheeks flabby, is to lie for a while each day with the feet raised eighteen to twenty-four inches higher than the head, and with the head hanging down slightly lower than the rest of the body. Their success in making older women look ten to twenty years younger has been almost miraculous.

Surgeons use this method in the operating room when they find a patient near collapse. They raise his legs, lower his head.

Now comes Brown Landone to tell of a food that "Makes cells grow younger!" In an article in Nautilus Magazine, he wrote—

"More than twenty years ago experiments were made on old decrepit rats. They were so old that, proportionately, they were about as old as a man of ninety years. These decrepit old rats were fed what were then called 'immature' foods, that is, foods which had not finished their growth, sprouting new stems and very young leaves. The results were amazing. The decrepit old rats were transformed, and their bodies began to grow younger!

"No one understood the cause of this. The experiments had been conducted to test effects of vitamins, but with larger amounts of vitamins in matured or full grown foods, the old rats did *not* grow younger. Hence, scientists knew there was something else, other than vitamins, which worked like magic in growing youthful cells.

"Several years passed, and no one tumbled to the spiritual significance of that experiment. Then, some five years ago, I began experimenting with young growing plants, in this case sprouts of bean seeds. I had used sprout foods for more than a generation, but had no proof of what caused them to be of value.

"At about the same time, other scientists discovered a root-auxin in plant roots. When they extracted this auxin from the tip of a young growing root, and pasted it on the edge of a leaf, roots grew even on the edge of the leaf! *This is the miracle of auxinon foods—they induce growth after their own kind of activity.* A root-auxin will grow roots; and a youth-auxinon will grow youthful cells.

"Youth-growing substances from new growing sprouts will induce cells to grow younger. That is, there is 'something' in the chemical substances of a youth-growing auxinon which, when you eat it as food, makes the cells of your body reproduce younger cells instead of older cells.

"The best auxinon foods I know of are found in *Mung Bean sprouts*. Mung Beans are Chinese beans."

But Landone went on to point out that foods are but one phase of growth and change. What you *think*—your emotions, your desires and ideals are even more important. Take hold of healing with your whole spirit, and like Jacob of old, make up your mind—"I will not let thee go except thou heal me." Join with all the hosts of heaven in declaring that only the good is true, and that good health everywhere is made manifest.

"Life abundant quickens me now. Love all-powerful heals me. God's strong, pure life is now active in and through every cell in my body. His perfect image of my every organ is now vitalized in me in perfect form. By the power and authority of Jesus Christ, every cell in my body is vitalized and restored. I have come to Him and I AM healed."

CHAPTER EIGHTEEN

LIFE BEGINS WITH MOVEMENT

SOME PHYSICIANS have said the only disease is CONGES-TION—that all other ailments are but an intensification of congestion.

Congestion means "over-crowding." When your lungs are congested, and you have difficulty getting enough air into them to breathe, it is not because there is any lack of air. There is just as much oxygen around you as there ever was. The trouble is that so much foreign matter has gotten into your lungs that the air cannot get in! They are no longer the clear, open channels that are needed to let in the oxygen to purify your blood.

All experiments in the perpetuation of life have shown that two things are necessary:

1. Food for renewing and rebuilding the cells.
2. Open pores, open passages through which to absorb it.

Dr. Carrel in his experiments with the chicken heart which he kept alive and growing for more than 30 years, and which seems able to live forever, showed that cleansing it of all impurities, keeping its pores and passages open, is just as important as giving it proper nourishment. For the cells cannot absorb that nourishment unless their pores and passages are open wide enough for its unobstructed passage.

All the air in the world will do you no good if your lungs are so congested that you cannot take it in. All the food in the world will give you no nourishment if your arteries and passages are so stopped up that nothing can get through them. You must throw off the old before you can absorb the new. You cannot pour water into a vessel already full. You must clean out the refuse of waste and worn out cells before you can hope for renewed life and strength and youthfulness.

And the first place where these must be cleaned out is in your mind. When you invite God to heal you, you must make way for Him and for the fulfillment of His law of love and peace. You can't let griefs or grievances, worries or fears, bitter feelings or resentments clutter up the passages, and still hope to see God's life flow through. The ancients used to call anger or resentment a "lump", and it is just that, for when it accumulates it is just like a great lump in the passages, effectively stopping the flow of life and good.

What is blocking off your health, your happiness, your prosperity? Every good thing in the Universe is all around you, as open to you as the air you breathe, as available to you as any radio program is to your radio receiver. The obstacles are all in YOU! Remove the negative thoughts, the fears, the resentments—and see how quickly the good will flow in! It is the old story that everything must be cured in your own mind first.

All external conditions are but the outward manifestation of your inner thoughts. Good is all around you, like the air you breathe. There is no more of the energy of the universe available to John D. Rockefeller or Henry Ford than there is to you. They have kept more of their passages open, that is all.

In an article in Nautilus Magazine, Kate F. Byrne told of a mechanic who had been given up by physicians as incurable. Since they could no longer offer him hope, he decided to study his own case and see if there was anything he could do for himself.

Being a mechanic, he naturally became interested in the methods the body used to nourish and renew its different organs. He learned about the white corpuscles and how they fought disease, and—most important of all—how the mind could send a flow of blood to any part of the body on which its thought was concentrated.

So he began consciously applying his thought to sending an extra flow of blood to the part of his body that was ailing. He ordered the white corpuscles in the blood to destroy the germs of disease and remove the waste matter from those parts. He commanded his subconscious to open wide the arteries to those affected parts, and send to them every bit of help that was needed. Within three months, he had lost all fear of the incurable condition. Within a year, he was back at work, cured!

When Kossuth was Governor of Hungary, he suffered greatly from a serious malady which the doctors of his day seemed unable to relieve. Yet when any urgent need arose, he showed that he had within himself the power to overcome it.

"At times when I was nailed to my bed with sickness," he wrote, "news would come from the army demanding all the strength of my activity, and I would say to my body—'Be well!'—and it would obey me."

You have seen the big electric cranes that are used for picking up scrap iron and metals of different sorts. There is a great metal disc at the end of the rope, which can be magnetized or de-magnetized at will. You drop the disc on a pile of scrap metal, turn on the current, and the disc picks up enormous quantities of the scrap. The crane carries it over to where you want the material dumped, you turn off the current and down plops the scrap iron.

You can magnetize any organ in your body in much the same way. You can send your blood flowing to it, have it cleanse away every obstruction, have it carry to it every bit of vitality that is needed to make it perfect.

Bless the Divinity in the affected organ. Send an increased blood stream coursing to it. Command the white corpuscles to destroy the germs of disease, to cleanse away the waste, to renew and revitalize every part. Feel them doing it. Then rest serenely in the consciousness that you are being made well. Don't work on disease—work on life! Stimulate the life—and the disease will vanish.

Remember, sickness is not a thing in itself. It is the negative result of the LACK of life or health. It is not something to be treated. It is like the darkness that disappears when you turn on the light. It is a waste of time to treat a condition. It is the CAUSE you want to get at.

In his Teachings and Addresses, Edward A. Kimball puts the whole idea so clearly that I quote it here:

"Suppose you have to treat an insane woman who believes she is covered with feathers. She says she has them. Would you treat her for the purpose of removing feathers? Are there any to deal with? Or would you know that you must abolish such a BELIEF?

"Now then, suppose your patient says that his lungs are half gone. Do you work any more in the realm of decayed lungs than in the realm of feathers? Do you have such a bodily condition to deal with or have you just to abolish the BELIEF in such a condition? Watch yourself. See that your treatments are not treatments for feathers.

"Do not treat fever any more than you would feathers in an insane woman. No pain, no claim of pain, only the action of mortal mind. Do not annihilate, but displace error with right ideas. The true idea is always the saviour."

If your image in the mirror showed a frowning face, you wouldn't try to rub off the frown. You would displace it with a smile. You don't have to fight sickness. All you need to do is to displace it with the healthy image of the affected organ. Do that, and the sickness will vanish of itself.

Go back to the Primary Cause, which is in your mind. Open wide the passages, clear them of doubts and fears and resentments, and LET God's perfect image of you shine through. Let the universal energy all around you flow into and through you like you let the air flow into your lungs. Don't accumulate lumps of anger or resentment or fear or worry to cause sickness by blocking off the passages to good.

The greatest problem of the body, physicians tell us, is to get rid of waste. We grow old, we get sick and die, not because we wear out, but because our passages get clogged so we cannot take in new life. How are we to get rid of all the decomposed matter, all the worn out cells, all the waste?

How does a Sanitary Engineer do it for a great city? He doesn't boil it or strain it or put strong drugs into it to kill off the harmful germs. He doesn't worry about the negative elements. He bends all his energies to encouraging the positive ones.

"The pollution in sewage," says Dr. John Arthur Wilson, "consists of bacteria and the soluble products of decomposition. The protozoa devour the bacteria and the polluting materials, and finally settle out with the sludge and become part of the resulting fertilizer. Through the introduction of oxygen, conditions are created favorable to the growth of the animal cells, and purification results. If the air supply is cut off, the animal cells succumb, the bacteria win and the sewage becomes foul again."

How is water purified before being turned into the mains of a great city? In the same way—by being sprayed into the air, thoroughly oxygenated, thus encouraging the growth of the protozoa and giving them the strength and numbers to devour any bacteria the water may contain.

How is your body kept healthy? You breathe in millions of germs with every breath in a crowded street. If your nostrils and throat were examined this minute, it would probably be found that a billion germs were making these passages their playground. But why worry? There are probably two billion friendly germs making a meal off those bacteria, ridding you of poisons, helping to keep your system clean and healthy.

Encourage the life, and the disease will vanish. Turn on the light and the darkness disappears. Keep your passages open—your mental ones even more than your physical—and LET the good come in.

Life is activity. Life is movement. Life is like a great stream that turns the wheels of every powerhouse along its banks. Its power lies in its movement. If it were still, it would generate no power. And the same is true of the powerhouses along its banks. If they do not let the water flow THROUGH them, they get no power. If they plug up their outlets, the water stops flowing in. It is only as they keep their passages open and let the water flow through that they get the benefit of its activity and power.

What then is the answer? Isn't it that life is a continuous giving out of power? That the more we want, the more we must give? That just as we develop our muscles by using them, so must we develop vitality and riches and power of all kinds by giving out what we have?

You remember the experience of Job in the olden days, how his afflictions increased despite all his prayers and lamentations, but how he was promptly cured when he prayed for his friends. The moment he started giving out, new and perfect life flowed into him.

How can we use this principle to help ourselves and our friends and loved ones?

1st—By relaxing. Know that disease or accident or other misfortune is not something in itself that you have to fight. It is merely a LACK of the right condition. So relax. Stop resisting. Stop closing up your mental and bodily passages. Instead, open them wide to LIFE.

2nd, Bless the good. Stimulate the life in you. Encourage it. Praise and bless it. Praise, you know, brings increase. Whatever is praised and blessed, multiplies. Use the power of praise and blessing to multiply the life in you. The Hebrews of old observed that—"A merry heart causeth good healing, but a broken spirit drieth up the bones."

3rd, Open wide your passages by getting rid of everything that clogs them, mentally or physically. Get rid of your resentments by blessing all who have wronged you, and all you have ever wronged. Make way for life to flow into you. Rid your mind of anger and grief and worry and all resentments, start the life flowing by giving out thoughts of love, of helpfulness, of joy and thanksgiving. As long ago as ancient Greece, Plato wrote—"If the head and the body are to be well, you must begin by curing the soul."

The story is told of a woman who had gone to consult a physician. Looking around at all the pained and worried and miserable faces in his waiting room, the thought came to her—"Why do we sit here looking so miserable? Let's leap up into that other land where all is health and cheer." She went home and prayed—"I am in your hands, Lord. I have burned all my bridges behind me. What would you have me do—now, this very minute?" And the answer that came to her was—"Rise and sing, we are all God's happy little children."

4th, See in your mind's eye the perfect image of your body as you would have it be, and then "Believe that you HAVE it." First the Word, the mental image, you remember, then the creation. You can't have the perfect house without the perfect blue print. See yourself as you would have yourself be—then pour all your life into that image. Bless that image. Salute the Divinity in it. Pay no further attention to the disease or imperfect image you may now have. Give all your praise and blessing and thanksgiving to that new and perfect image.

5th, Start using that new and perfect image, no matter on how small a scale you must make the start. Do as the man did who was paralyzed. He found he could use only one finger. So he started the mental image of his new self with that one finger, and began using it just as much as he could. Before long, the fingers next to it began showing life. He used them. Soon the hand, the arm, the whole body responded to his determined urge for life, for activity. He had given all that he had, he had made way for life—and new life flowed into and through him.

When you want to help others, the same rules apply. Bless the life in them. Start with whatever of good and perfect life they have, and use that to make new life flow through them. Bless that perfect life, praise and give thanks for it. See in your mind's eye the perfect image of them that God made, and send the current of your life into that perfect image through your faith, your earnest desire to help them.

You remember when the woman with an emission of blood touched Jesus in the crowd and was healed, He said—"Virtue has gone out of me." Well, "virtue" or life must go out of you when you help others. You must give of your vital force—your prayers and praise and blessing and thanksgiving—there must be an outpouring of your spiritual energy, before you can put new life into the perfect image of the one you wish to help.

That is why, as in the case of Job, prayer for others so often helps one's self. You have given out life—so new life flows into you. You have opened the passages, so the stream flows more strongly through you.

It is true that you cannot heal another. But it is also true that you don't have to. The only place you can help another to be healed is through your own mind. When you can see him as healed there, when you can picture him in your mind's eye as perfect and then get the serene feeling of relief and thankfulness that he is healed, you have done your part towards bringing about that healing. Now start the life flowing through that perfect image by going through the movements and activities yourself that a perfect body such as his should be doing, at the same time visualizing him doing the same things.

There must always be someone to release power, someone with the understanding and faith to say—"Let this thing come to pass!" If some friend is afflicted, and seems unable to make the start himself, do you release the power for him, and thereby attain greater power for yourself.

In his book "After Everest," Dr. Howard Somervell tells of two patients whom he turned down as being incurable—cases of malignant cancer. Both were completely cured when groups of people prayed for their recovery.

Such cases have become so common that the Episcopal Church, some years ago, appointed a joint commission of leading medical men and clergymen to investigate and report upon the practicability of healing through prayer. Their report, signed among others by Dr. Charles H. Mayo, said that—

"Christian healing has passed beyond the stage of experiment and its value cannot be questioned. Spiritual healing is no longer the hope of a few, but the belief and practice of a large and rapidly increasing number of persons."

The New York American summed up their report in

these words: "It was the essence of the early Christian religion to save from sickness as well as sin. Christ's life is a long record of healing disease and raising from death. We have been calling His acts miracles. Now modern science and religion begin to suspect that He was demonstrating the operation of a principle which is eternal. Indeed, Christ told His disciples to go forth into the world and demonstrate this principle. He said:

"Verily, verily, I say unto you, he that believeth in Me, the works that I do, shall he do also; and greater works than these shall he do."

"More things are wrought by prayer
Than this world dreams of. Wherefore, let thy voice
Rise like a fountain for me night and day.
For what are men better than sheep or goats
That nourish a blind life within the brain,
If, knowing God, they lift not hands of prayer
Both for themselves and those who call them friend?
For so the whole round earth is every way
Bound by gold chains about the feet of God."

Exercise for Chapter Eighteen

The First Law of Nature

There is one law of Nature that was considered so important that it was repeated no less than six times in the very first chapter of the Bible, and is referred to in numerous places thereafter. That law is—"Everything increases after its kind."

Throughout all of Nature you will find no variations of this law. Take the mineral kingdom as a start. A group of cells shows "cohesion" or the ability to stick together. Why? Because all are of the same kind, the electronic life in them revolving at the same rate. In like manner, they possess the ability to *repel* any other kind of cell that might attempt to join the group, because the rate of motion in those other cells is different.

In the vegetable kingdom, the process of selection is greater. Each group of cells attracts to itself from its immediate environment all those cells that are exactly like those forming that particular plant, and it repels all others. Thus tomatoes and potatoes and beans and a dozen other vegetables can all grow side by side, yet remain entirely separate and distinct in their organisms. No part of the potato will be attracted by or absorbed into the tomato, or vice versa. Each uses its selective properties to remain true to type.

Like Attracts Like

It all goes back to the electrons and protons of which each individual cell—whether mineral, animal or vegetable—is made. Everything in Nature starts with this. A single electron is touched in just the right way to start it revolving on its axis. Its awakening affects other particles of a like nature, drawing them to it, setting them in motion likewise. Each electron is a small universe in itself, with revolving particles turning about a common center with the same motion and at the same relative distances that the earth and planets revolve around the sun.

It is in the RATE of movement that variation occurs. Those groups that have a higher rate of movement produce the higher forms of life. The moment that the rate of movement changes, form and color are changed, and in the case of complicated organisms like the human body, the change in the rate of movement of any part of the body may readily affect the harmony of the whole, for with differences in rotation, the faster units have a tendency to break away from and throw off the slower.

Something of this kind is going on in the body all the time. Older cells slow down, break away and are thrown out. That is how a dog follows the scent of its master— by the trail of old, discarded cells that he is continually throwing off. It is only when we *fail* to throw off the inharmonious cells that disease gets a foothold and we sicken or die.

Remember this: Starting with the individual cell, we attract to us only those elements that are identical in quality and character with ourselves and that are revolving at the same rate of speed. Our selective ability is such that we are able to pick such material as will preserve our quality and identity. This is true of our bodies, of our circumstances, of our environment. Like attracts like. If we are not satisfied with ourselves as we are, if we want a healthier body, more attractive friends, greater riches and success, we must start at the core—*within ourselves!*

And that core lies in our thoughts. Thought can speed up or slow down the rate of motion of the whole body. Thought can retard certain organs, and thus cause inharmony throughout the whole body. Thoughts of anger, fear, worry, envy, hatred or discouragement can create such inharmony as to bring about cancerous growths in the body as well as disaster in one's affairs. You can cut out such growths with a surgeon's knife, and thus help the body organism to throw off the inharmonious elements, but an easier way, a better way, is to bring the body back into harmony, bring the entire organism into tune.

In Tune with the Infinite

The first essential to putting yourself in harmony with the Infinite Good about you is to relax, to take off the brakes. For what is worry or fear or discouragement but a brake on your thinking and on the proper functioning

of your organs, a slowing down of your entire rate of
activity?

It is said that the Devil once held a sale of all the tools
of his trade. Everything was displayed—his keen-edged
daggers of jealousy, his sledge-hammer of anger, his bow
of greed, his arrows of lust and covetousness, his weapons
of vanity and fear and envy and pride. And under each
was its price.

But in the place of honor, framed and set apart from
all the rest was a small wedge, dented and marked with
use. The name of this wedge was "Discouragement," and
the price set upon it was higher than all the other tools
combined.

Asked the reason for this amazing difference, the Devil
explained—"It is because this is the one tool I can use
when all others fail. Let me get that little wedge into a
man's consciousness, and it opens the way for everything
else. That wedge has opened more doors to me than all
my other weapons combined."

Few things will slow down your rate of activity as
much as Discouragement. Few offer greater resistance to
the good that is trying to manifest through you.

You remember Ohm's Law in electricity. $C = E \div R$.
C is the amount of electrical energy to be delivered at the
point of use. E is the amount available from the power
house. R represents the resistance offered by all the things
through which the current must flow.

If there were no resistance, the full amount of current
generated by E would be delivered. But there is always
some resistance. Even the best conductor offers a little,
and you can't deliver current without a conductor. So the
amount actually delivered depends upon the power available, divided by the resistance.

All the energy of the universe is around you. You can
have anything of good you desire. But it must first go

through you—*and you won't let it.* You put up more resistance to good than all the non-conductors that ever
interfered with an electrical circuit. You can't believe that
good is so easily available. You feel that it can come to
you only after hard struggle, and disappointments and
pain. You insist upon putting these non-conductors in its
path. You add worries and fears and hates and envies, so
that by the time the good reaches you, its current is so
weak that there is little left.

Like attracts like. Hate brings hate, and all the ills that
follow in its wake. Envy and fear and worry attract discord and disease. If you want health, happiness, in your
life, if you are seeking riches and success, attune your
thoughts to these. BLESS the circumstances that surround you. Bless and praise those who come in contact
with you. Bless even the difficulties you meet, for by blessing them, you can change them from discordant conditions
to favorable ones, you can speed up their rate of activity
to where they will bring you good instead of evil.

It is only lack of RESPONSIVENESS to good that
produces the lacks in your life. Good works on the plane
of EXPANSION. Good revolves at a high rate of activity. You can key your activity to that same rate by an
expectant, confident state of mind. You can bring all your
surroundings and circumstances up to that same level by
BLESSING them, PRAISING the good in them.

Remember, the basic magnet lies in your own thoughts.
Upon the quality and activity of that magnet depend the
good or evil that will be drawn to you. You are the Master of your fate. You are the architect who determines the
materials that are to be used in making your life and your
circumstances. You have the power of SELECTIVITY.

Knowing that, can you afford to select any but the best
for the circumstances and the surroundings that YOU
must live in?

What we all want to externalize is health instead of sickness, abundance instead of limitation, joy instead of inharmony. That being so, why not use our power of selection to attract these to us instead of their opposites?

If your need is for health, take your thought completely away from contemplation of symptoms and conditions. Think of your body as HAVING the vigor and strength and vitality that it should. Hold to that thought in spite of every appearance, and you will presently find your rate of movement attuned to the point where it is drawing to you only health and vigor, throwing off everything unlike these.

In the Gospel of St. Mark, you will find it written—"Nothing outside a man can defile him by entering him." And Emerson expressed the same thought when he wrote —"Nothing outside me has any power over me."

The truth of these statements lies in our power of selection. Just as the very lowest forms of mineral life have the power to repel any other kind of cell that attempts to join their group, because of the difference in their rate of motion, so you—the highest form of life— have the power to throw off any condition or circumstance that tries to attach itself to you.

For you have far greater power than the minerals. You have the power not merely to throw off those things that differ in their rate of motion from yours, but you can go farther—*you can change your own rate of motion!* You can speed it up or slow it down at will. And all without outside aid—through the medium of your thoughts.

You have seen marching men, so tired they could hardly lift their feet off the ground, change their weary shuffle to a vigorous, swinging stride—when the band struck up a popular martial tune. You have seen hunters, dog-tired after a day of fruitless tramping, take on new energy instantly when the game suddenly sprang up before them. You have seen parents, ready to drop from exhaustion, forget all their tiredness when some loved child dropped in on them unexpectedly.

But you don't need outside aid to speed up your rate of motion and throw off all the Old Men of the Sea that have fastened themselves upon your shoulders. You can supply that speed-up yourself. And the quick way, the sure way, is through confident affirmations.

When you find yourself saying—"I am tired," or "I am sick," deny it at once. Say, instead—"No! I AM is the name given to the God in me. I AM strong, active, refreshed. I AM energy, I AM strength, I AM power. I AM one with God. His strong, free, pure life is now active in and through every cell in my body. I AM one with all the good in the universe."

When you unify the rate of motion of your body with all that is good in the universe, you attract that good to you—health, happiness, riches, love. But be sure to leave no obstructions between you and that good. Put no circuit-breakers of hatred or resentment, no insulation of jealousy or envy, in its path. Say frequently—"Dear Father, now I AM one with all the good in the universe. I freely forgive any who have ever seemed to harm me, and I ask forgiveness of all I may have seemed to harm."

Love attracts. Fear repels. Love draws the good to you. Fear acts as insulation that keeps all the good away from you.

When you are sick, what has happened? Certain organs or parts of the body have slowed down in their rate of movement. Result? Inharmony. The different parts of the body are discordant, fighting against each other, moving at different rates of speed.

What is the remedy? First, to relax. Just as a thoroughly relaxed man cannot be angry, so a body thoroughly relaxed in all its parts cannot fight against itself.

So relax. Relieve the tension. Stop worrying and put everything lovingly in the hands of the Father.

Then start to speed up the ailing parts by blessing them, praising them, thanking God for them. Of an aching ear, for instance, you might say—"Blessed is my ear, for it is strong and clear and I hear well." Then put it lovingly and unworriedly in the hands of the Father to bring into tune with the rest of the body.

If told that you are assailed by certain germs, just remember that there is only one power, and that is God—Good. There cannot be two powers, two rates of motion, in you. The stronger must throw off the weaker. So put all the power of your thought, of your beliefs, into Good. Be like the gardener who, when asked what he did about weeds, said—"Weeds? I never give them a thought. I just concentrate on the flowers."

Claim the good. You believe, I am sure, that if Christ were here today, He could heal you of any ailment. Well, He is here in the spirit just as much as He was in the body 1900 years ago. And your belief in Him can speed up your rate of motion and heal you of any infirmity today just as surely as it could then.

Tell yourself and know—"I AM together with God." Then LET God do the work. Relax utterly and put your body entirely in His hands. Let its rate of movement be at one with His. When you can do that, you don't need to worry about disease or any other discordant condition. They will be thrown off of themselves. They simply can't remain in any body that is at one with the rate of motion of God—Good.

And by the same token, you will attract to yourself every element of good, for all of good is attuned to the one rate of motion. It is like a radio where all the good programs are on one wave length. You tune in on that wave length, and you get everything of good. You dial the others, and you get all manner of evil. With such a choice as that, wouldn't you choose always to be tuned in on the Good?

> "Through me now flows the life stream,
> Free, its cleansing waves roll,
> I enter the current
> And I am made whole."

CHAPTER NINETEEN

THE KEY TO POWER

IN ONE OF HIS fascinating stories of the Indian Mutiny, Louis Tracy tells of a native officer named Mohammed Khan who was invulnerable in battle.

"He is a lion among brave men," the natives would say, "but steel or lead cannot touch him. He hath a jadu (a fetich or amulet)." And in 40 years' service, that jadu never failed him. In a dozen pitched battles and scores of hill fights, he never received a wound, though comrades fell all about him. Yet nothing would persuade him to give the secret of his invulnerability.

It seems that at the outbreak of the Mutiny, Mohammed Khan was a lad of nineteen in one of the native cavalry regiments of which his father was Rissaldar-Major. Though most of the regiment joined the mutineers, he and his father swore to be true to their salt, and with a couple of troops of horse they were stationed in a mud fort near Delhi to serve as a refuge for the whites who escaped the massacre, and to help in every way they could.

In a little town some miles away, the natives murdered the English Resident, but because of the hate of one of their number, they decided on a special refinement of cruelty in the killing of his wife and sister and the three little children.

They told them first they were not making war on women, and that they would escort them through the jungle to within a couple of miles of the fort, and leave them to make their way to their friends in safety. But they instructed the soldiers who were to form their escort that, after letting the women get a hundred yards' start across the plain towards the fort, just when safety was in sight and their fears gone, they were to shoot them down!

The soldiers carried through the program as directed. They conducted the women and children to the edge of the jungle. They bade them good-bye and saw them start joyfully towards the fort. Then they opened fire. Missing the first volley, they ran forward to do their murderous work with knives and clubbed muskets, when from the woods behind them came in rapid succession two shots, and the rearmost of the soldiers fell dead. Before the others could recover from their surprise, a native cavalryman was upon them, cutting and thrusting with his saber, and before five minutes had passed, every man of that treacherous escort was dead.

That young cavalryman was Mohammed Khan. He had been out on patrol the previous evening and lost his way. As he did not know the country well, he had tied his horse to a tree and slept until morning. Just as he was saddling at dawn to ride back to the fort, he heard the soldiers approaching, and cautiously waited to see who they were and what they were going to do. When they opened fire, he first emptied his carbine and pistol, then mounted and charged them with his saber.

When the fight was over, the women and children ran to him and fell on their knees and thanked him. When he protested, they made him kneel with them, and they prayed to God for him, weeping as they prayed, and making each child repeat the words after them. They prayed the King of Kings to safeguard him from all risks, to make him happy and prosperous, and to grant him a peaceful and honorable old age.

Never did that scene efface itself from Mohammed

Khan's memory—the tearful, hysterical women, the awe-struck children, the bodies lying about where they had fallen. And never did the sense of protection that seemed to enfold him then, leave him.

And as they prayed, so was it with him. Well might he have said with the Psalmist of old:

"He that dwelleth in the secret place of the most High shall abide under the shadow of the Almighty.

"He shall cover thee with His feathers, and under His wings shalt thou trust; His truth shall be thy shield and buckler.

"Thou shalt not be afraid for the terror by night; nor for the arrow that flieth by day; nor for the pestilence that walketh in darkness; nor for the destruction that wasteth at noonday.

"A thousand shall fall at thy side, and ten thousand at thy right hand; but it shall not come nigh thee.

"There shall no evil befall thee, neither shall any plague come nigh thy dwelling.

"For He shall give His angels charge over thee; to keep thee in all thy ways."

Yet he never told the story. No one in the regiment, even among his brothers, knew it. Why? Because to give the secret of his jadu would have dispelled its power! By keeping it stored safely in his own mind, it grew in strength until nothing could do him harm!

You have seen a kettle of water boiling away, the steam pouring out of the spout, scarce enough left to rattle the lid. Yet if you stop up the spout for a few minutes, what happens? The steam quickly attains such a pressure that it blows the lid off entirely!

Professor Sigmund Freud has shown how ideas work in much the same way, attaining a pressure that blows the top off things when they have no outlet for expression. He shows that fears, long held, are responsible for many nervous diseases; that sex repressions cause many others; and by the mere searching out in the patient's mind the reason for his fear or repression, and getting him to talk about it, he has released the pressure and saved many a person from nervous breakdown or even insanity.

That is the basis of all psychoanalysis—to locate the hidden reasons for the patient's fears or repressions, reasons that sometimes date so far back that the patient himself has forgotten them—and release the pressure by getting him to talk of them. That is why, so often, the telling of one's troubles to a doctor relieves them.

Talk is a safety valve. The water boils in the kettle of our mind, and the steam escapes through the spout of our mouth. When the boiling water contains noxious vapors like fears and repressions and thoughts of disease, the mouth is truly a safety valve. We let them out and when presently they have all boiled off, we can forget them.

Of course, that may be hard on those we tell them to, for we are putting similar noxious vapors into the minds of others. So when you want to get rid of such, it is well to do it to some practitioner of the mental sciences, who can dispel them from himself as well as from you.

The trouble with most people is that they do not stop when they have released all their noxious vapors. They let the steam escape in the same way—through the spout of their mouths. They have a constructive idea. And every idea, good or bad, tends to express itself in physical activity. But before this one can gather sufficient force to amount to anything, they dissipate all its steam by telling it to the first one who will listen to it!

You have an idea for a new and better way of doing your work, let us say. Instead of letting it simmer for a while, gathering force and power and seeking out channels that will make its accomplishment easy, you go off at half cock, as it were. You tell your plan to some of your fellow workers, and they pick holes in it and discourage you. Or you go to the boss with it before it is complete

and he can't see it. And when you are all through, you feel
like a pricked balloon.

Take a lesson from the experience of Samson. As we
have often said before, we believe the Bible to be the
greatest work of practical psychology ever written.
Whether or not Samson actually slew a thousand Philistines with the jaw-bone of an ass and pulled a lion apart
with his bare hands, from a psychological point of view
the account is sound. Just listen:

> "And the angel of the Lord appeared unto the woman, and
> said unto her . . .
> "Thou shalt conceive, and bear a son; and no razor shall come
> on his head; for the child shall be a Nazarite unto God from
> the womb; and he shall begin to deliver Israel out of the hand
> of the Philistines.'
> . . . "Then went Samson down to Timnath; and behold, a
> young lion roared against him. And the Spirit of the Lord
> came mightily upon him, and he rent him as he would have rent
> a kid, and he had nothing in his hand; *but he told not his
> father* or his mother what he had done.
> "And it came to pass afterward, that he loved a woman in
> the valley of Sorek, whose name was Delilah.
> "And the lords of the Philistines came up unto her, and said
> unto her, 'Entice him, and see wherein his great strength lieth,
> and by what means we may prevail against him, that we may
> bind him to afflict him; and we will give thee every one of us
> eleven hundred pieces of silver.'
> "And Delilah said to Samson, 'Tell me, I pray thee, wherein
> thy great strength lieth, and wherewith thou mightest be bound
> to afflict thee.'
> "And Samson said unto her, 'If they bind me with seven
> green withs that were never dried, then shall I be weak, and be
> as another man.'
> "Then the lords of the Philistines brought up to her seven
> green withs which had not been dried, and she bound him with
> them.

"Now there were men lying in wait, abiding with her in the chamber. And she said unto him, 'The Philistines be upon thee, Samson.' And he brake the withs, as a thread of tow is broken when it toucheth the fire. So his strength was not known.

"And Delilah said unto Samson, 'Behold, thou has mocked me, and told me lies; now tell me, I pray thee, wherewith thou mightest be bound.'

"And he said unto her, 'If they bind me fast with new ropes that were never occupied, then shall I be weak, and be as another man.'

"Delilah therefore took new ropes, and bound him therewith, and said unto him, 'The Philistines be upon thee, Samson.' And there were liers in wait abiding in the chamber. And he brake them from off his arms like a thread.

"And Delilah said unto Samson, 'Hitherto thou hast mocked me, and told me lies: tell me wherewith thou mightest be bound.' And he said unto her, 'If thou weavest the seven locks of my head with the web.'

"And she fastened it with the pin, and said unto him, 'The Philistines be upon thee, Samson.' And he awakened out of his sleep, and went away with the pin of the beam, and with the web.

"And she said unto him, 'How canst thou say, I love thee, when thine heart is not with me? Thou hast mocked me these three times, and hast not told me wherein thy great strength lieth.'

"And it came to pass, when she pressed him daily with her words and urged him, so that his soul was vexed unto death:

"That he told her all his heart, and said unto her, 'There hath not come a razor upon mine head; for I have been a Nazarite unto God from my mother's womb: if I be shaven, then my strength will go from me, and I shall become weak, and be like any other man.' "

It was not the loss of his hair that made Samson weak. It was the loss of his secret. That secret had been with him from birth. None had spoken of it to him but his mother and father, and he had never before mentioned it to a soul. It filled him like steam in a boiler. It gave him unlimited power to work havoc among his enemies. But when he opened the spout and loosed off all the pressure, he was no better or stronger than any other man and the Philistines took him and put out his eyes and threw him into prison. In the solitude of that prison, the strength came back to him. With no one to talk to, no way to release the pressure, the steam again accumulated, and when the Philistines would have made sport of him, he brought down their temple upon their heads!

And in solitary thought, strength will come to you, too. Don't tell your plans, your ideas. Let them simmer, and grow perfect, and accumulate strength until they force you to achieve your goal. Let them work up the pressure that blows off the lid and makes openings for you. Let them grow until they are like a mighty river which first sweeps over the dam, then carries dam and all before it!

Looking Backward

Life is filled with opportunities, and there is always room at the top in some line of endeavor for you, no matter how crowded the bottom may be. The God in You has a special genius for something and he is merely waiting to be directed into the right channels of service. Your job is to discover and develop that particular bent.

But do not meantime complain about your present work or position. Whatever it is, depend upon it, it is the right place for you until you have learned its lesson. Success is not some sudden achievement. Success is like any other great structure—it must be built up brick by brick, and all manner of skills and materials enter into its making. What you are doing now is just as necessary to it as the higher-paid work you will probably be doing a year from now.

Old wealth is always dying rapidly. In a recent letter, one of the big Economic Forecasting Services stated that 83% of those who have money when they are 35 years old, lose it by the time they are 60. Even the great fortune of the first Baron Rothschild, wizard of finance, had shrunk by 85% within the ten years after his death. Old wealth is continually dying, but God is always creating all things new, so use the prayer suggested by Brown Landone in a recent issue of Nautilus:

"O God, who maketh all things new, I will get in line with thee, I am this hour healed of my blindness of forever looking at all old things; I am healed of my dumbness of holding on to the old and letting new things pass by me. As all things are being made new, so I am made new. I arise, I come up out of my cellars of want. I walk forth into the fields of new wealth and live in the midst of their abundance."

The Chinese have a saying that—"The path of duty is near, yet men seek it afar off. Go home and seek it, and you will not lack teachers." Every job is an open door to a better one, but you can open that door only by doing your job better than anyone else has ever done it before—doing it as to the Lord, in a spirit of loving service.

There is a task for today which can be done NOW better than at any other time. Each minute, each day, has its share in the making of all your tomorrows. Your future will be richer or poorer to the extent that you do that work now, or leave it undone.

"Just where I am I must be brave;
This is my test, the test God gave.
Although I long for higher tasks,
Right here I must do what life asks."
—EVELYN GAGE BROWNE

So many of us keep looking back to our lost opportunities, lost fortunes, and think—"If only I had that chance again, what wonders I could do." Whatever the experience was, good or bad, it taught its lesson. Remember the lesson, and forget the rest. We go, you know, in the direction in which we are headed. "Look not behind thee." the Lord bade Lot in the olden days. And you remember what happened to Lot's wife when she failed to heed that command. Many a man today has met the same fate and become no better than a pillar of salt (or, in today's parlance, a "Dead one"), by hugging to himself his losses, bemoaning his altered position, instead of using the experience acquired from these to gain greater position, increased riches.

> "All have a share in the beauty;
> All have a part in the plan;
> What does it matter what duty falls
> To the lot of man?
> Someone has blended the plaster,
> And someone has carried the stone.
> Neither the man nor the Master
> Ever has builded alone;
> Making a roof for the weather,
> Building a house for the King;
> Only by working together
> Men have accomplished a thing."

In the paper some time ago appeared an account of the finding of the tomb of King Zoser, famous Pharaoh of the Third Dynasty, who lived about 4,000 B.C. King Zoser was the builder of the great step pyramid near Sakkara.

The Egyptians of Zoser's day were far more civilized than any of the nations around them. The Greeks, for instance, were still wandering tribes of freebooters and pirates. Rome was not even thought of.

But away off in Asia was a country as far ahead of Egypt, as Egypt was of its savage neighbors.

That country was China.

4,000 years before Christ, China was already a highly civilized country. People lived in houses, rode in carriages, dressed in rich silks, wore leather shoes, ate food from plates, measured time by sundials, even carried umbrellas!

In those days China was the seat of learning, of civilization, of progress. And do you know why?

Because China alone among all the earlier nations had developed a religion without fear and without priests, while other countries were still struggling along in deadly fear of fetich or taboo. When other nations were in the thrall of high priest or medicine man, China left every one to worship in his own way. Every man was free to progress. There were no taboos, no fetiches. There was nothing to hold man back.

So for thousands of years China went steadily forward, the vanguard of the nations. But then suddenly all progress stopped. For 2,500 years China has stood still while the world has passed her by. Today she stands—a tragic figure—one of the most backward of nations, prey of aggressors.

Why? Because She Looked Back!

That fearless, forward-looking religion of hers was turned backward—was ritualized! Instead of a religion of freedom of worship, it became one of forms and ceremonies. Instead of merely honoring one's ancestors, ancestor worship became the religion.

2,500 years ago there was born in China a man who so loved the ancient customs that he turned them into a state religion. His name was Kung-Fu-Tze, or, as we call it, Confucius.

Confucius spent all his early life collecting and editing the writings of his people. It was not until he was 51 years old that he was made Magistrate of the State of Chung-Tu. Within a year he had rid the city of crime—

not by rigorous penalties, not by a strong police force, but by an elaborate system of etiquette. Three hundred points of behavior, and three thousand points of etiquette—instead of the means, these became the end of existence.

Every action, under whatever circumstance, was worked out in its entirety, and rules laid down governing it. No initiative, no individual thinking was either wanted or tolerated. Men were divided into classes, and became merely animated dummies, to be worked in unison by the authorities above them who pulled the string.

No longer was the common man encouraged to better his condition. On the contrary, he was told by China's greatest religious teacher that there was no grosser guilt than to be discontented with his lot. There were but three jewels of character, and the choicest of the three was inactivity. Next to this was humility, and third, frugality.

No longer was the ambitious youth permitted to experiment, to progress. He was assured by China's most orthodox teacher that all change was injurious—that salvation could be attained only by adhering strictly to the religious and social order that was already established. Whatever had been was good. Whatever one's ancestors had done was to be revered. Whatever was new, untried, experimental, was bad.

Imagine the effect of such teachings, inculcated into the young of a nation for more than 2,500 years! A wonderful thing for those already rich, already in authority, but how about the poor workers? How about the millions of hopeless plodders? Is it any wonder China is backward?

From the beginning of time, the one unpardonable sin in Nature has been to stand still. When a nation or an institution or an individual becomes too complacent, when it feels that it has made all the progress that can be made, it is time to look for the undertaker. Its end is not far off. When a family takes more pride in its ancestors than in what it is doing today, you can write "Finis" across its history.

Lot's wife was not the first nor the last of mankind to be lost by looking backward. There is only one road for each of us. That is the road ahead. There is only one way to look. That is in front of you.

Forget what is past, except in so far as you can profit by the experience of past mistakes. Live in the present. Remember—"Each night I burn the records of the day. Tomorrow every soul is born again!"

Did you ever read Emerson's advice in his letter to his daughter? "Finish every day and be done with it. You have done what you could today; some blunders and absurdities no doubt crept in; but forget them as soon as you can. Tomorrow is a new day; you shall begin it well and serenely and with too high a spirit to be cumbered with your old nonsense. This day is for all that is good and fair. It is too dear to waste a moment on the forgotten yesterdays."

Life is Change—Progress

No single thing abides, but all things flow.
    Fragment to fragment clings; the things thus grow
Until we know and name them. By degrees
    They melt, and are no more the things we know.

Nothing abides. Thy seas in delicate haze
    Go off; those mooned sands forsake their place;
And where they are shall other seas in turn
    Mow with their scythes of whiteness other bays.

                      —LUCRETIUS

CHAPTER TWENTY

P-R-A-I-S-E

DID YOU EVER NOTICE that if you leave off the "P" from the word Praise, what you have left is *"Raise"?*

That is no mere accident, for wise men have realized for thousands of years that to praise is to raise the spirits and increase the power of the one praised. In the same way, praise of God and thankfulness for His gifts raises the spirits of the one who sings those praises to the heights of rare accomplishment.

Just as praise and thanksgiving freed Paul and Silas from the chains of the dungeon, so can they free you from worry and fear and the dungeons of dark despair. "I will sing unto Jehovah," sang the Psalmist of old, "because He hath dealt bountifully with me." And if we would have Him deal bountifully with us, it behooves us to praise and be thankful for the good we now have, no matter how small that good may seem to be.

"The righteous doth sing and rejoice," we are told in the Scriptures. And the Hebrew word used for "sing" means "to sing out loud, even to shout for joy." To sing with joy is one of the long-neglected truths of POWER. "The Sons of God shouted for joy."

The Kingdom of Heaven is the Kingdom of Expansion, and the way to expand what we have is through praise and joy and thanksgiving. Seldom indeed in the Bible do you find that God provides supply out of thin air. Almost always He requires the recipients of His bounty to start with what they have. The widow with the oil and meal, that other widow with a little oil, the feeding of the multitudes with the loaves and fishes, and scores of other cases, all started with the supply in hand. God expanded what they had. And God will expand what you have, if you rightly use the power of praise and thanksgiving.

But mere expansion is not enough. You might expand all the water in the world into steam, and get no good from it—if you had no engine in which to use the steam. You must have a purpose in mind if you are to get the utmost of good from your expansion. You must set a goal. You must plan the *form* in which that expanded energy is to make itself manifest. It can be in your body, in your circumstances, in your surroundings—in anything of good you may desire.

Some years ago the Journal of Education had a story that expressed this idea clearly. "There was once a prince," it read, "who had a crooked back. He could never stand straight up like even the lowest of his subjects. Because he was a very proud prince, his crooked back caused him a great deal of mental suffering.

"One day he called before him the most skilful sculptor in his kingdom and said to him: 'Make me a noble statue of myself, true to my likeness in every detail, with this exception—make this statue with a straight back. I wish to see myself as I might have been.'

"For long months the sculptor worked, hewing the marble carefully into the likeness of the prince, and at last the work was done, and the sculptor went before the prince and said: 'The statue is finished; where shall I set it up?' One of the courtiers called out: 'Set it before the castle gate where all can see it,' but the prince smiled sadly and shook his head. 'Rather,' said he, 'place it in a secret nook in the palace garden where only I shall see it.'

"The statue was placed as the prince ordered, and

promptly forgotten by the world, but every morning and every noon and every evening, the prince stole quietly away to where it stood and looked long upon it, noting the straight back and the uplifted head and the noble brow. And each time he gazed, something seemed to go out of the statue and into him, tingling in his blood and throbbing in his heart.

"The days passed into months and the months into years; then strange rumors began to spread throughout the land. Said one: 'The prince's back is no longer crooked or my eyes deceive me.' Said another: 'Our prince has the high look of a mighty man.' And these rumors came to the prince, and he listened with a queer smile.

"Then went he out into the garden to where the statue stood and behold, it was just as the people said, his back had become straight as the statue's, his head had the same noble bearing; he was, in fact, the noble man his statue proclaimed him to be."

2500 years ago, in the Golden Age of Athens, when its culture led the world, Grecian mothers surrounded themselves with beautiful statues that they might bring forth perfect children and that the children in turn might develop into perfect men and women.

Eleven months from now, YOU will have an entirely new body, inside and out. Not a single cell, not a single bit of tissue that is now in you will be there then. What changes do you want made in that new body? What improvements?

Then start right now getting that new model clearly in mind. Buy yourself a scrap book. Cut from the magazines a picture of the finest figure of a man or woman that you can find, and paste it on page one. Cut out other pictures, that show clearly different parts of your body that need developing or perfecting, and paste them on other pages. Then cut pictures of people doing the sort of things you would love to do—dancing, swimming, riding horseback, rowing, fishing, playing golf or tennis, anything you like—and paste them on different pages of your scrap book.

At the top and bottom of each page, or alongside the pictures, put such reminders and affirmations as these:

"Father God, I thank Thee for my glorious strength, my abiding health, my tireless energy."

"Vitalize Thy perfect image in me in perfect form."

"I am strong in the Lord and the power of His might."

"God made me in His own image. He is my strength and power. He maketh my way perfect. The joy of the Lord is my strength."

"Know ye not that ye are the temple of God and that the Spirit of God dwelleth in you?"

"Divine Love protects and sustains me. I am the open channel through which the healing currents of life are now flowing. God is my life. God is my health. In God is my trust."

Under a picture showing someone with a splendid chest, taking breathing exercises, put—

"The Spirit of the Lord hath made me, and the breath of the Almighty giveth me life."

Under one bathing—

"Wash me and I shall be whiter than snow."

Under a picture of the eyes—

"Open thou mine eyes, that in Thy light I may see the light."

Or, if your eyes are weak or troublesome, put—

"Jehovah openeth the eyes of the blind. Blessed are the pure in heart, for they shall see God. I see God in my eyes, in their perfect life and strength and wholeness. If thou can'st believe, all things are possible to him that believeth. According to thy faith be it done unto you."

Under picture at a well-filled table—

"Thou shalt eat thy bread with joy."

Under sleep—

"They that rest in the Lord shall renew their strength like the eagle. They shall walk and not faint, they shall run and not be weary. Thy Spirit strengthens both my soul and my body, and I rest in the peace of wholeness and health."

Under vigorous, happy, healthy older people—

"As my days, so shall my strength be. Behold, all things are becoming new. Thou shalt make me full of joy in Thy presence. Passing years have no effect upon my spiritual body. I am alive in Jesus Christ forever. I am a tower of strength and stability in the realization that God is my health. God's life is constant, unbroken, eternal. I am quickened in His consciousness of life. His constant power and strength sustain me and I am healed. I AM a perfect idea of God and all of life is with me now and always."

A long time ago, Epictetus said: "God has delivered YOU to YOUR care, and this is what He says to you— 'I have no fitter to trust than YOU. Preserve this body for me just as it is by nature; modest, beautiful, faithful, noble, tranquil.' "

You will find many affirmations to paste in your scrap book. Use any and all that seem helpful. But that saying of Epictetus is a good one to paste on the last page—a good one to bear always in mind. "God has delivered you to your care." And God gave you dominion. So think of yourself as well and strong. Think of your body as spiritual substance that is not subject to the ills of the flesh. Think of it as constantly changing, continually GROWING into the perfect image that you are holding before it.

The Kingdom of Heaven is the Kingdom of Expansion. If you have but a single perfect cell in your whole body, you can expand that cell into a perfect body, provided only that you hold before it the image of health and strength—not of sickness; provided only that you BELIEVE! "God made man but little lower than the Angels."

"Give Us This Day Our Daily Bread"

For your Prosperity and Abundant Supply Scrap Book, you cannot do better than start with that line from the Lord's Prayer—"Give us this day our daily bread."

Get a picture of a horn of plenty—a cornucopia—with all manner of good things pouring out of it, and paste it on the first page of your Scrap Book. Line the page with pictures of sparrows and lilies of the field, to remind you of Jesus' promise, and then put at the bottom of the page something like this:

"O God, beginning now I shall forever LET Thy Spirit Infinite become the sole dictator of my soul; and I shall never more take anxious thought of anything, but grow as the lilies grow, in peace and power, so that I shall have all I need, forever more."

The next page, I'd head with the line—"I can have what I want—*if I plant it.*" Under it, paste pictures of farmers or gardeners planting seed, only take a pen or pencil and change those seeds into $$$. Under these pictures, put—"The riches of the Spirit now fill my mind and affairs. I think prosperity, I talk prosperity and I know that prosperity and success are mine."

On other pages, show pictures of growing grain or other plants, with $$$ at the top instead of the usual grain or fruit. Use such affirmations as—"God is my inexhaustible and omnipotent source of abundant supply." "I accept the will of God, which is abundant prosperity for me." "If I continue to desire you, I shall have you, because I trust in God for all things I desire."

Then on succeeding pages, show pictures of great piles of money—bags of money, piles of paper money and currency all around the pages, and pictures of yourself pasted in the center, surrounded by riches. If you can find pictures of men digging up treasure hoards, put them in. Put in all kinds of pictures that imply riches and prosperity. Put in pictures of the sort of surroundings you will have, when you have manifested the riches you desire. Get pictures of a beautiful home—the home of your dreams. Show if possible, each room as you would have it furnished. Show the outside, with a wide driveway, bordered by a beautiful lawn, shrubbery around the house, trees in the background, the kind of car you would like to own drawn up before the house. Show even the wardrobes of fine clothes you would have, show horses or bicycles or whatnot for the children, show the flowers in your garden.

"When I got the Lessons of THE GOD IN YOU," wrote Mrs. Caroline Kroll of Indianapolis, in December, 1939, "I had only $12.00 a month. Now I have a nice home and everything is paid for. I am so happy." Mrs. Kroll had written us in the fall of '37 expressing her great desire for a home, and we suggested to her this Treasure Mapping method. She says in her last letter—"I never faltered in my home making, and tonight I am sitting in a good home of my own and never was any happier in my youth."

Remember, the first step in supplying a need is to know that it IS already supplied in the Mind of God. God has already given you all of good. It is yours for the taking, and the most perfect prayer is the deep realization that your need is already supplied. You don't have to waste energy wondering about the supply. All you have to do is to focus your energy upon *being* one with it.

Your desires are like acorns—visions of the mighty oaks they can grow to be. What you desire is and always has been yours. What man can conceive, man can achieve. It is the eye that makes the horizon. No man ever bettered his position by limiting himself in his own mind to the one he had. No man ever made a success of his business by thinking failure. Every success is achieved first in your own thoughts. You must work first on yourself, because all trouble, limitation and the like are states of consciousness. Change your thought and you change all. You get the conditions that belong to your consciousness. As Emerson put it—"No man was ever ridden down or talked down by anything but himself."

Look within yourself for the source of all power. I AM the great power of God expressing as ME. I AM the great abundance for all my needs and a surplus to spare. That to which I give my attention reveals itself. So give your attention to the things you want! Fill your Scrap Book with pictures of them. Put over and under and around them such affirmations as these:

"God is able to do exceeding abundantly above all that we ask or think, according to the Power that worketh in us. I rejoice in the bounty of God, constantly manifesting to meet my every need."

"If ye abide in Me and my words abide in you, ye shall ask what ye will and it shall be done unto you. For herein is the Father glorified, that ye bear much fruit." "Your Father knoweth what things ye have need of before you ask Him. Fear not, for it is the Father's good pleasure to give you the Kingdom. All that the Father hath is yours, and you are in all ways prospered."

"I will give thee hidden riches of secret places, that thou mayest know that I am the God of Israel." "If thou return to the Almighty, then shalt thou lay up gold as dust, and the gold of Ophir as the stones of the brooks." "I will sing unto Jehovah, because He hath dealt bountifully with me."

Remember that—"According to thy faith be it done unto you." So believe that you RECEIVE! If your beliefs are all for the future, you will get them in the distant future but never NOW. You will never quite catch up with them. "Now is the accepted time. Now is the day of salvation." Realize that all these good things are NOW coming into manifestation in your life. Bless and thank God for them NOW.

"Instead of pleading, 'God bless me,'
And making such a weary fuss,
How much better off we'd be
If we would smile awhile and say,
'I thank you, God, for blessing us today.'

"Instead of begging, 'God give me
And mine the things which our hearts crave,'
How much happier we'd be
If we would laugh with life, and say,
'We thank you, God, for what we have today.'"
                                    MARION B. SHOEN

"But what shall we do about pressing debts?" many will ask. First, make a list of all of them. Then, thank God for having sent such trustful people to your aid, thank Him for the confidence they have shown in you. Next, see yourself in your mind's eye going the rounds of all your creditors, paying them in full. See their thankful, smiling faces. Hear yourself expressing to them your appreciation of their courtesy and forbearance, hear them telling you that they were glad to be of help, will be glad to extend the same credit to you in the future. Get pictures of people paying money over to merchants, paste in your own features over those of the debtors, and under them put such affirmations as these:

"Divine Love prospers all of us together NOW. God is our supply, through each of us to all, and through all of us to each.

I speak for all of us the word that multiplies money to all of us. And my word accomplishes that whereunto I send it. In God is my trust."

"When I worry, I am not trusting God. When I trust God, I have nothing to worry about."

"I put the payment of these debts lovingly in the hands of the Father with a child-like trust. That which is for my highest good will come to me."

Then do your part by using some of whatever money you receive to pay these just debts, and as you pay out the money, bless it in some such wise as this: "I bless thee . . . and be thou a blessing! As I pay out this money, I bless it. May it enrich everyone who touches it. The value of this substance I hold in my hand is this day magnified, for I perceive that it is truly a symbol of my heavenly Father's inexhaustible riches. Go forth, increase, multiply and bring forth fruit an hundredfold!"

Here is a prayer suggested by R. A. D., in a recent issue of NAUTILUS, to be used in connection with your list of debts:

"Father, I thank Thee that thou hast opened the way for me to pay every bill on this list, sending the money for each one before it is due. I place this expense sheet absolutely and unconditionally in Thy hands, and from the depths of a rich consciousness, I thank and praise Thee that the money for each separate item already is provided, awaiting only my claim to bring it into evidence. The glory of Thy radiance shining before me, Infinite Father, has opened the way for my unfailing prosperity and for a success greater than I ever before have experienced. I put from me every thought of limitations or lack and go free to have an abundance of all good."

The right job is the most pressing problem for many people. And you can help yourself or others to that right work through "Treasure Mapping" in the same way that you can bring riches or health or any other good thing.

The first essential, of course, is to know what you want. What kind of work would you most like to do? What are you best fitted for? What is your ultimate ambition? Get a Scrap Book and paste in it first a picture of yourself. After deciding on the line of work you want to devote yourself to, take inventory of yourself and think in what position you are now fitted to start. Then get a picture from the magazines of someone working in that position, paste it in your Scrap Book, and if you have a snap-shot of yourself that you can substitute for the face in the picture, do so.

Decide then what is the next position you will be fitted for in the line of work you have adopted, and paste a picture of someone in that position on the next page of your Scrap Book. Fill succeeding pages with logical steps in your progress, right on up to the very top. When you feel that your work will entitle you to a private office, paste in a picture of someone representing yourself seated at a desk in a sumptuously furnished office, with his title lettered on the door or on the side of the desk, and then letter in your name over the title.

And remember, no one ever got a good job by limiting himself mentally to a poor one. Admit to yourself that you are good. Then let others find it out by the service you give. That is the key to any door you wish to unlock. Yourself PLUS is your fortune. Your affairs PLUS is success.

Paste over and under and around your pictures such affirmations as these: "God is with me in all that I do." "If God be for you, who can be against you?" "Know ye not that ye are Gods, sons of the Most High?" What should your situation be like? What is it like in the Divine Mind, in the Eternal Plan? "Your Father knoweth what things ye have need of before you ask Him. Fear not, for it is the Father's good pleasure to give you the Kingdom.

All that the Father has is yours, and you are in all ways prospered." "If ye abide in Me and My words abide unto you, ye shall ask what ye will and it shall be done unto you. For herein is the Father glorified, that ye bear much fruit." "With good will, doing service as to the Lord and not to man." "Whether therefore ye eat or drink, or whatever ye do, do all to the glory of God."

The same principles that help you to a better position will help you to make your business grow and prosper, when you have a business of your own. Many a man has started with practically nothing, and built a fortune, simply by taking God into partnership with him.

Start your Scrap Book with a picture of yourself and of your business as it is now. The . on each succeeding page, show it growing bigger and better. Picture the service you want to give your customers. Picture thousands of them taking advantage of that service. Picture yourself and your helpers serving ever greater numbers, picture your product in the hands of more and more users, picture its manufacture in great volume, its shipping, its sale, everything you can connected with it. And let every picture show progress, growth, *expansion*. See yourself serving the world.

Under those pictures, put inspiring affirmations. "I am a partner and co-worker with God." "It is the purpose of Universal Mind to see men prosper, that they may express more of life, love, happiness and understanding, thus reflecting more of God. Our product is the connecting link between this demand and God's supply. The need is expanding continually and we have the will and the intelligence to see and meet it. Therefore, there is a continually growing demand for our product, that increases as I realize the spiritual significance of my work and make better products for my customers. It is in my power to make my customers better qualified, through the equipment that I provide, for prosperity and success. I delight in that power. I increase that power by using it for the honor, glory and pleasure of my customers and myself."

"Father, this business has to be good, so You handle it for me. I put it and all my affairs lovingly in Your hands, with a child-like faith. That which is for my highest good will come to me. One on God's side is a majority, and I am together with You, so all things are working together for my good and I am working with them in the wisdom and the power of the Spirit."

"God is in control. God is Spirit, good omnipotent. Apart from Him, there is no overcoming power. God is life, love and peace. God's will now fulfilled in me is abundant work for our bu. iness."

"The Spirit that multiplied the loaves and fishes for Jesus increases my substance, and I manifest prosperity."

But remember to give "good measure" to all, customers and co-workers alike, for "All who joy would win must share it—*Happiness was born a twin.*"

Many who have no business to worry about have homes or pieces of property or whatnot that they wish to sell, and at times this is a problem. Yet it is a problem that lends itself to the same methods outlined above, as you can judge from the following letter dated May 15th, 1940, from one of the subscribers to THE GOD IN YOU:

"When I received Robert Collier's Course THE GOD IN YOU, we were in debt and sometimes wondered what the next meal was to be, even though we owned our cottage and three lots. It seemed we couldn't get a buyer, nor could we even borrow on the property, even though it was clear, as it was in a run-down neighborhood.

"Since reading the Course, we have sold all St. Louis County property and purchased this 96-acre farm at Belle. paying cash for it and clearing ourselves of debt, as we sold most of the property for cash, a thing we could not have done without the help of THE GOD IN YOU. I believe we are about to see another manifestation of God's goodness as we have deposits under our ground which may indeed show God's goodness through riches to us."

The first essential is to BLESS the property you wish to sell. Know that it is a perfect image in the Divine Mind, made for the express purpose of manifesting good to someone, and declare that it is now sold to the right party at the right price.

Paste a picture of it in your Scrap Book. Think of every possibility for its development, and paste such pictures in your book, too. Show pictures of people looking at similar properties, of a sale being made, of the developments that will take place on it.

L. C. B. told in a recent issue of UNITY how she put her house "lovingly in the hands of the Father", then used this affirmation: "You, Christ, will find for us the perfect purchasers, who will love our home as we have loved it and recognize it for theirs and have sufficient cash to pay for it and have it NOW. Only through You are we fully aware of our omnipresent good." Within a short time, the article states, the house was sold for cash, and at their own price!

In Nautilus sometime ago, there was a similar story, the affirmation used in that case being the following: "God's loving Presence in all of us brings the right buyer NOW, who will pay the right price for the property and who will make money on the deal, while at the same time I will make money, God's money, in the selling. Divine Love now multiplies God's money and His Good to both buyer and seller, so that all shall be satisfied. All things now work together for good to me and to the new buyer of his property. We are the open channels through which

Divine Love is now flowing to this property and through it to all the world. All the barriers are now dissolved by Divine Love and my customer comes quickly and gloriously. God is our prosperity here and now. In God I trust and I know that all things work together to manifest the good we desire."

Whatever your problem, whatever your difficulty, you can get guidance if you will seek it. Give the facts to the God in You, ask Him for the solution, then leave the problem with Him and FORGET it in the serene confidence that He can and will find the answer. Never force the issue. Have faith in that God in You, and wait for a leading. "And thine ear shall hear a voice behind thee saying, this is the path; walk ye in it."

Our physical senses are able to discern only such objects as are on the same or a lower material plane than ourselves. Our ears, for instance, are attuned to but a few octaves of sound. Those of higher or lower wave lengths are inaudible to us. Yet the radio has taught us that all about us are sounds of music, of laughter, of drama and instruction.

The same is true with our eyes. We see only those things that are on the median light waves. The air may be full of television pictures, yet with our unaided eyes, we get none of them. Is it therefore so hard to believe that when the servant of the Prophet Elisha was fearful, because of the enemies all around, Elisha prayed and said —"Lord, I pray thee, open his eyes, that he may see. And the Lord opened the eyes of the young man; and he saw: And behold, the mountain was full of horses and chariots of fire round about Elisha."

May not the air around you be just as full of God's angels? May not Elisha's advice be just as good today— "Fear not, for they that be with us are more than they that be with them."

The Psalmist of old testified, you remember—"I have been young, and now am old, yet have I not seen the righteous forsaken, nor his seed begging bread."

Paste in your Scrap Book some of those old Biblical pictures of Angels guiding the children of God, of Guardian Angels, and over and under them put such affirmations as these: "God goes before me and opens the way." "Infinite Wisdom tells me just what to do." "I thank you, God, that you are here with us, and no matter what happens, we are all right." "Thou shalt not be afraid for the terror by night, nor for the arrow that flieth by day. He will cover thee with his pinions, and under his wings shalt thou take refuge."

Grace Crowell had a beautiful little poem along these lines in Unity Weekly:

"So often through God's Holy Book there shines
Some clear-cut word, some strong and simple phrase
That gleams like diamonds gathered from deep mines,
Set polished there to light our earthly days;
'And God was with the lad.' The words, how brief,
And yet what vital meaning in their sound,
As spoken of that ancient child of grief
Once left to die upon the hot, parched ground.

" 'And God was with the lad.' One need not look
For further information; all is told.
No gifted hand on earth could pen a book
Of strange biography that would unfold
With clearer words, nor could it tell as well
The God-companioned life of Ishmael."

Such affirmations cannot help but bring you peace and serenity. In Esquire Magazine some time ago there was an article telling about the fear-scent the body gives off, which is exceedingly irritating to any animal that senses it. "It is this fear-scent," said the article, "which causes dogs to attack people who have not molested them. A dog will respond quickly both in friendship and in training when he is approached without fear, but no one can fool him for a minute with a fearless exterior concealing a quaking heart, for the fear-scent is there.

"It is usually the fear that a canoe will tip over that causes the occupant to move suddenly in the wrong direction and thereby upset it. The fear of drowning, when suddenly thrown into the water, causes one to struggle frantically, and incidentally force himself under. It is an interesting scientific fact that a baby, until 24 hours old, can swim. Beyond that, it starts to realize fear and will sink. Fear is really the mental hazard of crossing your bridges before you come to them."

Is it not likely that the strong odor of our "fear-scent" registers on all we come in contact with, even though it be but subconsciously with human beings? Certain it is that when we approach people fearfully, we seem to repel them, for we seldom make a favorable impression, seldom get from them what we want.

The remedy? To BLESS the Divinity in all we come in contact with. You remember how often Jesus used the greeting—"Peace!" "Peace I leave with you; my peace I give unto you." And to the wind and waves, He bade— "Peace! Be still." And immediately the storm abated. "Acquaint now thyself with God and be at peace."

When trouble threatens in your home or your business, bless all concerned and mentally affirm—"Peace! The love of God is at work here. All of my forces are peaceful and harmonious. There is no resistance in me against the Spirit of God's peaceful life. Every anxious thought is stilled. Thy mighty confidence and Thy peace enfold me. The Spirit of God fills my mind, and abundance is everywhere manifest." Then go up to the thing you fear, con-

fidently, serenely. Or if it is something you must do, do it!
Once you have lost the fear of it, you will find it easy.

Evil? There is really no such thing. It is merely the
lack of Good. Summon the Good and the evil vanishes.
The same is true of enemies. Summon love for them,
salute the Divinity in them and bless them, and you will
find hate turned to love. Say mentally to the Divinity in
those who appear to be your enemies—"I recognize you.
You can't disguise yourself. You are a radiant child of
God. God's creations are all excellent. I bless you in the
name of Jesus Christ. Because you are a child of God,
you speak the truth and you are ever honest, just and
harmonious. My world is filled with splendid people, and
I love them all."

Be noble, and the nobleness that lies in other men,
sleeping but never dead, will rise in majesty to meet thine
own. Trust men, and they will be true to you. Treat them
greatly, and they will show themselves great.

Love overcometh, for all motion is cyclic. It circulates
to the limits of its possibilities and then returns to its
starting point. Thus any unselfish expenditure of energy
returns to you laden with gifts. Any unselfish act done
for another's benefit is giving part of yourself. It is an
outward flow of power that completes its cycle and returns
laden with energy.

The thoughts that we send forth always return with a
harvest of their kind. That which we put into the thought
comes back into our life. For our every thought there is a
response, a return of the pendulum that we have started
swinging. It is Emerson's Law of Compensation.

So you can see the wisdom in the dictum—"Into whatsoever house ye enter, first say—'Peace be to this
house!'"

But do more than bless those you come in contact with.
Act the part. Think kindly of them as well.

"Believe not each accusing tongue,
As most weak people do;
But still believe that story wrong
Which ought not to be true."

It is as easy to add, you know, as it is to subtract. Love adds. Fear and hatred subtract. You can reinforce your efforts with all the universe through love, as easily as you can separate yourself from everyone through hatred and fear.

Remember, evil is usually in the eye of the beholder. There is an old poem that depicts this graphically:

"Mistress Polly Wittenhouse
Lived on Whetstone Alley,
And she was like an angel
To little orphan Sally,
And she was like a harlot
To the lass across the way,
A 'good 'un' to the slavey
Who made her bed each day.
And she was like a siren
With the devil in her eye
To any roving sailor man
As he was passing by.

"So Mistress Polly Wittenhouse
Was either good or bad,
According to the need or greed
Each of her judges had,
According as her living
Threw a shadow on their own.
The sailors flung her kisses
And the lass she cast a stone.
And Sally and the slavey
They prayed for her each night,
And all of them that judged her
Knew that they judged her right."

A Scrap Book on Love is probably the most valuable one you can make. Put in it pictures of all your friends, all those you would have for friends. Paste in it pictures of the home of your dreams, of each separate room in it, of the furnishings, of everything about it.

Put in it every motto of peace and love and happiness you can find. Put in it pictures of children and toys and fireside scenes, dinners and parties and all the intimate happy things you can think of. Love that house and everything about it. Live in it mentally. Believe in it, and before long you will find that you ARE in it in actuality.

> "God lights the way, no more we grope
> Nor stumble on in troubled hope.
> We sow no seeds of care or strife,
> But those of love and joy and life.
> No more we strive to plan our lot,
> The Father fills our cup, unsought."

Sow the seeds in your Scrap Book and in your life of love and joy and happiness, then leave it to the Father to provide the means of making these seeds grow and bear fruit. "I have planted, Apollos watered, but God gaveth the increase."

Remember, the I AM in you is your part of Divinity. Some sage put it—"Whatever the Creator is, I AM." How often have you said—"I AM poor, I AM sick, I AM ignorant, I AM weak"—and thus fastened these evils upon yourself? You acknowledged a lack of something. What can you build with minus quantities? Only emptiness, void.

Reverse all that. Whenever you say "I AM", whenever you thus call upon the God in You, make it something you WANT. "I AM rich. I AM powerful. I AM well and whole and strong. I AM happy. I AM perfect in every way."

Make an I AM Scrap Book, with your picture on the first page, then pictures of supermen or genii or whatever your idea of power may be scattered throughout the pages of the book. Put in it pictures of all the things you would like to be and do. And fill it with such affirmations as these:

"The Spirit of Prosperity fills my mind and overflows into my affairs. God is my perfect will; through me it is done." "There is only one Presence and one Power in my life—God, the Good Omnipotent. God is my inexhaustible source of abundant supply. The riches of the Spirit now fill my mind and affairs. I think prosperity. I talk prosperity, and I know that prosperity and success are mine."

"If we but touch the garment's hem,
  Comes power surging through.
Try—play the part—stretch out your hand,
  Then quiet—wait what comes to you."

God gave man power and dominion over all that is below him. "I said—Ye are Gods, and all of you Sons of the Most High." "As many as received Him, to them gave He power to become the Sons of God, even to them that believe on His name."

Will YOU receive Him? Will you believe in and accept the power He offers you? "God is able to do abundantly above all that we ask or think, according to the Power that worketh in us." Will you accept His Divine Sonship? Will you BE the God-man you were intended to be? Then cast off all fear of debt and lack and sickness and evil. Live in the world of love and plenty that was intended for you. Use the God-given power that is yours to first visualize the things you want— "In the beginning was the Word", the mental image, you remember—and then bring those mental images into actuality through your faith and your work.

Treasure Maps help to re-educate your mind, help you to visualize and hold in thought the images you wish to create. But visualizing and asking God's guidance is only half the battle. The other half is to make your start, to dig in and DO the first thing necessary towards bringing your desires into actuality.

The Kingdom of Heaven is the Kingdom of Expansion, but there must be something to expand. You can start a house with a single brick. You can start a fortune with a single dollar. But there must be that brick or that dollar or that first step to put your leaven into before you can make it expand and grow into the perfect structure of your dreams.

So do the thing, whatever it may be, that is necessary to your start. Make your picture, draw your Treasure Map, then take the first step that may be necessary towards bringing it into actuality. To begin is to be half done. You will be amazed how quickly you will reach your goal.

"To every man God gives a gift tonight;
To king and peasant and to you and me:
A shining year, clean, white, as crystal clear
As tropic pools or stars above the sea.

"Oh, let us promise all the coming days
To keep them pure, to keep them ever white!
As, heaven born, one comes to us each morn,
God, help us use it wisely in Thy sight.

"Whatever task, whatever joy be ours
Throughout the year that now has scarce begun,
Let us steadfastly claim in His own name
The promised presence of the Holy One."
                              —BERTHA M. RUSSELL

THE SECRET OF POWER

"I am the owner of the sphere,
 Of the seven stars and the solar year,
 Of Caesar's hand and Plato's brain,
 Of Lord Christ's heart
         And Shakespeare's strain."

INTRODUCTION

WHAT IS THE strongest political trend in the world today?

After the last war, it was towards democracy. But somehow democracy failed the average man. When the depression came and he found himself unable to provide food and shelter for his loved ones, he demanded something more than equality of opportunity. He demanded SECURITY from want.

To answer that demand came "Strong Men," so-called, Mussolinis and Hitlers and Antonescus and Francos and the like, and Fascism was born. Men achieved security, of a kind, but they bartered their freedom for it. And soon they learned that power feeds on power, and the only end of dictatorship is war, which destroys all.

So today the trend is to the other extreme—to Communism. All over the world you see signs of it. China has largely embraced it. All of eastern Europe is engulfed by it. France and Belgium are trending in that direction. Even here in the U. S., some labor unions are strongly Communistic, several political groups are dominated by it, it has its disciples in high places and for a time Democrats feared that their party would be taken over by the Communists.

And the reason? The same reason that has impelled man since time began—the longing for security, security for the home, security against want, security for old age.

Since time began, the search for security has been one of the strongest urges in all of nature. You see it in the animal in the way it conceals its nest and tries to make it safe from predatory creatures—man or animal. You see it in the records of early man in the caves he dug into the sides of the mountains, in the tree huts, in the cliff dwellings. You follow it down through the ages to the walled cities, the turreted castles, the inaccessible mountains in which men made their homes.

Throughout history, you see this search for security as one of the dominant characteristics of all human kind. And now that the common man has realized his power, you find him all over the world banding together to take over all property, to the end that he and his may find that security from want that he has so long worked for.

What he does not seem to realize is that the mere redistribution of property never has and never will solve his problem. It will provide him with temporary supply, yes—but supply is a continuing problem, and when his small share of the general distribution is gone, he will be worse off than he was before, because production will have either ceased or been greatly curtailed.

Redistribution is not the answer. It has been tried repeatedly, and always failed. You must go farther back than that. You must start with the source of things. And that is what we shall try to do in the following pages.

"Know this, ye restless denizens of earth,
 Know this, ye seekers after joy and mirth,
 Three things there are, eternal in their worth—
 LOVE, that outreaches to the humblest things:
 WORK, that is glad in what it does and brings;
 And FAITH, that soars upon unwearied wings.
 Divine the powers that on this trio wait,
 Supreme their conquest, over time and fate.
 LOVE, WORK and FAITH, these three alone are great."

CHAPTER TWENTY-ONE

THE CREATIVE FORCE

"The Spirit of the Lord is upon me,
Because he anointed me to preach good tidings to the poor:
He has sent me to proclaim release to the captives,
And recovering of sight to the blind,
To set at liberty them that are bruised,
To proclaim the acceptable year of the Lord."

"IN THE BEGINNING WAS THE WORD. And the Word was with God. And the Word was God."—St. John.

What is a word? A mental concept or image, is it not? In originating language, words were coined to represent certain images or objects. The word horse, for instance, calls to mind the image left upon the retina and the brain by what one has seen of that quadruped.

But what if there were no horses? What if one were called upon to create a horse, with no previous knowledge of such an animal? You'd have to build up a clear mental image of him first, would you not? You'd have to work out a mental picture of every part of his anatomy, every physical outline. You'd need a perfect mental concept of everything that is comprised in the word horse.

And that was what happened when God created the world. In the beginning was the "Word," the mental concept, the image in God's mind of what He planned. "And the Word was made flesh." It took on shape and substance. It grew into an habitable world. It developed creatures like the fish in the sea, the birds in the air, the beasts of the field. And finally man.

To every one of these creatures, in turn, was given a certain amount of creative power. The Creative Force of the Universe was working through them, and it did not look upon them as a completed job. It was and is still creating, still improving. The horse, for instance, was not originally the powerful animal we see today. It was little larger than a fox. It developed its present proportions and qualities as the need for these arose.

All life originally came from the sea, for in the beginning the waters covered the face of the earth. As volcanic action raised certain portions of the earth's surface above the waters, and as the moon's attraction caused the waters to rise or recede from the shores of these sections of dry land, certain creatures of the sea were left high and dry periodically.

What happened to them? Did they die? In the beginning, yes, but as this regular movement of the waters became perceptible to the rudimentary intelligence of the sea animals, certain of them began to use the Creative Force working through them to enable them to survive. Where they had only gills to breathe with in the water, they developed lungs that enabled them to breathe when left on dry land. And where the rough waters of the surf rolled them over and over on the rocky beaches, bruising and killing thousands of them, they developed calluses or shells, just as your feet or hands will develop calluses where they are subjected to hard wear.

Life then, as now, was a continually developing process. Those early forms of life were threatened by every kind of danger—from floods, from earthquakes, from droughts, from desert heat, from glacial cold, from volcanic eruptions—but each new danger was merely an incentive to finding some new resource, to putting forth their Creative Force in some new shape.

To meet one set of needs, the Creative Force formed the Dinosaur; to meet another, the Butterfly. Long before it worked up to man, we see its unlimited resourcefulness in a thousand ways. To escape danger in the water, some forms of Life sought land. Pursued on land, they took to the air. To breathe in the sea, the Creative Force developed gills. Stranded on land, it perfected lungs. To meet one kind of danger, it grew a shell. For another, it developed fleetness of foot, or wings that carried it into the air. To protect itself from glacial cold, it grew fur. In temperate climes, hair. Subject to alternate heat and cold, it produced feathers. But ever, from the beginning, it showed its power to meet every changing condition, *to answer every creature need.*

Had it been possible to stamp out this Creative Force, or halt its constant upward development, it would have perished ages ago, when fire and flood, drought and famine followed each other in quick succession. But obstacles, misfortunes, cataclysms, were to it merely new opportunities to assert its power. In fact, it required difficulties or obstacles to stir it up, to make it show its energy and resourcefulness.

The great reptiles, the monster beasts of antiquity, passed on as the conditions changed that had made them possible, but the Creative Force stayed, changing as each age changed, always developing, always improving.

When God put this Creative Force into His creatures, He gave to it unlimited energy, unlimited resource. No other power can equal it. No force can defeat it. No obstacle can hold it back. All through the history of life and mankind, you can see its directing intelligence rising to meet every need of life.

No one can follow it down through the ages without

realizing that the purpose of existence is GROWTH,
DEVELOPMENT. Life is dynamic, not static. It is ever
moving forward—not standing still. The one unpardonable sin in all of nature is to stand still, to stagnate. The
Gigantosaurus, that was over a hundred feet long and as
big as a house; the Tyrannosaurus, that had the strength
of a locomotive and was the last word in frightfulness;
the Pterodactyl or Flying Dragon—all the giant monsters
of pre-historic ages—are gone. They ceased to serve a
useful purpose. They stood still while the life around
them passed them by.

Egypt and Persia, Greece and Rome, all the great
empires of antiquity, perished when they ceased to grow.
China built a wall around herself and stood still for a
thousand years. Today look at her, dismembered, torn by
strife without and within. In all of Nature, to cease to
grow is to perish.

It is for men and women who are not ready to stand
still, who refuse to cease to grow, that this book is written.
Its purpose is to give you a clearer understanding of your
own potentialities, to show you how to work with and
take advantage of the infinite energy and power of the
Creative Force working through you.

The terror of the man at the crossways, not knowing
which way to turn, should be no terror for you, for your
future is of your own making. The only law of infinite
energy is the law of supply. The Creative Principle is
your principle. To survive, to win through, to triumph-
antly surmount all obstacles has been its everyday practice
since the beginning of time. It is no less resourceful now
than it ever was. You have but to supply the urge, to work
in harmony with it, to get from it anything you need. For
if this Creative Force is so strong in the lowest forms of
animal life that it can develop a shell or a poison to meet
a need; if it can teach the bird to circle and dart, to bal-

ance and fly; if it can grow a new limb on a spider or crab to replace a lost one; how much more can it do for YOU —a reasoning, rational being, with a mind able to work with this Creative Force, with energy and purpose and initiative to urge it on!

The evidence of this is all about you. Take up some violent form of exercise, and in the beginning your muscles are weak, easily tired. But keep on a few days, and what happens? The Creative Force in you promptly strengthens them, toughens them, to meet their need.

All through your daily life, you find this Force steadily at work. Embrace it, work with it, take it to your heart, and there is nothing you cannot do. The mere fact that you have obstacles to overcome is in your favor, for when there is nothing to be done, when things run along too smoothly, the Creative Force seems to sleep. It is when you need it, when you call upon it urgently, that it is most on the job.

It differs from Luck in this, that fortune is a fickle jade who smiles most on those who need her least. Stake your last penny on the turn of a card—have nothing between you and ruin but the spin of a wheel or the speed of a horse—and the chances are a hundred to one that luck will desert you.

It is just the opposite with the Creative Force in you. As long as things run smoothly, as long as life flows along like a song, this Creative Force seems to slumber, secure in the knowledge that your affairs can take care of themselves. But let things start going wrong, let ruin or death stare you in the face—then is the time this Creative Force will assert itself if you but give it the chance.

There is a Napoleonic feeling of power that insures success in the knowledge that this invincible Creative Force is behind your every act. Knowing that you have with you a force which never yet has failed in anything it

has undertaken, you can go ahead in the confident knowledge that it will not fail in your case. The ingenuity which
overcame every obstacle in making you what you are, is
not likely to fall short when you have immediate need for
it. It is the reserve strength of the athlete, the second wind
of the runner, the power that, in moments of great stress
or excitement, you unconsciously call upon to do the deeds
which you ever after look upon as superhuman.

But they are in no wise superhuman. They are merely
beyond the capacity of your conscious self. Ally your conscious self with that sleeping giant within you, rouse him
daily to the task and those superhuman deeds will become
your ordinary, everyday accomplishments.

It matters not whether you are banker or lawyer, business man or clerk, whether you are the custodian of millions or have to struggle for your daily bread. The
Creative Force makes no distinction between high and
low, rich and poor. The greater your need, the more
readily will it respond to your call. Wherever there is an
unusual task, wherever there is poverty or hardship or
sickness or despair, there this Servant of your mind waits,
ready and willing to help, asking only that you call upon
him. And not only is it ready and willing, but it is always
ABLE to help. Its ingenuity and resource are without
limit. It is mind. It is thought. It is the telepathy that
carries messages without the spoken or written word. It
is the sixth sense that warns you of unseen dangers. No
matter how stupendous and complicated, or how simple
your problem may be, the solution of it is somewhere in
mind, in thought. And since the solution does exist, this
mental giant can find it for you. It can know, and it can
do, every right thing. Whatever it is necessary for you to
know, whatever it is necessary for you to do, you can
know and you can do if you will but seek the help of this
Genie-of-your-mind and work with it in the right way.

To every living creature, God gave enough of this Creative Force to enable it to develop whatever it felt that it needed for survival. Behind and working through every living thing was this Creative Force, and to each was given the power to draw upon it at need. With the lower forms of life, that call had to be restricted to themselves, to their own bodies. They could not change their environment.

They could develop a house of shell in which to live, like the crustaceans or the snail or the turtle. They could use the Creative Force to develop strength or fleetness or teeth and claws—anything within or pertaining to themselves. But aside from building nests or caves or other more or less secure homes, they could not alter conditions around them. To man alone was given the power to make his own environment. To him alone was given dominion over things and conditions.

That he exercises this power, even today, only to a limited extent, does not alter the fact that he has it. Man was given dominion. "And God said—Let us make man in our image, after our likeness, and let them have dominion over the fish of the sea, and over the fowl of the air, and over the cattle, and over all the earth, and over every creeping thing that creepeth upon the earth."

Of course, few believe in that dominion. Fewer still exercise it for their own good or the good of all. But everyone uses the Creative Force in him to an extent. Everyone builds his own environment.

"Don't tell me," some will say indignantly, "that I built these slums around me, that I am responsible for the wretched conditions under which I work, that I had anything to do with the squalor and poverty in which my family have to live." Yet that is exactly what we do tell you. If you were born in poverty and misery, it was because your parents imaged these as something forced upon them, something they could not help, a condition that was necessary and to be expected. Thinking so, they used the Creative Force working through them to fasten those conditions upon themselves as something they were meant to suffer and could do nothing about.

Then you in your turn accepted those conditions as what you were born to, and fastened them upon yourself by your supine acceptance of them, by failing to claim better ones, by making no great or sustained efforts to get out of them.

All history shows that the determined soul who refuses to accept poverty or lack can change these to riches and power if he has the determination and the perseverance. The great men of the world have almost all come up from poverty and obscurity. The rich men of the world have mostly started with nothing.

"Always the real leaders of men, the real kings, have come up from the common people," wrote Dr. Frank Crane. "The finest flowers in the human flora grow in the woods pasture and not in the hothouse; no privileged class, no royal house, no carefully selected stock produced a Leonardo or a Michelangelo in art, a Shakespeare or Burns in letters, a Galli Curci or Paderewski in music, a Socrates or Kant in philosophy, an Edison or Pasteur in science, a Wesley or a Knox in religion."

It is the NEED that calls forth such geniuses, the urgent need for development or expression, and it is because these men drew powerfully upon the Creative Force within them that they became great. As the poet put it:

"There is Power within me which is Life itself;
  I can turn to it and rest on it;
  As I turn to it and rest on it,
  It helps me and heals me all the time.

"There is Wisdom itself within me which is Life itself;
I can turn to it and rest on it;
As I turn to it and rest on it,
It helps me and heals me all the time.

"There is Love itself within me which is Life itself;
I can turn to it and rest on it;
As I turn to it and rest on it,
It helps me and heals me all the time."

"Look within," said Marcus Aurelius. "Within is the fountain of all good. Such a fountain, where springing waters can never fail, do thou dig still deeper and deeper."

God gave to man, and to man alone, the power to make his own environment. He can determine for himself what he needs for survival, and if he holds to that thought with determination, he can draw whatever is necessary from the Creative Force working through him to make it manifest. First the Word, the mental image, then the creation or manifestation.

Professor Michael Pupin says—"Science finds that everything is a continually developing process." In other words, creation is still going on, all around you. Use your Creative Force to create the conditions you desire rather than those you fear. The life about you is constantly in a state of flux. All you have to do is create the mental mold in which you want the Creative Force to take form, and then hold to that mold with persistence and determination until the Creative Force in it becomes manifest.

Dr. Titus Bull, the famous neurologist, says—"Matter is spirit at a lower rate of vibration. When a patient is cured, it is spirit in the cell doing the healing according to its own inherent pattern. No doctor ever cured a patient. All he can do is to make it possible for the patient to heal himself."

And if that is true of the body, it is just as true of conditions around you. Matter—physical materials—is spirit or Creative Force at a lower rate of vibration. The spirit or Creative Force is all around you. You are constantly forming it into mental molds, but more often than not these are dictated by your fears rather than your desires. Why not determinedly form only good molds? Why not insist upon the things you want? It is just as easy, and it works just as surely.

> "There is no great and no small," writes Emerson,
> "To the soul that maketh all;
> And where it cometh, all things are;
> And it cometh everywhere.
> I am the owner of the sphere,
> Of the seven stars and the solar year,
> Of Caesar's hand, and Plato's brain,
> Of Lord Christ's heart, and Shakespeare's strain."

"Give me a base of support," said Archimedes, "and with a lever I will move the world."

And the base of support is that all started with *mind*. In the beginning was nothing—a fire mist. Before anything could come of it there had to be an idea, a mental model on which to build. *The God Mind* supplied that idea, that model. Therefore the primal cause is mind. Everything must start with an idea. Every event, every condition, every thing is first an idea in the mind of some-one.

Before you start to build a house, you draw up a plan of it. You make an exact blue-print of that plan, and your house takes shape in accordance with your blue-print. Every material object takes form in the same way. Mind draws the plan. Thought forms the blue-print, well drawn or badly done as your thoughts are clear or vague. It all goes back to the one cause. The creative principle of the universe is mind, and thought forms the molds in which its eternal energy takes shape.

But just as the effect you get from electricity depends upon the mechanism to which the power is attached, so the effects you get from mind depend upon the way you use it. We are all of us dynamos. The power is there—unlimited power. But we've got to connect it with something—set it some task—give it work to do—else are we no better off than the animals.

The "Seven Wonders of the World" were built by men with few of the opportunities or facilities that are available to you. They conceived these gigantic projects first in their own minds, pictured them so vividly that the Creative Force working through them came to their aid and helped them to overcome obstacles that most of us would regard as insurmountable. Imagine building the Pyramid of Gizeh, enormous stone upon enormous stone, with nothing but bare hands. Imagine the labor, the sweat, the heartbreaking toil of erecting the Colossus of Rhodes, between whose legs a ship could pass! Yet men built these wonders, in a day when tools were of the crudest and machinery was undreamed of, by using the unlimited power of the Creative Force.

That Creative Force is in you, working through you, but it must have a model on which to work. It must have thoughts to supply the molds.

There are in Universal Mind ideas for millions of wonders greater far than the "Seven Wonders of the World." And those ideas are just as available to you as they were to the artisans of old, as they were to Michelangelo when he built St. Peter's in Rome, as they were to the architect who conceived the Empire State Building, or the engineer who planned the Hell Gate Bridge.

Every condition, every experience of life is the result of our mental attitude. We can *do* only what we think we

can do. We can *be* only what we think we can be. We can
have only what we think we can have. What we do, what
we are, what we have, all depend upon what we think.
There is only one limit upon the Creative Force, and that
is the limit we impose upon it.

We can never express anything that we do not first believe in. The secret of all power, all success, all riches, is
in first thinking powerful thoughts, successful thoughts,
thoughts of wealth, of supply. We must build them in our
own mind first. As Edgar A. Guest so well expressed it,

> "You can do as much as you think you can,
>   But you'll never accomplish more;
> If you're afraid of yourself, young man,
>   There's little for you in store.
> For failure comes from the inside first,
>   It's there if we only knew it,
> And you can win, though you face the worst,
>   If you feel that you're going to do it."

William James, the famous psychologist, said that the
greatest discovery in a hundred years was the discovery
of the power of the subconscious mind. It is the greatest
discovery of all time. It is the discovery that man has
within himself the power to control his surroundings, that
he is not at the mercy of chance or luck, that he is the
arbiter of his own fortunes, that he can carve out his own
destiny. He is the master of the Creative Force working
through him. As James Allen puts it:

"Dream lofty dreams, and as you dream, so shall you
become. Your vision is the promise of what you shall one
day be; your Ideal is the prophecy of what you shall at
last unveil."

For matter is in the ultimate but a product of thought,
the result of the mold into which you have put the Creative Force working through you. Even the most material

scientists admit that matter is not what it appears to be. According to physics, matter (be it the human body or a log of wood—it makes no difference which) is made up of an aggregation of distinct minute particles called atoms. Considered individually, these atoms are so small that they can be seen only with the aid of a powerful microscope, if at all.

Until comparatively recent years, these atoms were supposed to be the ultimate theory regarding matter. We ourselves—and all the material world around us—were supposed to consist of these infinitesimal particles of matter, so small that they could not be seen or weighed or smelled or touched individually—but still particles of matter *and indestructible.*

Now, however, these atoms have been further analyzed, and physicists tell us that they are not indestructible at all—that they are mere positive and negative buttons of force or energy called protons and electrons, without hardness, without density, without solidity, without even positive actuality. In short, they are vortices in the ether —whirling bits of energy—dynamic, never static, pulsating with life, but the life is *spiritual!* As one eminent British scientist put it—"Science now explains matter by *explaining it away!*"

And that, mind you, is what the solid table in front of you is made of, is what your house, your body, the whole world is made of—*whirling bits of energy!*

To quote the New York Herald-Tribune: "We used to believe that the universe was composed of an unknown number of different kinds of matter, one kind for each chemical element. The discovery of a new element had all the interest of the unexpected. It might turn out to be anything, to have any imaginable set of properties.

"That romantic prospect no longer exists. We know now that instead of many ultimate kinds of matter there are only two kinds. Both of these are really kinds of electricity. One is negative electricity, being, in fact, the tiny particle called the electron, familiar to radio fans as one of the particles vast swarms of which operate radio vacuum tubes. The other kind of electricity is positive electricity. Its ultimate particles are called protons. From these protons and electrons all of the chemical elements are built up. Iron and lead and oxygen and gold and all the others differ from one another merely in the number and arrangement of the electrons and protons which they contain. That is the modern idea of the nature of matter. *Matter is really nothing but electricity.*"

Can you wonder then that scientists believe the time will come when mankind *through mind* can control all this energy, can be absolute master of the winds and the waves, can literally follow the Master's precept—"If ye have faith as a grain of mustard seed, ye shall say unto this mountain, Remove hence to yonder place; and it shall remove; and nothing shall be impossible unto you."

For Modern Science is coming more and more to the belief that what we call *matter is a force subject wholly to the control of mind.*

So it would seem that, to a great degree at least, and perhaps altogether, this world round about us is one of our mind's own creating. And we can put into it, and get from it, pretty much what we wish. "Nothing is," said Shakespeare, "but thinking makes it so." And the psychologist of today says the same in a different way when he tells us that only those things are real to each individual that he takes into his consciousness. To one with no sense of smell, for instance, there is no such thing as fragrance. To one without a radio, there is no music on the air waves.

To quote from "Applied Psychology," by Warren Hilton:

"The same stimulus acting on different organs of sense will produce different sensations. A blow upon the eye will cause you to 'see stars'; a similar blow upon the ear will cause you to hear an explosive sound. In other words, the vibratory effect of a touch on eye or ear is the same as that of light or sound vibrations.

"The notion you may form of any object in the outer world depends solely upon what part of your brain happens to be connected with that particular nerve-end that received an impression from the object.

"You see the sun without being able to hear it because the only nerve-ends tuned to vibrate in harmony with the ether-waves set in action by the sun are nerve-ends that are connected with the brain center devoted to sight. 'If,' says Professor James, 'we could splice the outer extremities of our optic nerves to our ears, and those of our auditory nerves to our eyes, we should hear the lightning and see the thunder, see the symphony and hear the conductor's movements.'

"In other words, the kind of impressions we receive from the world about us, the sort of mental pictures we form concerning it—in fact, the character of the outer world, the nature of the environment in which our lives are cast—all these things depend for each one of us simply upon how he happens to be put together, upon his individual mental make-up."

In short, it all comes back to the old fable of the three blind men and the elephant. To the one who caught hold of his leg, the elephant was like a tree. To the one who felt of his side, the elephant was like a wall. To the one who seized his tail, the elephant was like a rope. The world is to each one of us the world of *his individual perceptions*.

You are like a radio receiving station. Every moment thousands of impressions are reaching you. You can tune in on whatever ones you like—on joy or sorrow, on success or failure, on optimism or fear. You can select the particular impressions that will best serve you, you can hear only what you want to hear, you can shut out all disagreeable thoughts and sounds and experiences, or you can tune in on discouragement and failure and despair if these are what you want.

Yours is the choice. You have within you a force against which the whole world is powerless. By using it, you can make what you will of life and of your surroundings.

"But," you will say, "objects themselves do not change. It is merely the difference in the way you look at them." Perhaps. But to a great extent, at least, we find what we look for, just as, when we turn the dial on the radio, we tune in on whatever kind of entertainment or instruction we may wish to hear. Who can say that it is not our thoughts that put it there? And why shouldn't it be? All will agree that evil is merely the lack of good, just as darkness is the lack of light. There is infinite good all about us. There is fluid cosmic energy from which to form infinitely more. Why should we not use our thoughts to find the good, or to mold it from the Creative Force all about us? Many scientists believe that we can, and that in proportion as we try to put into our surroundings the good things we desire, rather than the evil ones we fear, *we will find those good things.* Certain it is that we can do this with our own bodies. Just as certain that many people are doing it with the good things of life. They have risen above the conception of life in which matter is the master.

Just as the most powerful forces in nature are the invisible ones—heat, light, air, electricity—so the most powerful forces of man are his invisible forces, his thought forces. And just as electricity can fuse stone and iron, so can your thought forces control your body, so can they win you honor and fortune, so can they make or mar your destiny.

From childhood on we are assured on every hand—by scientists, by philosophers, by our religious teachers, that "ours is the earth and the fulness thereof." Beginning with the first chapter of Genesis, we are told that "God said, Let us make man in Our image, after Our likeness; and let them have dominion over the fish of the sea, and over the fowl of the air, and over the cattle, and over all the earth—and over every living thing that moveth upon the earth." All through the Old and the New Testament, we are repeatedly adjured to use these God-given powers. "He that believeth on Me," said Jesus, "the works that I do shall he do also; and greater works than these shall he do." "If ye abide in Me, and My words abide in you, ye shall ask what ye will, and it shall be done unto you." "For verily I say unto you, that whosoever shall say unto this mountain, Be thou removed, and be thou cast into the sea; and shall not doubt in his heart, but shall believe that those things which he saith shall come to pass; he shall have whatsoever he saith." "The kingdom of God is within you."

We hear all this, perhaps we even think we believe, but always, when the time comes to use these God-given talents, there is the "doubt in our heart."

Baudouin expressed it clearly: "To be ambitious for wealth and yet always expecting to be poor; to be always doubting your ability to get what you long for, is like trying to reach east by travelling west. There is no philosophy which will help a man to succeed when he is always doubting his ability to do so, and thus attracting failure.

"You will go in the direction in which you face. . . .

"There is a saying that every time the sheep bleats, it oses a mouthful of hay. Every time you allow yourself to complain of your lot, to say, 'I am poor; I can never do what others do; I shall never be rich; I have not the ability that others have; I am a failure; luck is against me'; you are laying up so much trouble for yourself.

"No matter how hard you may work for success, if your thought is saturated with the fear of failure, it will kill your efforts, neutralize your endeavors, and make success impossible."

What was it made Napoleon the greatest conqueror of his day? Primarily his magnificent faith in Napoleon. He had a sublime belief in his destiny, an absolute confidence that the obstacle was not made which Napoleon could not find a way through, or over, or around. It was only when he lost that confidence, when he hesitated and vacillated for weeks between retreat and advance, that winter caught him in Moscow and ended his dreams of world empire. Fate gave him every chance first. The winter snows were a full month late in coming. But Napoleon hesitated—and was lost. It was not the snows that defeated him. It was not the Russians. It was his loss of faith in himself.

The Kingdom of Heaven

"The Kingdom of Heaven is within you." Heaven is not some faraway state—the reward of years of tribulation here. Heaven is right here—here and now! In the original Greek text, the word used for "Heaven" is "Ouranos." Translated literally, Ouranos means EXPANSION, in other words, a state of being where you can expand, grow, multiply, and increase. This interpretation is strengthened by Jesus' own description of what the Kingdom of Heaven is like. "The Kingdom of Heaven is like to a grain of mustard seed, which a man took, and sowed in his field; which indeed is the least of all seeds, but when it is grown, it is the greatest among herbs, and becometh a tree, so that the birds of the air come and lodge in the branches thereof." "The Kingdom of Heaven is like unto leaven, which a woman took and hid in three measures of meal, until the whole was leavened."

What is the property of a mustard seed? *It spreads*— a single seed will grow into a tree, a single tree will produce enough seeds to plant a great field. And what is the property of leaven or yeast? *It expands*—in a single night it can expand a hundred times in size. So when Christ said that Heaven was within us, He meant just what He said —the power to multiply our happiness, to increase our good, to expand everything we need in life, is within each one of us.

That most of us fail to realize this Heaven—that many are sickly and suffering, that more are ground down by poverty and worry—is no fault of His. He gave us the power to overcome these evils; the Kingdom of Expansion is within us, the power to increase anything we have. If we fail to find the way to use it, the fault is ours. If we expand the evil instead of the good, that is our misfortune. To enjoy the Heaven that is within us, to begin here and now to live the life eternal, takes only the right understanding and use of the Creative Force working through us.

Even now, with the limited knowledge at our command, many people control circumstances to the point of making the world without an expression of their own world within, where the real thoughts, the real power, resides. Through this world within, they find the solution of every problem, the cause for every effect. Discover it—and all power, all possession is within your control.

For the world without is but a reflection of that world within. Your thought *creates* the condition your mind images. Keep before your mind's eye the image of all you want to be and you will see it reflected in the world without. Think abundance, feel abundance, BELIEVE abundance, and you will find that as you think and feel and believe, abundance will manifest itself in your daily life. But let fear and worry be your mental companions, thoughts of poverty and limitation dwell in your mind, and worry and fear, limitation and poverty will be your constant companions day and night.

Your mental concept is all that matters. Its relation to matter is that of idea and form. There has got to be an idea before it can take form.

The Creative Force working through you supplies you with limitless energy which will take whatever form your mind demands. Your thoughts are the mold which crystallizes this energy into good or ill according to the form you impress upon it. You are free to choose which. But whichever you choose, the result is sure. Thoughts of wealth, of power, of success, can bring only results commensurate with your idea of them. Thoughts of poverty and lack can bring only limitation and trouble.

"A radical doctrine," you'll say, and think me wildly optimistic. Because the world has been taught for so long to think that some must be rich and some poor, that trials and tribulations are our lot. That this is at best a vale of tears.

The history of the race shows that what is considered to be the learning of one age is ignorance to the next age.

Dr. Edwin E. Slosson, Editor of SCIENCE SERVICE, speaking of the popular tendency to fight against new ideas merely because they are *new*, said: "All through the history of science, we find that new ideas have to force their way into the common mind in disguise, as though they were burglars instead of benefactors of the race."

And Emerson wrote: "The virtue in most request is conformity. Self-reliance is its aversion. It loves not realities and creators, but names and customs."

In the ages to come, man will look back upon the poverty and wretchedness of so many millions today, and think how foolish we were not to take advantage of the abundant Creative Force all about us. Look at Nature; how profuse she is in everything. Do you suppose the Mind that imaged that profuseness ever intended you to be limited, to have to scrimp and save in order to eke out a bare existence?

There are hundreds of millions of stars in the heavens. Do you suppose the Creative Force which could bring into being worlds without number in such prodigality intended to stint you of the few things necessary to your happiness or well-being?

Nature is prodigal in all that she does. Many insects increase at such a marvelous rate that if it were not for their almost equal death rate, the world would be unable to support them. Rabbits increase so rapidly that a single pair could have 13,000,000 descendants in three years! Fish lay millions of eggs each year. Throughout Nature, everything is lavish. Why should the Creative Force working through you be less generous when it comes to your own supply?

Take as an example the science of numbers. Suppose all numbers were of metal—that it was against the law to write figures for ourselves. Every time you wanted to do a sum in arithmetic you'd have to provide yourself with a supply of numbers, arrange them in their proper order, work out your problems with them. If your problems were too abstruse you might run out of numbers, have to borrow some from your neighbor or from the bank.

"How ridiculous," you say. "Figures are not things; they are mere ideas, and we can add them or divide them or multiply them as often as we like. Anybody can have all the figures he wants."

To be sure he can. And when you learn to use the Creative Force, you will find that you can multiply your material ideas in the same way. You will EXPAND the good things in your life even as Jesus did the loaves and fishes.

Thought externalizes itself, through the Creative Force working through us. What we are depends entirely upon the images we hold before our mind's eye. Every time we think, we start a chain of causes which will create conditions similar to the thoughts which originated it. Every thought we hold in our consciousness for any length of time becomes impressed upon our subconscious mind and creates a pattern which the Creative Force weaves into our life or environment.

All power is from within and is therefore under our own control. When you can direct your thought processes, you can consciously apply them to any condition, for all that comes to us in the world without is what we've already imaged in the world within.

The source of all good, of everything you wish for, is Mind, and you can reach it best through your subconscious.

Mind will be to you whatever you believe it to be—the kind and loving Father whom Jesus pictured, always looking out for the well-being of his children—or the dread Judge that so many dogmatists would have us think.

When a man realizes that his mind is part of the God Mind, when he knows that he has only to take any right aspiration to this Universal Mind to see it realized, he loses all sense of worry and fear. He learns to dominate instead of to cringe. He rises to meet every situation, secure in the knowledge that everything necessary to the solution of any problem is in Mind, and that he has but

to take his problem to Universal Mind to have it correctly answered.

For if you take a drop of water from the ocean, you
know that it has the same properties as all the rest of the
water in the ocean, the same percentage of sodium chlo-
ride. The only difference between it and the ocean is in
volume. If you take a spark of electricity, you know that
it has the same properties as the thunderbolt, the same
power that moves trains or runs giant machines in factories. Again the only difference is in volume. It is the
same with your mind and the God Mind. The only difference between them is in volume. Your mind has the
same properties as the God Mind, the same creative
genius, the same power over all the earth, the same access
to all knowledge. Know this, believe it, use it, and "yours
is the earth and the fulness thereof." In the exact proportion that you believe yourself to be part of the God Mind,
sharing in Its all-power, in that proportion can you demonstrate the mastery over your own body and over the
world about you.

All growth, all supply is from the Creative Force working through you. If you would have power, if you would
have wealth, you must first form the mold in this world
within, in your subconscious mind, through belief and understanding.

If you would remove discord, you must remove the
wrong images—images of ill health, of worry and trouble from within. The trouble with most of us is that we
live entirely in the world without. We have no knowledge
of that inner world which is responsible for all the conditions we meet and all the experiences we have. We have
no conception of "the Father that is within us."

The inner world promises us life and health, prosperity
and happiness—dominion over all the earth. It promises
peace and perfection for all its offspring. It gives you the

right way and the adequate way to accomplish any normal purpose. Business, labor, professions, exist primarily in thought. And the outcome of your labors in them is regulated by thought. Consider the difference, then, in this outcome if you have at your command only the limited capacity of your conscious mind, compared with the boundless energy of the subconscious and of the Creative Force working through it. "Thought, not money, is the real business capital," says Harvey S. Firestone, "and if you know absolutely that what you are doing is right, then you are bound to accomplish it in due season."

Thought is a dynamic energy with the power to bring its object out from the Creative Force all about us. Matter is unintelligent. Thought can shape and control. Every form in which matter is today is but the expression of some thought, some desire, some idea.

You have a mind. You can originate thought. And thoughts are creative. Therefore you can create for yourself that which you desire. Once you realize this, you are taking a long step toward success in whatever undertaking you have in mind. You are the potter. You are continually forming images—good or bad. Why not consciously form only good images?

More than half the prophecies in the scriptures refer to the time when man shall possess the earth, when tears and sorrow shall be unknown, and peace and plenty shall be everywhere. That time will come. It is nearer than most people think possible. You are helping it along. Every man who is honestly trying to use the power of mind in the right way is doing his part in the great cause. For it is only through Mind that peace and plenty can be gained. The earth is laden with treasures as yet undiscovered. But they are every one of them known to the God Mind, for it was this Mind that first imaged them there. And as part of Universal Mind, they can be known to you.

"To the Manner Born"

Few of us have any idea of our mental powers. The old idea was that man must take this world as he found it. He'd been born into a certain position in life, and to try to rise above his fellows was not only the height of bad taste, but sacrilegious as well. An All-wise Providence had decreed by birth the position a child should occupy in the web of organized society. For him to be discontented with his lot, for him to attempt to raise himself to a higher level, was tantamount to tempting Providence. The gates of Hell yawned wide for such scatterbrains, who were lucky if in this life they incurred nothing worse than the ribald scorn of their associates.

That is the system that produced aristocracy and feudalism. That is the system that feudalism and aristocracy strove to perpetuate.

What was it that Jesus taught which aroused the wrath of the Priests and the Rulers? What was it that made them demand His blood? NOT the doctrine of the One God. NOT the teachings of love instead of hate. But the fact that He went up and down the length and breadth of the land teaching that all men were equally the Sons of God. That would never do. That would ruin their system, spread discontent, cause uprisings against their authority. It must be stopped at any cost.

Yet Jesus' teaching has lived to become the basis of all democracies—that man is not bound by any system, that he need not accept the world as he finds it. He can remake the world to his own ideas. It is merely the raw material. He can make what he will of it.

It is this idea that is responsible for all our inventions, all our progress. Man is satisfied with nothing. He is con-

stantly remaking his world. And now more than ever will
this be true, for psychology teaches us that each one has
within himself the power to use the Creative Force to
become what he wills.

LEARN TO CONTROL YOUR THOUGHT.
Learn to image upon your mind only the things you want
to see reflected there.

You will never improve yourself by dwelling upon the
drawbacks of your neighbors. You will never attain perfect health and strength by thinking of weakness or disease. No man ever made a perfect score by watching his
rival's target. You have to think strength, think health,
think riches. To paraphrase Pascal—"Our achievements
today are but the sum of our thoughts of yesterday."

For yesterday is the mold in which the Creative Force
flowing through us took shape. And cosmic energy concentrated for any definite purpose becomes power. To those
who perceive the nature and transcendency of this Force,
all physical power sinks into insignificance.

What is imagination but a form of thought? Yet it is
the instrument by which all the inventors and discoverers
have opened the way to new worlds. Those who grasp
this force, be their state ever so humble, their natural
gifts ever so insignificant, become our leading men. They
are our governors and supreme law-givers, the guides of
the drifting host that follows them as by an irrevocable
decree. To quote Glenn Clark in the ATLANTIC
MONTHLY, "Whatever we have of civilization is their
work, theirs alone. If progress was made, they made it. If
spiritual facts were discerned, they discerned them. If justice and order were put in place of insolence and chaos,
they wrought the change. Never is progress achieved by
the masses. Creation ever remains the task of the individual."

Our railroads, our telephones, our automobiles, our

libraries, our newspapers, our thousands of other conveniences, comforts and necessities are due to the creative genius of but two per cent of our population.

And the same two per cent own a great percentage of the wealth of the country.

The question arises, Who are they? What are they? The sons of the rich? College men? No—few of them had any early advantages. Many of them have never seen the inside of a college. It was grim necessity that drove them, and somehow, some way, they found a method of drawing upon their Creative Force, and through that Force they reached success.

You don't need to stumble and grope. You can call upon the Creative Force at will. There are three steps necessary:

First, to realize that you have the power.

Second, to know what you want.

Third, to center your thought upon it with singleness of purpose.

To accomplish these steps takes only a fuller understanding of the Power-that-is-within-you.

So let us make use of this dynamo, which is *you*. What is going to start it working? Your *Faith,* the faith that is begotten of understanding. Faith is the impulsion of this power within. Faith is the confidence, the assurance, the enforcing truth, the knowing that the right idea of life will bring you into the reality of existence and the manifestation of the All power.

All cause is in Mind—and Mind is everywhere. All the knowledge there is, all the power there is, is all about you—no matter where you may be. Your Mind is part of it. You have access to it. If you fail to avail yourself of it, you have no one to blame but yourself. For as the drop of water in the ocean shares in all the properties of the rest of the ocean water, so you share in that all-power, all-wisdom of Mind. If you have been sick and ailing, if poverty and hardship have been your lot, don't blame it on "fate." Blame yourself. "Yours is the earth and everything that's in it." But you've got to *take* it. The Creative Force is there—but *you* must *use* it. It is round about you like the air you breathe. You don't expect others to do your breathing for you. Neither can you expect them to use the Creative Force for you. Universal Intelligence is not only the mind of the Creator of the universe, but it is also the mind of MAN, *Your* intelligence, *your* mind. "Let this mind be in you, which was also in Christ Jesus."

I am success, though hungry, cold, ill-clad,
I wander for awhile, I smile and say,
"It is but for a time, I shall be glad
Tomorrow, for good fortune comes my way.
God is my Father, He has wealth untold,
His wealth is mine, health, happiness and gold."
—ELLA WHEELER WILCOX

So start today by *knowing* that you can do anything you wish to do, have anything you wish to have, be anything you wish to be. The rest will follow.

"Ye shall ask what ye will and it shall be done unto you."

CHAPTER TWENTY-TWO

THE URGE

"A fierce unrest seethes at the core
  Of all existing things:
It was the eager wish to soar
  That gave the gods their wings. . . .

"But for the urge of this unrest
  These joyous spheres are mute;
But for the rebel in his breast
  Had man remained a brute.

"When baffled lips demanded speech,
  Speech trembled into birth—
(One day the lyric word shall reach
  From earth to laughing earth.)

"When man's dim eyes demanded light,
  The light he sought was born—
His wish, a Titan, scaled the height
  And flung him back the morn! . . .

"I sing no governed firmament,
  Cold, ordered, regular—
I sing the stinging discontent
  That leaps from star to star."
                    —DON MARQUIS

WHAT IS THE STRONGEST force in life? What is the
power that carries those who heed it from the bottom-

most pits of poverty to the top of the world—from the slums and ghettos to governorships and presidencies and the rulership of kingdoms?

The URGE for SECURITY—for ASSURED SUBSISTENCE AND SAFETY!

When the first primitive water plants appeared, living in the saturated soil along the shores of the waters, you might think the Creative Force would have rested content for a while. It had created something that lived and grew and reproduced itself. It was the first form of life upon this earth—the thallophytes.

But with this Creative Force, that was merely the first experiment. Next it worked out the amphibious plants, such as the mosses. Both of these were one-celled plants, taking their food direct from the water in which they were immersed. They were the first forms of life, therefore the simplest. They could not live away from water. And they must be *in* the water; they would perish on land.

But if life was to spread over the earth, a form must be developed which could dig for its own water, reach up into the air for its sunlight and warmth, draw from the ground whatever it needed for nourishment. The principle of the cell had been worked out, and it was good. How hold on to this principle, yet enable it to live on dry land?

As always, the Creative Force found a way. First it banded together great groups of cells, as in moss. Then it worked out the idea of several layers of moss, the lowermost in the water, the upper layers getting their life-giving moisture from them by absorption. Finally it jumped from this to the fern, in which the lower layers of cells send roots down into the ground to pipe the water up, then the stem continues that piping process, carrying moisture to the uppermost leaves.

With that development, nothing more was necessary to

the invention of the tree, except to build ever bigger and greater groups, with stronger roots, more powerful stems. The Creative Force had attained perfection in the vegetable kingdom. It might vary the forms for all manner of climes and conditions, but the principle was established and further expression along this line was merely a matter of reproduction and development.

So the Creative Force turned to a higher form—*to life that was not rooted to one spot,* life that could seek its own subsistence wherever it could best be found.

It started, of course, as in the vegetable kingdom, with the simplest form—the one-celled amoeba, floating about upon the surface of the water, little higher in the scale than the vegetable life around—but still, *an animal,* the first form of animal life on earth!

As with the water plants, there came next the multiple-celled creature, each dependent for life upon drawing its own nourishment from the waters about. Then a central system corresponding with the stem and roots of the fern, finally evolving into distinct organs to take care of each function of life. And so was laid the foundation for all forms of animal life that have developed from this simple beginning. The principle had been perfected—it remained now only to develop every possible ramification of it, until the highest form should be reached.

Again as with the plant kingdom, different forms were developed to meet each new condition. When the water-living organisms were stranded by the tides high and dry half the time, they did not thereupon perish. On the contrary, they developed lungs to supplement their gills, that they might live either in the water or in the air.

When means of protection were found necessary for survival, the Creative Force developed these too. For those subject to the abrasive effects of sand and rocks, it developed shells. To the weak, it gave means of escape.

To the strong, teeth and claws with which to fight. It fitted each form to meet the conditions it had to cope with. When size was the paramount consideration, it made the Gigantosaurus, over a hundred feet long and as big as a house, and all the other giant monsters of antiquity. When smallness was the objective, it developed the tiny insects and water creatures, so little that it takes a powerful microscope to see them, yet so perfectly made as to form organisms as exact and well-regulated as the greatest.

Size, strength, fierceness, speed—all these it developed to the last degree. It tried every form of life, but each had its weaknesses, each was vulnerable in some way. The Creative Force might develop forms that would grow, but nothing physical could be made that would be invulnerable, that would ever attain SECURITY.

No, there must be some better method, something above mere physical growth or propagation, in the realm of the intellect, of MIND! So the Creative Force turned its attention to this new channel of development. *And man was made.*

In the entire vegetable kingdom, and in all the animal kingdom excepting man, each form of life is confined in its expression to evolving more and more of its own kind, and attaining a degree of security for it. It may build its own shelter, it may find better ways of securing food, but these are largely means to an end—the end of propagating its species. The Creative Force works through them only to make more of the same.

And how it does work to that end! A single insect—the Stylonychia—increases so fast that if it were not for its almost equally rapid death rate, it would in a single week raise a mass of insects equal in size to the whole earth! Rodents breed so rapidly as quickly to become a pest when unchecked. Anyone who has read Ellis Parker But-

ler's story "PIGS IS PIGS," knows how quickly guinea
pigs increase, and the same is true of practically all the
lower forms of life. Where the Creative Force is confined to the physical, its only outlet is through reproduction.

Only in man can the Creative Force express itself
through other means than propagation. Only he has an
intellect capable of grasping concepts, ideas.

Where the lower forms of life must give their entire
time to finding shelter and sustenance and reproducing
their species, man has used his intellect to such good purpose that these elementary needs occupy but a small part
of his time. That leaves him leisure to express something
more than the mere animal in him—MIND.

To man has been given the job of emulating his Maker
—of becoming a creator, finding new and broader and
better ways through which to express the Creative Force
in him. His is the work of creating beauty, or bringing
more of comfort, of joy and happiness into the world.

To every living thing on earth is given a measure of
Creative Power. Of the lower forms of life all that is
required is that they bring forth fruit according to their
kind—"some thirty, some sixty, some an hundred fold."

Of you, however, much more is expected. To bring
forth fruit according to your physical kind is good—but
that is no more than the animals do. More is required of
you. You must bring forth fruit, according to your *mental*
kind as well! You are a son of God, a creator. Therefore
creation is expected of you. You are to spread seeds not
merely of human kind, but of the intellect as well. You are
to leave the world a better place than you found it, with
more of joy in it, more of beauty, of comfort, of understanding, of light.

The real purpose of Life is expression, the constant
urge onward and upward. Even in the smallest child, you

see evidence of this. It plays with blocks. Why? To express the urge in him to build something. The growing boy makes toys, builds a hut. The girl sews dresses, cares for dolls, cooks, plays house. Why? To give vent to the inner urge in each, struggling for expression.

They reach the period of adolescence. They dance, they motor, they seek all manner of thrill. Why? Again to satisfy that constant craving of the Creative Force in them for *expression!*

True—at the moment, it is mostly a physical urge. But in some way, that urge must be translated into a mental one—*and satisfied!* It must be given an outlet for expression. It must be brought into the light of day, given useful, uplifting work to do, and it will then bring forth abundant fruit of happiness and accomplishment. Because no matter how it is repressed, no matter how deep it is buried in dark cellars, the Creative Force will still bring forth fruit—only then it may be fungus growths of sin and misery.

Through every man there flows this Creative Force, with infinite power to draw to itself whatever is necessary to its expression. It doesn't matter who you are, what your environment or education or advantages, the Creative Force in you has the same power for good or evil. Mind you, that Force never brings forth evil. Its life is good. But just as you can graft onto the trunk of the finest fruit tree a branch of the upas tree, and thereupon bring forth deadly fruit, so can you engraft upon the pure energy of your Creative Force any manner of fruit you desire. But if the fruit be bad, it is *you* who are to blame, not the perfect Force that flows through you.

> "To every man there openeth
> A high way and a low,
> And every man decideth
> The way his soul shall go."

What is it makes a poor immigrant boy like Edward Bok overcome every handicap of language and education, to become one of the greatest editors the country has ever known?

Isn't it that the more circumstances conspire to repress it, the stronger becomes the urge of the Creative Force in you for expression? The more it lacks channels through which to expand, the more inclined it is to burst its shell and flow forth in all directions.

It is the old case of the river that is dammed generating the most power. Most of us are so placed that some opportunity for expression is made easy for us. And that little opportunity serves like a safety valve to a boiler—it leaves us steam enough to do something worth while, yet keeps us from getting up enough power to burst the shell about us, and sweep away every barrier that holds us down.

Yet it is only such an irresistible head of steam as that which makes great successes. That is why the blow which knocks all the props from under us is often the turning point in our whole career.

As Walt Whitman put it—

"Oh, while I live, to be the ruler of life,
    Not a slave.
To meet life as a powerful conqueror . . .
And nothing exterior shall ever take command of me."

You cannot stand still. You must go forward—or see the world slide past you. This was well illustrated by figures worked out by Russell Conwell years ago. Of all the thousands who are left fortunes through the deaths of relatives, *only one in seventeen dies wealthy!*

Why?— Because the fortunes left them take away the need for initiative on their part. Their money gives to them easy means of expressing the urge in them, without effort on their part. It gives them dozens of safety valves, through which their steam continually escapes.

The result is that they not only accomplish nothing worth while, but they soon dissipate the fortunes that were left them. They are like kettles, the urge of life keeping the water at boiling point, but the open spout of ease letting the steam escape as fast as it forms, until presently there is not even any water left.

Why do the sons of rich men so seldom accomplish anything worth while? Because they don't have to. Every opportunity is given them to turn the Creative Force in them through pleasant channels, and they dissipate through these the energies that might carry them to any height. The result? They never have a strong enough "head of steam" left to carry through any real job.

"What shall I do to be saved?" begged the rich young man of Jesus. "Sell all that thou hast, give it to the poor and follow Me," the Master told him. Churches have used that to prove that poverty is necessary to salvation. But is that the lesson the Biblical writer meant to convey? If so, why is there no record of Jesus having ever given similar advice to Nicodemus, or Joseph of Arimathea, or any others of the rich who sought counsel of Him and at whose houses He frequently stopped?

Isn't the difference that these latter had made their mark in the world—expressed the Creative Force in them to some worth-while purpose—and in the expressing of it, the Creative Force had increased and multiplied and brought back to them goodly harvests of riches?

The young man, on the other hand, had done nothing to earn all the good things that were his. His life had been cast in pleasant places. The Spirit in him urged its need of expression, but Jesus saw that only by getting away from his life of ease was any worth-while expression possible. And the young man had not courage enough for that. Truly it is harder for a camel to go through the eye of the needle than for such a rich man to enter into the Kingdom of Heaven—the Land of Accomplishment.

"You will be what you will to be;
Let failure find its false content
In that poor word 'environment,'
But Spirit scorns it, and is free.

"It masters time, it conquers space,
It cows that boastful trickster Chance,
And bids the tyrant Circumstance
Uncrown and fill a servant's place.

"Be not impatient in delay,
But wait as one who understands;
When *Spirit* rises and commands
The gods are ready to obey."
—ELLA WHEELER WILCOX

You are a channel for power. There is no limit to the amount of Creative Force that will flow through you. The only limit to what you *get*, is the amount that you *use*. Like the widow's cruse, no matter how much you pour out, there is just as much still available, but unlike the cruse of oil, your channel and your power grow with use!

What are *you* doing to satisfy the urge in you? What are you doing to give expression—*and increase*—to the Creative Force working through you?

Many a man and woman has the urge to write—or paint—or sing—or do some other worth-while thing. But does he? No, indeed. He is not well enough known, or has not the right training, or lacks education or opportunity or influence. Or else he has tried once or twice and failed.

What does that matter? It is not your responsibility if

others fail in their appreciation. Your job is to express
the Creative Force surging through you, to give it the
best you have. Each time you do that, *you* are the better
for it, whether others care for it or not. And each time
you will give more perfect, more understanding expression to the Creative Force working through you, until
sooner or later ALL appreciate it.

You don't suppose the great writers, the successful artists, were born with the ability to write or paint, do you?
You don't suppose they had all the latest books or finest
courses on the art of expression? On the contrary, all that
many of them had was the URGE! The rest they had to
acquire just as you do.

The Creative Force flowing through you is as perfect
as the rose in the bud. But just as the life in the rose bush
evolved through millions of less beautiful forms before
it perfected the rose, so must you be satisfied to model but
crudely at first, in the sure knowledge that if you keep
giving of your best, eventually the product of your hands
or your brain will be as perfect as the rose.

Every desire, every urge of your being, is Creative
Force straining at the bonds of repression you have put
upon it, straining for expression. You can't stand still.
You can't stop and smugly say—"Look what I did yesterday, or last week, or last year!" It is what you are doing
now that counts.

The Creative Force is dynamic. It is ever seeking expression—and when you fail to provide new and greater
outlets for it, it slips away to work through some more
ambitious soul who will. Genius is nothing but the irresistible urge for one particular channel of expression—an
urge so strong that it is like a mountain torrent in flood,
sweeping trees and bridges and dams and everything else
before it.

So don't worry about whether those around you recognize your talents. Don't mind if the world seems indifferent to them. The world is too busy with its own little ways of expressing life to pay much attention to yours. To get under its skin, you must do something to appeal to its emotions.

You see, the world in the mass is like a child. Prod it, and you make it angry. Preach to it, or try to teach or uplift it, and you lose its attention. You bore it. But appeal to its emotions—make it laugh or weep—and it will love you! Love you and lavish upon you all the gifts in its power to give. That is why it pays a Crosby millions, and a great educator only hundreds. Yet the name of the educator may live for ages, while the entertainer will be remembered only until a better one displaces him.

So forget the immediate rewards the world has to offer, and give your energies to finding ways of better expressing the Creative Force in you. You are expressing it every day and hour. Try to express it better, to find ever greater channels through which to work. If your urge is to write a story, put into it the best you have, no matter if you know you could get by with a third of the effort. Work always for perfection, knowing that thus only can you be sure of the greatest help of the Creative Force working through you. "I can do all things through Christ which strengtheneth me," said Paul. And you can do all things through the Creative Force working through you.

That Creative Force is striving for a perfect body, perfect surroundings, perfect work. It is not its fault when you manifest less than these. Depend upon it, it is not satisfied with anything less. So don't *you* be! If you have the courage to refuse anything short of your ideal, if you have the dogged perseverence to keep trying, there's no power in the heavens or the earth that can keep you from success!

It's the way every great success has been won. Do you

suppose if Michelangelo or Da Vinci had an off day and painted some imperfect figures into a painting, he left them there? Do you think he explained to his friends that he was under the weather that day, and so, while he was sorry it spoiled the picture, he could not be held accountable for it?

Just imagine one of these great painters letting something less than his best go over his name! Why, he would cheerfully destroy a year's work rather than have that happen. The moment he noticed it, he would hasten to scratch out the offensive figure, lest others might see it and judge his work by it. Or even if no one was ever to see it, he would do it because it failed to express the genius that was his!

That is how you must feel about your work before ever it can attain greatness. The Creative Force working through you is perfect, all-powerful, without limit. So don't ever be satisfied with less than its best! Follow its urge. Use every atom of strength and skill and riches you have to express it, serene in the knowledge that, like Paul, you can do anything through the Christ working in you.

Andrew Carnegie said:

> "Here is the prime condition of success, the great secret: Concentrate your energy, thought, and capital exclusively upon the business in which you are engaged. Having begun on one line, resolve to fight it out on that line, to lead in it, adopt every improvement, have the best machinery, and know the most about it. Finally, do not be impatient, for, as Emerson says, 'No one can cheat you out of ultimate success but yourself.'"

Have you ever climbed a high mountain? Did you notice, as you kept getting higher and higher, how your horizon rose with you? It is the same with life. The more you use the Creative Force, the more you have to use.

Your skill and power and resources grow with your use of them.

From earliest infancy, the Creative Force is trying to express something through you. First it is purely physical —a perfect body, and through it the generation of other perfect bodies. But gradually it rises above the physical plane, and strives to express itself in some way that will leave the world a better place for your having been in it— a memory of noble thoughts, of splendid deeds, of obstacles conquered and ideals won.

Do your part by never falling short of your best, no matter in how small a thing you may express it. Perfection, you remember, is made up of trifles, but perfection is no trifle.

It doesn't matter how small or seemingly unimportant your job may be. You have the same chance to attain perfection in it as the greatest artist has in his work. It doesn't matter how little others may believe that any good or great thing can come from you. It was said in the Scriptures of a far greater than you—"Can there any good thing come out of Nazareth?"

Who knows what good things may come from you?

> "There's nothing to fear—you're as good as the best,
> As strong as the mightiest, too.
> You can win in every battle or test;
> For there's no one just like you.
> There's only one *you* in the world today;
> So nobody else, you see,
> Can do your work in as fine a way;
> You're the only *you* there'll be!
> So face the world, and all life is yours
> To conquer and love and live;
> And you'll find the happiness that endures
> In just the measure you give:

There's nothing too good for you to possess,
Nor heights where you cannot go;
Your power is more than belief or guess—
It's something you have to *know*.
There's nothing to fear—*you can and you will,*
For you're the invincible *you.*
So set your foot on the highest hill—
There's nothing you cannot do."

—Anonymous

CHAPTER TWENTY-THREE

THE MENTAL EQUIVALENT

"All the world's a stage,
And all the men and women merely players."

WHAT PART ARE YOU acting in the theater of life? What place have you assigned to yourself on that stage? Are you one of the stars? Do you bear one of the important parts? Or are you merely one of the "mob" scene, just background for the action, or one of the "props" for moving the scenery around?

Whatever part is yours, it is you who have given it to you, for as Emerson says, and the whole Bible teaches from one end to the other, "Man surrounds himself with the true image of himself."

"Every spirit builds itself a house," writes Emerson, "and beyond its house a world, and beyond its world a heaven. Know then that the world exists for you. For you is the phenomenon perfect. What we are, that only can we see. All that Adam had, all that Caesar could, you have and can do. Adam called his house, heaven and earth. Caesar called his house, Rome; you perhaps call yours a cobbler's trade; a hundred acres of plowed land; or a scholar's garret. Yet line for line and point for point, your dominion is as great as theirs, though without fine names. Build therefore your own world. As fast as you conform your life to the pure idea in your mind, that will unfold its great proportions."

All men are created free and equal, in that all are given the only tool with which you can really build your life. That tool is your thought. All have the same material with which to build. That material is the Creative Force working through you. As your interior thought is, so will your exterior life be. The Creative Force takes shape in the mold your thoughts give it. "We think in secret and it comes to pass; environment is but our looking glass."

"In all my lectures," declared Emerson, "I have taught one doctrine—the infinitude of the private man, the ever-availability to every man of the divine presence within his own mind, from which presence he draws, at his need, inexhaustible power."

> "Think big, and your deeds will grow;
> Think small, and you'll fall behind;
> Think that you can, and you will—
> It's all in the state of mind."

"What sort of mental image do you hold of yourself?" Emmett Fox asks in one of his helpful books. "Whatever your real conviction of yourself is, that is what you will demonstrate.

"Whatever enters into your life is but the material expression of some belief of your own mind. The kind of body you have, the kind of home you have, the kind of job you have, the kind of people you meet with, are all conditioned by and correspond to the mental concept you are holding. The Bible teaches that from beginning to end.

"About twenty years ago, I coined the phrase 'mental equivalent.' And I am going to say that anything that you want in your life, anything that you would like to have in your life—a healthy body, a satisfactory vocation, friends, opportunities, above all the understanding of God—if you want these things to come into your life, you

must furnish a mental equivalent for them. Supply yourself with a mental equivalent and the thing must come to
you. Without a mental equivalent, it cannot come to you."

And what is this "Mental Equivalent"? What but your
mental image of what you hope to be, plan to be. "Think
and forms spring into shape, will and worlds disintegrate."

God hid the whole world in your heart, as one great
writer tells us, so when any object or purpose is clearly
held in thought, its manifestation in tangible and visible
form is merely a question of time. Cause and effect are as
absolute and undeviating in the hidden realm of thought
as in the world of visible and material things. Mind is the
master weaver, both of the interior garment of character
and the outer garment of circumstance. Thinking for a
purpose brings that purpose into being just as surely as a
hen's "setting" on an egg matures and brings the chicken
into being.

"Amid all the mysteries by which we are surrounded,"
wrote Herbert Spencer, "nothing is more certain than
that we are ever in the presence of an infinite and eternal
energy from which all things proceed."

That infinite and eternal energy or Creative Force is
molded by our thought. For thousands of years, men of
wisdom have realized this and have molded their own
lives accordingly. The Prophets of old did their best to
impress this fact upon their people. "My word (my
thought or mental image) shall not come back to me
void, but shall accomplish that whereunto it was sent,"
says one. And in a hundred places, you will find the same
thought expressed. You are molding your tomorrows,
whether you realize it or not. Make them the good you
desire—not the evil you fear.

Clarence Edwin Flynn expresses something of the
power of thought in his little poem:

"Whenever you cultivate a thought
Remember it will trace
With certain touch, its pictured form
A story on your face.

"Whenever you dwell upon a thought,
Remember it will roll
Into your being and become
A fiber of your soul.

"Whenever you send out a thought,
Remember it will be
A force throughout the universe,
For all eternity."

Remember that this holds good in all of your affairs. In your own thoughts, you are continually dramatizing yourself, your environment, your circumstances. If you see yourself as prosperous, you will be. If you see yourself as continually hard up, that is exactly what you will be. If you are constantly looking for slights, if you seek trouble in your thoughts, you will not be long in finding them in your daily life. Whatever part you give yourself in the drama of life in your own thought, that part you will eventually act out on the stage of life.

So give yourself a good part. Make yourself the hero of the piece, rather than the downtrodden member of the mob or the overworked servant. Set your lines in pleasant places. It is just as easy as laying them in the slums. As long as you are bound to dramatize yourself and your surroundings and circumstances anyway, try this:

1. Dramatize yourself, in your mind's eye, with the people and surroundings and things you want most, doing the things you would like most to do, holding the sort of position you long for, doing the work you feel yourself best fitted to do. Some may call it day-dreaming, but make it day-dreaming with a purpose. Make the picture

as clear in your mind's eye as though you saw it on the screen of a motion picture theater. And get all the enjoyment out of it that you can. Believe in it. Be thankful for it.

2. Prove your faith in your dream by making every logical preparation for the material manifestation of your desires. Just as the kings of old did when they prayed for water, dig your ditches to receive it.

3. Alter minor details of your drama as you like, but stick to the main goal. Make it your objective, and like Grant in his successful campaign, resolve to stick to it "though it takes all summer."

4. Be a finisher as well as a beginner. Remember that one job finished is worth a dozen half finished. The three-quarter horses never win a prize. It is only at the finish that the purse awaits you. So complete your drama mentally before you begin to act it out, and then stick to it actually until you've made it manifest for all to see.

5. Keep that mental drama to yourself. Don't tell it to others. Remember Samson. He could do anything as long as he kept his mouth shut. Most people's minds are like boilers with the safety valve wide open. They never get up enough of a head of steam to run their engines. Keep your plans to yourself. That way they'll generate such power that you won't need to *tell* others about them —they'll see the result for themselves.

"The imagination," says Glenn Clark in "The Soul's Sincere Desire," "is of all qualities in man the most God-like—that which associates him most closely with God. The first mention we read of man in the Bible is where he is spoken of as an 'image.' 'Let us make man in our image, after our likeness.' The only place where an image can be conceived is in the imagination. Thus man, the highest creation of God, was a creation of God's imagination.

"The source and center of all man's creative power—

the power that above all others lifts him above the level of brute creation, and that gives him dominion, is his power of making images, or the power of the imagination. There are some who have always thought that the imagination was something which makes-believe that which is not. This is fancy—not imagination. Fancy would convert that which is real into pretense and sham; imagination enables one to see through the appearance of a thing to what it really *is*."

There is a very real law of cause and effect which makes the dream of the dreamer come true. It is the law of visualization—the law that calls into being in this outer material world everything that is real in the inner world by directing your Creative Force into it. Imagination pictures the thing you desire. VISION idealizes it. It reaches beyond the thing that is, into the conception of what can be. Imagination gives you the picture. Vision gives you the impulse to make the picture your own by directing your Creative Force into it.

Make your mental image clear enough, picture it vividly in every detail, then do everything you can to bring that image into being, and the Creative Force working through you will speedily provide whatever is necessary to make it an everyday reality.

The law holds true of everything in life. There is nothing you can rightfully desire that cannot be brought into being through visualization and faith.

The keynote of successful visualization is this: See things as you would have them be instead of as they are. Close your eyes and make clear mental pictures. Make them look and act just as they would in real life. In short, day-dream—but day-dream purposefully. Concentrate on the one idea to the exclusion of all others, and continue to concentrate on that one idea until it has been accomplished.

Do you want an automobile? A home? A factory? They can all be won in the same way. They are in their essence all of them ideas of mind, and if you will but build them up in your own mind first, complete in every detail, you will find that the Creative Force working through you can build them up similarly in the material world.

"The building of a trans-continental railroad from a mental picture," says C. W. Chamberlain in "The Uncommon Sense of Applied Psychology," "gives the average individual an idea that it is a big job. The fact of the matter is, the achievement, as well as the perfect mental picture, is made up of millions of little jobs, each fitting in its proper place and helping to make up the whole.

"A skyscraper is built from individual bricks, the laying of each brick being a single job which must be completed before the next brick can be laid."

It is the same with any work, any study. To quote Professor James:

"As we become permanent drunkards by so many separate drinks, so we become saints in the moral, and authorities and experts in the practical and scientific spheres, by so many separate acts and hours of working. Let no youth have any anxiety about the upshot of his education whatever the line of it may be. If he keep faithfully busy each hour of the working day he may safely leave the final result to itself. He can with perfect certainty count on waking some fine morning, to find himself one of the competent ones of his generation, in whatever pursuit he may have singled out. . . . Young people should know this truth in advance. The ignorance of it has probably engendered more discouragement and faintheartedness in youths embarking on arduous careers than all other causes taken together."

Remember that the only limit to your capabilities is the

one you place upon them. There is no law of limitation. The only law is of supply. Through mind you can draw upon the Creative Force for anything you wish. Use it! There are no limitations upon it. Don't put any on yourself.

Aim high! If you miss the moon, you may hit a star. Everyone admits that this world and all the vast firmament must have been thought into shape from the formless void by some God-Mind. That same God-Mind rules today, and it has given to each form of life power to attract to itself as much of the Creative Force as it needs for its perfect growth. The tree, the plant, the animal—each one finds supply to meet its need.

You are an intelligent, reasoning creature. Your mind is part of the great God-Mind. And you have the power to *say* what you require for perfect growth. Don't be a niggard with yourself. Don't sell yourself for a penny. Whatever price you set upon yourself, life will give. So aim high. Demand much! Make a clear, distinct mental image of what it is you want. Hold it *in your thoughts*. Visualize it, see it, *believe it!* The ways and means of satisfying that desire will follow. For supply always comes on the heels of demand.

It is by doing this that you take your fate out of the hands of chance. It is in this way that you control the experiences you are to have in life. But be sure to visualize *only what you want*. The law works both ways. If you visualize your worries and your fears, you will make them real. Control your thought and you control circumstances. Conditions will be what you make them.

To paraphrase Thackeray—

"The world is a looking glass, and gives back to every man the reflection of his own thought."

Philip of Macedon, Alexander's father, perfected the "phalanx"—a triangular formation which enabled him to center the whole weight of his attack on one point in the opposing line. It drove through everything opposed to it. In that day and age it was invincible. And the idea is just as invincible today.

Keep the one thought in mind, SEE it being carried out step by step, and you can knit any group of workers into one homogeneous whole, all centered on the one idea. You can accomplish any one thing. You can put across any definite idea. Keep that mental picture ever in mind and you will make it as invincible as was Alexander's phalanx of old.

> "It is not the guns or armament
> Or the money they can pay,
> It's the close cooperation
> That makes them win the day.
> It is not the individual
> Or the army as a whole
> But the everlasting team work of every bloomin' soul."
> —J. Mason Knox

The error of the ages is the tendency mankind has always shown to limit the power of Mind, or its willingness to help in time of need.

"Know ye not," said Paul, "That ye are the temples of the Living God?"

No—most of us do not know it. Or at least, if we do, we are like the Indian family out on the Cherokee reservation. Oil had been found on their land and money poured in upon them. More money than they had ever known was in the world. Someone persuaded them to build a great house, to have it beautifully furnished, richly decorated. But the Indians, while very proud of their showy house, continued to *live in their old sod shack!*

So it is with many of us. We may know that we are

"temples of the Living God." We may even be proud of that fact. But we never take advantage of it to dwell in that temple, to proclaim dominion over things and conditions. We never avail ourselves of the power that is ours.

The great prophets of old had the forward look. Theirs was the era of hope and expectation. They looked for the time when the revelation should come that was to make men "sons of God." "They shall obtain joy and gladness, and sorrow and sighing shall flee away."

Jesus came to fulfill that revelation. "Ask and ye shall receive, that your joy may be full."

The world has turned in vain to materialistic philosophy for deliverance from its woes. In the future the only march of actual progress will be in the mental realm, and this progress will not be in the way of human speculation and theorizing, but in the *actual demonstration* of the power of Mind to mold the Creative Force into anything of good.

The world stands today within the vestibule of the vast realm of divine intelligence, wherein is found the transcendent, practical power of Mind over all things.

> "What eye never saw, nor ear ever heard,
> What never entered the mind of man—
> Even all that God has prepared for those who love him."

CHAPTER TWENTY-FOUR

I AM

THIRTY YEARS AGO, Emile Coué electrified the world
with his cures of all manner of disease—solely through
the power of SUGGESTION!

"Nobody ought to be sick!" he proclaimed, and proceeded to prove it by curing hundreds who came to him
after doctors had failed to relieve them. Not only that,
but he showed that the same methods could be used to
cure one's affairs—to bring riches instead of debts, success instead of drudgery.

Originally, Coué was a hypnotist. In his little drug
store, he found occasional patients whom he could hypnotize. He hypnotized them—put their conscious minds
to sleep—and addressed himself directly to their subconscious.

To the subconscious, he declared that there was nothing wrong with whatever organ the patient had thought
diseased, and the subconscious accepted the statement and
molded the Creative Force within accordingly. When the
patient came out from under the hypnotic influence, he
was well! It remained then only to convince his conscious
mind of this, so he would not send through new suggestions of disease to his subconscious, and the patient was
cured!

How account for that? By the fact that the disease or
imperfection is not so much in your body as in your mind.

It is in your rate of motion, and this is entirely mind-controlled. Change the subconscious belief, and the physical manifestations change with it. You speed up your rate of motion, and in that way throw off the discordant elements of disease. Doctors recognize this when they give their patients harmless sugar pills, knowing that these will dispel fear, and that when the images conjured up by fear are gone, the supposed trouble will go with them.

But Coué found many patients whom he could not hypnotize. How treat them? By inducing a sort of self-hypnosis in themselves. It is a well-known fact that constant repetition carries conviction—especially to the subconscious mind. So Coué had his patients continually repeat to themselves the affirmation that their trouble was passing, that they were getting better and better. "Every day in every way I am getting better and better." And this unreasoning affirmation cured thousands of ills that had been troubling them for years.

What is back of that success? A law as old as the hills, a law that has been known to psychologists for years—the law that the subconscious mind accepts as true anything that is repeated to it *convincingly* and *often*. And once it has accepted such a statement as true, it proceeds to mold the Creative Force working through it in such wise as to MAKE IT TRUE!

You see, where the conscious mind reasons inductively, the subconscious uses only deductive reasoning. Where the reasoning mind weighs each fact that is presented to it, questions the truth or falsity of each, and then forms its conclusions accordingly, the subconscious acts quite differently. IT ACCEPTS AS FACT ANY STATEMENT THAT IS PRESENTED TO IT CONVINCINGLY. Then, having accepted this as the basis of its actions, it proceeds logically to do all in its power to bring it into being.

That is why the two most important words in the English language are the words—"I AM." That is why the Ancients regarded these two words as the secret name of God.

You ask a friend how he is, and he replies carelessly —"I am sick, I am poor, I am unlucky, I am subject to this, that or the other thing,"—never stopping to think that by those very words he is fastening misfortune upon himself, declaring to the subconscious mind within him that he IS sick or poor or weak or the servant of some desire.

"Let the weak say—'I am strong!'" the Prophet Joel exhorted his people thousands of years ago. And the advice is as good today as it was then.

You have seen men, under hypnotic suggestion, perform prodigies of strength. You have seen them with their bodies stretched between two chairs, their heads on one, their feet on another, supporting the weight of several people standing on them, when they could not ordinarily hold up even their own bodies in that position. How can they do it? Because the hypnotist has assured their subconscious that they CAN do it, that they have the strength and power necessary.

"Therefore I say unto you, what things soever ye desire when ye pray, BELIEVE THAT YE RECEIVE THEM, and ye shall HAVE them." That was the assurance given us by the Master Psychologist of all time, the Great Healer, the Worker of Miracles. Again and again He told those He healed that it was their FAITH that made them whole. And where such faith was lacking, as when He went back to Nazareth, the home of his childhood, it is written that "There He did no mighty works."

How can you work up the necessary faith to accomplish the things you desire? By taking the advice of the wise men of old, of the Prophet Joel, of Jesus—by *claiming* it as yours, and setting your subconscious mind to work making those claims come true.

It is a sort of self-hypnosis, but so is all of prayer. Away back in 1915, the head of the Warsaw Psychological Institute conducted a series of experiments from which he concluded that the energy manifested by anyone during life is in direct ratio with his power for plunging himself into a condition of auto-hypnosis. In simple language, that means convincing yourself of the possibility of doing the things you want to do.

The subconscious in each of us HAS the knowledge, HAS the power to do any right thing we may require of it. The only need is to implant in it the confidence—the "BELIEVE THAT YOU RECEIVE" which Jesus taught.

In a case cited by Baudouin, the famous psychologist, a woman after using autosuggestion as a means of helping herself, declared: "I can do twice as much work as before. During vacation, I have been able to go through two extensive tasks, such as a year ago I should never have attempted. This year I systematized my work and said, 'I can do it all; what I am undertaking is materially possible, and therefore must be morally possible; consequently I ought not to experience, and shall not experience, discouragement, hesistancy, annoyance, or slackness.'" As a result of these affirmations, the way to her inner powers was opened and she was able to say truly, "Nothing could stop me, nothing could prevent my doing what I had planned to do; you might almost have said that things were done by themselves, without the slightest effort on my part." Not only did she find herself working with a high degree of success heretofore unknown, but with a certainty and calmness of mind beyond her previous attainment.

Emerson, with his genius for condensing great truths into a few words, wrote—"Do the thing and you shall have the power."

The wise men of old learned thousands of years ago that life is like an echo. It always returns the call sent out. Like the echo, the response is always the same as the call, and the louder the call, the greater the response.

You say—"I am sick, I am poor," and your words are forerunners of your circumstance. "Every idle word that men shall speak, they shall give account of in the day of judgment." And that day of judgment comes sooner than most people think.

Be careful to speak only those words which you are willing to see take form in your life, for remember the words of wise old Job: "Thou shalt also decree a thing, and it shall be established unto thee." Never speak the word of lack or limitation, for—"By thy words shalt thou be justified, and by thy words shalt thou be condemned."

Affirm constantly—"I have faith in the power of my word. I speak only that which I desire to see made manifest." Remember, "Behind you is Infinite Power, before you is endless possibility, around you is endless opportunity. Why should you fear?"

C. G. Tanner expresses the idea beautifully—

"If you have faith in what you want to do,
 If you behold yourself a king's own son,
 Then you have asked God's power to work through you,
 And pledged yourself to see that it is done.
 'With faith I place it in God's hands,' you say?
 God's hands are yours! Your good must come through you!
 God has no other hands with which He may
 Give unto you your sonship's rightful due.

"Faith and persistence travel hand in hand,
  The one without the other incomplete.
  If you would reach success, then take the stand,
  'This I will try once more,' and no defeat
  Can cloud that beacon gleaming bright and clear,
  Or conjure up dread failure's haunting wraith!
  You rest secure with God. No thought of fear
  Can dim the shining armor of your faith."

Most people seem to think that we work to live, but there is a deeper purpose in life than that. What we really work for is to call forth the talents that are within our own soul, to give expression to the Creative Force working through us. That is the one big purpose for which we were born—to express the Creative Force in us, to give God the chance to express Himself through us. And we CAN do it. As the famous English poet Shelley put it—"The Almighty has given men arms long enough to reach the stars, if they would but put them forth."

And the first step lies in using what you have. The key to power lies in using, not hoarding. Use releases still more power for ever greater works. Hoarding builds a hard shell around the thing hoarded and prevents more from coming in. You may have what you want, if you are willing to use what you have now. You can do what you want to do if you are willing to do what there is to do right now. "The one condition coupled with the gift of truth," says Emerson, *"is its use."*

Professor William Bateson of the British Society for Scientific Research said: "We are finding now beyond doubt that the gifts and geniuses of mankind are due not so much to something added to the ordinary person, but instead are due to factors which in the normal person INHIBIT the development of these gifts. They are now without doubt to be looked upon as RELEASES of powers normally suppressed."

And why are they suppressed? Because of doubt, of fear of failure, of procrastination, of putting things off till the morrow. "Straight from a mighty bow this truth is driven: They fail, and they alone, who have not striven."

> "Tomorrow you will live, you always cry;
> In what far country does this morrow lie,
> That 'tis so mighty long ere it arrive?
> Beyond the Indies does this morrow live?
> 'Tis so far fetched, this morrow, that I fear
> 'Twill be both very old and very dear.
> Tomorrow I will live, the fool does say;
> Today itself's too late; the wise lived yesterday."
> —ABRAHAM COWLEY

"To begin," said Ausonius, "is to be half done." "Greatly begin!" wrote another sage. "Though thou have time for but a line, be that sublime." And the Easterners have a proverb that the road of a thousand miles begins with one step.

So make your start, and don't allow any thought of failure to stop you. Have faith—if not in yourself—then in the Creative Force working through you. Many a splendid work has been lost to mankind because the faith of its originator was not strong enough to release the Creative Force that would have enabled him to make his dream come true.

Remember that you cannot talk failure, or think failure, and reap success. You'll never reach the top of the ladder if doubt and fear and procrastination make you hesitate to put your foot on the first rung.

There is a Power working through you that can accomplish any aim you may aspire to. But to energize that power, you must harness it up with Faith. You must have the will to believe, the courage to aspire, and the profound conviction that success is possible to anyone who works for it persistently and believingly.

Three hundred and forty years ago, there sailed from Spain the mightiest fleet the world had ever known, Spanish galleasses, Portuguese caracks, Florentine caravels, huge hulks from other countries—floating fortresses, mounting tier upon tier of mighty cannon—140 great ships in all, manned to the full with sailors and soldiers and gentlemen adventurers.

The treasure of the Incas, the Plunder of the Aztec, had gone into the building and outfitting of this vast Armada. No wonder Spain looked upon it as invincible. No wonder England feared it. For this was the Armada that was to invade England and carry fire and sword through town and countryside. This was the Armada that was to punish these impudent Britons for the "piratical" raids of Sir Francis Drake, Morgan and all those hardy seamen who had dared death and slavery to pull down treasure ships on the Spanish Main.

The iron hand of Philip II of Spain rested heavily upon the Netherlands. It dominated all of Europe. Now he confidently looked forward to the time when England, too, would groan beneath its weight.

But he reckoned without one thing—faith! He put in charge of this invincible Armada, the Duke of Medina Sidonia, a man who had no faith in himself, no faith in his ability, no faith in his men. And when he did that, he blunted the point of every pike; he dulled the cutting edge of every sword; he took the mightiest naval weapon ever forged, and deliberately drew its sting.

Is that putting it too strongly? Just listen. Here is the letter the Duke wrote to the King, upon being notified of his appointment to the command:

"My health is bad and from my small experience of the water I know that I am always seasick. . . . The expedition is on such a scale and the object is of such high importance that the person at the head of it ought to understand navigation and sea fighting, and I know nothing of either. . . . The Adelantado of Castile would do better than I. The Lord would help him, he is a good Christian and has fought in naval battles. If you send me, depend upon it, I shall have a bad account to render of my trust."

He had everything to succeed with—everything but faith in himself. He expected failure—and disastrous failure met him at every turn.

One hundred and forty mighty ships—the greatest ever built. And England, to meet that splendid Armada, had only 30 small ships of war and a few merchantmen outfitted and manned by private gentlemen. Yet England, while alarmed, was yet courageous and hopeful. For had not England Sir Francis Drake? And Lord Charles Howard? And a dozen other mighty fighters who had met and bested the Spaniards a score of times on the Spanish Main? And could they not do the same again?

So said England, believing in her leaders. And her leaders echoed that sentiment. Are not English sailors the hardiest seamen and finest fighters afloat, they asked. And believed in their men.

The English had 30 or 40 little ships against the Spaniards' 140 mighty men-of-war. The English had scarce two days' powder aboard—so penurious was their Queen—while the Spanish were outfitted with everything a ship-of-war could ask.

But Howard and Drake were not depending upon any Queen to fight their battles. They were not worrying about the size of the enemy. They were thinking—"There are the Spaniards. Here are we. We have fought them and whipped them a dozen times before. We can do it now. So let's get at them!"

They went out expecting victory. And victory met them at every turn.

From the Lizard in Cornwall to Portland, where Don Pedro de Valdes and his mighty ship were left; from Portland to Calais, where Spain lost Hugo de Moncado with the galleys which he captured; from Calais, out of sight of England, around Scotland and Ireland, beaten and shuffled together, that mighty Armada was chased, until finally the broken remnants drifted back to Spain.

With all their vast squadron, they had not taken one ship or bark or pinnace of England. With all those thousands of soldiers, they had not landed one man but those killed or taken prisoner.

Three-fourths of their number lost or captured, their mighty fleet destroyed. And why? Because one man lacked faith. Spanish soldiers were proving on a dozen fields that no braver fighters lived anywhere. The "Spanish Square" had withstood infantry, cavalry, artillery—then carried all before it. Yet these same soldiers, afloat in their huge fortresses, were utterly defeated by less than a fourth their number.

And the reason? Because they were a spear without a head—an army without a leader—riches and power without faith. Was ever a better example of the power of belief?

Men go all through life like the Duke of Medina Sidonia—looking ever for the dark side of things, expecting trouble at every turn—and usually finding it. It is really lack of courage—courage to try for great things, courage to dare disappointment and ridicule to accomplish a worthy end. Have you ever sat in a train and watched another train passing you? You can look right on through its windows to the green fields and pleasant vistas beyond. Or you can gaze at the partitions between the windows and see nothing but their dingy drabness.

So it is with everything in life. You can look for the good, the joyful and happy—and not merely see only these but manifest them in your daily life. Or you can look for trouble, for sickness and sorrow—and find them awaiting you around every corner.

Pessimists call this the "Pollyanna Age" and ridicule such ideas as this. But ridicule or not, it works—in one's personal life as well as in business—and thousands can testify to its efficacy.

Perhaps one of the best examples of the difference that outlook makes is in the lives of Emerson and Thoreau. Emerson's philosophy of living can best be expressed in his own words—"Nerve us with incessant affirmatives. Don't bark against the bad, but chant the beauties of the good." And his tranquil and serene life reflected that attitude throughout.

Thoreau, on the other hand, was constantly searching out and denouncing evil. With motives every whit as high as Emerson's, he believed in attacking the problem from the opposite angle, with the result that he was constantly in hot water, yet accomplished not a tenth of the good that Emerson did. Like the man in d'Annunzio's play, LA CITTA MORTA—"Fascinated by the tombs, he forgot the beauty of the sky."

It is necessary at times to clean up evil conditions in order to start afresh. It is necessary to hunt out the source of pollution in order to purify a stream. But it should be merely a means to an end. And the end should always be—not negative like the mere destruction of evil, but the positive replacing of evil with good.

If you have ever walked across a high trestle, you know that it doesn't pay to look down. That way dizziness and destruction lie. You have to look forward, picking out the ties you are going to step on ten or twenty feet ahead, if you are to progress.

354 THE LAW OF THE HIGHER POTENTIAL

Life is just such a trestle. And looking downward too much is likely to make one lose his balance, stumble and fall. You must gaze ever forward if you are to keep your perspective.

There's a little poem by Edgar Guest * that exemplifies the idea:

> "Somebody said that it couldn't be done,
>   But he with a chuckle replied
> That 'maybe it couldn't,' but he would be one
>   Who wouldn't say so till he'd tried.
> So he buckled right in with the trace of a grin
>   On his face. If he worried he hid it.
> He started to sing as he tackled the thing
>   That couldn't be done, AND HE DID IT."

Most of the world's progress has been made by just such men as that. Men like Watt, who didn't know that steam could not be made to accomplish any useful purpose, and so invented the steam engine. Men like Fulton, who didn't know that it was foolish to try to propel a boat with wheels—and so invented the steamboat.

Men like Bell, Edison, Wright, who didn't know how foolish it was to attempt the impossible—and so went ahead and did it.

"For God's sake, give me the young man who has brains enough to make a fool of himself!" cried Stevenson. And when they succeed, the whole world echoes that cry.

There is no limit upon you—except the limit you put upon yourself. You are like the birds—your thoughts can fly across all barriers, unless you tie them down or cage them or clip their wings by the limitations you put upon them.

There is nothing that can defeat you—except yourself.

* From "The Path to Home." The Reilly & Lee Co.

You are one with the Father. And the Father knows everything you will ever need to know on any subject.

Why then, try to repress any right desire, any high ambition? Why not put behind it every ounce of energy, every bit of enthusiasm, of which you are capable?

Mahomet established a larger empire than that of Rome on nothing but enthusiasm. And Mahomet was but a poor camel-driver. What then can *you* not do?

Men repress their power for good, their capacity for success, by accepting suggestions of inferiority; by their timidity or self-consciousness; by fear; by conservatism.

Never mind what others think of you. It is what *you* think that counts. Never let another's poor opinion of you influence your decisions. Rather, resolve to show him how unfounded is his opinion.

People thought so poorly of Oliver Cromwell that he could not win permission to emigrate to the Colonies. When he raised his regiment of cavalry, that later won the name of "Ironsides" because of its practical invincibility, the old soldiers and the dandies of the day laughed at it. Seldom had a lot of more awkward-looking country-men been gathered together.

Any soldier might have trained them. But the thing that made them invincible, the thing that enabled them to ride over and through all the legions of King Charles, was not their training, but their fervent belief in the justice of their cause, in their leader and in their God.

"Hymn-singing hypocrites," their enemies called them. But here were no hypocrites. Here were men who were animated by a common faith that God was with them as with the Israelites of old—and that with God on their side, nothing could withstand them.

That was the faith of Cromwell. And he instilled that faith into every man in his regiment.

And while Cromwell lived to keep that faith alive,

nothing *did* withstand them. They made the man who was not good enough to emigrate to America, Ruler of England!

Nothing worth while ever has been accomplished without faith. Nothing worth while ever will.

Why do so many great organizations go to pieces after their founder's death? Why do they fail to outlive him by more than a few years?

Because the ones who take up his work lack the forward look, the faith, to carry on. His idea was one of service—theirs is to continue paying dividends. His thought was to build ever greater and greater—theirs to hold what he won.

"The best defensive is a strong offensive." You can't just hold your own. You can't stand still. You've got to go forward—or backward!

Which is it with you? If forward, then avoid the pessimist as you would the plague. Enthusiasm, optimism, may make mistakes—but it will learn from them and progress. Pessimism, conservatism, caution, will die of dry rot, if it is not sooner lost in the forward march of things.

So be an optimist. Cultivate the forward look.

> "The Optimist and Pessimist,
>   The difference is droll,
>   The Optimist sees the doughtnut,
>   The Pessimist—the *hole!*"

The good is always there—if you look for it hard enough. But you must look for *it*. You can't be content to take merely what happens to come into your line of vision. You have got to refuse to accept anything short of good. Disclaim it! Say it is not yours. Say it—*and believe it.* Then keep a-seeking—and the first thing you know,

the good you have been seeking will be found to have
been right under your nose all the time.

What is the backbone of all business? Credit. And
what is credit but faith—faith in your fellow-man—faith
in his integrity—faith in his willingness and his ability to
give you a square deal?

What do you base credit-faith upon? Upon hearsay—
upon what your prospective customer has done for others,
his promptness in paying them, his willingness to co-
operate with them. In many cases you have never seen
him—you can't be certain of your own personal knowledge that such a person exists—but you believe in him,
you have FAITH. And having faith, your business grows
and prospers.

If you can have such faith in a man you have never
seen, as to trust large portions of your earthly goods in
his hands, can you not put a little trust in the Father,
too?

True, you have not seen Him—but you have far
greater proof of His being than of that of your customer
thousands of miles away. You have far greater proof of
His reliability, of His regard for you, of His ability and
His willingness at all times to come to your assistance in
any right way you may ask. You don't need money with
Him. You don't need high standing in your community.
You don't need credit.

What is it makes a successful salesman? Faith in his
house. Faith in the goods he is selling. Faith in the service they will render his customers. Faith in himself.
Have you faith in your "house"—in your Father—in the
manifold gifts He offers you so freely?

Men can sell for a little while solely on faith in their
own ability, they can palm off anything that will show a
profit to themselves. But they never make successful salesmen. The inevitable reaction comes. They grow cynical,

lose all faith in others—and eventually lose faith in them-selves as well. The successful salesman must have a four-fold faith—faith in his house, faith in his product, faith in the good it will do his customer, faith in himself. Given such a faith, he can sell anything. Given such a faith in the Father, *you* can do anything.

It wasn't superior courage or superior fighting ability that enabled Washington's half-trained army to beat the British. English soldiers were showing all over the world that they were second to none in fighting qualities. And the American soldiers were, for the most part, from the same sturdy stock. It was their faith in a greater Power outside themselves.

What is it differentiates the banker from the pawn-broker? Both make loans. Both require security. But where the pawn-broker must have tangible, material property that he can resell before he will lend a cent, the really great banker bases his loans on something big-ger than any security that may be offered him—his faith in the borrower.

America was built on faith. Those great railroad builders who spanned the continent knew when they did it that there was not enough business immediately available to make their investment profitable for a long time to come. But they had faith—a faith that was the making of our country.

That same faith is evident on every hand today. Men erect vast factories—in the faith that the public will find need for and buy their products. They build offices, apart-ments, homes—in the faith that their cities will grow up to the need of them. They put up public utilities capable of serving twice the number of people in their territories —in the faith that the demand will not only grow with the population, but the availability of the supply will help to create new demands.

Faith builds cities and businesses and men. In fact, everything of good, everything constructive in this old world of ours is based on faith. So if you have it not, *grow it*—as the most important thing you can do. And if you have it, *tend it,* water it, cultivate it—for it is the most important thing in life.

"When nothing seems to help, I go and look at a stonecutter hammering away at his rock, perhaps a hundred times without as much as a crack showing in it. Yet at the hundred and first blow, it will split in two, and I know it was not that blow that did it, but all that had gone before."—J. A. RIIS.

CHAPTER TWENTY-FIVE

TALISMAN

"Like the waves of the sea are the ways of fate
As we voyage along through life.
'Tis the set of the soul which decides its goal
And not the calm or the strife."
—ELLA WHEELER WILCOX

WHAT IS THE ETERNAL QUESTION which stands up and looks you and every sincere man squarely in the eye every morning?

"How can I better my condition?" That is the real life question which confronts you, and will haunt you every day until you solve it.

The answer to that question lies first in remembering that the great business of life is thinking. Control your thoughts and you mold circumstance.

Just as the first law of gain is desire, so the first essential to success is FAITH. Believe that you *have*—see the thing you want as an existent fact—and anything you can rightly wish for is yours. Belief is "the substance of things hoped for, the evidence of things not seen."

You have seen men, inwardly no more capable than yourself, accomplish the seemingly impossible. You have seen others, after years of hopeless struggle, suddenly win their most cherished dreams. And you've often wondered, "What is the power that gives new life to their dying ambitions, that supplies new impetus to their jaded desires, that gives them a new start on the road to success?"

That power is belief—*faith*. Someone, something, gave them a new belief in themselves and a new faith in their power to win—and they leaped ahead and wrested success from seemingly certain defeat.

Do you remember the picture Harold Lloyd was in some years ago, showing a country boy who was afraid of his shadow? Every boy in the countryside bedeviled him. Until one day his grandmother gave him a talisman that she assured him his grandfather had carried through the Civil War and which, so she said, had the property of making its owner invincible. Nothing could hurt him, she told him, while he wore this talisman. Nothing could stand up against him. He believed her. And the next time the bully of the town started to cuff him around, he wiped up the earth with him. And that was only the start. Before the year was out he had made a reputation as the most daring soul in the community.

Then, when his grandmother felt that he was thoroughly cured, she told him the truth—that the "talisman" was merely a piece of old junk she'd picked up by the roadside—that she knew all he needed was *faith in himself*, belief that he could do these things.

Stories like that are common. It is such a well-established truth that you can do only what you think you can, that the theme is a favorite one with authors. I remember reading a story years ago of an artist—a mediocre sort of artist—who was visiting the field of Waterloo and happened upon a curious lump of metal half buried in the dirt, which so attracted him that he picked it up and put it in his pocket. Soon thereafter he noticed a sudden increase in confidence, an absolute faith in himself, not only as to his own chosen line of work, but in his ability to handle any situation that might present itself. He

painted a great picture—just to show that he *could* do it.
Not content with that, he visioned an empire with Mexico
as its basis, actually led a revolt that carried all before
it—until one day he lost his talisman. Then the bubble
burst.

It is your own belief in yourself that counts. It is the
consciousness of dominant power within you that makes
all things attainable. *You can do anything you think you
can.* This knowledge is literally the gift of the gods, for
through it you can solve every human problem. It should
make of you an incurable optimist. It is the open door to
welfare. *Keep it open*—by expecting to gain everything
that is right.

You are entitled to every good thing. Therefore expect
nothing but good. Defeat does not *need* to follow victory.
You don't have to "knock wood" every time you con-
gratulate yourself that things have been going well with
you. Victory should follow victory.

Don't limit your channels of supply. Don't think that
riches or success must come through some particular job
or some rich uncle. It is not for you to dictate to the
Creative Force the means through which it shall send Its
gifts to you. There are millions of channels through which
It can reach you. Your part is to impress upon Mind your
need, your earnest desire, your boundless belief in the
resources and the willingness of the Creative Force to
help you. Plant the seed of desire. Nourish it with a clear
visualization of the ripened fruit. Water it with sincere
faith. But leave the means to the Creative Force.

Open up your mind. Clear out the channels of thought.
Keep yourself in a state of receptivity. Gain a mental
attitude in which you are constantly *expecting good.* You
have the fundamental right to all good, you know. "According to your faith, be it unto you."

The trouble with most of us is that we are mentally

lazy. It is so much easier to go along with the crowd than to break trail for ourselves. But the great discoverers, the great inventors, the great geniuses in all lines have been men who dared to break with tradition, who defied precedent, who believed that there is no limit to what Mind can do—and who stuck to that belief until their goal was won, in spite of all the sneers and ridicule of the wiseacres and the "It-can't-be-doners."

Not only that, but they were never satisfied with achieving just one success. They knew that the first success is like the first olive out of the bottle. All the others come out the more easily for it. They realized that they were a part of the Creative Force and Intelligence of the Universe, and that the part shares all the properties of the whole. And that realization gave them the faith to strive for any right thing, the knowledge that the only limit upon their capabilities was the limit of their desires. Knowing that, they couldn't be satisfied with any ordinary success. They had to keep on and on and on.

Edison didn't sit down and fold his hands when he gave us the talking machine. Or the electric light. These great achievements merely opened the way to new fields of accomplishment.

Open up the channels between your mind and the Creative Force, and there is no limit to the riches that will come pouring in. Concentrate your thoughts on the particular thing you are most interested in, and ideas in abundance will come flooding down, opening up a dozen ways of winning the goal you are striving for.

But don't let one success—no matter how great—satisfy you. The Law of Life, you know, is the Law of Growth. You can't stand still. You must go forward—or be passed by. Complacency—self-satisfaction—is the greatest enemy of achievement. You must keep looking forward. Like Alexander, you must be constantly seeking new worlds to conquer. Depend upon it, the power will come to meet the need. There is no such thing as failing powers, if we look to the Creative Force for our source of supply. The only failure of mind comes from worry and fear—and disuse.

William James, the famous psychologist, taught that— "The more mind does, the more it can do." For ideas release energy. You can *do* more and better work than you have ever done. You can *know* more than you know now. You know from your own experience that under proper mental conditions of joy or enthusiasm, you can do three or four times the work without fatigue that you can ordinarily. Tiredness is more boredom than actual physical fatigue. You can work almost indefinitely when the work is a pleasure.

You've seen sickly persons, frail persons, who couldn't do an hour's light work without exhaustion, suddenly buckle down when heavy responsibilities were thrown upon them, and grow strong and rugged under the load. Crises not only draw upon the reserve power you have but they help to create new power.

It Couldn't be Done

It may be that you have been deluded by the thought of incompetence. It may be that you have been told so often that you cannot do certain things that you've come to believe you can't. Remember that success or failure is merely a state of mind. Believe you cannot do a thing— and you can't. Know that you *can* do it—and you *will.* You must *see yourself doing it.*

> "If you think you are beaten, you are;
> If you think you dare not, you don't;
> If you'd like to win, but you think you can't,
> It's almost a cinch you won't;

If you think you'll lose, you've lost,
For out in the world you'll find
Success begins with a fellow's will—
It's all in the state of mind.

"Full many a race is lost,
Ere even a race is run,
And many a coward fails
Ere even his work's begun.
Think big, and your deeds will grow,
Think small and you fall behind,
Think that you can, and you will;
It's all in the state of mind.

"If you think you are outclassed, you are;
You've got to think high to rise;
You've got to be sure of yourself before
You can ever win a prize.
Life's battle doesn't always go
To the stronger or faster man;
But sooner or later, the man who wins
Is the fellow who thinks he can."

There's a vast difference between a proper understanding of one's own ability and a determination to make the best of it—and offensive egotism. It is absolutely necessary for every man to believe in himself, before he can make the most of himself. All of us have something to sell. It may be our goods, it may be our abilities, it may be our services. You've got to believe in yourself to make your buyer take stock in you at par and accrued interest. You've got to feel the same personal solicitude over a customer lost, as a revivalist over a backslider, and hold special services to bring him back into the fold. You've got to get up every morning with determination, if you're going to go to bed that night with satisfaction.

There's mighty sound sense in the saying that all the

world loves a booster. The one and only thing you have to win success with is MIND. For your mind to function at its highest capacity, you've got to be charged with good cheer and optimism. No one ever did a good piece of work while in a negative frame of mind. Your best work is always done when you are feeling happy and optimistic.

And a happy disposition is the *result*—not the *cause*—of happy, cheery thinking. Health and prosperity are the *results* primarily of optimistic thoughts. *You* make the pattern. If the impress you have left on the world about you seems faint and weak, don't blame fate—blame your pattern! You will never cultivate a brave, courageous demeanor by thinking cowardly thoughts. You cannot gather figs from thistles. You will never make your dreams come true by choking them with doubts and fears. You've got to put foundations under your air castles, foundations of UNDERSTANDING AND BELIEF. Your chances of success in any undertaking can always be measured by your BELIEF in yourself.

Are your surroundings discouraging? Do you feel that if you were in another's place success would be easier? Just bear in mind that your real environment is within you. All the factors of success or failure are in your inner world. *You* make that inner world—and through it your outer world. You can choose the material from which to build it. If you've not chosen wisely in the past, you can choose again now the material you want to rebuild it. The richness of life is within you. No one has failed so long as he can begin again.

> "For yesterday is but a dream,
> And tomorrow is only a vision.
> And today well-lived makes
> Every yesterday a dream of happiness,
> And every tomorrow a vision of hope."

Start right in and *do* all the things you feel you have it in you to do. Ask permission of no man. Concentrating your thought upon any proper undertaking will make its achievement possible. Your belief that you *can* do the thing gives your thought forces their power. Fortune waits upon you. Seize her boldly, hold her—and she is yours. She belongs rightfully to you. But if you cringe to her, if you go up to her doubtfully, timidly, she will pass you by in scorn. For she is a fickle jade who must be mastered, who loves boldness, who admires confidence. Remember, you can have what you want if you will use what you have now. You can do what you want if you will do what there is to do right now. Take the first step, and your mind will mobilize all its forces to your aid. But the first essential is that you *begin*. Once the battle is started, all that is within and without you will come to your assistance, if you attack in earnest and meet each obstacle with resolution. But *you* have to start things. As the poet so well expresses it:

> "Then take this honey from the bitterest cup,
> There is no failure save in giving up—
> No real fall so long as one still tries—
> For seeming set-backs make the strong man wise.
> There's no defeat, in truth, save from within:
> Unless you're beaten there, you're sure to win."

The men who have made their mark in this world all had one trait in common—*they believed in themselves!* "But," you may say, "how can I believe in myself when I have never yet done anything worth while, when everything I put my hand to seems to fail?" You can't, of course. That is, you couldn't if you had to depend upon your conscious mind alone. But just remember what One far greater than you said—"I can of mine own self do nothing. The Father that is within me—He doeth the works."

That same "FATHER" is within you, and back of Him and of you is all the Creative Force in the universe. It is by knowing that He is in you, and that through Him you can do anything that is right, that you can acquire the belief in yourself which is so necessary. Certainly the Mind that imaged the heavens and the earth and all that they contain has all wisdom, all power, all abundance. With this Mind to call upon, you know there is no problem too difficult to undertake. The *knowing* of this is the first step. *Faith*. But St. James tells us—"Faith without works is dead." And Emerson expressed it in the modern manner when he said: "He who learns and learns, and yet does not what he knows, is like the man who plows and plows, yet never sows." So go on to the next step. Decide on the one thing you want most from life, no matter what it may be. There is no limit, you know, to Mind. Visualize this thing that you want. See it, feel it, BELIEVE in it. Make your mental blue-print, and *begin to build!* And not merely a mental blue-print, but make an actual picture of it, if you can. Cut out pictures from magazines that symbolize what you want. Paste them on a large sheet of paper and pin them up where you can see them often. You'll be surprised how such pictures help you to form the mental mold, and how quickly the Creative Force will take shape in that mold.

Suppose some people DO laugh at your idea. Suppose Reason does say—"It can't be done!" People laughed at Galileo. They laughed at Henry Ford. Reason contended for countless ages that the earth was flat. Reason said—or so numerous automotive engineers argued—that the Ford motor wouldn't run. But the earth *is* round—and some millions of Fords did run—and are running.

Let us start right now putting into practice some of

these truths that you have learned. What do you want most of life right now? Take that one desire, concentrate on it, impress it upon your subconscious mind in every way you can, particularly with pictures. Visualizing what you want is essential, and pictures make this visualizing easier.

Psychologists have discovered that the best time to make suggestions to your subconscious mind is just before going to sleep, when the senses are quiet and the attention is lax. So let us take your desire and suggest it to your subconscious mind tonight. The two prerequisites are the earnest DESIRE, and an intelligent, understanding, BELIEF. Someone has said, you know, that education is three-fourths encouragement, and the encouragement is the suggestion that the thing can be done.

You know that you can have what you want, if you want it badly enough and can believe in it earnestly enough. So tonight, just before you drop off to sleep, concentrate your thought on this thing that you most desire from life. BELIEVE that you have it. SEE it in your mind's eye, and see YOURSELF possessing it. FEEL yourself using it.

Do that every night until you ACTUALLY DO BELIEVE that you have the thing you want. When you reach that point, YOU WILL HAVE IT!

"Do you accept the Power within,
Or do you say—'Tomorrow,
Or after that, I will begin,'
And try from time to time to borrow
Sweet, precious moments, quickly sped,
On futile paths by error led?

"Our God has willed a legacy
To all of those believing.

So why not change your 'it might be'
To just 'I am receiving
A guiding hand in every task,
And full returns for all I ask.'

"Do you desire success to win?
Humbly accept the Power within."
—JOHN GRAHAM

CHAPTER TWENTY-SIX

THE PERFECT PATTERN

IN CHAPTER IV, we quoted Baudouin to show how a person can hypnotize himself into health, happiness, success.

This is not as foolish as it sounds, for self-hypnosis is nothing more nor less than deep concentration, and it is a well-known fact that we go in the direction of our thoughts. What we long for, or dread or fear—that we are headed towards.

You see, man is inseparable from the Creative Force. God has incarnated Himself in man, and God is dynamic —not static. He cannot be shut up. He must be expressed in one way or another. We put His power into all that we do—whether towards failure or success.

How then can we use this Creative Power for good? How can we put it into our efforts toward success?

First, by convincing ourselves that we ARE successful, that we are on the road to riches or health or power. We must "believe that we receive." And the quickest, easiest, surest way to do this is through repetition. It is now generally known and accepted that one comes to believe whatever one repeats to oneself sufficiently often, whether the statement be true or false. It comes to be the dominating thought in one's mind.

Such thoughts, when mixed with a strong feeling of desire or emotion, become a magnet which attracts from all about similar or related thoughts. They attract a host of their relatives, which they add to their own magnetic power until they become the dominating, motivating master of the individual.

Then the second law begins to work. All impulses of thought have a tendency to clothe themselves in their physical equivalent. In other words, if the dominating thought in your mind is riches, that thought will tend to draw to you opportunities for riches that you never dreamed of. Just as the magnet attracts iron, so will you attract money and ways of making more money. Or if health be your dominating thought, ways and means of winning new health and strength will come to you. The same is true of love, of happiness, of anything you may greatly desire of life.

On the other hand, if you fill your mind with fear, doubt and unbelief in your ability to use the forces of Infinite Intelligence, these in turn will become your dominating thought and form the pattern for your life.

You will be lifted up, or pulled down, according to the pattern of your thought. There are no limitations upon the Creative Force working through you. The limitations are all in you, and they are all self-imposed. Riches and poverty are equally the offspring of your thought.

So if you desire anything of good, the first and most important thing you must do is to develop your faith that *you can have that good.* Faith, like any other state of mind, can be induced by suggestion, by repetition. Tell yourself often enough that you HAVE faith, and you will have it, for any thought that is passed on to the subconscious often enough and convincingly enough is finally accepted, and then translated into its physical equivalent by the most practical method available.

You remember the story of the king who felt that his child, if brought up in the court, would be spoiled by overmuch attention. So he put him in the family of an honest peasant, and had him raised as the peasant's own child.

The boy had all the power, all the riches of the kingdom at his disposal—yet he knew it not. He was a great prince, yet because he knew nothing of it, he worked and lived as a lowly peasant.

Most of us are like that young prince, in that we are ignorant of our Divine parentage. We know nothing of the power that is ours, so we get no good from it. God is working through us, and there is nothing He cannot do, yet because we know nothing of Him, we are powerless.

There is no such thing as a human nobody. All have the Divine spark in them, all can kindle it into a glowing flame through faith. People let themselves be hypnotized by fear and anxiety, fear of poverty, of failure, of disease. They continually visualize these, and thus make them their dominant thought, using it as a magnet to draw these things to them.

Whatever form your thoughts and beliefs take, the Creative Force working through you uses as a mold in which to form your life and your surroundings. If you want to be strong, think of yourself as perfect. If you want to be prosperous, think not of debts and lacks, but of riches and opportunity. We go in the direction of our dominating thought. It strikes the keynote of our life song.

"The chief characteristic of the religion of the future," wrote Dr. Eliot, "will be man's inseparableness from the great Creative Force." We are in partnership with the Fountain Head of all good.

Emerson said that Christ alone estimated the greatness and the divinity of man. Christ constantly emphasized man's unlimited possibilities. He saw that God incarnated Himself in man.

Emerson goes on to say that man is weak when he looks for help outside himself. It is only as he throws himself unhesitatingly upon the Creative Force within himself that he finds the springs of success, the power that can accomplish all things. It is only when he realizes that all outside help amounts to nothing compared with the tremendous forces working through him that he stands erect and begins to work miracles.

Nearly every man has a habit of looking back and saying—"If I had that period of my life to live over again, if I could go back and take advantage of the chance at fortune I had then, I'd be rich and successful today."

Yet a year from now, or five or ten years from now, most of you who read this will be saying the same thing of today.

Why? Because your future depends upon the foundations you are digging NOW. Yesterday is gone. There is no recalling it. And tomorrow has not come. The only time you have to work with is right now, and whether you will go up or down tomorrow, whether you will be rich or a failure, depends upon your thoughts today.

It took mankind thousands of years to learn how to control matter, how to provide comfort and safety and some degree of financial security. It has taken less than a generation to learn how to control one's own future. The knowledge is so new that most people are not yet aware of it. As David Seabury put it in his book—"They know that science and mechanics have made over the face of the earth. They do not know that psychology and its kindred sciences are making a like change in man's handling of his own nature."

Do you know why so few people succeed in life? Because it is so EASY that most people cannot believe in the methods that really make men successful. They prefer to look upon success as something arduous, something practically impossible for them to attain—and by looking upon it that way, they make it so for themselves.

YOU CAN HAVE WHAT YOU WANT—if you
know how to plant the seeds of it in your thought. To
know that is the most important thing that anyone can
learn. It is not fate that bars your path. It is not lack of
money or opportunity. It is yourself—your attitude towards life. Change it—and you change all.

Ask yourself this important question: Are you a victim
of self-pity? Are you embittered at life and at those more
successful than yourself? Do you think fortune has played
you a scurvy trick? Or are you cheerfully, steadfastly,
confidently working out ways of meeting and bettering
the situations that life presents to you?

Most people will dodge that question. They are more
concerned in defending their ego and putting the blame
for their failures on something outside themselves than
they are in getting ahead. Failure comes from the inside
first. It cannot be forced upon a resolute, dauntless soul.

How about YOU? Will you give yourself an honest
answer to this important question—"Are you a victim of
self-pity?"

Think of the times when you have yearned for a future
—when you have grown impatient with the barriers that
seemed to hold you down—when you have heard of the
success of some acquaintance whom you knew to be inwardly no more capable than yourself. Are you willing to
keep on *wishing* and *envying* and looking to the future for
your success? Or will you start that success in the only
time that will ever be yours to work with—the everlast-
ing NOW?

Remember what Emerson told us: "There is one Mind
common to all individual men. Every man is an inlet to
the same and to ALL of the same. He that is once admit-
ted to the right of reason is a freeman of the whole estate. What Plato has thought, he may think; what a
Saint has felt, he may feel; what has at any time befallen

any man, he can understand. Who hath access to this Universal Mind is a party to all that is or can be done; for this is the only and sovereign agent—of this Universal Mind each individual is one more incarnation."

The Creative Force of the Universe is working through you. You can be as great an outlet for IT as anyone who has ever lived. You have only to provide the mold in which it is to take shape, and that mold is formed by your thoughts. What is your dominant desire? What do you want most? *Believe in it*—and you can have it. Make it your dominating thought, magnetize your mind with it, and you will draw to you everything you need for its accomplishment.

"There is not a dream that may not come true," wrote Arthur Symons, "if we have the energy which makes or chooses our own fate. We can always in this world get what we want, if we *will* it intensely and persistently enough. So few people succeed because so few can conceive a great end and work towards it without deviating and without tiring. But we all know that the man who works for money day and night gets rich; and the man who works day and night for no matter what kind of material power, gets the power. It is only the dreams of those light sleepers who dream faintly that do not come true."

Knowing these things, can you ever again limit yourself, when you have such unlimited possibilities? Sure, there are times when you feel inferior. Everyone does. Just remember that, and realize that *you* are superior, one of the efficient few who take advantage of the Infinite Power inside them to carry you on to the heights of success.

Plato held, you remember, that in the Divine Mind are pure forms or Archetypes according to which all visible beings are made. And most of the great Mystery Schools of the older world held similar opinions. They taught growth by intent rather than by accident, a development from birth all through life towards the perfect image or Archetype of each of us that is held in Divine Mind. They visioned each of us growing into a destiny that had been imaged for him long before he was born.

Progress was movement in the direction of the perfect Archetype. Man became nobler as the interval between him and his perfect pattern grew less. To the Greeks, happiness meant peace between a man and his pattern, whereas if you lived in a manner inconsistent with your Archetype, you suffered from inharmonies of various kinds. They believed that it was not so much what you do that causes you to suffer, as it is the inharmony between what you do and what you SHOULD DO to match your perfect pattern.

There is a perfect pattern for YOU in the Divine Mind, a perfect Archetype that you CAN match. It has perfect form, perfect intelligence, all power necessary to make your surroundings perfect. Why not make yourself like it?

You CAN! Just let your Archetype be your model. Fill your mind with thoughts of its perfection, make it your dominant thought, and you can draw to yourself whatever elements you need to manifest that perfect image. And not merely the perfect image of yourself, but all that goes to make your surroundings and circumstances just as perfect. Remember, the only limit upon the Power working through you is the limit you impose.

Bear these facts in mind:

1. Your subconscious mind is constantly amenable to control by the power of suggestion.
2. Its power to reason deductively from given premises to correct conclusions is practically perfect.

3. It is endowed with a perfect memory.
4. It is the seat of your emotions.
5. It has the power to communicate and receive intelligence through other than the recognized channels of the senses.
6. Its activity and power are inversely proportionate to the vigor and healthfulness of the physical organism.
7. It is endowed with the faculties of instinct and intuition, and under certain conditions with the power of intuitive cognition or perception of the laws of Nature.

"Man contains all that is needful within himself," wrote Emerson. "He is made a law unto himself. All real good or evil that can befall him must be from himself. The purpose of life seems to be to acquaint a man with himself. The highest revelation is that God is in every man."

CHAPTER TWENTY-SEVEN

TO HIM THAT HATH

JESUS GAVE US the Fundamental Law of Increase when He told us that—"Unto everyone that hath shall be given, and he shall have abundance, but from him that hath not shall be taken away even that which he hath."

Sounds simple, doesn't it, yet it is the basic law of all success, all riches, all power. It is the way the whole universe is run. You live by it, whether you like it or not, or you die by it.

To many, this law seems unfair, but in this, as in all things, Nature is logical, and when you understand exactly how the law works, you will agree that it is eminently just and right.

You see, everything consists primarily of electricity—of tiny protons and electrons revolving about each other. It is of these that your body is made, it is of these that all plant life is made, it is of these that all so-called inanimate life is made. Wherein, then, is the difference between all these forms of life? Largly in their RATE OF MO-TION!

Remember this: Starting with the individual cell in your mother's womb, you attract to yourself only those elements that are identical in quality and character with yourself, and that are revolving at the same rate of speed. Your selective ability is such that you are able to pick such material as will preserve your quality and identity.

This is true of your body, of your circumstances, of your environment. Like attracts like. If you are not satisfied with yourself as you are, if you want a healthier body, more attractive friends, greater riches and success, you must start at the core—within YOURSELF!

And the first essential to putting yourself in harmony with the Infinite Good all about you is to relax, to take off the brakes. For what is worry or fear or discouragement but a brake on your thinking and on the proper function-ing of your organs, a slowing down of your entire rate of activity.

"Get rid of your tensions!" says the modern psycholo-gist. By which he means—think more about the agreeable things and less about the disagreeable ones. You know how martial music stirs your pulses, wakes even the tired-est man into action. Why? Because it tends to increase the rate of motion in every cell in your body. You know how good news has often cured sick people, how sudden ex-citement has enabled paralyzed people to leap from their beds. Why? Because good news makes you happy, speeds up your rate of motion, even as sudden excitement stirs up the whole organism. You know how fear, hatred, and discouragement slow you down. Why? Because those feel-ings put a definite clamp upon your rate of motion.

Remember this: Hatred, anger, fear, worry, discour-agement—all the negative emotions—not only slow down your rate of motion, and thus bring on sickness and make you old before your time, but they definitely keep the good from you. Like attracts like, and the good things you desire have a different rate of motion from these negative ones.

Love, on the other hand, attracts and binds to you the things you love. As Drummond tells us—"To love abun-dantly is to live abundantly, and to love forever is to live forever." And Emerson expresses the same idea—"Love and you shall be loved. All love is mathematically just, as much as the two sides of an algebraic equation."

"Whate'er thou lovest, man,
That, too, become thou must;
God, if thou lovest God,
Dust, if thou lovest dust."

And that, again, is strictly logical, strictly in accord with Nature's law that like attracts like. Whatever your rate of motion, the elements of like quality with that rate of emotion will be attracted to you.

Which brings us back to the law enunciated by Jesus— "Unto everyone that hath shall be given, and he shall have abundance, but from him that hath not shall be taken away that which he hath."

Read the parable of the Talents, which brought forth this pronouncement of Jesus, and you will see that it is not mere money or possessions that attracts more money —it is the USE to which these are put. You can't bury your talent and expect increase. You must put it to good use. It is the rate of motion that attracts increase, what the modern merchant would call the "turn-over." The oftener he turns over his stock of goods, the more money he makes on his invested capital. But if he fails to turn it over, if his goods lie dormant on his shelves, they will gather dust or mold and presently be worthless.

The servant in the parable who had five talents put them to work and attracted five more; the servant with two talents did likewise and increased his by two more. But the servant with only one talent buried his in a field and let it lie idle. He got nothing, and the talent he had was taken away from him.

We see the same thing happening every day. Statistics show that of all those who inherit money, only one in seventeen dies with money; of all those possessed of fortunes at the age of 35, only 17% have them when they reach 65.

The old adage used to be—"Three generations from shirtsleeves to shirtsleeves," but the modern tempo has speeded this up until now most fortunes hardly last out a single generation. Why is this? Because of the old law of the Rate of Motion. The man who makes the money has set in motion some idea of service that has attracted riches to him. More often than not, it is the idea or the service that is important in his mind. The money is incidental, and is attracted to him with other things of good because he has set in motion an idea that is bringing good to others.

But when he dies, what happens? Too often the business is carried on solely with the thought of how much money can be made out of it. Or the business is sold, and the money put out at interest, with the sole idea of hanging on to the money in hand. Naturally its rate of movement slows down. Naturally it begins to disintegrate and its parts are gradually drawn away by the stronger forces around it, until of that fortune there is nothing left.

You see exactly the same thing in Nature. Take any seed of plant life; take an acorn, for instance. You put it in the ground—plant it. What happens? It first gives of all the elements it has within itself to put forth a shoot, which in turn shall draw from the sun and the air the elements that they have to give; and at the same time, it puts out roots to draw from the earth the moisture and other elements it needs for growth. Its top reaches upward to the sun and air, its roots burrow deeply into the ground for moisture and nourishment. Always it is reaching out. Always it is creating a vacuum, using up all the materials it has on hand, drawing to itself from all about every element it needs for growth.

Time passes. The oak tree stops growing. What happens? In that moment, its attractive power ceases. Can it then live on the elements it has drawn to itself and made a part of itself through all those years? No, indeed! The moment growth stops, disintegration starts. Its component elements begin to feel the pull of the growing plants around them. First the moisture drains out of the tree. Then the leaves fall, the bark peels off—finally the great trunk crashes down, to decay and form soil to nourish the growing plants around. Soon of that noble oak, nothing is left but the enriched soil and the well-nourished plants that have sprung from it.

The Fundamental Law of the Universe is that you must integrate or disintegrate. You must grow—or feed others who are growing. There is no standing still. You are either attracting to yourself all the unused forces about you, or you are giving your own to help build some other man's success.

"To him that hath, shall be given." To him that is using his attractive powers, shall be given everything he needs for growth and fruition. "From him that hath not, shall be taken away even that which he hath." The penalty for not using your attractive powers is the loss of them. You are de-magnetized. And like a dead magnet surrounded by live ones, you must be content to see everything you have drawn to yourself taken by them, until eventually even you are absorbed by their resistless force.

That is the first and fundamental Law of the Universe. But how are you to become an Attracter? How are you to make your start? In the same way that it has been done from the beginning of time.

Go back to the first law of life. Go back to the beginning of things. You will find Nature logical in all that she does. If you want to understand how she works, study her in her simplest, most elementary forms. The principles established there hold good throughout the universe. The methods there used are used by all created things, from the simplest to the most complicated.

How, for instance, did the earliest forms of cell life, either plant or animal, get their food? By absorbing it from the waters around them. How does every cell in your body, every cell in plant or tree or animal, get its food today? In exactly the same way—by absorbing it from the lymph or water surrounding it! Nature's methods do not change. She is logical in everything. She may build more complicated organisms, she may go in for immense size or strange combinations, but she uses the same principles throughout all of life.

Now, what is Nature's principle of Increase? From the beginning of Time, it has been—

Divide—and Grow!

That principle, like every other fundamental Law of Nature, is the same in all of life. It has remained unchanged since the first single-celled organism floated on the surface of the primordial sea. It is the fundamental Law of Increase.

Take the lowest form of cell life. How does it grow? It DIVIDES—each part grows back to its original size—then they in turn divide and grow again.

Take the highest form of cell life—MAN. The same principle works in him in exactly the same way—in fact, it is the only principle of growth that Nature knows!

How does this apply to your circumstances, to the acquisition of riches, to the winning of success?

Look up any miracle of increase in the Bible, and what do you find? First division—then increase.

When Russell Conwell was building the famous Baptist Temple in Philadelphia, his congregation was poor and greatly in need of money. Through prayer and every other means known to him, Conwell was constantly trying to help his flock.

One Sunday it occurred to him that the old Jewish custom had been, when praying to God, to first make an offering of the finest lamb of the flock, or of some other much prized possession. Then, after freely giving to God, prayer was made for His good gifts.

So instead of first praying, and then taking up the collection, as was the custom, Conwell suggested that the collection be taken first and that all who had special favors to ask of the Creator should give freely as a "Thank Offering."

A few weeks afterwards, Conwell asked that those who had made offerings on this occasion should tell their experiences. The results sounded unbelievable. One woman who had an overdue mortgage on her home found it necessary to call in a plumber the following week to repair a leak. In tearing up the boards, he uncovered a hiding place where her late father had hidden all his money—enough to pay off the mortgage and leave plenty over!

One man got a much-needed job. A servant some dresses she badly needed. A student the chance to study for his chosen vocation. While literally dozens had their financial needs met.

They had complied with the law. They had sown their seed—freely—and they reaped the harvest.

"Except a kernel of wheat fall into the ground and die," said the Master, "it abideth alone. But if it die, it beareth much fruit." You can't put strings on your seeds. You can't sow them and say—"I'll give you a chance to sprout and bring forth increase, but if you fail, I'll take you back and use you to make bread." You must give that seed freely, fully. It must be dead to you, before you can hope to get back from it a harvest of increase.

Many people will tell you—"I don't see why God does not send me riches, I have prayed for them, and promised

that if I get them, I will use them to do good." God enters into no bargains with man. He gives you certain gifts
to start, and upon the way you use these depends whether
you get more. You've got to start with what you have.

And the place to start is pointed out in a little poem
by Nina Stiles:

"The land of opportunity
Is anywhere we chance to be,
Just any place where people live
And need the help that we can give."

The basis of all work, all business, all manufacturing,
is SERVICE. Every idea of success must start with that.
Every nucleus that is to gather to itself elements of good
must have as its basis service to your fellow man. Carlyle
defined wealth clearly when he said that "the wealth of a
man is the number of things he loves and blesses, which
he is loved and blessed by."

And that is the only kind of wealth that endures. Love
and blessings speed up your rate of motion, keep your
nucleus active, keep it drawing to you every element of
good that you need for its complete and perfect expression. They are, in effect, a constant prayer—the kind of
prayer Coleridge had in mind when he wrote—

"He prayeth well who loveth well
Both man and bird and beast.
He prayeth best who loveth best
All things both great and small;
For the dear God who loveth us,
He made and loveth all."

Remember that the only word often used in the Old
Testament to signify "prayer" means, when literally
translated—"To sing a song of joy and praise." In other
words, to speed up your rate of motion with joy and

thanksgiving. And you have only to read the Old Testament to know how often the great characters of the Bible had recourse to this method.

What do *you* want from life? Speed up your rate of motion and overtake it. Is it health you want? Then start by relaxing, by letting go of all your fears and worries. In a recent article, I read: "Dr. Loring Swaim, director of a famous clinic in Massachusetts, has under observation 270 cases of arthritis which were cured when they became free from worry, fear, and resentment. He has come to the conclusion after some years that no less than 60% of his cases are caused by moral conflict."

In the Reader's Digest some months ago, it was stated that "Personal worry is one of the principal causes of physical ailments which send people to hospitals. It is literally possible to worry yourself sick; in fact, the chances are better than even that if you are ill, worry is causing the symptoms."

That is not a modern discovery, by any means. In Proverbs, you will find the statement—"A merry heart causeth good healing, but a broken spirit drieth up the bones." And Plato observed 19 centuries ago—"If the head and the body are to be well, you must begin by curing the soul."

So the first essential in curing yourself of any ailment would seem to be to let go of your resentments, your worries and fears. Make peace within yourself, within your thoughts. Laugh a little, sing a little. Dance a little, if you can. Exercise speeds up your rate of motion, but it should be joyous exercise. Do something you enjoy, something that speeds up your mind as well as your muscles. Dance, if you like dancing. Swim, ride horseback, play tennis—do something exhilarating to the spirit as well as the body. Mere routine exercises that soon become a chore do little good and often are harmful. Unless you can get mental as well as physical exhilaration out of your exercise, don't bother with it at all.

Do you want money, riches? Then use what you have, no matter how little it may be. Speed up your rate of turnover, as the merchant speeds the turnover of his stocks. Money is now your stock. Use it! Pay it out joyfully for any good purpose, and as you pay it, BLESS IT! Bless it in some such wise as this:

"I bless you . . . and be thou a blessing; May you enrich all who touch you. I thank God for you, but I thank Him even more that there is unlimited supply where you came from. I bless that Infinite Supply. I thank God for it, and I expand my consciousness to take in as much of it as I can use . . . As I release this money in my hand, I know that I am opening the gates of Infinite Supply to flow through my channels and through all that are open to receive it. The Spirit that multiplied the loaves and fishes for Jesus is making this money attract to itself everything it needs for growth and increase. All of God's channels are open and flowing freely for me. The best in myself for the world—the best in the world for me."

There is no quicker way of speeding up your rate of motion than by *giving*. Give of your time, of your money, of your services—whatever you have to give. Give of that you want to see increased, for your gift is your seed, and "everything increaseth AFTER ITS KIND!"

Solomon was the richest man of his day, and he gave us the key to his riches and success when he wrote:

"There is that scattereth, and increaseth yet more. And there is that witholdeth more than is meet. The liberal soul shall be made fat, and he that watereth, shall be watered himself."

And one even wiser than Solomon told us: "Give, and it shall be given unto you, good measure, pressed down and shaken together and running over, shall men give into your bosom. For with the same measure that ye mete withal, it shall be measured to you again."

Do you want power, ability, greater skill in what you are doing? Then use what you have, use it to the greatest extent of which you are capable. The Sunshine Bulletin had an excellent little piece along these lines:

"There is a task for today which can be done now better than at any other time. It is today's duty. And we are writing now a judgment upon our lives by our faithfulness or unfaithfulness at the present moment.

"This moment has its own priceless value, and if wasted, it can no more be recovered than jewels that are cast into the depths of the ocean.

"Each day has its share in the making of our tomorrow; and the future will be nobler or meaner by reason of what we now do or leave undone."

What is ambition but the inner urge that speeds up your rate of motion and makes you work harder and longer and more purposefully to the end that you may accomplish something worth while? What is perseverance but the will to carry on in spite of all difficulties and discouragements? Given that ambition and that perseverence, there is nothing you cannot accomplish, nothing with a rate of motion so high that you cannot overtake it.

> "It is in loving, not in being loved,
>   The heart is blessed.
> It is in giving, not in seeking gifts,
>   We find our quest.
>
> "If thou art hungry, lacking heavenly bread,
>   Give hope and cheer.
> If thou art sad and wouldst be comforted,
>   Stay sorrow's tear.

"Whatever be thy longing or thy need,
That do thou give.
So shall thy soul be fed, and thou indeed
Shalt truly live."

—M. ELLA RUSSELL

CHAPTER TWENTY-EIGHT

EVERYTHING HAS ITS PRICE

"Dear God, help me be wise enough to see
That as I give so it is meted out to me!
Help me to know that with my every thought
The good or ill that's mine myself I've wrought!
Help me to place all blame of lack on *me,*
Not on my fellow man, nor yet on Thee.
Give me the courage, God, truly to know
That as I'd reap in life thus must I sow!"
—VERA M. CRIDER

IN HIS ESSAY on Compensation, Emerson says:

"What will you have?" quoth God.
"Pay for it, and take it!"

How can we buy the things we want at the counter of God? What pay can we offer?

Perhaps the answer lies in the ancient Law of Karma. Karma is Sanskrit, you know, and means "Comeback." It is one of the oldest laws known to man. It is the law of the boomerang. Jesus quoted it when He said—"Whatsoever a man soweth, that shall he also reap."

In the parlance of today, it is—"Chickens come home to roost." Even in science we find it, as Newton's Third Law of Motion—"Action and reaction are equal to each other." Ella Wheeler Wilcox expressed the Law beautifully when she wrote—

"There are loyal hearts, there are spirits brave,
There are souls that are pure and true;
Then give to the world the best you have,
And the best will come back to you.

"Give love, and love to your heart will flow,
A strength in your utmost need;
Have faith, and a score of hearts will show
Their faith in your word and deed.

"For life is the mirror of king and slave,
'Tis just what you are and do,
Then give to the world the best you have
And the best will come back to you."

One of the best illustrations of the working of the Law lies in the two seas of Palestine, the Sea of Galilee and the Dead Sea. The Sea of Galilee contains fresh water and is alive with fish. Green trees adorn its banks and farms and vineyards spread all around it. The River Jordan flows into it, and all the little rivulets from the hills around feed its sparkling waters.

The Dead Sea, on the other hand, knows no splash of fish, has no vegetation around it, no homes, no farms or vineyards. Travelers give it a wide berth, unless forced by urgent business to use its shores. The air hangs heavy, and neither man nor beast will drink of the waters.

What makes the difference? The River Jordan empties the same good waters into both seas. So it is not the river. And it is not the soil or the country round about.

The difference lies in the fact that the Sea of Galilee gives as it receives; for every drop of water that flows into it, another flows out. Whereas the Dead Sea holds on to all it receives. Water leaves it only through evaporation and seepage. It hoards all it gets, and the result is that the water stagnates, turns salt, and is good for naught.

"Unless a kernel of wheat fall into the ground and die," Jesus told us, "it abideth alone. But if it die, it beareth much fruit." In other words, if you put your kernel of wheat safely away to keep, you will never have anything but a kernel of wheat, and in time it will mould and rot away, but if you sow it freely (let it die to you), it will bear much fruit. It is another way of saying—"Cast thy bread upon the waters and it will return to you after many days increased an hundredfold."

In all of Nature, the only known law of increase is that you must give to get. If you want to reap a harvest, you must first plant your seed. If you want to increase your strength, you must first break up the muscle cells, and stimulate them to divide and grow.

Division and growth is the way that all of life increases. Watch a single cell at work in your body, in a plant, or in any form of life. What happens? It first divides, then each half grows until it reaches its normal size, when it divides and starts growing again. Without division, there is no growth—only atrophy and decay. You must divide to grow, you must give to get.

John Bunyan knew nothing of the law of cell growth, but he expressed it just as well when he wrote—

> "A man there was and they called him mad;
> The more he gave, the more he had."

And Moffatt had the same thought in his couplet:

> "One gives away, and still he grows the richer;
> Another keeps what he should give, and is the poorer."

Even the thoughts we send forth return to us laden with a harvest of their kind. That which we put into our thought comes back into our own lives, because for every thought there is a response, a return of the pendulum we have started swinging. It is the Einstein doctrine of the extended line, which must return to its source.

There is no use saying you have not enough money or abilities to be worth starting with. Just remember the parable of the talents. The servant who was given five talents put them out at interest and made more, as did the one who was given two talents. But the servant who received only one talent felt that it was too little to do much with, so he buried it. And you know what happened to him when the Master came back.

Start with what you have and plant your seed, no matter how small and unimportant it may seem. You remember Jesus told us that the Kingdom of Heaven (or Expansion) is like a mustard seed—"Which indeed is the least of all seeds, but when it is grown, it is the greatest among herbs, and becometh a tree, so that the birds of the air come to lodge in the branches thereof."

What you have to start with can hardly be smaller than the tiny mustard seed. If it can grow into a tree, think what your seed may grow into.

"*Do the thing* and you shall have the power," says Emerson. "But they that do not the thing have not the power. Everything has its price, and if the price is not paid—not that thing but something else is obtained. And it is impossible to get anything without its price. For any benefit received, a tax is levied. In nature, nothing can be given—all things are sold. Power to him who power exerts."

> "You are not higher than your lowest thought,
> Or lower than the peak of your desire.
> And all existence has no wonder wrought
> To which ambition may not yet aspire.
> Oh man! There is no planet, sun or star
> Could hold you, if you but knew what you are."

The key to power lies in using what you have, for use releases more power, just as using your muscles builds them into greater muscles, and failing to use them makes them weak and useless. "The one condition coupled with the gift of truth," Emerson tells us, "is its USE! That man shall be learned who reduces his learning to practice."

And Goethe expressed it even more strongly when he wrote—

"Lose this day loitering, it will be the same story
Tomorrow, and the rest more dilatory;
Thus indecision brings its own delays
And days are lost tormenting over other days.
Are you in earnest? Seize this very minute;
What you can do, or dream you can, begin it;
Boldness has genius, power, and magic in it;
Only engage and then the mind grows heated;
Begin, and then the work will be completed."

CHAPTER TWENTY-NINE

YESTERDAY ENDED LAST NIGHT

"I said to the man who stood at the gate of the year: 'Give me a light that I may tread safely into the unknown.' And he replied: 'Go out into the darkness and put your hand into the hand of God. That shall be to you better than a light and safer than a known way.' "

WHAT DO YOU WANT from life? Whatever it is, you can have it—and you have the word of no less an authority than Jesus for that.

"Seek ye first the Kingdom of God and His Righteousness," He told us, "and all these things (all the riches and power and other material things you have wanted) shall be added unto you."

Does that mean that you must become saintly in order to amass material possessions? Experience would seem to indicate that it seldom works out that way. The saintly are not often burdened with worldly goods. No, saintliness is not the answer. Then what is?

Let us examine the meaning of "righteousness" and see if the answer does not lie in it. The word used for "righteousness" in the ancient Greek text of the original Gospels is "dikaiosune," which, literally translated, means the absolute dictatorship of the spirit within you.

Translated thus, the passage reads—"Seek ye first the Kingdom of God and His absolute dictatorship of the spirit within you, and all these things shall be added unto you." In other words, put the problem up to the God in You, the part of Divinity that is the Creative Force in you, and leave it to Him to work it out while you rest in serene faith that it IS done.

How would this work out in practice? There was an article in UNITY recently that exemplified the idea so well that I quote it here:

"Let us say we are planning a business venture, or a social event, or a religious meeting, or the recovery of the sick. We are ready to pray over the situation. Now instead of futurizing our prayers and asking for something to take place tomorrow, let us imagine (imagination is an aid to the release of faith power) that everything has turned out just as we desired it. Let us write it all down as if it were all past history. Many of the Bible predictions are written in the past tense. Let us try listing our desires as if they had already been given us.

"Of course we shall want to write down a note of thanksgiving to God for all that He has given us. He has had it for us all the time or else we should not have received it. More than this, God has it for us or we could not even desire it now or picture it in our imagination.

"What happens? After we have written down our desires in the past tense, read them over carefully, praised God for them, let us then put away our paper and go on about our business. It will not be long before we actually see the desired events taking place in ways so natural that we may even forget that God is answering our prayers.

"Imagination helps us to have faith, for it pictures the thing desired and helps make it real. After we have tried this experiment a few times we shall find that our imagination has increased our faith, and faith has turned to praise, and praise has opened our eyes to see what God has for us."

The habit of thanking God ahead of time for benefits about to be received has its firm basis in past experience. We can safely look upon it as a sure formula for successful prayer because Christ used it. David always praised and thanked God when he was in trouble. Daniel was saved from the lions through the praise of God. Paul sang songs of praise and liberated himself from prison. And don't you, and everyone else, find satisfaction in being praised for a task well done?

Wrote William Law:

> "If anyone could tell you the shortest, surest way to all happiness and all perfection, he must tell you to make it a rule yourself to thank and praise God for everything that happens to you. For it is certain that whatever seeming calamity happens to you, if you thank and praise God for it, you turn it into a blessing. Could you therefore work miracles, you could not do more for yourself than by this thankful spirit; for it . . . turns all that it touches into happiness."

And Charles Fillmore adds:

> "Praise is closely related to prayer; it is one of the avenues through which spirituality expresses itself. Through an inherent law of mind, we increase whatever we praise. The whole creation responds to praise, and is glad. Animal trainers pet and reward their charges with delicacies for acts of obedience; children glow with joy and gladness when they are praised. Even vegetation grows better for those who love it. We can praise our own ability, and the very brain cells will expand and increase in capacity and intelligence, when we speak words of encouragement and appreciation to them."

So don't let anything that has happened in your life discourage you. Don't let poverty or lack of education or past failures hold you back. There is only one power—the I AM in you—and it can do anything. If in the past you have not used that power, that is too bad as far as the past is concerned, but it is not too late. You can start NOW. "Be still, and know that I AM God." What more are you waiting for? God can do for you only what you allow Him to do through you, but if you will do your part, He can use you as a channel for unlimited power and good.

In "Personal Achievement" (published by the Mc-Graw-Hill Book Co., 330 W. 42nd St., New York), J. C. Roberts tells us:

"A man wins success not with his feet or his hands or his eyes but with his brain and his soul. As long as his brain keeps functioning, as long as his soul keeps driving his will to action, he will achieve his aims.

"Nor need he be discouraged if his record at school or college has not been particularly brilliant. Some of the most amazing successes in human history have been achieved by 'stupid boys.'

"The Waverley novels were written by a man who in his school days was called the 'great blockhead.'

"Oliver Goldsmith, in the words of his teacher, 'seemed impenetrably stupid.'

"Newton was a 'dull boy'; Shakespeare made a bad record at school; while George Stephenson, inventor of the locomotive, could not read or write at twenty.

"There's a gold mine in every man. Diligent prospecting will uncover it—intelligent application will bring forth its riches.

"Don't let anything discourage you—don't admit for a moment that the thing you have set your heart upon can't be done. It can be done, if you say it can!"

There was a little article along similar lines by Kathleen Masterson in THIS WEEK magazine:

"It's inspiring to read about the achievements of the great, but it's rather comforting to know that: Beethoven found his first music lessons very distasteful and cried bitterly when subjected to them. . . . Albert Einstein was slow in learning to talk and did so only after great difficulty . . . Benjamin Franklin was such a dunce in arithmetic his father took him out of school when he was ten and sent him to work . . . Paderewski used to run from the house and hide in a tree when he saw his music teacher coming to give him a lesson . . . Balzac was thirty before he wrote a novel that won any acclaim. He had been writing steadily since he was twenty.

"Sir Walter Scott, Thomas Edison, Robert Burns, Daniel Webster, Henry Ward Beecher and Friedrich Froebel were all regarded as dumbbells by their teachers. . . . Sandro Botticelli, Italian painter, was such a poor student he was taken out of school at an early age and apprenticed to a goldsmith . . . Irvin S. Cobb was a flop as an insurance salesman, and at the close of his first day on the job his boss told him with tragic finality: 'You were not cut out to sell insurance. Good night!' . . . As a child Daniel Webster was so shy he couldn't stand up in school to speak pieces . . . Franklin D. Roosevelt failed in his final exams at law school.

"The Duke of Wellington was considered the dunce of his family . . . Richard Wagner's first piano teacher told him flatly that he would never amount to anything as a musician . . . Charles Darwin's teachers considered him slow and dull.

"In his youth Edison lost job after job because of his inattention to duty. Once when working as a telegraph operator at a Canadian station he was so busily engaged in something other than his work, he almost caused a wreck on the road. . . . Learning to drive one of the first horseless carriages, the very young Mrs. Franklin D. Roosevelt knocked down a gatepost and took off a corner of the house."

The difference between failure and success is measured only by your patience and faith—sometimes by inches, sometimes by minutes, sometimes by the merest flash of time.

Take Lincoln. He went into the Black Hawk War a Captain—and came out a private. His store failed—and his surveyor's instruments, on which he depended to eke out a livelihood, were sold for part of the debts. He was defeated in his first try for the Legislature. Defeated in his first attempt for Congress. Defeated in his application for Commissioner of the General Land Office. Defeated for the Senate. Defeated for the nomination for the Vice Presidency in 1856. But did he let that long succession of defeats discourage him? Not he. He held the faith—and made perhaps the greatest President we have ever had.

Then there was Grant: He failed of advancement in the army. Failed as a farmer. Failed as a business man. At 39, he was chopping and delivering cordwood to keep body and soul together. Nine years later he was President of the United States and had won a martial renown second in this country only to Washington's.

Search the pages of history. You will find them dotted with the names of men whom the world had given up as failures, but who held on to their faith, who kept themselves prepared—and when their chance came they were ready and seized it with both hands.

Napoleon, Cromwell, Patrick Henry, Paul Jones— these are only a few out of thousands.

When Caesar was sent to conquer Gaul, his friends found him one day in a fit of utter despondency. Asked what the matter was, he told them he had just been comparing his accomplishments with Alexander's. At his age, Alexander had conquered the entire known world—and what had Caesar done to compare with that? But he presently roused himself from his discouragement by resolving to make up as quickly as might be for his lost time. The result? He became the head of the Roman Empire.

The records of business are crowded with the names of middle-aged nobodies who lived to build great fortunes, vast institutions. No man has failed as long as he has faith in the Father, faith in the great scheme of things, faith in himself.

Yesterday Ended Last Night

When Robert Bruce faced the English at the battle of Bannockburn, he had behind him years of failure, years of fruitless efforts to drive the English out of Scotland, years of heart-breaking toil in trying to unite the warring elements among the Scotch themselves. True, at the moment a large part of Scotland was in his hands, but so had it been several times before, only to be wrested from him as soon as the English brought together a large enough army.

And now in front of him stood the greatest army England had ever gathered to her banners—hardy veterans from the French provinces, all the great English nobles with their armored followers, wild Irish, Welsh bowmen —troops from all the dominions of Edward II, over 100,000 men.

To conquer whom Bruce had been able to muster but 30,000 men, brave and hardy, it is true, but lacking the training and discipline of the English.

Was Bruce discouraged? Not he. What though the English had the better archers. What though they were better armed, better trained, better disciplined. He was fighting for freedom—and he *believed* in himself, he believed in his men, he believed in the God of battles.

And, as always, weight, numbers, armament, proved of no avail when confronted with determination and faith. The vast English host was completely defeated and dispersed. Bruce was firmly seated upon the throne of Scotland, and never more did an invading English army cross its borders.

It matters not how many defeats you have suffered in the past, how great the odds may be against you. Bulow put it well when he said—"It's not the size of the dog in the fight that counts, so much as the size of the fight in the dog." And the size of fight in you depends upon your faith—your faith in yourself, in the Creative Force working though you and in your cause. Just remember that yesterday ended last night, and yesterday's defeats with it.

Time after time throughout the Bible we are told that the battle is not ours—but the Lord's. But like all children, we know better than our Father how our affairs should be handled, so we insist upon running them ourselves.

Is it any wonder they get so tangled as to leave us in the depths of discouragement?

When the Black Prince with his little army was penned in by Philip of France, most men would have felt discouraged. For the hosts of France seemed as numerous as the leaves on the trees. While the English were few, and mostly archers. And archers, in that day, were believed to stand no chance against such armored knights as rode behind the banners of Philip.

The French came forward in a great mass, thinking to ride right over that little band of English. But did the Black Prince give way? Not he. He showed the world that a new force had come into warfare, a force that would soon make the armored knight as extinct as the dodo. That force was the common soldier—the archer.

Just as the Scotch spearmen overthrew the chivalry of England on the field of Bannockburn, just as infantry have overthrown both cavalry and artillery in many a later battle, so did the "common men" of England—the archers—decide the fate of the French at Crecy. From being despised and looked down upon by every young upstart with armor upon his back, the "common men"—the spearmen and archers—became the backbone of every successful army. And from what looked like certain annihilation, the Black Prince by his faith in himself and his men became one of the greatest conquerors of his day.

Troubles flocked to him, but he didn't recognize them as troubles—he thought them opportunities. And used them to raise himself and his soldiers to the pinnacle of success.

There are just as many prizes in business as in war—just as many opportunities to turn seeming troubles into blessings. But those prizes go to men like the Black Prince who don't know a trouble when they meet it—who welcome it, take it to their bosoms, and get from it their greatest blessings.

What is the use of holding on to life—unless at the same time you hold on to your faith? What is the use of going through the daily grind, the wearisome drudgery—if you have given up hoping for the rewards, and unseeing, let them pass you by?

Suppose business and industry did that? How far would they get? It is simply by holding on hopefully, believingly, watchfully—as Kipling put it: "Forcing heart and nerve and sinew to serve your turn long after they are gone, and so hold on when there is nothing in you except the will which says to them: 'Hold on'!"—that many a business man has worked out his salvation.

It is not enough to work. The horse and the ox do that. And when we work without thought, without hope, we are no better than they. It is not enough to merely hold on. The poorest creatures often do that mechanically, for lack of the courage to let go.

If you are to gain the reward of your labors, if you are to find relief from your drudgery, you must hold on hopefully, believingly, confidently—knowing that the answer is in the great heart of God, knowing that the Creative Force working through you will give it to you, the moment you have prepared yourself to receive it.

It is never the gifts that are lacking. It is never the Creative Force that is backward in fulfilling our desires.

It is we who are unable to see, who fail to recognize the good, because our thoughts are of discouragement and lack.

So never let yesterday's failure discourage you. As T. C. Howard wrote in Forbes Magazine:

"Yesterday's gone—it was only a dream;
Of the past there is naught but remembrance.
Tomorrow's a vision thrown on Hope's screen,
A will-o'-the-wisp, a mere semblance.

"Why mourn and grieve over yesterdays ills
And paint memory's pictures with sorrow?
Why worry and fret—for worrying kills—
Over things that won't happen tomorrow?

"Yesterday's gone—it has never returned—
Peace to its ashes, and calm;
Tomorrow no human has ever discerned,
Still hope, trust, and faith are its balm.

"This moment is all that I have as my own,
To use well, or waste, as I may;
But I know that my future depends alone
On the way that I live today.

"This moment my past and my future I form;
I may make them whatever I choose
By the deeds and the acts that I now perform,
By the words and thoughts that I use.

"So I fear not the future nor mourn o'er the past
For I do all I'm able today,
Living each present moment as though 'twere my last;
Perhaps it is! Who knows? Who shall say?"

"Duty and today are ours," a great man once wrote. "Results and the future belong to God." And wise old Emerson echoed the same thought. "All that I have seen," he said, "teaches me to trust the Creator for all I have not seen." In short, a good daily prayer might be one I read in a magazine recently—"Lord, I will keep on rowing. YOU steer the boat!"

Easy enough to say, perhaps you are thinking, but you never knew such disaster as has befallen me. I am broken down with sickness, or crippled by accident, or ruined financially, or something else equally tragic. Shakespeare wrote the answer to your case when he told us—"When Fortune means to man most good, she looks upon him with a threatening eye."

In the town of Enterprise, Ala., there is a monument erected by its citizens for services done them. And you could never guess to whom it is dedicated. To the Boll Weevil!

In olden days, the planters living thereabouts raised only cotton. When cotton boomed, business boomed. When the cotton market was off—or the crop proved poor—business suffered correspondingly.

Then came the Boll Weevil. And instead of merely a poor crop, left no crop at all. The Boll Weevil ruined everything. Debt and discouragement were all it left in its wake.

But the men of that town must have been lineal descendants of those hardy fighters who stuck to the bitter end in that long-drawn-out struggle between North and South. They got together and decided that what their town and their section needed was to stop putting all their eggs into one basket.

Instead of standing or falling by the cotton crop, diversify their products! Plant a dozen different kinds of crops. Even though one did fail, even though the market for two or three products happened to be off, the average would always be good.

Correct in theory, certainly. But, as one of their number pointed out, how were the planters to start? They were over their heads in debt already. It would take money for seeds and equipment, to say nothing of the fact that they had to live until the new crops came in.

So the townsfolk raised the money—at the Lord only knows what personal sacrifices—and financed the planters.

The result? Such increased prosperity that they erected a monument to the Boll Weevil, and on it they put this inscription:

"In profound appreciation of the Boll Weevil, this monument is erected by the citizens of Enterprise, Coffee Co., Ala."

Many a man can look back and see where some Boll Weevil—some catastrophe that seemed tragic at the time —was the basis of his whole success in life. Certainly that has been the case with one man I know.

When he was a tot of five, he fell into a fountain and all but drowned. A passing workman pulled him out as he was going down for the last time. The water in his lungs brought on asthma, which, as the years went on, kept growing worse and worse, until the doctors announced that death was only a matter of months. Meantime, he couldn't run, he couldn't play like other children, he couldn't even climb the stairs!

A sufficiently tragic outlook, one would say. Yet out of it came the key to fortune and success.

Since he could not play with the other children, he early developed a taste for reading. And as it seemed so certain that he could never do anything worth while for himself, what more natural than that he should long to read the deeds of men who had done great things. Starting with the usual boy heroes, he came to have a particular fondness for true stories of such men as Lincoln, Edison, Carnegie, Hill and Ford—men who started out as poor boys, without any special qualifications or advantages, and built up great names solely by their own energy and grit and determination.

Eventually he cured himself completely of his asthma —but that is another story. The part that is pertinent to this tale is that from the time he could first read until he was seventeen, he was dependent for amusement almost entirely upon books. And from his reading of the stories of men who had made successes, he acquired not only the ambition to make a like success of himself, but the basic principles on which to build it.

Today, as a monument to his Boll Weevil, there stands a constantly growing, successful business, worth millions, with a vast list of customers that swear by—not at—its founder.

And he is still a comparatively young man, healthy, active, putting in eight or ten hours at work every day, an enthusiastic horseman, a lover of all sports.

"There is no handicap, either hereditary or environmental, which cannot be compensated, if you are not afraid to try." Thus wrote one of New York's greatest psychiatrists. "No situation in our heredity or in our environment can compel us to remain unhappy. No situation need discourage one or hold him back from finding a degree of happiness and success."

Age, poverty, ill-health—none of these things can hold back the really determined soul. To him they are merely stepping stones to success—spurs that urge him on to greater things. There is no limit upon you—except the one you put upon yourself.

> "Ships sail east, and ships sail west,
>   By the very same breezes that blow;
> It's the set of the sails,
> And not the gales,
>   That determine where they go."

Men thought they had silenced John Bunyan when they threw him into prison. But he produced "Pilgrim's Progress" on twisted paper used as a cork for the milk jug.

Men thought that blind Milton was done. But he dictated "Paradise Lost."

Like the revolutionist of whom Tolstoy wrote—"You can imprison my body, but you cannot so much as approach my ideas."

You cannot build walls around a thought. You cannot imprison an idea. You cannot cage the energy, the enthusiasm, the enterprise of an ambitious spirit.

This it is that distinguishes us from the animals. This it is that makes us in very truth Sons of God.

> "Waste no tears
> Upon the blotted record of lost years,
> But turn the leaf
> And smile, oh, smile to see
> The fair, white pages that remain for thee."
> —ELLA WHEELER WILCOX

CHAPTER THIRTY

THE UNDYING FIRE

"I want to do one kindly deed each day
To help someone to find a better way.
I want to lend a hand to one in need
Or find some lonely stray that I may feed.
I want to sing for someone a loved song
To give them courage when the road is long.
If just one smile of mine can lighten pain
Then I shall feel I have not lived in vain."
—LENA STEARNS BOLTON

IN AN OLD NEWSPAPER CLIPPING, I read of a fire on the hearth of a farmhouse in Missouri, that has not been out for a hundred years.

When the builder of that old homestead left Kentucky with his young bride a hundred years ago, he took with him some live coals from the home fireplace, swinging in an iron pot slung from the rear axle of his prairie schooner.

Matches were unknown in those days, and the making of fire from flint and steel was too uncertain. So all through the long trek from Kentucky to Missouri, he kept that little fire alive, finally transferring it to his new log cabin home.

There his children grew and prospered. There he lived and there he died—by the light and warmth of that living fire. And so it must be with love—an undying fire.

The ancient Greeks had a legend that all things were

created by love. In the beginning, all were happy. Love reigned supreme, and life was everywhere. Then one night while Love slept, Hate came—and everything became discordant, unhappy, dying.

Thereafter, when the sun of Love rose, life was renewed, happiness abounded. But when the night of Hate came, then came discord also, and sorrow and ashes. And truly without love, life would be dead . . . a thing of wormwood and death.

> "I have seen tenderness and pity trace
> A line of beauty on a homely face,
> And dull and somewhat ordinary eyes
> Made brilliant by a flash of glad surprise,
> And lips relax and soften happily
> At unexpected generosity.
> But, oh, what strange, delightful mystery
> Is there in love's breath-taking alchemy,
> With power to take a drab, gray chrysalis
> And form such radiant loveliness as this!"
> —OPAL WINSTEAD

The most fascinating women in history—Cleopatra, Helen of Troy, Catherine the Great, Queen Elizabeth, the Pompadour—none of them had beautiful features. Cleopatra's nose was much too big—but that didn't keep her from holding the ruler of the then-known world under her thumb for ten long years, and after his death, subjugating Anthony in his turn.

Of course, she had something else—as did all these famous women of history—something stronger, more subtle, more fascinating than beauty. She had charm—that enticing, bewildering thing called feminine charm. The same charm that is born in every daughter of Eve who has the brains to use it.

What is charm? Charm is something in the glance of

the eyes, the turn of the head, the touch of the hand, that sends an electric thrill through every fiber of the one at whom it is directed, that speeds up his rate of motion. Charm is taking the gifts that God has given you and keeping them supernally young and fresh and alive. Charm is being so exquisitely buoyant and full of life, *keeping the magnet within you so surcharged with the joy of life,* that even poor features are lost sight of in the bewitching attraction of the whole.

Charm is keeping your loveliness all through life. It is holding on to your ability to stir the pulses and speed up the rate of motion of the one you love.

"For those we love, we venture many things,
The thought of them gives spirit flaming wings,
For those we love, we labor hard and long,
To dream of them stirs in the heart a song.
For those we love, no task can be too great,
We forge ahead, defying adverse fate.
For those we love, we seek Life's highest goal,
And find contentment deep within the soul."

"Though we travel the world over to find the beautiful," wrote Emerson, "we must carry it with us or we find it not." Charm is not to be bought in jars or bottles. Nor is beauty. Both must come from within. Both spring from that magnet of life which is the Creative Force within us.

There are women who seem to have been born tired—never exactly sick, never entirely well. They don't go out because they don't get any fun out of play. They are sallow, listless, having neither charm nor personality, because they have allowed the magnet of life within them to run down. To them I would say—renew your health first, renew your energy and vigor, renew your interest in those around you, speed up your own rate of motion—*then* begin to look for love. "For love," says Browning, "is energy of life."

> "For life, with all it yields of joy or woe
>   And hope and fear,
> Is just our chance of the prize of learning love—
>   How love might be, hath been indeed, and is."

How to inspire love in another? By first cultivating it in yourself. Love begets love, you know. Charge your mental magnet with thoughts of unselfish love and devotion, give to the loved one in your thoughts the admiration, the appreciation, the idealized service you would like to give in reality—and as you give, love will come back to you.

Love is giving. It cannot be jealous, for it seeks only the good of the one loved.

"Blessed is he that truly loves and seeketh not love in return," said St. Francis of Assisi. "Blessed is he that serves and desires not to be served. Blessed is he that doeth good unto others and seeketh not that others do good unto him."

Love such as that is never lost or wasted. It comes back as surely as the morrow's sun—oftentimes not from the one to whom you send it, but it comes back, nevertheless, blessed and amplified. As Barrie says—"Those who bring happiness into the lives of others, cannot keep it from themselves."

And Ella Wheeler Wilcox wrote—

> "Who giveth love to all
> Pays kindness for unkindness, smiles for frowns,
> And lends new courage to each fainting heart,
> And strengthens hope and scatters joy abroad.
> He, too, is a Redeemer, Son of God."

A woman once went to Krishna and asked him how to find the love of God. He inquired of her—"Whom do you love most?" "My brother's child," she answered. "Then go," he told her, "and love the child still more!" She did so, and behind the figure of the child, she presently saw the form of the Christ child.

> "True happiness doth lie in store
> For those who love their neighbor more;
> 'Tis blessed more to give than get.
> Come, do your part, our cause abet."

'Tis blessed more—and it does more to speed up your rate of motion. Though that statement would seem to be belied, at times, by young mothers who work so hard over their families.

Why is it that many married women grow old quickly, lose their youthful lines and rounded cheeks, get sallow and wan while their husbands are still in their prime?

Bearing children? There are thousands of women with three and four and five children who still look as youthful as when they married.

Work? A reasonable amount of work is good for every woman.

Then what is the reason?

STRAIN—unending, unceasing strain. There is not a servant in this country that you could hire to work every day and all day, without any period of freedom, any day of rest. Yet many men think nothing of making their wives do it.

When Taylor, the great efficiency engineer, was called in to re-organize the work of a certain foundry, he found a number of men with wheel-barrows engaged in carting pig iron from the pile in the yard to the cupola. They worked continuously, without rest except for lunch, and careful checking showed that each man carted from twelve to fifteen tons of pig iron a day. At the end of the day they were worn out.

Taylor took one of the men (an entirely average man), stood over him with a watch, and had him work exactly in accordance with his directions. He would have him load his barrow with pig iron, wheel it over to the cupola, dump it—then sit down and rest, utterly relaxing for a minute or more. When the minute was up, he would go through the same performance—and again rest.

It took two or three days to figure out the best periods of rest, but at the end of the week, Taylor's man was carting forty-five tons of pig iron every day, where before he had carted twelve to fifteen! And at the end of the day he was still fresh, where before he had been worn out.

If you have ever seen an army on the march, you know that no matter how great the hurry, the men are allowed to fall out for five minutes in every hour, and completely relax. Why? Because it has been found that this relaxation and rest enables them to march farther and faster.

There is not an organ in the body that does not require and take its period of rest, from the heart and lungs to the stomach and digestive tracts. Yet many a wife and mother goes all day and every day with never a moment of relaxation, never a minute when her nerves are not taut with strain. Is it any wonder they grow old years before their time? Is it any wonder they are nervous and irritable, unhappy themselves and making those around them depressed and unhappy?

To every such mother, I would say, first—relax! Sit down, lie down, every chance you get—*and just let go!* Don't listen for the baby—don't worry about dinner. Just blissfully relax—even if only for a minute or two at a time. If you can multiply those minutes by a dozen times a day, you will be surprised how much better you feel when night comes.

Give your inner magnet a chance to renew itself. Remember, the first essential toward speeding up your rate of motion is to relax, to get rid of your tensions, to LET the Creative Force work through you. Only then can you draw to you kindred elements of good.

"I pray the prayer the Easterns do,
May the peace of Allah abide with you.
Wherever you stop—wherever you go—
May the beautiful palms of Allah grow;
Thru days of love and nights of rest
May the love of sweet Allah make you blest.
I touch my heart as the Easterns do
May the love of Allah abide with you."

CHAPTER THIRTY-ONE

PRAYER

"But the stars throng out in their glory,
  And they sing of the God in man;
  They sing of the mighty Master,
  Of the loom His fingers span,
  Where a star or a soul is part of the whole,
  And weft in the wondrous plan."

                                        —ROBERT SERVICE

IF YOU WOULD know the surest way of speeding up your rate of motion, and overtaking the things you desire, try PRAYER!

But when I say "prayer", I don't mean the begging kind. I don't mean a lot of vain repetitions, that seldom have the attention even of the one repeating them, much less of the Lord. Go to the Bible, and you will learn how to pray.

Out of 600,000 words in the Old Testament, only six, when literally translated, mean to "ask for" things in prayer, and each of these six is used but once.

Against that, the word "palal" is used hundreds of times to signify "to pray." And "palal" means—"To judge yourself to be a marvel of creation; to recognize amazing wonders deep within your soul."

Wouldn't that seem to indicate that prayer was meant to be a realization of the powers deep within you? Wouldn't you judge that all you need to do is to expand your consciousness to take in whatever it is that you desire?

"What things soever you ask for when you pray, believe that ye receive them, and ye shall have them." You are not to think of your lacks and needs. You are to visualize the things you want! You are not to worry about this debt or that note, but mentally see the Infinite Supply all about you. "All that you need is near ye, God is complete supply. Trust, have faith, then hear ye, dare to assert the 'I'."

Remember this: If you pray to God, but keep your attention on your problem, you will still have your problem. You'll run into it and continue to run into it as long as you keep your attention focussed upon it. What you must do is fix your attention upon God—upon His goodness, His love, His power to remedy any ill or adjust any untoward condition. Focus your attention upon these, and these are the conditions you will run into.

Prayer is expansion, and expansion of yourself into the Godself all around you. As Kahlil Gibran describes it in his great book "The Prophet"—"For what is prayer but the expansion of yourself into the living ether. When you pray, you rise to meet in the air those who are praying at that very hour, and whom save in prayer you may not meet. Therefore let your visit to the temple invisible be for naught save ecstasy and sweet communion. I cannot teach you to pray in words. God listens not to your words save when He Himself utters them through your lips."

Prayer is a realization of your Oneness with God, and of the infinite power this gives you. It is an acceptance of the fact that there is nothing on earth you cannot have—once you have mentally accepted the fact that you CAN have it. Nothing you cannot do—once your mind has grasped the fact that you CAN do it.

Prayer, in short, is thanksgiving for the infinite good God *has* given you. The word most often used for "prayer" in the Old Testament means—"To sing a song of joy and praise."

And how often you see that method used by every great character of the Bible. Running through all of Jesus Christ's acts, as well as His teachings, you find the glowing element of praise and thanksgiving. When He looked at five loaves and two small fishes and realized that He had a multitude to feed, His first thought was a thought of praise. "And looking up to Heaven, He blessed." When He raised Lazarus from the dead, He first praised and thanked God.

When Paul and Silas lay in jail, bound with chains, did they repine? Did they get down on their knees and beg for help? On the contrary, they sang hymns of praise, and the very walls were shaken down and they were set free. "The righteous doth sing and rejoice." "The sons of God shouted for joy."

Go back over the Old Testament and see how often you are adjured to "Praise the Lord and be thankful, that THEN shall the earth yield her increase." Probably no life chronicled in the Scriptures was more beset with trials and dangers than that of King David. And what was his remedy? What brought him through all tribulations to power and riches? Just read the Psalms of David and you will see.

> "Jehovah reigneth; let the earth rejoice;
> Let the multitude of isles be glad.
> Bless Jehovah, O my soul;
> And all that is within me, *bless* His holy name . . .
> Who forgiveth all thine iniquities;
> Who healeth all thy diseases."

Throughout the Bible we are told—"In everything by

prayer and supplication WITH THANKSGIVING let your requests be made known unto God." Again and again the root of inspiration and attainment is stressed: *Rejoice, be glad, praise, give thanks!* "Prove me now herewith, saith the Lord of Hosts, if I will not open you the window of Heaven and pour you out a blessing, that there shall not be room enough to receive it."

The most complete interpretation of prayer I have heard came from the man who wrote—"Once I used to say 'Please.' Now I say, 'Thank you.' " "Enter into His gates with thanksgiving," the Psalmist bade us, "and into His courts with praise. Be thankful unto Him and bless His name." And Christ's apostles tell us the same thing—"Let us offer up a sacrifice of praise to God continually. In everything by prayer and supplication *with thanksgiving* let your requests be made known unto God."

Someone has said that prayer is the spirit of God pronouncing His works good. "This is the day Jehovah hath made. We will rejoice and be glad in it." It is sound psychology as well, as Prof. Wm. James of Harvard testified. "If you miss the joy," he wrote, "you miss all."

Complete, wholehearted reliance upon God—that is the prayer of faith. Not an imploring of God for some specific thing, but a clear, unquestioning recognition that the power to be and do and have the things you want is inherent in you, that you have only to recognize this power and put your trust in it to get anything of good you wish.

But perhaps you have prayed long and fervently for some particular thing, and it has not come? What then? Has it ever occurred to you that the answer was there, but you didn't receive it because you were not ready or willing to accept it?

God always answers prayer. Over and over He tells us this. The answer to your prayer is as sure as tomorrow's sunrise. YOU are the one who is not sure. You are not sure, and so you do not accept the answer.

If you accepted it, you would act on it, wouldn't you? Did you ever act upon the answer to those long and fervent prayers of yours? Yet that is the way it must be, if you are to pray for an answer—and GET it. If you pray for health, you must accept health. You must act as though you already had it. If you pray for other things, you must accept them at once and start doing—even on the smallest scale—the things you would do when the answer to your prayer became evident.

Dr. Alexis Carrel, the brilliant scientist who for many years headed the Rockefeller Institute, stated that "prayer is the most powerful form of energy one can generate."

"The influence of prayer on the human mind and body," Dr. Carrel went on to say, "is as demonstrable as that of secreting glands. Its results can be measured in terms of increased physical buoyancy, greater intellectual vigor, moral stamina, and a deeper understanding of the realities underlying human relationships. . . . Prayer is as real as terrestrial gravity. As a physician, I have seen men, after all other therapy had failed, lifted out of disease and melancholy by the serene effort of prayer. It is the only power in the world that seems to overcome the so-called 'laws of nature', the occasions on which prayer has dramatically done this have been termed 'miracles.' But a constant, quieter miracle takes place hourly in the hearts of men and women who have discovered that prayer supplies them with a steady flow of sustaining power in their daily lives."

An old peasant was kneeling alone in a village church, long after the services had ended. "What are you waiting for?" the priest asked him. "I am looking at Him," the peasant replied, "and He is looking at me." That is prayer, of the kind that Emerson said—"No man ever prayed without learning something."

"I never try to do my work by my own power alone.
When I begin I make my prayer before God's holy throne.
I ask that His Almighty power may work its will through me,
And so each task is done with ease; I'm charged with power,
  you see."

—HANNAH ORTH

In the eighteenth chapter of St. Matthew, Jesus gives us a method of praying that He assures us will bring us anything we ask for: "Again I say unto you, that if two of you shall agree on earth as touching anything they shall ask, it shall be done for them of My Father which is in Heaven. For where two or three are gathered together in My name, there am I in the midst of them."

That would seem simple enough, for two or three to gather together and agree upon some one thing that all should ask for. It is simple, too, and when properly done, it works wonders. In "The Magic Word," we give a number of true experiences in which little groups of people got together and prayed for the particular needs of some one of their number, with seemingly miraculous results.

It is the most effective method of prayer known, and the only reason it is not used oftener is that people so seldom agree upon what they shall ask for. They will get together and agree to pray for the health of some of their number, but where one may be thinking of health and strength, another will be dwelling upon his suffering, or the hardships it has brought upon his family or any one of a dozen other negative images. To get results, all must think of the health and strength they are praying for —not the sickness. They must dwell upon the power of God to heal the sick one, not upon the misery his sickness has caused.

Two thousand years before Christ, it was said in the

Vedas that if two people would unite their forces, they could conquer the world, though singly they might be powerless. And psychologists and metaphysicians everywhere agree that the power of two minds united in a single cause is not merely their individual powers added together, but multiplied manifold.

Perhaps this can best be explained in terms of electrical power. Take an ordinary magnet capable of lifting, let us say, 10 pounds of iron. Wrap this magnet with wire and charge it with the current from a small battery, it will lift—not merely ten pounds, but a hundred pounds or more!

That is what happens when one person prays and believes, and another adds his prayer and his faith. Why did Jesus send out his disciples, two and two? Why was it that on the one occasion He went alone among a crowd of scoffers, He was able to do no mighty works—on the occasion of His visit to His home town of Nazareth? You find the answer written in the Bible—"Because of their unbelief!"

Before a miracle could be wrought, there had to be faith—not only on Jesus' part, but on the part of someone around Him. Read how often He told those He cured—"Thy faith hath made thee whole."

If you were stuck in a muddy road with a heavily loaded two-horse wagon, and I were stuck with another right behind you, what would be the quickest way out? To unhitch my horses, would it not, couple them on to your wagon tongue and let the two teams pull you out. They could then take my wagon in its turn and pull it onto solid ground. What neither team could accomplish alone, the two pulling together could easily do.

Have you ever noticed a locomotive pulling a long train of cars? To START such a train takes 90% of the locomotive's power. To keep it running on a smooth stretch takes less than 1%. So a freight locomotive must have nearly a hundred times as much power as it needs for ordinary smooth running.

You are like a locomotive in that. To start you on the road to success requires every bit of energy you can muster. To keep you there, once you have reached the top, needs only a fraction of your abilities. The locomotive must carry its extra 99% of power as a reserve, to start it again when it stops for orders or water or to pick up or unload freight, or to carry it over a heavy grade. It can do nothing with all that extra energy at other times, except blow off steam.

But what about you? You need your full 100% to get started. Probably there are many times when you draw upon all of it to carry you through some grave difficulty, to push aside some obstacle that bars your way. But for the most part, you just carry that extra energy as reserve. What can you do with it? Find outlets for it!

All around you are men and women—earnest, hardworking men and women—who have put their hearts into their work, but lack some of the 100% energy that would start them on the road to success. They are like freight locomotives that are perfect engines, but not quite up to the task of starting as heavy a train as has been given them. Give them a push, help them to get started or over the hump of some obstacle or difficulty, and they will go far. But getting started is too much for them alone.

Why should you do this? Because only thus can you profit from that excess energy you have to carry for emergencies, but which you so seldom use. How do you profit? Through the additional reserve power it brings you. A stalled train is a useless thing. Worse than that, it is an encumbrance, in the way of everything else that uses the line. It may be generating all but 10% of the power required to move it, but without that 10%, the 90% is useless. So the 10% you furnish to get it started is of as much value to it as the 90% it furnishes, and is entitled to as great reward. When you help another in that way, you have in effect grub-staked him, and you share in the spiritual power that his success brings him. As Edwin Markham put it in his little poem—

"There is a destiny that makes us brothers;
  No man goes his way alone;
  All that we send into the lives of others
  Comes back into our own."

So whenever you have some earnest purpose, or want to help a friend or loved one to accomplish some greatly-cherished ambition, follow the advice Jesus gives us and unite in prayer for a few minutes each day until you have brought about the answer to that desire.

And when praying alone, remember:

First, center your thoughts on *the thing that you want* —not on your need.

Second, read the 91st and the 23rd Psalms, just as a reminder of God's power and His readiness to help you in all your needs.

Third, *be thankful,* not merely for past favors, *but for granting of this favor you are now asking.* To be able to thank God for it sincerely, in advance of its actual material manifestation, is the finest evidence of belief.

Fourth, B E L I E V E! Picture the thing that you want so clearly, see it in your imagination so vividly, that you can actually B E L I E V E T H A T Y O U H A V E I T!

It is this sincere conviction, registered upon your subconscious mind, that brings the answer to your prayers. Once convince your subconscious mind that you HAVE the thing that you want, and you can forget it and go on to your next problem. Mind will attend to the rest. So "sing and rejoice" that you HAVE the answer to your prayer. Literally shout for joy, as did the Sons of God in days of old.

Fifth, remember Emerson's advice—"Do the thing and you shall have the power." Start doing—even on a small scale—whatever it is that you will do when the answer to your prayer is materially evident. In other words, ACCEPT the thing you have asked for! Accept it—and start using it.

> "If you have faith in God, or man, or self,
> Say so; if not, push back upon the shelf
> Of silence all your thoughts till faith shall come.
> No one will grieve because your lips are dumb."
> —ELLA WHEELER WILCOX

THE LAW OF THE HIGHER POTENTIAL

INTRODUCTION

IF YOU HAVE ever seen a blacksmith trying to hammer a piece of cold iron into shape, you know how much chance he would have of repairing a broken tool or annealing the corners of a wrought iron frame, without the fusing power of heat.

Yet every day, physicians and healers of all kinds are working themselves into as great a sweat over "cold" patients as ever blacksmith did over cold iron, and then wondering why they can't get more satisfactory results!

You have heard of miracles of healing at shrines and revivals all over the world. No doubt you have actually seen cases that seemed little short of miraculous. Do you know what is back of these "miracles"? Not faith alone. Faith by itself never did anything. As St. Paul put it— "Faith without works is dead." It needs an additional factor to make faith effective. Do you know what that factor is?

When you want to release the energy in a boiler of water, what do you do?

You heat it, do you not? You resolve that water into its higher potential—steam. Then you can turn it to any useful purpose. Then you can release the energy in it to work for you.

Steam is free energy. Condensed into water, it still has a certain amount of active energy, but not nearly as much as in steam. Condensed further into ice, its energy is static. It can be used only as you release it.

Your body is much like water in this respect. Your bones and flesh are frozen energy. Your blood is liquid, but still condensed, energy. The pure energy, the highest potential, lies in your thought.

When you move, what happens? You send your thought to a certain set of muscles, with instructions to contract or expand. To do either means that they must break up a certain amount of condensed energy and release it into a liquid state. The result? Movement—turning energy to useful purpose. Every move you make requires the breaking up of a certain number of cells. But breaking up means opportunity for expansion and growth.

Breaking up must always precede growth. As the Master put it—"Except a corn of wheat fall to the ground and die, it abideth alone. But if it die, it bringeth forth much fruit."

A kernel of wheat is frozen energy. Swallow it, and it will go through your digestive organs intact, doing you no good. It must be broken up, the energy in it must be released, before the nutriment in it can be turned to useful purpose.

The same is true of planting it in the ground. It must heat and expand to burst its outer shell and send forth its stalk to bear fruit and multiply.

In all of Nature and all of Life, to change any substance, you must release the energy in it. If the substance is solid (condensed) like iron or glass, it must be liquefied. If it is already liquid, it may have to be vaporized.

The Law is that power flows only from the higher potential into the lower. And to release power, you must break up the lower form, and let the energy in it expand into a higher state. It is The Law of the Higher Potential.

That law is the basic law not only of mechanics and riches and success, but of *health and healing!*

You have, let us say, hardened arteries. How are you

going to cure them? Go to a Doctor? All right, what does he do? Tries to release the "frozen" energy in those arteries through his drugs or his diet.

But back in your subconscious mind is a solvent greater than any drug or diet, a solvent which can release every cell in your whole body into free energy, and then condense it again in the form God intended it.

That mind of yours is like a foundry. If you have ever been in a stove foundry, you know that they put tons of pig iron into a cupola, heat it until it melts, then pour the molten iron into molds formed in wet sand. If a puddler happens to be careless and spills the iron, or if a customer sends back his stove because it cracks or buckles, the founder doesn't waste time tinkering over the imperfect casting. He just throws it into the next "heat," melts it down again and tries once more to pour it into the perfect form he had imaged of it.

And that is what God gave *you* the power to do—with your life, your circumstances, your body—melt them down and re-cast them. The heat which does the melting, which releases the energy and brings it into flux, comes from two things; Faith is one of them.

That faith may be in a Doctor. It may be in a drug, or diet, or treatment. Or it may be in the Creator who first released the energy, who imaged the perfect You. If it is in God, then here are ways to release it.

CHAPTER THIRTY-TWO

THE OLD MAN OF THE SEA

FOUR THOUSAND YEARS AGO, when sickness fell upon the household of Abimelech the King, he had recourse to Abraham for help. "So Abraham prayed to God, and God healed Abimelech, and his wife, and his maid servants."

Throughout the Old Testament and the New, you will find only one remedy for sickness—Understanding PRAYER.

"Is any among you afflicted?" asked the Apostle James. "Let him pray. Is any sick among you? Let him call for the elders of the Church; and let them pray over him. And the prayer of faith shall save the sick and the Lord shall raise him up. Pray for one another, that ye may be healed. The effectual prayer of a righteous man availeth much."

Conversely, the fate of those who put their trust in nostrums is given neatly and graphically in the story of Asa, King of Israel: "And Asa was diseased in his feet, until his disease was exceeding great; yet in his disease he sought not to the Lord, but to the physicians. And Asa slept with his fathers."

Humanity can be divided into three groups:

1. Those who, through ignorance or folly, work against the Creative Law of the Universe, and suffer misery and sickness in consequence.

2. Those who know something of the law, but are too mentally lazy to co-operate with it, and are therefore frequently among the sufferers.
3. Those who understand the Law, work with it, and live a life of contentment and health.

Ignorance of a Law does not save you from its effects—in either the Law Courts or life. So if you are suffering from weakness or disease, it behooves you to acquaint yourself with the Law as speedily as may be.

What is this Law? It is the Law that power must always pass from a higher to a lower potential. Try to reverse this Law in electricity, and your machine will go "dead". Try to reverse it in your body, and like Asa the King, you will "sleep with your fathers."

Scientists have discovered hundreds of ways of destroying life. They know a thousand methods of killing us. But though they have sought it since time began, they know no way to create life. Life comes only from God.

Many try to simulate new life by stimulating the cells of the body with drugs and medicaments but the greatest physicians content themselves with keeping the passages open so that *new life may flow in!* They are like good gardeners—they loosen the soil that moisture and warmth may get to the roots, but they leave the growing to the life-giving forces of Nature.

Life is the higher potential, and life is all around, seeking expression. How can we draw it to us? How but by providing channels for its expression. Fearlessly releasing the life we have, secure in the knowledge that as fast as we make room, more will flow in.

The Law of Life is the law of division and growth. Our life cells divide, grow and divide again. Use them—break them up—and the more you release, the more the life in you will expand and draw new life to you.

The Law of Life is no different from the Law of Supply. You must give to get. All of life is around you— but it is unappropriated life, life uncondensed. It is the sunlight, the air, the water. But you can make it a part of you only as you make yourself like to it!

Ice does not mix with water. It floats in water, but it mixes only to the extent that it liquefies and loses its substance as ice, and becomes water. Water does not mix with steam, until it gives up its properties as water and becomes steam.

You do not become one with the unappropriated life around you until you mentally release the energy condensed into your body as flesh and blood and bone, and let it work as pure life in its highest potential, mixing with the pure God-life all about you.

A man who tinkers with stoves might repair a broken one by riveting two broken parts together. But if you took that stove back to its maker, he would put it into his cupola and melt it down until it mixed perfectly with the rest of the molten metal in his "heat", so that no one could tell which was old metal and which new. Then he would pour that metal into the perfect mold and bring forth a new stove.

A Doctor can tinker with an imperfect organ. And perhaps put a patch upon it that will enable it to function. But he is working with life in condensed form. To get a new organ, you must resolve that condensed life into its higher potential, mix it with the unappropriated God-life all about, and then pour it into God's perfect mold of that organ.

How can you do it? How has it been done all through the ages? Through the prayer of faith!

"My old disorder returned as violently as ever," wrote John Wesley in his journal. "The thought came to my mind, why do I not apply to God at the beginning rather than at the end of my illness? I did so and found immediate relief, so that I needed no further medicine.

"My horse was exceedingly lame and my head ached more than it had done for some months (which I here aver is the naked fact. Let every man account for it as he sees good.) I then thought, cannot God heal either man or beast, by any means or without any? Immediately my headache and weariness ceased, and my horse's lameness in the same instant, nor did he halt any more either that day or the next."

There is a story by Stewart Edward White called "Free, Wide and Handsome." It tells of a man who lay dying—whom the Doctor considered dead. And the thought that came to him as he lay thus was this—

"You know these pictures sent by radio? They are all made up of a lot of separate dots, you know. If you enlarged the thing enough, you'd almost lose the picture, wouldn't you? And you'd have a collection of dots with a lot of space between them. Well, that's how I seemed to myself.

"I could contract myself, bring all the dots close together, and there I'd be, solid as a brick church, lying in bed; and I could expand myself until the dots got separated so far that there were mostly spaces between them. And when I did that my body in the bed got very vague to me, because the dots were so far apart they didn't make a picture; and I—the consciousness of me—was somehow the thing in the spaces that held the dots together at all. I found it quite amusing contracting and expanding like that.

"Then I began to think about it. I began to wonder whether I held the dots together, or whether the dots held me together; and I got so interested that I thought I'd try to find out. You see, I wasn't the dots: I—the essence of me, the consciousness of me—was the spaces between the dots, holding them together. I thought to myself, 'I wonder if I can get away from these dots?' So I tried it; and I could. I must say I was a little scared. That body made of dots was a good, solid container. When I left its shelter, it occurred to me that I might evaporate into universal substance, like letting a gas out of a bottle. I didn't; but I certainly was worried for fear I'd burst out somewhere. I felt awfully thin-skinned!"

That man was in a mental state of flux. And it is for a degree of that mental state you must try when you are in the grip of disease or accident, when pain assails you or some organ seems incapable of performing its functions.

Instead of patching an injured or diseased part, throw it into the "melt" and re-cast it anew from the original, perfect pattern. Instead of trying to change the condensed energy after it is frozen into its solid form, liquefy it and release it into what mold you like.

How can you liquefy a rheumatic joint or aching tooth? "The thing that hath been," says the Bible, "it is that which shall be; and that which is done is that which shall be done; and there is no new thing under the sun."

So let us see how it was done aforetime. "I called upon Mr. Kingsford," reads John Wesley's Journal, "a man of substance as well as of piety. He informed me: 'Seven years ago I so entirely lost the use of my ankles and knees that I could no more stand than a new born child. Indeed, I could not be in bed without a pillow laid between my legs, one of them being unable to bear the weight of the other. I could not move from place to place, but on crutches. In this state I continued about six years. At Bath I sent for a physician, but before he came, as I sat reading the Bible, I thought, Asa sought to the physicians and not to God; but God can do more for me than any physician; soon after I heard a noise in the street, and rising up, found I could stand. Being much surprised I walked several times around the room. Then I walked into the square and afterwards on the Bristol road and from that time on I have been perfectly well.' "

In recent years, such cases have become so common that the Episcopal Church, some years ago, appointed a joint commission of leading medical men and clergymen to investigate and report upon the practicability of healing through prayer. Their report, signed among others by the famous surgeon, Dr. Chas. H. Mayo, says that:

"Christian healing has passed beyond the stage of experiment and its value cannot be questioned. Spiritual healing is no longer the hope of a few, but the belief and practice of a large and rapidly increasing number of persons."

As the New York American put it in summing up their report:

"It was the essence of the early Christian religion to save from sickness as well as sin. Christ's life is a long record of healing disease and raising from death. We have been calling his acts miracles. Now modern science and religion begin to suspect that he was demonstrating the operation of a principle which is eternal. Indeed, Christ told his disciples to go forth into the world and demonstrate this principle. He said:

" 'Verily, verily, I say unto you, he that believeth in Me, the works that I do, shall he do also; and greater works than these shall he do; because I go unto My Father.' "

What was it healed the sick, the halt and the blind in Jesus' day? Their faith, coupled to His understanding of the God-life in them. Their perfect faith in Him released the energy which had condensed into images of sickness and helplessness, and His understanding then guided that energy into God's perfect images of them. As the Bible puts it, He "unstopped" their ears, removed the "scales" from the eyes of the blind, "cleansed" the leper, "released" the woman who was bound by disease, "awaked" the dead.

And He told us repeatedly that we could do the same.

You see, it is not as though disease were something sent by God to punish us. On the contrary, it is something we inflict upon ourselves! If a foundryman let the fire go out in his furnace, and all his "melt" congealed into one solid mass of iron, you wouldn't say that God had afflicted him, would you? Yet when you let the same thing happen to some organ of your body, you blame it on God!

He never sent sickness or accident to anyone. Sickness is the LACK of life. Sickness means that you have allowed the life-energy in you to congeal. New life can't come in because the old life won't make way for it. It is like a freezing river—the current becomes sluggish, slows up, stops. Doctors will tell you that the reason most people die is because their arteries become clogged, their eliminatory organs sluggish. They can't take hold of new life because they don't release the old.

God put infinite life here upon earth. He made it equally available to all. But He gave us free will—freedom to avail ourselves of His generous gifts or to ignore them, as we like. He doesn't punish us for failing to draw upon His fountain of life, any more than the sun punishes us if we choose to live in a dark cellar. We may suffer for lack of the sun, but we need only to come up out of our cellar to enjoy again its beneficent rays. It does not withhold a single ray from us because we slighted it. It radiates just as much warmth and light over us as over the most faithful of its devotees.

Just so it is with God. He doesn't punish us with disease when we neglect Him. We punish ourselves. And the quickest and surest way to relieve ourselves of our troubles is to go back to Him, and let His ever-present life re-vitalize our failing sinews.

Don't bother about what you have had. Don't worry about the diseases that seem to trouble you now. *Let go of them!* RELEASE THEM! Raise that condensed energy to a higher potential. Throw it into flux. Then turn to God for His perfect image in which to re-cast your life-energy.

That means work—mental work. It means burning all your old molds of ill-health and deformity, and using only God's perfect patterns. And so few will take the trouble to do this. As one great writer expressed it—"People will adopt any expedient to avoid the work of using their minds."

It is so much easier to tinker with the casting than to re-cast it. It is so much easier to pay a Doctor $5 or $10 than to make the mental effort ourselves. Yet if we put the same faith in prayer that we put in Doctors and their drugs, we would be—not repaired *but made whole!*

When you want to become rich, what is the first thing you must do? BE rich in your thoughts, in your actions, even though you must start it on the most modest of scales. Take your life out of all images of limitation and lack, and put it into the pattern of opulence and plenty. *Act the part!*

When you want to become well and strong, what is the first thing you must do? BE well and strong, even though you must start that BEING with only one finger. BE the man or woman you want to be. BE it in your own mind first. Get your pattern right. Then start breaking down the condensed life in the diseased images, until your body and your new mental image are one.

Your body is the sum-total of your beliefs—objectified. It is God's life, condensed into your patterns. As I see it, God has a perfect pattern for your body. Every night, you are supposed to go to Him, compare your body with that perfect pattern, throw into the furnace all worn and diseased parts, and re-make your body for the new day.

But that is too much mental effort for most of us. We'd rather "leave well-enough alone," patch the worn parts and be on our way. We forget all about the original pattern and work only on the casting we have. Is it any wonder that after a while parts wear out, the machine goes to pieces?

"I will praise thee," sang the Psalmist, "for I am fearfully and wonderfully made. Marvelous are Thy works: and that my soul knoweth right well. My substance was not hid from Thee when I was made in secret and curiously wrought in the lowest parts of the earth. Thine eyes did see my substance, yet being unperfect, and in Thy book all my members were written, which in continuance were fashioned, when as yet there was none of them."

Have you ever known a Master Sculptor to turn out an imperfect statue? Have you ever known a great artist to paint a distorted picture? God is the greatest Sculptor, the finest Artist conceivable. Is it likely He failed in His conception of your body.

His record in the "book where all your members are written" is perfect. His pattern for them, "when as yet there was none of them," was flawless. His work is forever. The image He formed of you before you were fashioned, the pattern He held of you when you were being made, was the same perfect picture He sees in you now.

When you fail to manifest that perfect image, when sickness or accident mirrors a different picture to your eyes, get rid of it. Throw it back into the "melt" and release the life in it. If a photographer took a picture of you that made you look like a gargoyle (and it can be done), you would refuse it, of course. You would tell him to throw it away and take another—and keep on taking others until he had one that imaged the perfect contours of your face.

That is what you must do with the life in you—refuse to accept any image it may show you that is unlike the perfect image of you that is in Divine Mind.

No thing which comes from God can hurt you, for in His picture, everything is harmonious. We have Jesus' word for it that when we have the right idea, nothing shall by any means do us harm. Therefore when anything seems to harm you, know that it is not from God, and refuse to accept it. Don't keep it as part of your picture. Don't claim it as yours. Don't tell others you HAVE it. Send it back for another image—and another—until you are reproducing the perfect original.

You don't need to treat a disease or an ache or an ulcer. On the contrary, you need to REFUSE them—to refuse to regard them as yours. To take your life out of them, and use it to make manifest God's perfect image of you.

Jesus, of all who ever appeared upon this earth, never failed to heal any who came to him in faith. How did He do it? Not through drugs or treatments. Not through scientific diagnoses. He never asked what was wrong with the diseased ones. He commanded the devil to get out of them—*He released the hold those wrong images had on the life in them*—He directed it into the perfect image the Father had of them—*and they were healed.*

They did not need to know anything about hygiene or laws of health—they did not even need to understand how He healed them—they needed only the faith to take their life out of the old image, to raise that condensed life to a higher potential while He turned the molten energy into right channels.

"These signs shall follow them that *believe*," said

Jesus. "They shall lay hands on the sick, and they shall recover."

Faith and emotion—these are the two requisites for mental healing. Faith takes one back to the perfect image that is in Divine Mind. Emotion (the FEELING that you *have* this perfect image) melts every particle of congealed energy and makes it malleable.

The trouble with the faith of most of us is that it comes only in flashes, and immediately is obscured by doubts and fears. You know what chance you would have of melting iron if your fire burned only by fits and starts. Your flame must be steady, your heat intense.

Jesus had the perfect image always in mind, but you know how often He told those whom He healed—"Thy *faith* hath made thee whole!"

A mere momentary belief is not enough—you must *hold* to that belief like the blind man who kept calling until Jesus harkened to him, or the woman who persisted until she touched the hem of His garment. First, reject the imperfect image, break it up and release your life-energy from it by disowning it. Next, go back to the Father for His perfect picture of you. Third, KNOW THAT YOU HAVE THAT PERFECT MOLD—and hold to that knowledge until your life-energy has condensed in it.

The only essential difference between those who believe in drugs and treatments, and those who put their faith in the power of Mind, lies in the fact that the former look upon their present bodies as the only ones they will ever have in this world, whereas the latter know they can get new ones each day if they need them.

The followers of the old school are like a Robinson Crusoe with only one stove to his name, and no means of getting spare parts, therefore he spends much time and care patching damaged parts and repairing breaks.

The followers of the new school, on the other hand, are like people living next door to a stove foundry, knowing they can get spare parts or a new stove any time, therefore wasting no time or worry over wear and tear.

To these followers of the new idea, as to their Master, whose precepts they follow, the crippled body, the defective organ, the fevered touch, are no more permanent, no more cause for worry, than is a broken or imperfect casting to a founder. *"Re-melt it"*—that's all he would say. And re-melt it is all you need to do. The life in it is perfect—it is only that your molding of that life was wrong. So let us, each night before we go to sleep, throw into the melt everything we have, everything we are—our bodies, our possessions, our circumstances and surroundings, blessing them in some such wise as this:

> I bless the life in me, and I baptize it God's creative, intelligent Life, seeking to express through me His perfect idea of my body, my surroundings, my work.
>
> And I freely release it from all its present confines—in my body and my possessions. I release it to expand and mix with the infinite, unappropriated God-life all about, and I pray the Creator then to pour it into His perfect images of my body, my surroundings and my work. I cast that burden upon Him, and I go free.

Then SEE every imperfect form in which your life-energy has become condensed, melting away like ice before a summer sun. SEE it flowing into the perfect mold, condensing again into God's perfect image. Know that you HAVE this image—and keep knowing it (try to get the *feeling* of it) until you make it manifest.

Then start ACTING the part. The finest theoretical knowledge in the world will do you no good unless you have faith enough to put it into action.

You must BE the perfect man or woman you image

yourself—no matter on how small a scale you make the start. You must start to USE the life-energy in you before you can break up your condensed energy to expand and draw more energy to you.

So don't worry about the diseases you have had. They don't count. Just disclaim them, and release your life-energy from them. Release it—and put it into the perfect images God holds of you.

"O Son of Spirit, I have made thee mighty. How is it thou art weak? Turn thy sight to thyself that thou mayest find ME standing in thee—MIGHTY, POWERFUL, SUPREME!"

CHAPTER THIRTY-THREE

THE KING'S TOUCH

WHAT IS IT THAT ACCOUNTS for the miracles of healing which take place at shrines all over the world? What is it that gives revivalists, faith healers, practitioners, power to dispel sickness, power to "make the blind see, the deaf hear, the lame walk"?

All of these wonders do occur—make no mistake about that. At St. Anne de Beaupre, at Lourdes, at thousands of shrines, at hundreds of meetings like those in the Angelus Temple, the sick have been, and every day new ones are being, cured of their infirmities. Why?

It cannot be merely because of the power of the "healer" or the holiness of the relic, for in olden times thousands of so-called "relics" were no more parts of the bodies of the Saints they were supposed to represent than they were of yours or mine. Yet in many cases they proved just as potent for good! Why?

If you have read much of history, you know that the Kings in the Middle Ages were a pretty scoundrelly lot, yet the "King's Touch" healed hundreds every year. Why?

Religions which we piously regard as pagan have on record almost as many cases of miraculous healings as have we. Again, why? If we have the only truth, how is it that they, many of whom never heard of the Christ, should be able to use the truth in another form to accomplish the same result?

445

Why? Because the Laws of God are universal laws. Whether we follow them blindly or understandingly, they work just the same. They are as impartial as the sunshine. They require only conformity to them.

Everything in this universe is made up of energy. That energy manifests itself in three different states—solid, liquid and vapor.

When you want to change the form in which any solid manifests itself, you have only two methods open to you:

1st, you can carve or break or burn off parts until the remainder is in the form you desire.

2nd, you can break up the whole mass (by heat or mixing with liquid or vapor) until you have liquefied or vaporized it, and then mold it into the shape you desire.

Those methods are universal. They apply to wood or rock or iron or flesh. They are the only two ways known to man of changing the form of any solid substance.

How, then, are miracles of healing achieved? In the same way as miracles of turning lumps of iron into useful tools—by breaking up the solid mass, resolving it into its higher potential, then molding it into the form you desire.

But you can't take your flesh and resolve it into liquid by putting it into a furnace as you do with iron. And you can't break it up and mix it with water, as you do with wheat. What, then, can you do with flesh and bone?

Liquefy it through EMOTION! The heat of a strong emotion is the only power that will resolve the cells of your body into a higher potential. Understanding faith that God's image of you is perfect, is the only power that will mold them into the pattern God intended.

It matters not what may ail you, it matters not how close to death's door you may be, fervent emotion can loosen all your condensed energy, faith can bring it back into the perfect mold. Mind you, by "fervent emotion" we do not mean hysteria or wild excitement. We mean deep feeling—*the conviction that you have received* the healing you are praying for.

Of course, every emotion has a tendency to raise the life in us temporarily to a higher potential. And every emotion has, at times, been used unwittingly to heal the sick and afflicted. Brown Landone, for instance, told of having been an invalid for seventeen years, his whole time spent in bed or in a wheel chair, his knees swollen as large as water pails, his heart organically diseased. Then one day the house caught fire, and this man who could not climb a flight of stairs without fainting away, not only ran up steps like an athlete, *but carried down one after another three heavy trunks!*

In the New York *Times* a couple of years ago, there was an account of a paralytic who had not stirred from his bed for five years. The patient in the cot next his own suddenly went crazy and attacked him, and the paralytic wrenched himself loose and ran up three flights of stairs!

More conclusive even that these was an *Associated Press* dispatch recounting the unexpected visit of a boa constrictor to the paralytic ward of the Guayaquil Hospital in Ecuador. When the snake arrived—through the window—there were eight patients in the ward, all helplessly paralyzed. Ten seconds later, the snake was the ward's sole occupant.

Every bed was emptied, every patient "miraculously" cured! One, who had not moved from his bed in two years, jumped six feet to a window, and then took easily the eight-foot jump from the window to the ground. And in each of the eight cases, *a complete cure was effected!*

The dumb have been made to talk, the deaf to hear, just by taking them in an aeroplane and doing "stunts" that worked them into a high state of excitement.

But an outside stimulus is in no wise necessary to stir

the emotions. It can be done as effectively from within, through the stimulus of a strong conviction. Starting a fire or importing a snake to cure a paralytic is almost as wasteful as the old Chinese custom of burning down a house just to roast a pig. There are less expensive and more effectual ways.

Go to any of the more popular shrines, and you will see men carried in on stretchers or limping along on crutches, lifted to a high emotional pitch through preaching or music or just the contagion of the emotional excitement around them, then walking away as well and strong as you or I.

There is nothing miraculous about it, any more than life itself is miraculous. The miraculous part is that mankind has not long ago discovered the perfectly natural laws governing such "miracles".

Why are the Churches beautifully decorated, in rich colors? Why do they give us such wonderful music? Why do they have congregational singing? Because beauty and color and music and singing all appeal strongly to the emotions, all have a tendency to awaken the dormant life in us, stirring it out of the congealed form in which sickness or accident has left it, giving us the chance to pour it anew into God's perfect image.

How did Jesus heal the sick? By first commanding the "devil" to get out of them. In other words, by first loosening the congealed life from its diseased form. Then it flowed easily into the perfect pattern he held of it: "Satan hath bound this woman," He said of one, and then proceeded to loosen the bonds.

Who is "Satan"? Who but the devils of fear and worry, who "bind" the life in so many poor souls into all manner of diseased forms. What is mankind's greatest ill today? Ask any Doctor, and he will tell you—"Congestion." And what is congestion but *congealed* life, life bound into constricting limits by worry and fear?

Dr. G. Dumas, of Paris, discovered recently that *writh-ing* acts as an anaesthetic for pain. Why? Because writh-ing means strain, and strain has a tendency to make the muscles hard, to *congeal* the life in them, deadening it so there is no longer feeling in it. Continued strain brings unconsciousness or death. Why? Because the congealing process reaches the seat of the nerves or the heart, and it stops functioning. The "potential" becomes too low for life to act.

When that potential is raised by drugs or alcohol, the release is only temporary, for it is merely a chemical re-lease. When the chemical reaction ceases, the particles of life will settle again, with the poison of the chemicals to trouble them in addition.

Treating with drugs is working upon conditions. To cure those conditions, you must go back to the parent causes. "Heal me, O Lord, and I shall be healed," prayed the Prophet Jeremiah. And when you work through Mind to reach the causes of your trouble, you are truly healed.

That is the way Jesus worked. He first preached. He gave His hearers the necessary understanding. He worked up their faith, their emotion—then He healed them.

Two requisites there are without which there can be no healing. The first is understanding faith. The second is emotion.

But how can you work up your emotions to the proper pitch? How do you work them up to the pitch of asking a girl to marry you? You don't wait for a brass band to stir you up. You don't dive from an aeroplane or jump up and down to work up the necessary heat. You get your heat from within. You dwell upon her every perfect qual-ity in your thoughts, do you not? You think of her in your embrace, you picture your happy life together, you live it all in your imagination.

You must make the thought of your perfect body just as real. You must visualize your perfect organs, you must so fervently desire them that you can see yourself *using* them, you must actually FEEL THE THRILL of it! When you can work up that FEELING, and hold it long enough to bless the organ and baptize it God's perfect image, YOU WILL HAVE THAT PERFECT IMAGE FOR ALL TO SEE!

CHAPTER THIRTY-FOUR

THE KINGDOM OF EXPANSION

HERE IS A SECRET of riches and success that has been buried 1,900 years deep.

Since time began, mankind has been searching for this secret. It has been found—and lost again—a score of times. The Ancients of all races have had some inkling of it, as is proven by the folktales and legends that have come down to us, like the story of Aladdin and his wonderful lamp, or Ali Baba and his "Open Sesame" to the treasure trove.

Every nation has such legends. Every nation has had its Wise Men, its men of genius and vision who glimpsed the truth that is buried in these old folktales and who understood at least something of how it works.

But it remained for Jesus to re-discover this secret in its entirety and then to show us clearly, step by step, how we might use it to bring us anything of good we might desire.

Make no mistake about this: The miracles of Jesus were not something super-natural that could be performed only by Him, else how could He have picked seventy disciples—ordinary men, uneducated, untaught, fishermen, farmers, tax-gatherers and the like—and sent them out two by two to perform miracles and wonders second only to His own, so that they returned to Him with joy, saying, "Lord, even the devils are subject to us through Thy name." How could He have assured us— "The things that I do shall ye do also, and greater things.

than these shall ye do." The miracles of Jesus were divinely NATURAL. Instead of being departures from
natural law, they were demonstrations of what the law
will do for you—if you understand how to use it!

God does not deal in exceptions. Every force in Nature
works along definite, logical lines, in accord with certain
principles. These forces will work for anyone who possesses the key to their use, just as Aladdin's fabled Genie
would respond to the call of anyone who rubbed the
magic lamp. They can be neglected and allowed to lie
idle, they can be used for good or evil, but the laws themselves do not change. It is merely the methods of using
them that change.

An aeroplane or an automobile would have seemed as
great a miracle to the people of Jesus' day as the curing
of a leper. Sending sound waves through the ether, to be
picked up by a little box called a radio, would have been
as wonderful to our fathers as is the sending of our voice
over a beam of light to us today. Yet there is nothing
super-natural about either of these. The forces of Nature
have always been there, ready for our use. It is our understanding of them that has changed, our knowledge of
how to USE them.

Man in ancient times looked upon the lightning as the
wrath of God, just as many deeply religious people look
upon poverty and sickness and calamities today in the
same way, as visitations of God. Yet man has learned to
harness the lightning and make it serve him.

The laws governing electricity were there all the time,
waiting only for the understanding of someone wise
enough to show us how to put them to good use. Just so
the power to BE and HAVE what you want is right here,
needing only for you to learn how it works.

Nineteen hundred years ago, there came to this earth
a Son of Man who proclaimed that His mission was—

"That ye might have LIFE, and have it more ABUN-DANTLY."

NOT, mind you, that you might learn how to die, and thus reach Heaven and a life of comfort, but that you might have LIFE—here and now. Over and over again He told us—"What things soever ye desire . . . ye shall have them," and lest you might think that this referred to some future state, He assured us—"If two of you shall agree ON EARTH as touching anything they shall ask, it shall be done for them."

Furthermore, He gave exact instructions as to how to go about getting the things you desire. When you want more of the good things of life, when happiness or success or riches seem to elude you, there is a definite formula for you to use. "Seek ye first the Kingdom of Heaven," Jesus directed, "and all these things shall be added unto you."

"Ah ha!" you say. "There it is. You do have to die and go to Heaven in order to get the good you want." But Jesus must have anticipated that you might think just that, for He pointed out specifically that the Kingdom of Heaven is not afar off, in the clouds or in the next world. "The Kingdom of Heaven cometh not with observation," He said. "Neither shall they say, Lo here, lo there! For behold, the Kingdom of Heaven is within you."

What Is Heaven?

That word "Heaven" is perhaps the most misunderstood word in the Bible. In the original Greek text, the word used for "Heaven" is OURANOS, which, translated literally, means EXPANSION. And what is expansion? It is increasing, spreading out, multiplying, is it not? "Seek ye first the Kingdom of EXPANSION, and all these things shall be added unto you." Seek a place or a state of being where you can expand, grow, increase, multiply, bring forth fruit.

But we don't need to seek such a place, for Jesus assured us that the Kingdom of Heaven is already within us. We must therefore look within ourselves for this faculty of expansion.

Now what, within us, has unlimited power to expand? Our muscles are elastic, our lungs and many of our organs can be expanded to an extent, but none of them can expand greatly without harm to itself and to the body.

The only thing in this body of ours that can expand without limit is our MIND, our imaging faculties. So Jesus' advice might be paraphrased—"Seek ye first the Kingdom of Mind, of imagery, and all these things shall be added unto you."

That would seem to fit in with Jesus' own description of what the Kingdom of Heaven is like. "The Kingdom of Heaven is like to a grain of mustard seed, which a man took, and sowed in his field; which indeed is the least of all seeds, but when it is grown, it is the greatest among herbs, and becometh a tree, so that the birds of the air come and lodge in the branches thereof." "The Kingdom of Heaven is like unto leaven, which a woman took and hid in three measures of meal, until the whole was leavened."

What is the property of a mustard seed? *It spreads*— a single seed will grow into a tree, a single tree will produce enough seeds to plant a great field. And what is the property of leaven or yeast? *It expands*—in a single night it can expand a hundred times in size.

Go back over any of the miracles of increase in the Bible and see if they are not all miracles of EXPANSION. How did Elijah make the oil and meal last, so that one measure of oil and a little meal fed him and the widow and her son for an indefinite period? How did

Elisha increase the pot of oil for that other widow who came to him to save her sons from bondage, so that she had enough to fill all the vessels she could borrow from her neighbors?

By EXPANDING them, did they not? And that is how you can increase your substance, your happiness, your every good thing.

When the disciples asked Jesus how to pray, what did He teach them? "Our Father which art in Heaven, hallowed be Thy name, Thy Kingdom come, *Thy will be done on earth as it is in Heaven."* In other words, may the good that you have imaged for me in the Heaven of your consciousness be made manifest here on earth.

God is MIND, and He dwells in the Kingdom of Mind or Heaven. There—in the mind and thoughts of God—all is good. He images you as perfect, your surroundings pleasant and comfortable, all your ways cast in pleasant places. He does not think up sickness and troubles for you. He images you as His perfect child, happy and care-free, with everything of good that makes life desirable. He is your Father, and what father, even among us here on earth, would plan anything but good for his children? As Jesus reminded us—"What man is there of you, whom if his son ask bread, will he give him a stone? Or if he ask a fish, will he give him a serpent? If ye then, being evil, know how to give good gifts unto your children, how much more shall your Father which is in heaven give good things to them that ask Him?"

In short, when you pray . . . "Thy will be done . . ." you are asking that everything of good that the Father has imaged for you in His mind should be made manifest for you here on earth. For His will, like that of every father, is that His children should be contented and happy, that they should have everything that is for their good.

How can we help to bring this about? By putting our own lives and especially our thoughts on the plane of the Kingdom of Heaven—in other words, by starting here and now to *live* in that Kingdom of Heaven.

When you meet evil on its own level, you meet it at a disadvantage. You may overcome it, but only after a terrific struggle. The only sure way to overcome evil is to get above it—to use the Law of the Higher Potential not merely to defeat the evil that confronts you, but to replace it with the perfect condition you desire.

That is what Jesus bade us do when He told us to "Seek first the Kingdom of Heaven (of expansion, of mind, of the imaging faculties)."

Seek in your own mind the ideal condition you would have, expand your thoughts to image it in every detail, see it as part of the Kingdom of Heaven, so that you can be thankful for it and praise God for it. See it, believe in it, until you can be happy over it and no longer fearful or worrying about seeming conditions around you.

In the beginning all was void—space—nothingness. How did God construct the planets, the firmaments, the earth and all things on and in it from this formless void? By first making a mental image on which to build.

That is what you, too, must do. You control your destiny, your fortune, your happiness to the exact extent to which you can think them out, VISUALIZE them, SEE them, and allow no vagrant thought of fear or worry to mar their completion and beauty. The quality of your thought is the measure of your power. Clear, forceful thought has the power of attracting to itself everything it may need for the fruition of those thoughts. As W. D. Wattles puts it in his "Science of Getting Rich":

"There is a thinking stuff from which all things are made and which, in its original state, permeates, penetrates, and fills the interspaces of the universe. A thought in this substance produces the thing that is imagined by the thought. Man can form things in his thought, and by impressing his thought upon formless substance, can cause the thing he thinks about to be created."

The connecting link between your conscious mind and the Kingdom of Heaven is thought, and every thought that is in harmony with progress and good, every thought that is freighted with the right idea, can penetrate to the Heaven Mind. And penetrating to it, it comes back with the power of God to accomplish it. You don't need to originate the ways and means. God knows how to bring about any necessary results. There is but one right way to solve any given problem. When your human judgment is unable to decide what that one right way is, turn to the Lord for guidance. You need never fear the outcome, for if you heed His advice you cannot go wrong.

Always remember—your mind is but a conductor— good or poor as you make it—for the power of the Universal Mind or God. And thought is the connecting energy. Use that conductor, and you will improve its conductivity. Demand much, and you will receive the more. The Lord is not a niggard in any of His gifts. "Ask and ye shall receive, seek and ye shall find, knock and it shall be opened unto you."

That is the law of life. And the destiny of man lies not in poverty and hardship, but in living up to his high estate in unity with the Heaven Mind, with the Power that governs the universe.

To look upon poverty and sickness as sent by God and therefore inevitable, is the way of the weakling. God never sent us anything but good. What is more, He has never yet failed to give to those who would use them the means to overcome any condition not of His making. Sickness and poverty are not of His making. They are not evidences of virtue, but of weakness. God gave us everything in abundance, and he expects us to manifest that abundance. If you had a son you loved very much, and you surrounded him with good things which he had only to exert himself in order to reach, you wouldn't like it if he showed himself to the world half-starved, ill-kempt and clothed in rags, merely because he was unwilling to exert himself enough to reach for the good things you had provided. No more, in my humble opinion, does God.

Man's principal business in life, as I see it, is to establish a contact with the Heaven Mind. It is to acquire an understanding of this power that is in him. "With all thy getting, get understanding," said Solomon.

> "Happy is the man that findeth wisdom,
> And the man that getteth understanding.
> For the gaining of it is better than the gaining of silver.
> And the profit thereof than fine gold.
> She is more precious than rubies:
> And none of the things thou canst desire are to be compared
>   unto her.
> Length of days is in her right hand:
> In her left hand are riches and honor.
> Her ways are ways of pleasantness,
> And all her paths are peace.
> She is a tree of life to them that lay hold upon her.
> And happy is every one that retaineth her."
>   —*Proverbs*

When you become conscious, even to a limited degree, of your one-ness with this God Mind, your ability to call upon It at will for anything you may need, it makes a different man of you. Gone are the fears, gone are the worries. You know that your success, your health, your happiness will be measured only by the degree to which you can impress the fruition of your desires upon mind.

The toil and worry, the wearisome grind and the back-breaking work, will go in the future as in the past to those who will not use their minds. The less they use them, the more they will sweat. And the more they work only from the neck down, the less they will be paid and the more hopeless their lot will become. It is Mind that rules the world.

You see, from an ordinary earthly point of view, any savage or even many animals are to all intents as good as you or I. They are stronger, have greater vitality, live longer comparatively, and some are surer of their sustenance. The only faculty in which we are their superior is our mind.

And the only faculty that can make us superior to those around us, that can keep us from being the sport of circumstance and lift us above all danger of want or sickness, is that same mind.

Why is it that fervent prayer often works what seems to us to be a miracle? Why does Treasure Mapping bring such marvelous results? Because both put us upon the Heaven-plane, the plane where the Father works with us to bring about the object we desire.

When you pray earnestly, you see in your mind's eye the condition or result you desire. When you Treasure Map, you picture on paper the condition you want to see realized. And that is exactly how God worked when He created the world. "In the beginning was the word (the mental image)." In the beginning, He formed a picture in His own mind of what He wanted to create. "And the word (the mental image) was made flesh." It was made manifest, became reality for all to see.

Your word—your mental image—can be made flesh in the same way. All it needs is to get on the same plane that God is on when He creates—the plane of the Kingdom of Heaven—of imagery and faith. Remember the words of the Psalmist—"In Thy Book, all my members were written, *when as yet there was none of them."* And elsewhere in the Scriptures, you find—"The Lord made the earth and the heavens, and every plant of the field *before it was in the earth,* and every herb of the field *before it grew."*

That is the way you must create the conditions you desire. Create them in your own mind first.

"The imagination," says Glenn Clark in "The Soul's Sincere Desire," "is of all qualities in man the most God-like—that which associates him most closely with God. The first mention we read of man in the Bible is where he is spoken of as an 'image.' 'Let us make man in our image, after our likeness.' The only place where an image can be conceived is in the imagination. Thus man, the highest creation of God, was a creation of God's imagination.

"The source and center of all man's creative power— the power that above all others lifts him above the level of brute creation, and that gives him dominion, is his power of making images, or the power of the imagination. There are some who have always thought that the imagination was something which makes-believe that which is not. This is fancy—not imagination. Fancy would convert that which is real into pretense and sham; imagination enables one to see through the appearance of a thing to what it really is."

There is a very real law of cause and effect which makes the dream of the dreamer come true. It is the law of visualization—the law that calls into being in this outer material world everything that is real in the inner world. Imagination pictures the thing you desire. VISION idealizes it. It reaches beyond the thing that is, into the conception of what can be. Imagination gives you the picture. Vision gives you the impulse to make the picture your own.

CHAPTER THIRTY-FIVE

AS A MAN THINKETH

WE CANNOT CHANGE the past experience, but we can determine what the new ones shall be like. We can make the coming day just what we want it to be. We can be tomorrow what we think today. For the thoughts are causes and the conditions are the effects.

Thought is the only force. Just as polarity controls the electron, gravitation the planets, tropism the plants and lower animals—just so thought controls the action and the environment of man. And thought is subject wholly to the control of mind. Its direction rests with us.

Walt Whitman had the right of it when he said— "Nothing external to me has any power over me."

Each of us makes his own world—and he makes it through mind.

Thoughts are the causes. Conditions are merely effects. We can mold ourselves and our surroundings by resolutely directing our thoughts towards the goal we have in mind.

Ordinary animal life is very definitely controlled by temperature, by climate, by seasonal conditions. Man alone can adjust himself to any reasonable temperature or condition. Man alone has been able to free himself to a great extent from the control of natural forces through his understanding of the relation of cause and effect. And now man is beginning to get a glimpse of the final freedom that shall be his from all material causes when he shall acquire the complete understanding that mind is the only cause and that effects are what he sees.

"We moderns are unaccustomed," says one talented writer, "to the mastery over our own inner thoughts and feelings. That a man should be a prey to any thought that chances to take possession of his mind, is commonly among us assumed as unavoidable. It may be a matter of regret that he should be kept awake all night from anxiety as to the issue of a lawsuit on the morrow, but that he should have the power of determining whether he be kept awake or not seems an extravagant demand. The image of an impending calamity is no doubt odious, but its very odiousness (we say) makes it haunt the mind all the more pertinaciously, and it is useless to expel it. Yet this is an absurd position for man, the heir of all the ages, to be in: Hag-ridden by the flimsy creatures of his own brain. If a pebble in our boot torments us, we expel it. We take off the boot and shake it out. And once the matter is fairly understood, it is just as easy to expel an intruding and obnoxious thought from the mind. About this there ought to be no mistake, no two opinions. The thing is obvious, clear and unmistakable. It should be as easy to expel an obnoxious thought from the mind as to shake a stone out of your shoe; and until a man can do that, it is just nonsense to talk about his ascendancy over nature, and all the rest of it. He is a mere slave, and a prey to the bat-winged phantoms that flit through the corridors of his own brain. Yet the weary and careworn faces that we meet by thousands, even among the affluent classes of civilization, testify only too clearly how seldom this mastery is obtained. How rare indeed to find a man! How common rather to discover a creature hounded on by tyrant thoughts (or cares, or desires), cowering, wincing under the lash.

"It is one of the prominent doctrines of some of the

oriental schools of practical psychology that the power of expelling thoughts, or if need be, killing them dead on the spot, must be attained. Naturally the art requires practice, but like other arts, when once acquired there is no mystery or difficulty about it. It is worth practice. It may be fairly said that life only begins when this art has been acquired. For obviously when, instead of being ruled by individual thoughts, the whole flock of them in their immense multitude and variety and capacity is ours to direct and despatch and employ where we list, life becomes a thing so vast and grand, compared to what it was before, that its former condition may well appear almost ante-natal. If you can kill a thought dead, for the time being, you can do anything else with it that you please. And therefore it is that this power is so valuable. And it not only frees a man from mental torment (which is nine-tenths at least of the torment of life), but it gives him a concentrated power of handling mental work absolutely unknown to him before. The two are co-relative to each other."

There is no intelligence in matter—whether that matter be electronic energy made up in the form of stone, or iron, or wood, or flesh. It all consists of Energy, the universal substance from which Mind forms all material things. Mind is the only intelligence. It alone is eternal. It alone is supreme in the universe.

When we reach that understanding, we will no longer have cause for fear, because we will realize that Universal Mind is the Creator of life only; that death is not an actuality—it is merely the absence of life—and life will be ever-present. Remember the old fairy story of how the Sun was listening to a lot of earthly creatures talking of a very dark place they had found? A place of Stygian blackness. Each told how terrifically dark it had seemed. The Sun went and looked for it. He went to the exact spot they had described. He searched everywhere. But he could find not even a tiny dark spot. And he came back and told the earth-creatures he did not believe there was any dark place.

When the sun of understanding shines on all the dark spots in our lives, we will realize that there is no cause, no creator, no power, except good; evil is not an entity—it is merely the absence of good. And there can be no ill effects without an evil cause. Since there is no evil cause, only good can have reality or power. There is no beginning or end to good. From it there can be nothing but blessing for the whole race. In it is found no trouble. If God (or Good—the two are synonymous) is the only cause, then the only effect must be like the cause. "All things were made by Him; and without Him was not anything made that was made."

CHAPTER THIRTY-SIX

THE MASTER OF YOUR FATE

ORISON SWETT MARDEN WROTE—"A highly magnetized piece of steel will attract and lift a piece of unmagnetized steel ten times its own weight. De-magnetize that same piece of steel and it will be powerless to attract or lift even a feather's weight.

"Now, my friends, there is the same difference between the man who is highly magnetized by a sublime faith in himself, and the man who is de-magnetized by his lack of faith, his doubts, his fears, that there is between the magnetized and the de-magnetized pieces of steel. If two men of equal ability, one magnetized by a divine self-confidence, the other de-magnetized by fear and doubt, are given similar tasks, one will succeed and the other will fail. The self-confidence of the one multiplies his powers a hundred-fold; the lack of it subtracts a hundred-fold from the power of the other."

When Frank A. Vanderlip, former President of the National City Bank, was a struggling youngster, he asked a successful friend what one thing he would urge a young man to do who was anxious to make his way in the world. "Look as though you have already succeeded," his friend told him. Shakespeare expresses the same thought in another way—"Assume a virtue if you have it not." Look the part. Dress the part. Act the part. Be successful in your own thought first. It won't be long before you will be successful before the world as well.

David V. Bush, in his book "Applied Psychology and

Scientific Living," says: "Man is like the wireless operator. Man is subject to miscellaneous wrong thought currents if his mind is not in tune with the Infinite, or *if he is
not keyed up to higher vibrations* than those of negation.

"A man who thinks courageous thoughts sends these
courageous thought waves through the universal ether
until they lodge in the consciousness of someone who is
tuned to the same courageous key. Think a strong
thought, a courageous thought, a prosperity thought, and
these thoughts will be received by someone who is strong,
courageous and prosperous.

"It is just as easy to think in terms of abundance as to
think in terms of poverty. If we think poverty thoughts
we become the sending and receiving stations for poverty
thoughts. We send out a 'poverty' mental wireless and it
reaches the consciousness of some poverty-stricken 'receiver.' We get what we think.

"It is just as easy to think in terms of abundance, opulence and prosperity as it is to think in terms of lack,
limitation and poverty.

"If a man will *raise his rate of vibration* by faith currents or hope currents, these vibrations go through the
Universal Mind and lodge in the consciousness of people
who are keyed to the same tune. Whatever you think is
sometime, somewhere, received by a person who is tuned
to your thought key.

"If a man is out of work and he thinks thoughts of success, prosperity, harmony, position and growth, just as
surely as his thoughts are things—as Shakespeare says—
someone will receive his vibrations of success, prosperity,
harmony, position and growth.

"If we are going to be timid, selfish, penurious and
picayunish in our thinking, these thought waves which we
have started in the universal ether will go forth until they
come to a mental receiving station of the same caliber.

'Birds of a feather flock together,' and minds of like thinking are attracted one to the other.

"If you need money, all you have to do is to send up your vibrations to a strong, courageous receiving station, and someone who can meet your needs will be attracted to you or you to him."

When you learn that you are entitled to win—in any right undertaking in which you may be engaged—you will win. When you learn that you have a right to a legitimate dominion over your own affairs, you will have dominion over them. The promise is that we can do all things through the Mind that was in Christ.

The Heaven Mind plays no favorites. No one human being has any more power than any other. It is simply that few of us *use* the power that is in our hands. The great men of the world are in no wise SUPER Beings. They are ordinary creatures like you and me, who have stumbled upon the way of drawing upon their subconscious mind—and through it upon the God Mind. Speaking of Henry Ford's phenomenal success, his friend Thomas A. Edison said of him—"He draws upon his subconscious mind."

The secret of being what you have it in you to be is simply this: Decide now what it is you want of life, exactly what you wish your future to be. Plan it out in detail. Vision it from start to finish. See yourself as you are now, doing those things you have always wanted to do. Make them REAL in your mind's eye—feel them, live them, believe them, especially at the moment of going to sleep, when it is easiest to reach your subconscious mind— and you will soon be seeing them in real life.

It matters not whether you are young or old, rich or poor. The time to begin is NOW. It is never too late. Remember those lines of Appleton's: *

* From "The Quiet Courage." D. Appleton & Co., New York.

"I knew his face the moment that he passed
Triumphant in the thoughtless, cruel throng—
I gently touched his arm—he smiled at me—
He was the Man that Once I Meant to Be!

"Where I had failed, he'd won from life, Success;
Where I had stumbled, with sure feet he stood;
Alike—yet unalike—we faced the world,
And through the stress he found that life was good.
And I? The bitter wormwood in the glass,
The shadowed way along which failures pass!
Yet as I saw him thus, joy came to me—
He was the Man that Once I Meant to Be!

"We did not speak. But in his sapient eyes
I saw the spirit that had urged him on,
The courage that had held him through the fight
Had once been mine. I thought, 'Can it be gone?'
He felt that unmasked question—felt it so
His pale lips formed the one-word answer, 'No!'

"Too late to win? No! Not too late for me—
He is the Man that Still I Mean to Be!"

The secret of power lies in understanding the infinite resources of your own mind. When you begin to realize that the power to do anything, to be anything, to have anything, is within yourself, then and then only will you take your proper place in the world.

As Bruce Barton put it—"Nothing splendid has ever been achieved except by those who dared believe that something inside them was superior to circumstance."

CHAPTER THIRTY-SEVEN

THE MASTER MIND

THE CONNECTING LINK between the human and the Divine, between the formed universe and formless energy, lies in your imaging faculty. It is, of all things human, the most God-like. It is our part of Divinity. Through it we share in the creative power of the Heaven Mind. Through it we can turn the most drab existence into a thing of life and beauty. It is the means by which we avail ourselves of all the good which God is constantly offering to us in such profusion. It is the means by which we can reach any goal, win any prize.

Do you want happiness? Do you want success? Do you want position, power, riches? *Image* them! How did God first make man? "In his image created He him." He "imaged" man in His Mind.

And that is the way everything has been made since time began. It was first imaged in Mind. That is the way everything you want must start—with a mental image.

So use your imagination! Picture in it your Heart's Desire. Imagine it—day-dream it so vividly, so clearly, that you will actually BELIEVE you HAVE it. In the moment that you carry this conviction to your subconscious mind—in that moment your dream will become a reality. It may be a while before you realize it, but the important part is done. You have created the model. You can safely leave it to your subconscious mind to do the rest.

Every man wants to get out of the rut, to grow, to

develop into something better. Here is the open road—
open to you whether you have schooling, training, position, wealth, or not. Remember this: Your subconscious
mind knew more from the time you were a baby than is in
all the books in all the colleges and libraries of the world.

So don't let lack of training, lack of education, hold
you back. Your mind can meet every need—and will do so
if you give it the chance. The Apostles were almost all
poor men, uneducated men, yet they did a work that is
unequalled in historical annals. Joan of Arc was a poor
peasant girl, unable to read or write—yet she saved
France! The pages of history are dotted with poor men,
uneducated men, who thought great thoughts, who used
their imaginations to master circumstances and became
rulers of men. Most great dynasties started with some
poor, obscure man. Napoleon came of a poor, humble
family. He got his appointment to the Military Academy
only through very hard work and the pulling of many
political strings. Even as a Captain of Artillery he was so
poverty-stricken that he was unable to buy his equipment
when offered an appointment to India. Business today is
full of successful men who have scarcely the rudiments of
ordinary education. It was only after he had made his
millions that Andrew Carnegie hired a tutor to give him
the essentials of an education.

So it isn't training and it isn't education that make you
successful. These help, but the thing that really counts is
that gift of the Gods—Creative Imagination!

You have that gift. Use it! Make every thought, every
fact, that comes into your mind pay you a profit. Make
it work and produce for you. Think of things—not as
they are but as they MIGHT be. Make them real, live
and interesting. Don't merely dream—but CREATE!
Then use your imagination to make that CREATION of
advantage to mankind—and, incidentally, yourself.

Get *above* your circumstances, your surroundings. Get above your troubles—no matter what they may be. Remember, the Law is that Power flows only from a higher to the lower potential. Use your imaging faculty to put yourself and keep yourself on a higher plane, *above* trouble and adversity. "Circumstances?" exclaimed Napoleon when at the height of his power. "I make circumstances!" And that is what you too must do.

"As the rain cometh down and the snow from heaven, and returneth not thither, but watereth the earth, and maketh it bring forth and bud, and giveth seed to the sower and bread to the eater; so shall my word be that goeth forth out of my mouth: it shall not return unto me void, but it shall accomplish that which I please, and it shall prosper in the thing whereto I sent it."—Isaiah.

Do You Have Money Worries?

Say to yourself and believe—"There is no lack in the Kingdom of Heaven." Then make a Treasure Map as suggested in The Magic Word, showing all the riches and supply you may long for. All this must start, you know with an idea, a mental image.

"All that the Father hath is mine," said Jesus. And all that the Father hath is yours, too, for all He has to begin with is IDEAS, *mental images,* and you can create these as easily as He. Make your mental image of the thing you want, picture it on paper in so far as you can to make it more real and vivid to you, then have FAITH!

Faith starts you DOING the things you need to do to bring your ideas into realities. Faith brings to you the opportunities and people and things you need to make your images realities.

All that the Father hath is yours—all the ideas, all the mental images, all the power to make them manifest.

Do you want riches? They are yours for the making. The ancient Alchemists who spent their lives trying to turn base metals into gold were trying and working from the bottom up. Power does not flow that way. You must start ABOVE the thing you want, working from the higher potential to the lower.

Riches, health, happiness, power, all are yours if you work for them in the right way—if you make them yours in Heaven first and then use your faith and your abilities to make them manifest here on earth.

"Thy will be done on earth as it is in Heaven," God's will for you is for riches, for happiness, for health. If you haven't these now, deny the lack. Deny the wrong conditions. Say to yourself—"There is no lack in Heaven. There is no disease there, no weakness, no trouble or conflict, no worries of any kind. There is only love and plenty."

Then take your beliefs out of the images around you, which are merely the result of your previous belief objectified and put all your faith, all your hopes, all your strength and abilities into making your new Heaven images come true.

You CAN do it. But you must believe so firmly that you can actually ACT the part. As the Prophet Noel told us "Let the weak say—I am strong!" And the poor say, I am rich. And the sick say, I am well. And the miserable say, I am happy. Say it, repeat it until you believe it—then *ACT the part!*

In one of Edgar Rice Burroughs' Martian stories, he told of a great walled city that had outlived its usefulness and was now peopled by only a few old men. But every time an invading army appeared before this city, it was driven away by hordes of archers that manned every foot of the walls and even swarmed out through the gates to meet the enemy in the open. When the enemy fled, the archers disappeared!

Where did the archers come from? According to the story, they came entirely from the minds of the old men who still lived in that almost-deserted city. These old men remembered the huge armies that had garrisoned the town in its heyday. They remembered former invasions when their soldiers had repelled every assault and then dashed out through the gates and swept the invaders into the sea. And by gathering together and visualizing those mighty armies of theirs as once more existent, they brought them into being so that their enemies too could see them and be driven into flight by them.

Does that sound far-fetched? Then remember that you have only to go back to the Bible to find a parallel. Just turn to II Kings, Chapter 6, and you will read how the King of Syria sent his horses and chariots and a great host to capture the Prophet Elisha, and how in the night they compassed him around.

"And when the servant of the man of God was risen early, and gone forth, behold, an host compassed the city both with horses and chariots. And his servant said unto him, Alas, my master, what shall we do?

"And he answered, Fear not! For they that be with us are more than they that be with them.

"And Elisha prayed, and said, Lord, I pray thee, open his eyes, that he may see. And the Lord opened the eyes of the young man; and he saw: and behold, the mountain was full of horses and chariots of fire around Elisha."

Again, when the High Priest sent his soldiers to seize Jesus, and Peter struck one of the soldiers with his sword, Jesus rebuked him, saying: "Thinkest thou that I cannot now pray to My Father, and He shall presently give Me more than twelve legions of angels?"

The mountains can be full of chariots of fire for you, too. The Father can send to your help as many legions of angels as you may need. All it requires is the power to visualize what you want, the faith to believe that you receive, the serenity to sit back and LET God work through you.

"However meager be my worldly wealth,
Let me give something that shall aid my kind,
A word of courage, or a thought of health,
Dropped as I pass for troubled hearts to find.
Let me tonight look back across the span
'Twixt dawn and dark, and to my conscience say—
Because of some good act to beast or man—
The world is better that I lived today."

ELLA WHEELER WILCOX

Printed in the United States
34696LVS00003B/84